street KINGDOM

street KINGDOM

FIVE YEARS INSIDE THE FRANKLIN AVENUE POSSE

DOUGLAS CENTURY

WARNER BOOKS

A Time Warner Company

Library of Congress Cataloging-in-Publication Data

Century, Douglas.
    Street kingdom : five years inside the Franklin Avenue Posse /
Douglas Century.
        p. cm.
        ISBN 0-446-52266-X BT 25.00/13.48 2/99
        1. Gangs—New York (N.Y.)—Case studies. 2. Brooklyn (New York,
N.Y.) I. Title.
HV6439.U7N436 1999
364.1'06'6097471—DC21   98-15083
                                                                CIP

Book design by H. Roberts Design

FOR *Jack and Marcia*
AND FOR *Crystal*

WITH LOVE AND GRATITUDE

Contents

Author's Note

This is a work of nonfiction: all of the events depicted are factual and the characters real. Any material not derived from my own observation and firsthand experience is the result of interviews with the principal participants—more precisely, numerous tape-recorded interviews conducted over a considerable period of time.

The writing of this book presented several technical problems, not the least of which stemmed from the fact that, for the earliest years covered by the chronology, I had no notion that I was ever going to write it. The narrative, therefore, reflects this hybrid status: partly a work of reportage, partly a memoir of events which occurred at a time when I had no conscious—or at least premeditated—plan to document them.

I first stumbled onto this terrain when I met a young aspiring rapper called Big K in June 1992, following an impromptu performance he'd given in a small club on the Lower East Side of Manhattan. But it wasn't until the spring of 1995 that, with K's consent, I began systematically gathering source material for use in some form of journalistic project—at the time, I was thinking only of a magazine article or long newspaper story.

It's difficult, of course, to encapsulate several years of complex human interaction in a single sentence; put simply, that initial period—'92–'95—consisted primarily of hanging out with K in recording studios, going to after-hours hip-hop parties, engaging in a good deal of aimless, rambling chatter in pizzerias and Burger Kings. After a time, as K struggled in his pursuit of a career as a recording artist, I found myself, at his request, acting as his daily sounding board and confidant; his mouthpiece in his dealings with various producers, lawyers and record companies; his guide in navigating the minefield of the music business—a task for which I found myself, in the end, abjectly ill-suited.

While there was no clear journalistic road map in those first few years, it would be false not to acknowledge that there was, from the outset, a literary nexus to our relationship. In the beginning, it was K's intense lyric-writing that fascinated me (he'd asked me to type dozens of his lyrics into my computer one day in the summer of '92); and my interest gradually broadened to include the world described in those lyrics:

Brooklyn streets, Brooklyn battles, many cryptic Brooklyn tales detailing
the violent exploits of K and his old Crown Heights crew—known as the
Franklin Avenue Posse.

Some readers may remark on the dichotomy between the urgent,
raging language of K's hip-hop and reggae lyrics and the more detached,
articulate, self-reflective voice of his interview segments. This is easily
explained: K, like many of us, is something of a verbal chameleon,
coloring his syntax, accent and slang to suit a given setting. (Linguists use
two highfalutin terms, code-shifting and diglossia, to describe this
unconscious tendency to adapt our speech to the appropriate social
context.)

Such code-shifting is especially pronounced in the case of someone like
K; he is, after all, a Caribbean-American—the descendant of Jamaicans
who migrated to Panama in the days of Canal building; but also wholly a
product of urban America—born in Philadelphia, raised on the fast
streets of East Flatbush and Crown Heights, Brooklyn. His spoken
language reflects these diverse influences: in conversation he swerves
effortlessly, like some aerodynamic sportscar hitting open highway,
between dense Jamaican patois, the latest hip-hop argot, bits of
Panamanian Spanish and also—as evidenced by his live studio interview
on CBS This Morning in September 1993—an urbane and measured
brand of Standard English which would sound natural on the tongue of
any college-educated American.

When recounting or dramatizing events at which I was not present—
events from K's childhood and adolescence in the '70s, or the Franklin
Avenue Posse's "heyday" in the mid to late '80s—I have interspersed the
text with sections of verbatim transcripts culled from many taped
interviews, conducted with K between May '95 and April '97. The
intended effect is of a cinematic voice-over, lending those sections a
firsthand immediacy I found impossible to achieve solely through pages of
third-person rendering. Wherever possible, I've footnoted these italicized
reflections, giving a clear indication of the time and place the interviews
were conducted.

street KINGDOM

Look round you: everywhere blood flows in torrents, and what's more, as merrily as if it was champagne.

—Dostoyevsky, *Notes from Underground*

SECOND MURDERER   I am one, my liege,
    Whom the vile blows and buffets of the world
    Have so insensed that I am reckless what
    I do to spite the world.

FIRST MURDERER   And I another
    So weary with disasters, tugg'd with fortune,
    That I would set my life on any chance,
    To mend it or be rid on 't

—*Macbeth* (III, i)

JUDGE DREAD   *Order! Now this court is in session and I order all you rudeboys*
to stand! You are brought here for gun-shooting, ratchet-using
and bomb-t'rowings. Now—tell me rudeboys—what have you
to say for yourselves?

THE RUDEBOYS   *Your Honor!*
Rudies don't fear!
Rudies don't fear, no boys
Rudies don't fear
    Rougher than rough
    Tougher than tough
    Strong like lion
    We are iron
Rudies don't fear . . .

—"Tougher than Tough" (1967) by Derrick Morgan,
a pioneer of Jamaican popular music

the
tombs

He is the monster created by the American republic, the present awful sum of generations of oppression; but to say that he is a monster is to fall into the trap of making him subhuman and he must, therefore, be made representative of a way of life which is real and human in precise ratio to the degree to which it seems to us monstrous and strange.
—James Baldwin, *Notes of a Native Son*

NOVEMBER '94. He enters the visiting room of the Tombs with his Brooklyn badboy swagger, throwing a scowl back at the corrections officer who's been assigned the unhappy job of escorting him today. The walk is slow and deliberate—an exaggerated wobble in his stride—giving him time to stare hard at the other inmates, to let them acknowledge that he's by far the biggest and most menacing man in the visiting room.

There's no gray jail jumpsuit big enough for his 270 pounds of top-heavy muscle; he strides toward us wearing a tight white tank top that makes plain the bullet scars in his shoulders and arms. Bunched ropelike around his neck, a thick jumble of multicolored beads serves notice—to anyone who knows the code—that he is watched over by the orishás, by the mysterious powers of santería.

Little K—a round-faced one-year-old in miniature black work boots and black ski cap—squirms out of my lap when he sees his father approaching. His mother, Faith, leans back in one of the Day-Glo plastic chairs that would seem more appropriate in a playschool than a jailhouse. Like most of the other women here in the Tombs— the storied Manhattan House of Detention, home to some eight hundred inmates remanded into the custody of the Department of Corrections while awaiting trial—Faith, a brown-skinned twenty-one-year-old from Harlem, has done herself up properly for visiting day: bright lipstick, braided extensions, faded jeans stretched tight across her hips and thighs. Her belly is round. She is seven months pregnant.

"My little man!" he says, scooping his son up in his hands, throwing Little K high onto his shoulder, making the boy squeal with delight. Then with his free arm he reaches out and gives me a powerful hug. He doesn't even lean over to kiss Faith. When you're locked up, he'll later tell me, it's more painful to have a brief moment of bodily contact with your woman than no contact at all.

He hands Little K back to me and I hold the boy in my lap. There's a strong scent of lemon-lime deodorant as the big man drops his weight heavily in his chair, leaning forward on the plastic table, glaring at me, unsmiling, head cocked to one side.

"You tryin' to fuck my head up, duke?"

"Fuck your head up how?"

"I'm not depressed enough without you givin' me some shit about a nigga who ends up on Death Row?" He turns to Faith now, shaking his head in disbelief. "He leaves me this shit called *Native Son,* right? 'Bout this cat out there in Chi-town. I start readin'—it's a little slow at first, but then, *boom,* it gets good: my nigga's caught up in some manslaughter shit, has to take it on the lam. Now I'm *into* it—thinkin' there's gotta be a twist comin', knowmsayin'? Cat's gonna get off *somehow:* either he gonna beat trial, or escape, or get a last-minute pardon from the governor. But no—you got me readin' five hundred tightly spaced pages just to find out that they put my nigga to *death?*"

Faith looks at me and then lets out a loud throaty laugh.

"What was the point even *readin'* it?" he says. "Just another story of a fucked-up life? Nigga does the crime, nigga goes to jail, nigga *never* comes home . . ."

"I didn't mean to depress you."

"Word, I don't *never* wanna read no shit like that again."

Staring at his son and reaching out to take Little K's hand, the big man finally cracks a mischievous grin. His skin is a dark toffee-brown; his eyes are bright and playful; when he smiles his upper lip curves in a perfect cupid's bow. He'd be conventionally handsome but for obvious battle scars on his face: the bridge of his nose savagely thrust to one side, broken during his brief career as a prizefighter; the shiny, raised keloid bump on his left cheek, marking the spot where he was gouged by a 007 knife during a teenage brawl. ("You wanna be Scarface so bad?" his Panamanian-born mother had chided him at his hospital bed. "Bwoy, you surely Scarface *now!*")

"That other book I could appreciate, though. *Wiseguy?* I could appreciate that one like a muthafucka. At least them cats brought some savvy to the game. You wanna bring me some criminal-minded shit, bring me another joint like that . . . Them Lucchese cats wasn't *bull-shittin'* . . ."

Tirelessly struggling to get out of my lap, huffing, grunting, his feisty son now produces a prodigious dollop of drool which dangles in midair before swinging down, like some lazy spider, to land on the leg of my jeans. With this clever diversionary tactic, and a nifty half twist, Little K manages to squeeze out of my hands. Arms held high, he bursts off on a toddling jail break across the visiting room, pursued by a Puerto Rican guard with a colorfully tattooed forearm.

"This little boy," Faith says with an exasperated kiss of her teeth. "He's too rude!" It's the second time she's said this today. The first was out in the waiting area when, again under my watch, Little K wandered off and pulled a thick stack of paperwork and a binder down from the guard's desk, causing the guard to warn—only half jokingly—that he might have to snap cuffs on the kid.

Zigzagging, shrieking joyously, the boy continues his carefree run, under the surveillance of several video cameras and the somber, watchful eyes of Marcus Garvey, Malcolm X and Martin Luther King.

Finally the muscular Puerto Rican snatches Little K up and returns him, dangling and dog-paddling, to his father's care.

"Rude Lil K! You really livin' up to that name, duke!" He laughs proudly, lifting his son high overhead. "Knowledge *Born*!" The big man has bestowed his favorite street alias on the boy, the name from his Five Percenter days . . . a name still uttered in fear on the streets of Brooklyn . . . From the Vanderveer projects to the heart of Crown Heights, people still talk about the days when Knowledge Born and the Franklin Avenue Posse stood knee-deep in drug money, when they kept the whole borough of Brooklyn running red . . .

Three tables away, a commotion breaks out: guards rushing over to apprehend one of the inmates and drag him off for a strip search. A female CO leads away the inmate's girlfriend. The surveillance cameras have caught her trying to pass him a packet of weed with her tongue during that long soulful reunion kiss.

The big man shakes his head at their stupidity.

"Y'all left somethin' on my books?"

"A few bucks."

"Word, I gotta get myself some more Tang and Right Guard."

He begins to talk about all the felony cases he's facing. New Jersey will have to come extradite him for that pistol-whipping, but before that, he has to answer to three outstanding New York bench warrants that date back to the height of the crack wars. In one case he stands accused of firing a Tec-9 out of the sunroof of a vehicle while speeding recklessly down a sidewalk in Queens.

His first court date is still weeks away, and he'll soon be transferred to Rikers Island, where well-armed mobs of Latin Kings, Ñetas, Bloods and other new-breed gangsters have the run of the jail. But he seems in relatively good spirits—in spite of his agitation about Faith's impending due date and his anxiety over how she'll feed the new baby without him being there to help out.

I ask him if he's having any problems here in the Tombs. "You crazy?" he says, glancing disdainfully around at his fellow prisoners. "Jail done *changed*—even the suckers in here got jewelry on nowadays. Word, this is like some little-kid shit. Brings me back to Spofford," he says, meaning the juvenile facility in the South Bronx where he was first incarcerated as a juvenile offender.

He sits recalling the heyday of Rikers Island madness in the late '80s. "Soon's you set foot in C-95, muthafucka steps to you, shank out already, talkin' 'bout: *Nigga, what size them sneakers?*" He laughs heartily at the memory, then tells us that the only battling going on in the Tombs is the freestyle rhyme cipher the guys have every afternoon in the dayroom. He yanks off Little K's ski cap, kisses his sweaty forehead, then begins to rap a rhyme he wrote as a lullaby for his son:

My little man
Forty grand, pots & pans, steak & ham
My little man.

He stops rapping suddenly and stares hard at Faith's swollen belly, shaking his head slowly. It looks, just for a moment, as if the big man's stony facade might dissolve into tears. Faith's face remains locked in an impassive grin. "I'm too old to be goin' through all this bullshit again," he tells her quietly.

Our visiting time in the Tombs is cut short. After only twenty minutes, the shadow of the Puerto Rican guard falls over us. "Time, big man, time." Seeing his father get up, Little K begins to screech.

"Yo, I'm a holler at you tomorrow," he tells me as he's led back to the lockup, to the indignity of the strip search.

I hold Little K's hand in a tight, sweaty grip. The boy does his best to wave and mouth the word: *Fazzah.*

Father flashes a goodbye look, his hardrock smirk—but as he's led away I can see that he's still fighting back the tears, clenching his teeth, wondering if his little man will be a full-grown one by the time he gets back out in the world.

ONE

enter the
cipher

The basic creed of the gangster, and for that matter of any other type of criminal, is that whatever a man has is his only so long as he can keep it, and that the one who takes it away from him has not done anything wrong, but has merely demonstrated his smartness.

—Herbert Asbury, *The Gangs of New York*

One time for your mind. He stepped on the tiny stage of the Nuyorican Poets Cafe as if entering a prize ring: chin tucked tight against his chest, glowering into the bright red lights, shifting his weight from foot to foot as he waited to attack his rhymes. *One-two, one-two.* He nodded to the soundman, mumbled another mike check, then introduced himself to the crowd as Big K the American Dread. The heavy thud of the breakbeats kicked in and he threw his whole musculature into the flow of his lyrics. Eyes downcast, microphone pressed close to his lips, he nodded his head and beat his chest from time to time with the flat of his hand.

ci•pher[1] [sīfər] *n.* 1. symbol indicating a value of zero; 2. person or thing of no importance or value; 3. a code or system of secret writing meant to be understood only by those who have the key to it; 4. the key to such a code.

ci•pher[2] [sīfər] *n.* (*urban slang late 20th century*) 1. a circle of teaching or study, esp. among members of the Five Percent Nation; 2. a circle in which freestyle rap is improvised; 3. a loosely organized clique or crew; 4. one's frame of mind or mental state ("My cipher keeps movin' like a rollin' stone"—Erykah Badu).

One moment he was rapping Brooklyn-style, describing himself as *The mike John Gotti / Prince of the lyrics / Son to no man;* and then there was a breathless surge and he was rhyming in the island boasts of a Jamaican badman, calling himself a *don gorgon* and the *dread mad-hatter;* and then a breath later I began to hear snippets of Spanish slang thrown into the mix, like bits of hot pepper added to his already thick verbal stew.

He was staring straight at me as he rhymed. The red spotlight lit up the weltlike scar on his face. The gangster poetry spilled from him so quickly, so furiously, that it was impossible to grasp all the images before they scattered.

I sat transfixed as he bounded across the stage. His ferocious gaze and athletic movements seemed out of place in the smoke-filled East Village coffeehouse, his words booming and echoing off the cavernous ceiling and bare brick walls, over the heads of the smattering of people gathered here for a night billed as RAP MEETS POETRY. I looked over at my girlfriend, Crystal. She was bobbing her head to the beat as the big man rhymed.

Straight and simple
My shit be mental
Comin' for your temple
Soon as they put on instrumental

When he finished his verses he stepped offstage and sat at a round table with several friends. I approached him, told him that I liked his lyrics. He nodded his thanks and introduced me to his wife, Faith, and to his homeboy, the Grand Wizard Shabazz, who he described as "the wickedest DJ in the whole borough of Brooklyn."

I commented on the reggae inflection of his rhymes, and asked him if his background was Jamaican.

"Panamanian," he said, sipping his bottled water.

Crystal smiled beside me in the darkness. She told him that her grandparents had also been immigrants from Panama. "My sister," he said, and he offered her the handshake of a perfect gentleman.

I wrote my number down on the inside flap of a pack of matches—telling him to call me whenever he was going to be doing another hip-hop show—and then asked him to write down his. He leaned in close and spoke directly in my ear: "I ain't got no number right now. I'm homeless."

He said it without embarrassment. He was simply stating a fact: he had no home. He spent his nights riding the Number 2 train end to end, from 241st Street in the Bronx to New Lots Avenue in East New York. He'd lost everything: the drug money, the boxing money, even his jewelry—he didn't have *shit* now. Faith was staying at her mother's crib up on the Hill in Harlem, but he didn't get along too well with his mother-in-law and he didn't need any more headaches. (He didn't actually use the words *mother-in-law*; I assumed that's whom he meant when he referred to a woman as *the hungry hippo*.)

"So you sleep on the trains?"

His laugh was humorless. "Sometimes I don't be sleepin' at all."

He asked me if I was someone in the record business; I looked like someone he had met once before: a producer or an agent or somebody. I shook my head and told him I was a journalist. He raised an eyebrow.

"Word? So be a journalist. Ask me a fuckin' question."

He enjoyed playing this game in the darkness, rocking heavily back in his chair while I sat across from him, Bic in hand, pretending to be making notes on the apricot-colored flyer.

The first thing that mystified me was that odd appendage to his name: Why "American Dread"? He didn't *look* like a dread; his hair was woven in a dozen short, neat braids—not the matted tendrils of a Rastafarian.

"The 'American' is 'cause I'm fuckin' American," he said, shrugging with mild impatience, taking another long swig of his bottled water. Then he narrowed his gaze at me, smirking, suddenly shifting again to his island patois: "True mi no Rasta—but a *dread* mi dread same way. Yunno when a Yardman seh sumting dread? It mean a ting serious an' powerful an' *wicked*."

"Serious and powerful and wicked," I said.

"Yes, star." He gave a small nod. "A so mi dread."

Crystal was still smiling at me as we drove home: she said she really liked this American Dread and what he was saying in his lyrics. He reminded her of so many of the guys she'd grown up with back in the Bronx. He reminded her of those long summer nights, back when she was still a little Catholic School girl, sneaking out with her buddies to the jams in Echo Park and Bronx River to hear Flash and Bambatta spin. He reminded her of dancing in the Fever and T-Connection as the MCs battled it out on the mike. But those nights were different, of course. They seemed always to end in shootouts.

One-two. His words echoed in my ears for a long time. Lying in bed that night, Crystal and I continued to talk about the big man: the white heat of his gaze as he leapt across the stage, looping cables of the microphone trailing behind him like the coils of a snake's tail . . . *And you don't stop.* I let my mind drift off to sleep that night to the insistent echo of his rhymes.

My mind was drifting a lot that summer. I'd just dropped out of graduate school—the very reason I'd come to New York in the first place—and though I was making a meager living as a journalist, writing freelance stories and reviews, I was actually spending more time running around nightclubs in the East Village and SoHo than I was looking for steady work.

I'd been living in the city for four years now, promised myself that this was going to be the last feckless summer, the last summer of clubs and parties, of sleepwalking and looking for Kerouac's "mongrel America"—vaguely chasing down the dream of being a writer—until I found myself sleepwalking square into that towering Panamanian with the eyes burning like live coals . . . and from that day on the labyrinth of New York began to unfold in turns too strange to be imagined.

I t was in a party called Medusa that I first saw the darkness. Crystal had been teasing me as we left our apartment that night, telling me that I'd become a bad influence; for the second time in two weeks I'd managed to drag her away from her textbooks and dissertation research.

Medusa was an underground Tuesday night party that roamed from space to space; lately it had settled in a narrow two-level bar on West Broadway. I knew one of the party's promoters, a lanky Englishman with blond shoulder-length dreadlocks. His real name was Norman but everyone called him Bunny. He was a part-time reggae musician and a full-time poseur. Through the crowded doorway, I caught a glimpse of Bunny grinning cheesily for a Polaroid, leaning back against a pillar with his latest Scandinavian girlfriend.

I did a double take when I saw who was working the door: Big K. He was wearing a Kansas City Royals baseball cap, holding a guest list clipboard, sitting open-legged on a tall stool. Face lighting up, he leapt from his seat when he saw me. I went to shake his hand, but instead he grabbed me by the forearm and enveloped me in a remarkable, smothering hug.

"Yes, don dada! Get in here, muthafucka! Naw, put your fuckin' wallet away—you and your pretty Pana lady ain't payin' a dime."

I asked him how he came to be working the door at Medusa; he told me that he and Bunny had linked up. Bunny was going to be shopping his demo tape to various record labels. He said that, before the summer was out, Bunny had promised he was going to land him a record deal.

This did not bode well. I had known Bunny for several years now, and I knew that his only connection to the record company executives whose names he dropped with annoying regularity was in his capacity as their weekly supplier of weed.

But I didn't dare tell Big K that Bunny was a bullshit artist. I assumed he would learn the truth in his own time. And hopefully I wouldn't be present when he did.

The DJ in Medusa was spinning a mix of old reggae and hip-hop and acid jazz, and Crystal was having a good time dancing. She said she had forgotten how much she loved dancing to reggae music. She said it reminded her of high school. She said all this time in graduate school had made her boring.

We were dancing to Barrington Levy's "Too Experienced" and I had both hands on the small of her back and I thought there was nothing like close-dancing to lovers' rock to make you feel that the summer had finally arrived.

And then, around two, Big K appeared and put his hand on my shoulder.

"Gettin' ready to bounce, baby-paw?"

"No, not yet."

"Good, 'cause I'm gonna fuck your head up right about now. Bunny says he's gonna let me get on the mike and bust some freestyles."

We were dancing in the back corner of the club; I watched Big K and Bunny go over to talk to the DJ. A queue of young guys had formed—some white, some black, all in the requisite baggy jeans and ballcaps and dreadlocks. Like Big K, they were all eager to drop freestyle rhymes on the mike.

We stopped dancing when we heard the loud commotion. At first I thought it must be laughter, but I soon saw that it wasn't. Body language suggested that the DJ did not want anyone touching his microphone or his equipment. He kept shaking his head and waving his hand dismissively at Bunny. Bunny started to argue with him, and I could lip-read the DJ saying *fuck you* to Bunny and then suddenly I saw that Big K had stepped into the argument and that Big K was extremely enraged. His voice had risen powerfully over the sound of the music. He was waving his arms and growling the word *bumboclaat* over and over.

Bumboclaat is an especially ugly West Indian curse word. On my first trip to Kingston in the mid-'80s I had been taught the word by a Jamaican expatriate—my freshman-year roommate at Princeton—who then advised me that to use the word around the wrong people could result in grievous bodily injury. It was a highly charged word, my roommate warned, a fighting word, far more inflammatory than its literal meaning (a menstrual rag) would suggest.

By this time I'd spent enough time in West Indian circles to know that when you start hearing the unmistakable sound of *bumboclaat* echoing across a crowded dance floor, it's advisable to set down your unfinished drink and make your way toward the nearest exit. But before I could do that I heard the horrifying screech of feedback, then the scrape of a stylus on vinyl—and then the sound system went completely dead.

The party was over. I saw Big K hovering over the DJ's turntables, clutching the DJ's microphone in one hand.

The sudden silence only amplified the sound of him shouting his curses and threats at tremendous volume throughout the club. It was a nearly unintelligible howl—but I could decipher a few snippets: one threat involved doing damage to the DJ's turntable set, and another, doing damage to the DJ himself.

At this point dozens of people began to leave the party very rapidly.

For some absurd reason I felt compelled to try to talk to him. Leaving Crystal behind, I moved against the stream of rapidly departing dancers, stepped toward him, touched him on the arm, trying to tell him to calm down—

He whirled around and stared at me: it was like he had never set eyes on me before. His face was hardened in a mask of rage. His mouth was clenched tight, his upper lip bulging like a taut bow. The whites of his eyes seemed to have vanished.

I stood frozen. He reared back.

"Get the *fuck* away from me!" he said.

I felt Crystal touching my arm. "Let's go," she said.

In the mob milling around at the upstairs exit, I bumped into my friend Jack, a clinical psychologist, born and raised on Colombia's Caribbean coast. He was quite somber and buttoned-up by day, but at night he shed the professional stiffness and became a baggy-jeans-and-Airwalk-wearing tornado on the downtown party scene. (A much-needed release from the hours spent counseling East Harlem psychotics who believed they were Jesus Christ?) Jack shrugged in the red glow of the EXIT sign and, as we stepped out into the night air, murmured an admittedly rudimentary diagnosis: "Well, your man has extremely poor impulse control."

Crystal's appraisal was a little more personal. Walking through SoHo, she said she couldn't stand him: he was *just* like the guys from the old neighborhood. That temper was just like Tommy's, she said. The guy was a walking time bomb just like Tommy.

We walked down to Crystal's Skyhawk and an enormous river rat crossed our path, looking up at us lazily before ducking under a parked car. Crystal grabbed my arm when she saw the rat and it began to rain lightly on our heads and I squeezed Crystal's hand and wondered why she was so cold when I was so hot. The sounds of Big K shouting *bumboclaat* and threatening the DJ were echoing in my head and when I went to open the car door I noticed that my fingers were trembling.

Crystal wasn't frightened. She was quiet and looked a little sad.

She touched the rosary beads that hung in a twisted loop from the dashboard ashtray. She always touched the rosary beads before starting up her car. When she finally spoke, as we sat in the idling Skyhawk, waiting for the engine to warm up, she said that it was like going back ten years, ten years she didn't want to go back, back to her days with Tommy, to those crazy Bronx nights of guns and shootouts and running home trembling to cry alone in her bedroom . . .

They'd all grown up on the edge of the Belmont section of the Bronx, back in the height of the gang days, when you had the Ching-a-Lings owning this block, and you couldn't walk down that block because the Savage Nomads were known for raping girls down there.

But Tommy never got down with the gangs.

Tommy was always his own show.

He was her childhood sweetheart. They'd grown up in the same co-op complex on Crotona Avenue. And the unusual thing about Tommy was that he actually came from a solid family. His parents were together; his father worked for the Transit Authority; they kept an extremely strict home. They were Pentecostal and Tommy used to be in church for five hours every Sunday. His older brother had an old-fashioned Singer machine and used to sew everybody clothes. He promised he was going to sew Crystal the most beautiful wedding gown one day.

Tommy hated being in church for so many hours. He used to come and tell Crystal how his mother had been taken by the Holy Spirit and started speaking in tongues. Then when Tommy started getting in a lot of fights in the neighborhood, his mother would tell him that there was a demon inside him. They'd scream at him like he was a demon.

That only made Tommy worse. He put his energy into body-building and boxing for a while, but that didn't last long and soon he was out sticking people up and getting in shootouts. Every Saturday night was another fight with him. If he took Crystal to the movies and someone even glanced at her bare legs, Tommy'd start shouting and fighting.

It was easy for me to look at the superficial facts of Crystal's life today—a doctoral candidate at Columbia University whose favorite diversion from her studies was her Wednesday night ballroom dancing group—and imagine that she'd always been cocooned from the darker side of life in the Bronx. After all, hadn't she told me that she'd often been teased by the other kids in her old neighborhood for speaking so properly, for dressing so prissily, that the tough girls from nearby Garden Street were forever yanking off their earrings and smearing Vaseline on their faces, wanting to fight her for supposedly trying to "act white" all the time?

She realized now that she'd been fooling herself, that she hadn't wanted to accept the telltale signs of Tommy's transformation. Even when she'd witnessed it with her own eyes. Like the night of his senior prom.

Tommy'd asked Crystal to be his date even though she went to Cardinal Spellman and he went to DeWitt Clinton. And then for some reason Tommy's crazy cousin Mike was riding along like a third wheel all through the prom. As wild as Tommy was, his cousin Mike was even wilder. In those days Tommy was still mostly a streetfighter, handling situations with his fists, but Mike was known for carrying a switchblade and stabbing people for the most trivial of reasons.

The prom night began badly, and ended worse. After the dance, they came to Arthur Avenue—Crystal wanted to eat at Mario's, her favorite Italian restaurant—but the manager at Mario's wouldn't seat them, claiming the restaurant was booked for a private function. Mike started cursing and acting wild right in Mario's and Tommy had to forcibly drag his stupid cousin out into the street.

In those days there was still a line spray-painted on the pavement, just off Arthur Avenue, that said NO NIGGERS NO SPICS. And here they were, three teenagers of the wrong complexion, walking on the wrong side of the line. It was a hot night and they were hungry and sweaty in their prom outfits. The night was so hot that some of the Italian kids were playing at the hydrant with one of those Chock Full o' Nuts coffee cans with the bottom cut out. There were lots of old people sitting outside playing cards and dominoes. When they came down the block in their prom outfits, some of the Italian kids started to point and laugh.

"Look at the niggers! Look at the niggers in their monkey suits!"

Then one of them leaned back with the coffee can and directed the wide stream of water at them. They were all soaked. Crystal's black-and-red prom dress was dripping. Tommy's rented tuxedo was dripping. Mike's afro was soaked and flattened on his head. The Italian kids were all laughing at them and pointing.

And then someone screamed.

Crystal turned and saw that Mike had pulled a small pistol out of his powder-blue tuxedo—he was doing this crazy two-step, aiming the gun at the Italian kids.

"Keep laughin'!" he was shouting. "Laugh at *this,* ya greaseball muthafuckas!"

Leveling his gun at the crowd, he started to squeeze off shots. There was pandemonium on the block: young kids screaming, everybody running, playing cards flying, old people falling out of lawn chairs.

Mike stood there howling with laughter, firing shots over their heads as everybody scattered. And there was Tommy, laughing right alongside his cousin.

She couldn't believe it was really happening. Sure, she was furious at the racist kids who'd sprayed them with the coffee can; but there were old women and old men and little five-year-olds out there too and they were just minding their own business, playing pinochle, playing hearts, trying to get some air on a hot night. And Crystal knew some of the old people's faces. They used to see her coming to take confession at Our Lady of Mount Carmel.

Mike stood there firing off his gun and getting such a kick out of making everybody run. And then she felt Tommy push her in the back. "Run!" he said, laughing wildly, and there she was trying to run through Belmont in her ruined prom dress and her pumps, thinking she wasn't even going to make it home—all three of them were going to die in the street that night.

*   *   *

In the two years Crystal and I'd been living together, the subject of Tommy had precipitated one of our worst fights—the night I found out that he was incarcerated in an upstate prison, still dreaming about Crystal, still staring at her little high school graduation photo taped up on his cell wall. I couldn't accept the fact that she had a violent felon for an ex-boyfriend. I sat staring at her, shaking my head. She lashed out defensively. *I* was the one with the problem, she said, people like me, people who knew just a *little* bit about something but thought they knew it *all.* She said she didn't care how many rap records I bought or how many midnight reggae parties I went to, I was still a white, middle-class Jewish guy from the wilds of Canada, and what the *hell* could I possibly know about the streets? Who was I— living my sheltered little life—to sit there smugly judging her?

Tommy was one guy, she said, just one guy from the neighborhood; there was Spike and Finesse and Van and all the other guys who'd been busted for drugs, for stickups, for carrying guns. And what about all the girls she'd known since childhood, what about Shanice and Lashonda and Naomi, all the sweet little Bronx schoolgirls who'd turned into gun-toting gang girls or hookers or crackheads?

What about the crack fiends who roamed the halls of her parents' old building now that the neighborhood was going downhill, knocking on Crystal's mom's door at all hours, and she naively letting them in and feeding them because to her they aren't faceless fiends, they aren't the hollow-cheeked ghouls you see on the news, they're just the kids down the hall she's watched grow up her whole life, the same kids who used to be dressed up in bow ties for church Sunday morning, the same kids who used to play skelly and hot-peas-and-butter in front of the building, who used to offer to help Crystal's mother carry in her grocery bags.

What, Crystal wanted to know, her gaze fixing tightly on mine, *what* did I want her to do? Stop caring about all the guys she'd played tag with, the guys who'd taught her to lace up her sneakers, who'd chased her screaming down the block back in the days when she was barely big enough to pedal her trike?

That was Crystal's way: forever giving Tommy the benefit of the doubt, holding out hope that he was going to change. She'd encouraged Tommy to go to pharmacy school—he was always very good at chemistry—but she soon saw that he didn't have the patience, or the desire, to study. Her brother found Tommy a job down at the mailroom of his Wall Street office; but Tommy just stopped showing up for work. The years passed and she moved on with her life—getting out of the Bronx, going away to an upstate campus, Pace University in Pleasantville. Tommy traveled upstate as well, on the first of several penitentiary bids.

Finally, she had to accept the truth: that he didn't really want to work at anything, that he really didn't want to change. He'd always choose the easy route, wanting to be the big shot, the big drug dealer in the neighborhood. Here she was, working two part-time jobs, doing home-care work, wiping old people's butts for four dollars an hour, *and* going to school—and Tommy wasn't even trying. He kept going in and out of jail, kept calling her collect, making excuses for himself, and then finally she realized that jail was the perfect place for him—it was the one place that seemed to give his life any structure.

She'd tried to tell him goodbye a few times. But Tommy was living in a state of suspended animation; he kept calling for her at her parents' apartment, thinking nothing had changed since they were in high school.

She'd penned him a short goodbye note several years ago, during one of his previous stretches in prison. She wrote him to say that, since she wasn't with him anymore, he should stop wasting so much energy thinking about her.

When he got out of prison, he shot straight up to Pleasantville to find her. Coming home from the library one night, she saw him waiting for her in the shadows of the dorm. She was out of breath. He'd been secretly following her all night; he said he'd watched her talking to another guy. He said, "I still love you. I still wanna marry you." Finally, she told him to his face: "Tommy, look, we can be friends—but I can't be *with* you anymore."

She would never forget the way his face darkened then; he looked so *evil* standing there in the shadows of her dorm, neck clenched tight, flexing that bodybuilder's physique. You'd never believe he could've been that little bow-tie-wearing churchboy on Crotona Avenue. He hissed at her: "Look, you're still *mine*. You'll always be *mine*. If I can't have you, *no one* will."

And after that night in Medusa, after seeing Big K grabbing for the microphone, howling those badman curses, Crystal could never look at him the same way again. From that night on, she could see K only as another Tommy.

In the coming years she would continue to caution me, whisper about getting too close to the flame. Never chiding—she always spoke about it in a tone of weary fatalism. *Every time you think you can predict his actions, he'll throw you for a sudden loop. Every time you think you've glimpsed the real person behind that tough-guy facade, he'll force you to face the fact that you don't know a damn thing about him.*

Call it voyeurism—compulsion, lunacy—but something was driving me forward, forcing me to see it with my own eyes. One sunny Saturday in July, K called me from a pay phone, wondering if I was doing something important right then—besides jerking off to *Soul Train*, of course. Did I want to go get some money with him? I thought I must have misheard—what was he suggesting? Robbery? Some kind of illicit hustle? I began to whisper conspiratorially into the receiver, but he cut me short, cackling crazily in my ear: "You a funny muthafucka, you know that? You straight-up *stoopid!*"

It turned out I had him all wrong: *gettin' money* was simply slang for lifting weights.

Two hours later I met him under the Empire State Building and we walked to the gym I belonged to on the East Side. I quickly realized that it was going to be a strange Saturday. I emptied my pockets and put the contents on the top shelf of my gym locker: key ring, sixty-three cents in loose change, a half pack of lint-covered Life Savers.

K carried no keys and no paper money. He took off his two-finger diamond-encrusted ring that said FAITH.

And then, from his waistband, I watched as he drew out a gun, an enormous pearl-handled, chrome-plated .45, which he proceeded to slide under my folded-up jeans in the gym locker. He did it so smoothly and unselfconsciously, no one else in the bustling locker room even noticed.

I stared at him for an instant; then I stared at the pearl handle of the gun. At that point in my life, I had never held a real pistol, and I'd certainly never expected to see one tucked under my faded Levi's in the locker room of this overpriced East Side health club.

The changing room was crowded with nude sweaty white men, toweling off and pulling down their underpants, naked accountants and stockbrokers, scurrying in all directions, trying not to step in the nasty puddles that were always forming on the green-tiled floor. I looked at K again but didn't speak. I realized that to say the words that were in my mind—*Why did you put a loaded .45 in my locker?*—might trigger a potentially hazardous commotion in the health club, some frightful stampede of naked sweaty stockbrokers slipping and falling and racing for the locker room exit.

So I said nothing. I closed up the locker and clicked my combination lock shut.

"Let's go get that money," K said, and then he slapped me hard on the chest.

He worked out with a large white towel dangling from his back pocket: it was a fashion I'd often seen West Indian tough guys affect. The right leg of his navy blue pants was hiked up to his knee and he wore a faded stretched tank top that said BALLY'S LAS VEGAS, exposing his long hard biceps and his cantaloupe-sized shoulders.

As we began to lift I noticed the dark shiny penny of a scar just above his right shoulder blade. He caught me staring at it. A love bite from that bitch named nine-milli, he explained, puffing, completing a repetition of preacher curls. When he set down the weights, he turned and lifted one side of his tank top to show me several more hideous circular and mushroom-shaped scars on his back and side and belly.

"How many times have you—"

He shrugged matter-of-factly. He said he had picked up lead four times. Seven gunshot wounds to his body, that is. Four separate occasions.

He suddenly lowered himself to the floor, saying he wanted to show me an exercise he called the C-74 push-up—C-74 being the adolescent jail facility on Rikers Island—that combined a regular push-up with a calisthenic jumping jack. A deceptively simple combination. I copied him, tried to keep pace. Soon I was doubled over on the dirty rubber floor, panting and trying not to throw up.

In between sets, K kept limber by shadowboxing, bobbing and weaving, rifling five or six left-hand jabs at himself in the mirror, ducking down savagely and exploding with a short left hook. His reflexes were astonishing; as big as he was, he moved with the speed and grace of a welterweight. And as he shadowboxed, everyone in the gym stopped to stare.

K, for his part, did not appreciate all the masculine attention.

"No offense," he said, panting for breath, still snapping crisp jabs, "but what's with all the Sodomite business up in this piece?"

"What?"

"On the strength," he said. "You ain't notice? This place is *crawlin'* with fish."

I was sure that the pretty-boy bodybuilders—with their gelled hair and their Lycra workout shorts, posing and studying the horseshoe indentations of their triceps in the full-length mirrors—were no less thrilled by the presence of K, what with those gang-style braids and the way he kept calling me a *punk bitch* as he urged me to complete whatever repetition I was struggling to get off my chest. None of the conventional *c'mon, buddy, that's all you!* exhortations you generally get from a spotting partner in a gym. K kept hurling abuse at me as if we were a couple of drug dealers on the street. "Gimme my muthafuckin' money, *bitch!* Word, that's *my* money!"

He disappeared suddenly, saying that he had to find a pay phone to call Faith. I was gulping down water at the fountain when he came bounding back into the gym.

"We gotta break the fuck out!" he said. "We gotta be at the Circle Line in less than an hour! You know where the fuck that is?"

"West 42nd Street. West Side Highway. W-w-why? What's on the Circle Line?"

"Crazy Sam and them niggas from *Video Music Box* called lookin' for me. They havin' a cruise tonight and we supposed to be on it."

In the locker room, getting dressed after our showers, I asked him how he'd come to know Crazy Sam and the guys from *Video Music Box*—toweling my hair dry, all the while trying, without much success, to keep my eyes from drifting back to the dark healed-up bullet holes in his body.

He explained that the *Video Music Box* crew had been shooting a segment in Central Park the previous weekend. The segment featured the three young ladies called Imago or Indigo—he couldn't remember the precise name of the group. They were three young high-school-aged honeys, doing some dance steps for the cameras—and then, all of a sudden, a group of rowdy uptown guys started disrespecting the girls, coming too close, grabbing at them, and finally Crazy Sam had to tell them to cut that bullshit out.

K shrugged, carefully adjusting the drape of his baggy khaki pants. "So then this one nigga starts talkin' shit to Sam like he's some real badman and, boom, I just stepped to him and knocked him the fuck out. *Pa-pow!* Cracked that punk bitch in the cranium, put him to bed. Ever since then them *Video Music Box* niggas have been on the dick."

He smiled at himself in the mirror; I noticed that his teeth looked extremely white and well cared for. I watched as he took his Colt .45 from my locker and then furtively tucked it back in the waist of his pants.

From his gym bag he took two different deodorants, first a Ban roll-on, then a Right Guard aerosol spray. He had borrowed them from one of his babies' mothers, he said. I watched as he patted his chest and underarms with baby powder. For a guy who didn't have a regular place to sleep, I thought, he was pretty meticulous about the way he smelled.

We took a cab over to the West Side to meet the guys from *Video Music Box*. *Video Music Box* was the pioneering rap program in New York City, playing hip-hop videos years before the programmers at MTV had ever heard of Run-DMC or LL Cool J. It broadcast every weekday afternoon on UHF channel 31, and had an avid following in the hundreds of thousands, mostly in the poorer sections of the city where many buildings still weren't wired for cable.

Crazy Sam was one of the show's most popular and colorful personalities, with his wild matted-up head of hair and his gap-toothed smile; he was forever growling and jumping around as he hosted the weekly episode known as "Nervous Thursdays."

Within the hour we were standing beside Crazy Sam on board the Circle Line boat, slowly rocking back and forth in the Hudson River. K had hoped that there would be an open mike on the cruise, that he'd have a chance to drop some lyrics in the party; but he soon learned, much to his disappointment, that he was only there to provide muscle, to bodyguard some skantily clad dancing girls. According to the flyer I caught fluttering in the wind, the night was billed as a DOO DOO BROWN CRUISE FEATURING DA BRONX'S LEGENDARY LOVEBUG STARSKI ON DA WHEELS OF STEEL. Doo Doo Brown was the latest and lewdest hip-hop dance style out of Miami; I'd seen it a few times in videos: the women dancers bent-over and gyrating their backsides in a pantomine of doggy-style sex.

We had a private corner of the ship—Crazy Sam, K, the other security men, along with a group of six professional dancing girls wearing skintight catsuits and Lycra miniskirts. Crazy Sam was explaining to K and the other security men what their mission for the night would be: at the appointed hour, the dancers would strip down to their thong bikinis and begin to shake; the security men would have to form a human ring around them, to protect their bodies from the groping hands of male partyers.

By the time we pulled out of the West Side piers, the ship's main deck was packed; there was barely a place to stand comfortably on the makeshift open-air dance floor. Throughout the cruise, Crazy Sam and the *Video Music Box* camera crew would set up their bright lights and microphones in various parts of the deck, and there was good-natured shrieking and jostling as people tried to get on camera and make their dedications heard over the sound of the music.

"Shoutout to all my peeps in Edenwald, Gun Hill Road, Baychester Ave—the whole of the Boogie Down!"

"One love to my man J.B. on Rikers—hold it down, God!"

"Yo, Marcy Projects in full effect! *Brooklynnn!* Represent, represent!"

Everyone shifted suddenly to the leeward side of the ship. At first I was afraid that someone had gone overboard, but then I realized they were just trying to get a good look at the Statue of Liberty as we passed. I stayed on the other side of the boat, leaning against the railing, mesmerized by one of the Doo Doo Brown dancers. She wore a shimmering white bodysuit with wide black stripes curving demonically over the sweep of her hips and thighs. She was doing the Jamaican dance known as The Butterfly and as she danced her black-and-white-striped body began to look like an optical illusion.

A little later in the cruise, when Lady Liberty was no longer in view, I found myself talking to the optical illusion. Her name was

Robin. She smiled at me a lot with her large white teeth. Her lips were full and painted a glossy red. Her false fingernails were about four inches long and also painted a glossy red.

She asked me if I was a hip-hop junkie. I told her I'd never thought of myself as a hip-hop junkie. She said I would have to be a hip-hop junkie to be on a cruise like this. She asked me if I'd noticed that the only other white people on board were the ship's crew, and they'd now disappeared to some cabin with the door safely bolted shut.

I gave a tentative nod. Then Robin asked me if I'd seen her dancing in that Wreckxs-n-Effect video. Of course, I said. (As if even an ass connoisseur could distinguish one close-up shot of bouncing buttocks from the next.) A lot of people recognized her from the Wreckxs-n-Effect video, she said. But she was now more of a choreographer. In September she was going to go back to school to study dance and choreography full-time.

Robin was bored. She said she was only doing this cruise for the money. She clapped one time and began to rap along to the Nice & Smooth song blaring from the overhead speakers:

I left my Philly at home
Do you have another?

We were somewhere in the middle of the Hudson River when K landed the punch. It happened so quickly that at first I thought I hadn't seen what I'd seen. Like catching a glimpse of the stuttered movements of a dancer through the flashes of a strobe light.

The ruckus began with some big-time drug dealers from Harlem. K had pointed them out to me earlier in the cruise. K knew them— and they knew K—from his own days in the drug game. But since K was no longer wearing the type of heavy gold jewelry or designer clothes they sported, the uptown dealers weren't showing him much respect. Actually, they weren't showing anyone much respect. They staggered drunkenly around the boat, swigging from their bottles of champagne, loudly slapping the asses of women they didn't know.

I could overhear snippets of the argument as it began. Apparently the posse of uptown dealers felt Lovebug Starski wasn't showing their crew adequate respect. Why weren't they receiving more shoutouts from his microphone?

They made a mad rush for the DJ's table, trying to wrest the mike from Starski, but K and Crazy Sam and the rest of the security team cut them off and got into a jawing match with them. The argument grew louder and louder. I was standing about five feet away when one of the uptown badboys, a pissy-drunk hustler called Trigga Trig, reached into his waistband to pull out his pistol.

But before Trigga Trig could even raise the gun, K sprang forward and landed a lightning left hook, followed, instantly, by a right cross that left Trigga Trig sprawled and dazed at the boat's railing.

By the time Trigga Trig got to his feet, Crazy Sam had drawn his own Glock 9-mm with its thirty-two-round banana clip from his baggy pants (pants so wondrously baggy, I later reflected, it would not have been all that surprising to see him standing on the bow of the boat brandishing a bazooka). Sam didn't need to level his Glock at anyone; he simply held it in his hands as a peacemaker. And it kept the peace until the boat was safely docked back at the West Side pier.

Once we got to the parking lot, the beef with Trigga Trig erupted again. Someone was toting a sawed-off shotgun. K had his .45 ready in his right hand. They began to follow Trigga Trig to the dark end of the Circle Line parking lot. K told me to wait for him in the van but, with more Heineken than good sense in my system, I couldn't wait: I got out and followed him into the dark end of the parking lot. As I approached I could hear Trigga Trig spitting out his drunk bravado: "Shoot me, muhfucka! G'head an' shoot me if you gon' shoot me!"

K was furious when he saw me standing in the darkness behind him. "Muthafucka, I told you wait in the fuckin' *van!* Shit gettin' ready to pop off!"

*   *   *

I sat in the dark of the van with the dancing girls. No one was speaking. One of the dancers was snapping her gum in a way that reminded me, vaguely and for some unknown reason, of my mother. I looked at the dancer named Robin. She was no longer an optical illusion. She was half asleep with her head on another girl's shoulder. All the girls looked bored and tired and ready to go home. It was quiet enough that I could hear the ticking of my glow-in-the-dark Swatch. There was no sound of gunfire.

After a few minutes, K and Crazy Sam and the rest of the security guys returned. Laughing at some private joke, they piled into the van and we squealed out of the parking lot. K shoved himself heavily down next to me. I whispered in his ear: "What happened?"

"We squashed that shit," he said loudly.

"Squashed it?"

"Why even *distress* the nigga? Trig was too fuckin' drunk for his own good."

With the loud crackle of gravel under rubber, the driver swung a hard uptown turn onto the West Side Highway. Everyone was laughing again, the dancing girls, the security guys; Crazy Sam was telling some funny story I could only half hear over the blaring stereo.

I caught a glimpse of my ghostly reflection in the van's side window: I expected to see something different, *someone* different—shouldn't a person be instantaneously changed by such proximity to casual gunplay? But nothing looked or felt any different; the green-glowing second hand of my watch was still clicking off notches at its usual pace; K was still smiling beatifically beside me in the shifting shadows.

I heard a sound I hadn't expected to hear: my own laughter. Yes, that was me laughing along with Crazy Sam's story . . . and now it was so easy to forget that there'd nearly been a wild shootout on the cruise, that these large men around me had nearly turned the West Side piers into the O.K. Corral. We were just an ordinary vanful of people pressed together tightly in the darkness, laughing at some half-assed joke, rumbling home from a party on a steamy summer night.

After the incident on the Circle Line cruise I resolved that it would be best not to spend too much time around K. But barely one week later I was out at an after-hours reggae party in the basement of the Time Café when I felt catlike footsteps creeping up behind me in the shadows.

"Yush, ragamuffin!" called the voice, and when I turned I saw him, looming over me, looking even taller than I remembered, his form dark and menacing in a shimmering black sweat suit. "One love," he said, and I nodded and he held out his fist for me to bump gently with my own. He wore a black nylon doo-rag on his head. There was a playful gleam in his eyes. The scar on his left cheek looked translucent and wet in the dark light of the club. "You need a beer?" No, he reminded me, he never touched alcohol.

I asked him about Bunny and the music business. He kissed his teeth, said he'd found out the hard way what Bunny was about. Bunny was about a bunch of bullshit. Bunny was strictly about trying to impress the bitches.

He was sipping a bottle of Evian water and he danced, rubbing his back lazily against the wall in the classic Jamaican badman skank. *Cool an' deadly.* When he stopped dancing he asked me to look close, real close, and see if I could spot Scobey.

Scobey? I began to scan the wall beside him, but then he grabbed my shoulder, took my hand, touched it to his hip. I felt the cold metal bulge and then I understood: Scobey was his pet name for his .45. He smiled, and continued to dance, very pleased with himself, pleased that he'd been able to bring Scobey to the dance without detection.

We stood side by side with our backs against the wall. It was a night of heavy dub: strictly drum and bass. I closed my eyes and stood swaying to the snare drum hammering out the militant rockers rhythm and then the echo chamber sound effects pulsing through you like X rays and then the bass so low you could no longer hear it, you could only feel it, feel it entering your chest like a demon, wrestling your own heartbeat away from you.

We left the Time Café together at ten minutes past one. There was a painful ringing in my ears and I couldn't even hear the traffic anymore. K asked me if I felt like walking. He said he needed to walk in order to think. We wandered the dark streets of the Lower East Side, talking about Meyer Lansky and Bugsy Siegel and how the feds had railroaded the Dapper Don—Gotti'd finally been convicted of murder and racketeering a few weeks earlier—and then we veered west and wandered through the dead-fish-reeking streets of Chinatown, then through shuttered-up SoHo and over into the West Village, me swaying slightly under the influence of four Red Stripes, he, as always, cold sober, rhyming to the rhythm of his own footsteps, working out a lyric—*"Pack it up, pack it up"*—about how he and Faith had been on the lam over in New Jersey. The police hated him over there in Jersey, he said. He could not go back to Jersey without having *big* problems.

The back of his black nylon doo-rag fell well below his shoulders, billowing backward in the breeze. It made him look like an Arab sheik who'd decided to take up midnight jogging. It also made him look particularly scary.

Everywhere we went that night, I caught those fearful glances, witnessed his uncanny capacity to turn people to stone. Walking alongside him, stride for stride, I could almost feel, for one flashbulb instant, what it was like to be in his skin—not simply possessing an inherent power to terrorize, but never *escaping* from that power. Even laughing good-naturedly, he needed only to appear in a bodega or on a subway platform to see the blanched faces recoiling from him in mute terror. To them, he was nothing more than the cartoon criminal cutout from every eleven o'clock newscast, the specter who haunted the dreams of all decent New Yorkers: gunman, drug dealer, home invader . . . Shouldn't a man that scary, the faces seemed to be saying, a man that irredeemably *bad*, be locked up someplace behind bars?

K knew this was how the world perceived him; he acknowledged as much in one of the Jamaican lyrics he used to rhyme in those days: *Jah know mi dangerous*. Dangerous, yes, but I liked better the phrase I heard later in the summer, from one of his admiring homeboys, standing inside the Arab-owned bodega on the corner of Franklin Avenue, twisting the cap off a foaming forty-ounce bottle of St. Ides malt liquor. Big K was the ultimate street terror, said the admirer: a natural-born thug with Golden Gloves skills *and* a heart of stone.

But behind the sheer danger in his badman stride, behind the natural-born thugishness, I perceived something else, something those blood-less, terrorized faces could never see. Could they have imagined the capricious humor, the childlike wonder, the constant eagerness to learn, to inquire, to decipher the mysteries of a code just slightly be-yond his reach? Riding the subway one afternoon, I felt him elbowing me hard on the shoulder, leaning his lips close to my ear so I could hear him over the din of the train.

"Ay yo, this is something I never understood. Why do white peo-ple—as much as y'all be *hatin'* black people—why do you always hire one of us to look after your kids?"

Just as I was trying to figure out why the hell he was asking me this, I saw, seated on the next bank of subway seats, the young nanny with her dreadlocks tied up in a blue tie-dyed scarf, holding the hand of a small blond girl. The little girl looked about three and wore a shiny purple Barney the dinosaur raincoat with purple barrettes in her hair. Her little sneakers barely dangled over the edge of the seat. No doubt the pride and joy of some East Side ophthalmologist.

"Why are you saying *you?*" I said.

"I don't mean *you* you—I mean white cats in general."

"Shhh." He was talking so loudly. "I don't know about anybody *in general*," I said. "First off, how do you know that *that* little girl's par-ents hate black people?"

"I'm just sayin'," he said. "Not all white people—maybe not her parents—but whatever percent of white cats—cats that's rich enough so that they can afford to pay somebody to take care of their kids all day long. And then you know they ain't got *no* black friends. They ain't got no black colleagues comin' over to the crib on Friday night for chocolate-filled croissants and cappuccino and all that ol' good shit. So why pick one of us?"

I shrugged. "Some of them don't. They pick Mexicans, Salvadorans—"

"Same shit," he said. "They black too. They just don't know it."

He held his head close to mine, waiting for me to respond. The train continued on its rumbling, jostling underground course.

"Don't they know how impressionable kids is at that age? Look at her—everything that little kid's learnin' about the world—how a cash register rings when the drawer kicks out . . . why worms come out of the ground when it rains—all that crucial shit she's learnin' from one of *us.*"

I nodded and, since I couldn't answer his question, I asked him one of my own.

"What about you?" I said.

"What about me?"

"You ever hate white people?"

"Come again?"

"You ever hate—"

"I *heard* you, muthafucka—I just can't believe you got the balls to ask me that question."

If I was happy to trespass on his turf, he seemed equally happy to trespass on mine. When he wasn't in his relaxed homeboy mode, when he was trying too hard to impress, he had a habit of mangling and misusing proper English—saying, for example, *intelligentsia* when he was simply trying to describe someone's intelligence. At first I was hesitant to point out these malapropisms. But one night I overheard him, standing in the basement of Nell's, butchering language in a conversation with some goateed and Kangol-wearing music industry leech. When we had a private moment together, I leaned over and told him that he had the wrong idea about certain words.

"What, intelligentsia ain't a real word?"

"It's a real word, but not the word you think it is."

I thought he might be offended by my pedantry; but he simply stared back at me, wide-eyed, and asked me to explain where he'd been wrong. As it turned out, he'd long been trying to improve his vocabulary. When I finished talking, he nodded his head. "You see, *that's* what I've been tryin' to fuckin' tell you," he said. "Each one, teach one. Any person who ain't open to new game is a muthafuckin' fool."

Brooklyn beckoned. Flickering dreams of the borough so vast, so impenetrable, its many secrets could be known—in Thomas Wolfe's impeccable phrase—only by the souls of the dead. Until that summer, everything I knew about Brooklyn had been culled from books or films or family stories; in short, I knew *nothing* about Brooklyn. I wanted to see the borough firsthand, walk the broad avenues and leafy parkways, stand in the dark, dangerous corners where tourists never ventured.

Brooklyn was where my mother'd been born, where my immigrant grandfather had worked as a stevedore during the Depression. His name was Velvl—the Yiddish diminutive for Wolf—but we always called him Grandpa Willie. Born into the radical industrial ferment of Bialystok, he was an avowed anarchist who read the writings of Bakunin in Russian; a short broadbacked man with forearms that felt like wrought iron; a self-taught intellectual who, in his younger years, had been a fierce fistfighter.

Working on the Brooklyn waterfront, he'd been routinely taunted by bigger men who spat out that hated epithet, the one he'd heard so often in Polish and Russian: *dirty Jew*. But Willie's temper was so bad that some nights, after those waterfront brawls, showing up bruised

and bloody, my grandmother would cry and yell at him in Yiddish—
"One day you'll come home a murderer!"—so afraid was she that, in
his blinding rage, he'd end up strangling one of those Jew-baiting
goons with his bare hands.

K was intrigued to hear that I too had Brooklyn bloodlines. As the
weeks rolled into months, I envisioned him as my intrepid guide
through the borough, taking me out to the block in Coney Island
where my grandparents used to live. My mother had described playing on an idyllic street of modest but lovingly maintained wood-frame
homes, a close-knit block of Jews and Italians, not a stone's throw
from Steeplechase Park—23rd Street just off the Coney Island Boardwalk. It couldn't have been a fantasy; I'd seen the shady verandas myself in one of my mother's blurry black-and-white snapshots.

"Well, ain't no *homes* out there now," K said with a scornful laugh.
"Long as I've been alive that's been some rude fuckin' projects. I wouldn't
show my face out there without no biscuit and no bulletproof vest."

If my grandfather's Brooklyn had vanished, I would have to discover
whichever side of the borough K could show me. I had to master a
whole new lexicon for my first journey to Crown Heights. For starters,
K called the neighborhood *Crime Heights;* he referred to the borough
variously as *Crooklyn* or *Medina.* The heart of *his* Brooklyn was the corner of Franklin Avenue and Eastern Parkway on the western fringe of
the Heights. This corner, this infamous crossroads, was the home base
to his crew: the Franklin Avenue Posse.

Emerging from the subway station, I asked him if I had to worry
about any of his old crew mistaking me for an undercover cop.

"If you rolled out of the train alone—*hell yeah.* They'd make you for
a DT in about, oh, half a second." He looked me up and down, glancing
at my sweat-stained baseball cap, my knapsack, my busted-up Adidas.
"Shit, you got the mark of the beast all over you. But you gotta figure they
all know my pedigree—they all know what time it is with me. They
know I'm one nigga who never had *no* love for no muthafuckin' beast."

The sunshine on Eastern Parkway was blinding. The summer heat hit us like a desert wind. We passed under the red-and-green neon tubing of a drugstore called Maiman's. A small amplifier was set up on the corner of Franklin Avenue, blasting a melodic reggae beat over which a gospel singer was wailing some tune called "One True God."

Traveling through the Crown Heights streets that first day, I noticed something strange: my walking companion was known by many different aliases. Some people called him Knowledge Born; others called him Gato. But mostly they called him K-God. *K-God! K-God! What's poppin', Big K?* (Later, I'd learn of his other aliases: Tony Speng—*speng* being rudeboy slang for a gun; and Tunda, an apparent reference to the thunderous report of that Colt .45 on his hip.)

I asked him why people in Crown Heights didn't call him American Dread. "That's just my rap name," he said. His voice dropped to a whisper and he explained the necessity for so many aliases. "When shit gets hot, and beast is all over askin' a bunch of questions about Knowledge Born or K-God, you got no choice but to start operatin' under a fresh name. See, it's good because—like muthafuckas over in Red Hook"—he waved his arm expansively toward the west side of Brooklyn—"over in Red Hook they only know me as Gato, and they might hear my crimies over here talkin' about K-God and not even know it's the same *me* they talkin' 'bout."

"Can I ask you something personal?"

"Depends."

"What's your real name?"

"Whatcha sayin'? Knowledge Born ain't a *real* name? 'Merican Dread ain't a *real* name?"

"You know what I'm saying. What's it say on your birth certificate?"

He stopped walking, stood dead still, the better to focus his laser-like gaze and force me to stop walking as well. "You bugged the fuck out, duke? I ain't lettin' you know my fuckin' government name."

I shrugged; it made no difference to me what I called him.

"Shit!" he said, still very agitated. "I got niggas out here that's known me they *whole* life and still don't know my fuckin' government name!"

"Okay. I understand. Dead issue."

*   *   *

Whatever name you called him, he was certainly infamous on the block, the subject of dozens of street corner anecdotes. Some spoke about his remarkably precocious fistfighting skills (as an eleven-year-old boy he'd had the power to knock out a grown man), or his uncanny ability to survive gunshot wounds. ("Kill K-God? *What!* This nigga got more lives than *twenty-two* cats!") Still others droned on about his extravagant lifestyle back in the drug days, all the excessive gold jewelry, the diamond-encrusted Rolexes, the Fila track suits, all the kitted-up candy-colored sports cars that would appear, mysteriously, like phantom chariots on the block. "This nigga used to change his rides just to match his sneakers," someone said.

There were people on Franklin who hadn't seen K since he went out to California and Nevada to box. "Niggas up north told me you was out in Vegas, letting niggas *have* it!" said Drévon, a short stocky guy who'd just come out of prison, who stood hugging K for at least five minutes before letting go. (Drévon was never a member of the Franklin Avenue Posse, I learned, but of the nearby, affiliated crew called N.A. Rock—Nostrand Avenue Rock.) "I said, 'My nigga was doin' that out in the street for *nothin*'—'bout time he got paid for it.'"

But K didn't like to talk about the boxing days. He told me that boxing had left a bitter taste in his mouth. He felt like he'd been chumped. He'd never been beaten in the ring—he had sixteen professional fights—but he'd been badly beaten by his managers: they'd screwed up his money, left him with nothing but bills. He'd stopped boxing in disgust, taking a Greyhound bus home from Vegas, went right back to a career he could understand, back to selling drugs.

Throughout that first summer, I got to know many of the other Posse members—both the living and the dead. There was the tale of poor Infinite, who'd died in '86, right in that building across the Parkway, blown himself up, soldering iron in hand, while constructing a pipe bomb packed with C-4 explosives. Infinite had always been a bomb freak, K explained matter-of-factly. There was the late, great Kool Aid (he and K had reputedly exchanged a hail of automatic gunfire during a financial dispute back in the '80s); big Kool Aid, who could not be felled by .45-caliber bullets, but who'd recently died of AIDS, acquiring the fatal virus during a seemingly routine blood transfusion. ("Faggot-ass muthafuckas," Drévon angrily growled, referring, I assumed, to the doctors who'd given Kool Aid his transfusion.)

There was Shabazz, the renowned DJ, currently out on bail, charged with assaulting several police officers and inciting a riot right on the corner of Franklin Avenue and President Street. To hear Shabazz tell the story, he'd been minding his own business, drinking a bottle of malt liquor with some of the other guys on the corner. They weren't doing *shit* that day, he said, except hanging on the corner and being black. A squad car of uniformed cops from the 71st Precinct drove past in pursuit of another call. Suddenly, the car stopped and one of the cops advised them to get off the corner. Shabazz told the cops he wasn't going anywhere; this was *his* neighborhood. Unlike them, he lived on this block.

The cops said they could write him a citation for drinking that malt liquor in public. They told Shabazz to get rid of the bottle. Shabazz tried to hook-shot the malt liquor bottle into the garbage can. He caught the rim and the bottle shattered on the pavement.

The police claimed that Shabazz had been trying to throw the bottle at their squad car. A violent altercation ensued during which a car windshield was smashed in. The police said Shabazz smashed the windshield with his fist. Neighborhood eyewitnesses disputed this story. They said that, in fact, the police had smashed the windshield with Shabazz's head.

The only fact not in dispute was that, when the altercation ended, Shabazz was in the hospital. And when he regained consciousness, the police informed him that he was under arrest for a host of felony charges, including, bizarrely, grand larceny (after the altercation, one of the cops claimed that his radio was missing from his belt).

Against the advice of K and some of the other Posse members, Shabazz had turned down the DA's plea bargain offer. He wanted to take his case to trial. There were plenty of eyewitnesses—and these were people who worked nine-to-fives, mind you—who could back up his side of the story. There was a nurse who'd seen the whole thing through her living room window. She was willing to come to court and testify that she'd seen the police throw Shabazz through the windshield when he was already in handcuffs. Shabazz was confident he'd beat the case in court because, he said, he was quite simply in the right.

K kept shaking his head. "Right ain't got shit to do with it. You cannot take that shit to trial, Bazzy. You ain't never gonna beat them lyin'-ass beast in court."

K often said that he lived to rhyme, that his truest love was for the "art of hip-hop." For me, it was more of an infatuation. How could it be otherwise? I grew up in *Canada,* after all—I hadn't even heard of rap until my freshman year in college. But by that Brooklyn summer of '92, I was clearly smitten, watching Shabazz skillfully working his crossfader, finding magic in the crackling vinyl grooves—he was indeed the Grand Wizard of the Technics 1200s. His bedroom was his private sound lab, a claustrophobic cavern of turntables and massive outdoor speakers and milk crates filled with hundreds of vintage records. The Gemini mixer boldly labeled with the name of his sound system, MAGNUM FORCE PRODUCTIONS, and, on the ledge above the turntables, neatly lined up, a dozen empty Moët & Chandon bottles: trophies of parties past.

"Stop loafin', Heliumhead! Let's *roll* with this shit!" K was shouting with typical impatience.

"Why do you keep calling him Heliumhead?"

"You *blind?* Look at his muthafuckin' head, man. Don't it look inflated—like it should say *Happy Birthday* 'cross the front?"

"Man, *fuck* you!" said Shabazz, even as K pointed to the bumped scar on his homeboy's forehead, just below the hairline, where a bullet had made a valiant effort to penetrate brain tissue but been denied entrance by the thick bone of his skull.

I watched Shabazz's nimble wrists at work on the turntables, delicately fingering the vinyl of Biz Markee's "Vapors" back and forth. *Big-*

bubba-big. Bubba-big-drug-dealer. Someone was puffing on a sensimillia blunt and, through the rising whorls of weed smoke, the half-light
from the window illuminated the ghostly fingerprint smudges on the
spinning vinyl.

Crystal had described the minimalist beauty of this scene for me:
as a little Bronx kid, after all, she'd been there to watch it all unfolding; her uncle had been the promoter—Godfather Productions—of
some of the early hip-hop parties at the Disco Fever and the T-Connection and Harlem World. ("Uncle Bundy!" she'd cry. "Eddie *Cheeba?*
Kurtis *Blow? Again? C'mon!* Book someone *new!*") But now I was seeing it with my own eyes. So this was how hip-hop had sounded,
looked—felt—back in the days of the Bronx pioneers, before sam-
plers and synthesizers had reduced everything to sterile kilobytes and
computerized sound waves.*

Shabazz's bedroom lab had no MPC-60 drum machine or DX-7
keyboard. If he needed to extend the four-bar instrumental break in a
given song, he had to do it the old-fashioned way, using two copies of
the record, his crossfader switch and a panther's reflexes. He'd isolate
an instrumental break in the Sugar Hill Gang's "Eighth Wonder" and,
quickly switching back and forth between two well-worn copies, provide K with a crackling bed on which to drop his rhyme. K would hold
the microphone close to his mouth and drop a flow he called "Hustler."

Criminal justice system
They just missed him
Forget about the homicide victim

---

*Although the terms *rap* and *hip-hop* are often used interchangeably in the press, there is
a clear connotative distinction: to many aficionados, *rap* is a pejorative, referring (as in "the
rap game") to corporate America's newfound love affair with the music, its co-option by
the world of glass towers, computerized recording studios and glitzy TV commercials; *hip-
hop,* by contrast, is the pure, uncompromised, ever-mutating street culture, bedroom
turntable sets and impromptu rhyme ciphers sparked on dimly lit street corners. *Hip-hop*
can also be used as an umbrella term, encompassing all four of the primary cultural expressions born simultaneously in the early '70s Bronx: breakdancing, graffiti art (tagging),
DJing (cutting and scratching) and MCing (rapping).

The glory days of the Magnum Force sound system—like the glory days of the Franklin Avenue Posse—were now long gone. Shabazz rarely rallied the guys to haul those mammoth speakers down to the park, or the street corner, so that he could give a free performance, have all the neighborhood girls shrieking and shaking their sexy round rumps to the sonic boom of his turntable sorcery. But there were plenty of live recordings of his parties, plenty of battle tapes stacked in a corner; listening to them on my Walkman, I could imagine myself there in the park, back in '88 or '89, on the crowded dance floor of Club Illusion, or the Empire Roller Rink, as Shabazz dropped the latest reggae groove, as Posse men like K and Fuquan and Naquan stepped up, like conquering heroes, to take control of the microphone. On one muffled, unlabeled tape, I could hear K—then billing himself as Knowledge Born—arrogantly commandeering the mike, barking out his humorous, echoing, rudeboy-style dedication to the packed dancehall:

Special request goin' out to all F.A. Posse an' all overseer! Yu nuh know? A so it go . . . Come down wit' de riddim, Bazzy! Now dis one kickin' like Bruce Lee—like Chef Boy-ar-dee—wit' de rav-i-o-li . . .

Every time K showed up on Franklin Avenue, he would soon be surrounded by several of the younger Posse members, approaching, eager-eyed, shuffling in their shabby sneakers, asking him vague questions—*So what you got goin' on, K?*—looking like they were waiting for a miracle, for manna to fall from the heavens.

What the hell were they waiting for? I wondered aloud, once K and I were walking alone, down toward the Tower Isle bakery to get some Jamaican beef patties.

Money, he said.

"They was always my little niggas—under my wing—when I was hustlin' I always used to hit 'em off with sneakers and jewelry and shit. Now I just gotta tell 'em straight-up—I ain't got *shit* no more—can't do *nothin'* for you, duke."

*   *   *

Sure, there was abject poverty on Franklin Avenue—you had only to stand in the corner bodega for a few minutes and watch the steady exchange of food stamps—but it wasn't the bombed-out destitution I'd seen, driving with Crystal, through those otherworldly stretches of Hunts Point and Soundview in her native Bronx. The architecture on Franklin was still intact: classic prewar brick buildings with impressive masonry work—so what if nearly every corner needed to be steamed clean of those omnipresent graffiti tags? The solace of the Brooklyn Museum and the Botanic Garden lay just up the block; the trees that lined Eastern Parkway were in full, fragrant bloom; the pigeons were cooing, fat bumblebees humming, happy kids were doing reckless, acrobatic stunts on skateboards and Rollerblades.

It didn't feel like desperation.

But just wait until nightfall: you'd soon see the desperation. Peer into the dull yellow eyes that haunted the midnight corner, willing to sell anything, sell *themselves,* for just one more hit of the white rock.

Once the sun had set on Franklin Avenue, and the glow of those darting, desperate eyes lit up the corner, I was always terrified that K might disappear from sight, leave me standing there alone, unprotected, on his block. But he was a loyal friend: he never once left my side.

Crime Heights. One of the strangest patches of New York City: this sprawling section of central Brooklyn where Rastafarians in bright hand-painted dashikis walk uneasily beside black-frocked Hasidim; where yarmulke-wearing boys on banana-seat bikes pedal past little bronze island faces sucking on stalks of sugarcane; where, on a gloriously sunny Saturday afternoon, the air over Eastern Parkway rings with the babble of Jamaican patois commingling with old-country Yiddish.

Of course, to many New Yorkers, the name Crown Heights evokes a darker image: the bloody riots of the summer of 1991, the worst episode of black-Jewish violence in the nation's history. The bare facts of those riots could never convey the complexities of the decades-old culture clash: a seven-year-old Guyanese boy killed by a reckless Hasidic driver; a twenty-nine-year-old Holocaust scholar from Australia stabbed to death by a mob chanting *Kill the Jew!*

When I first ventured into Crown Heights with K, I was surprised to feel the relative tranquillity, to find the streets blanketed by an eerie calm. Barely a year had passed since the riots, but like everything else in Crown Heights, those three ugly August nights were now lost in a *Rashomon* haze: to many Jews, the violence had been a *pogrom,* the actions of an organized anti-Semitic mob, aided by an ineffectual mayor and a criminally negligent police department; to many black residents, it had been an *uprising,* the inchoate rage of an impoverished community fed up with years of perceived inequity, political double standards and institutional neglect.

Two versions of history. Two versions of the truth. And between the warring camps, little dialogue, little contact, just a surplus of suspicious stares.

Standing on the corner of Franklin Avenue with K and the other Posse members, I felt like a solitary pawn pushed too far up the chessboard for its own good, surrounded by stronger pieces, pieces of a different hue. I would invariably become the target of passing Lubavitch Hasidim wanting to retrieve me, rescue me, bring me back into the bosom of the tribe. Our eyes would lock in a glance of recognition, then they'd approach, ignoring the glares of the Franklin Avenue badmen, rushing over, asking me, without introduction or preamble: "You're Jewish?" (That was always their first question; the second: *Would I be willing to make a mitzvah, bind my head and arm in the phylacteries and say the ancient prayers with them—right there in the street?*) I understood that this was all part of their Grande Rebbe's religious mission, to try to lure as many "unaffiliated" Jews as possible back into the fold; accordingly, I'd always try to engage the Hasidim as politely as I could; once or twice, I even agreed to come down to their World Headquarters at 770 Eastern Parkway to pray with them.

But eventually they became so annoying in their proselytizing zeal that whenever one would rush over to ask me if I was Jewish, I'd sim-

ply shake my head, avert my gaze, and let him continue on his way—
another bearded, bobbing black fedora, fast-striding down Eastern
Parkway toward the safety of the Kingston Avenue enclave.

"Not Jewish?" K stared hard at me the first time he saw me em-
ploying this self-defense strategy. "Denied your *boys?* That ain't right,
duke." Turning away, he kissed his teeth loudly, disapprovingly. Yes,
he was right: it was craven, cowardly; and I did feel the burn of shame
on my face, like Peter—wasn't it Peter? the Galilean?—denying *his*
rabbi three times before the crowing of the cock.

Late in the summer we crossed our Rubicon: K entrusted me with
all his precious rap lyrics—and with his government name. Kevin Antonio Thomas.* I felt strange typing it into my computer; he hadn't
seemed like a Kevin to me. All those other names had sounded *hard*—
Knowledge Born, K-God, Gato, Tony Speng. You could imagine the
icy click of an automatic when you said those aliases, a chilling holler
in an alleyway, the bitter screech of getaway rubber. *Kevin* made him
sound like a quiet little kid.

We'd been walking in the West Village one night when he asked
me to take all his lyrics from him, type them up in my computer, mail
them down to the copyright office in Washington. He was intent on
putting those folded-up, handwritten pages of looseleaf in my knapsack, but I wouldn't accept possession of them.

"What the fuck's wrong with you, D?"

"Those are your originals, right?"

"Yeah."

"What if I lose them? What if my bag gets stolen or something?
You're gonna want to kill me."

"True."

---

*In addition to his myriad street aliases, K is known to the authorities by several different
"government" names. Kevin Antonio Thomas is *not* one of them. See note on p. 403 regarding names changed in this book.

So then we set out on a mission, looking for someplace that could make photocopies of his lyrics at two o'clock on a deathly still Monday morning. At last we found an all-night corner store on Greenwich Avenue with a self-service photocopier in the back. It was an ancient Xerox machine, a refugee from some early '80s high school office: the blinding light flashed and the machine rattled and hummed and let out its close-to-dying groan. It worked on an honor system; you told the guy how many copies you'd made and then paid. I was being very meticulous about making sure each copy was legible. K got impatient with me and waited outside in the street.

When I finally finished making all the copies, the store's only employee had his back turned. He was splitting open a newly arrived bundle of tomorrow's newspapers with a box cutter. I had to clear my throat to get his attention.

When I came outside K was glaring at me. "What the fuck is your problem, D? Why the fuck you didn't just *step?* That Arab muthafucka wasn't even studyin' you."

I glared back at him. Why the hell would I want to rip the guy off for a few bucks' worth of photocopies?

He was so exasperated now that he seemed in pain: it made his brain ache just contemplating the depths of my idiocy. "This *corny* muthafucka!" he was hollering, loud enough that even the three yuppies staggering out of the bar across the street turned to stare at us. Then he turned to me suddenly and put his arm around my shoulder, pulled me in close against his chest like my big brother used to do, back when I was about six and we used to wrestle in the basement and he'd torture me by rubbing my cheeks raw with his bearded hippie's chin.

We walked and K held me tight in that big-brother clench, so tight that I could smell his Bazooka Joe bubblegum breath and feel the cold metallic bulge on his hip. "Lemme ask you somethin', duke," he said. "How you gonna be down with F.A.P. if you gotta be so muthafuckin' *honest* all the time?"

*   *   *

I'd told him that I wasn't interested in his Franklin Avenue Posse primer on petit larceny; but there were other lessons I did want to learn, mysteries imbedded in the cramped, scratched-out handwriting of his rap lyrics. Typing them into my computer, I was continually perplexed; the slang was too thick, his personal references too oblique for me to fathom. One lyric had been marked with a blotchy asterisk; beside which, a small parenthetical note—written to him or to me? who could tell?—(HANDLE THIS SHIT WITH CARE MY AUTOBIOGRAPHY.) The title was "American Dread a.k.a. the Born Loser." I began to enter the first few verses into my computer.

the impact of childhood sadness
keeps me anguished
as I unleash the madness
the scars of life on my body parts
they help me remember
when I was young and tender

the struggle the fight
my whole life I cried
thought about suicide
damn oh yo otherwise
to murder the bitch that cold kept the switch
evil and wicked witch
the little fat bitch

curse the day of October
lookin' over my shoulder
stuck no luck as I grew older
the maze the stage the cage
the whole outrage
was filled with Spofford nights
and Goshen days

the animal magnitude instinct
always kept me on the brink
and lookin' for the link

(hurry!) come catch him!
don't let him! (hurry!)
(hurry!) come catch him!
And let him learn his lesson

the sound of a cell block door
or an iron gate
fuck a doctor monk!
And send a nigga upstate
let him shape up ship out
but don't let him drop out
or go the right route

too late to pray for the Lord
to come my way
on a two-to-six bid
I was cursed from the first day

a total outcast
I would wax that ass
punks or chumps even badboys
they can't last

put 'em up stickup
buck-buck!
I'm totally fucked-up
cuz I lived corrupt

By this time he was no longer technically homeless, no longer riding the subway trains all night. He was sleeping at some girl's apartment in

Harlem. But Faith was never supposed to know where he was really staying. She was under the impression he was cotchin' at his man Jay's crib—Jay who, conveniently, had no phone. Boys being boys—and K being K—he'd sworn me to secrecy on this bit of sexual deception.

I hadn't finished typing the first page of the "Born Loser" lyric when I stopped to dig up that phone number and call him at the girl's apartment in Harlem.

"You've got me confused here," I admitted.

He sounded sleepy. He and the girl were watching *Scarface* for the sixty-seventh time.

"Whatcha need to know?"

What didn't I need to know? "This line, *Fuck a doctor monk*—"

"Yeah?"

"What's a doctor monk?"

"It's not a *what*—it's a who," he said. "It's a shrink."

"Doctor monk is slang for a shrink?"

"*No,* Doug! What the fuck is *wrong* with you? She's a *real* fuckin' person. Her last name was Monk. She was the shrink they had doing evaluations on me and shit when I first went in the system as a JO."

"JO?"

"Juvenile offender."

Sitting beside him on the sofa, overhearing this exchange, the girl now burst into riotous laughter. I tried to ignore her.

"So—Dr. Monk's the little fat bitch?"

"No, that's my stepmother."

"You thought about killing your stepmother?"

"Hell yeah. Thought about it all the time. For that shit she used to be doing to me."

I was staring at his words on my computer screen. The verses had now started to blur together. I began to ask another question but he cut me short by sighing loudly, impatiently, into my ear. If I was going to understand why he'd written this "Born Loser" lyric, he said, he would have to take me back to the very beginning.

T W O

gangster rules

This ain't funny so don't you dare laugh
Just another case about the wrong path . . .
    —Slick Rick

I t'll come to him sometimes as a vision: he can see his brother Julio standing over the ironing board—*One love, Julio César: your heart beats with my heart, nig!*—standing there doing the ironing in the living room of the old apartment on Washington Avenue.

It was a school day and he should've been sitting in his class at P.S. 316. But Julito didn't give a fuck about truancy, or any other law for that matter; the only lessons he had in mind for little Kevin that morning were gangster ones.

"Where we goin', Julito?"

Julio was dressing Kev up in his lime-green Jackson 5–style satin shirt and a crisply pressed pair of tan corduroys.

"We goin' on President," Julio said. "We goin' hang out on President. You wan' see Willie and T.C. and dem?"

"Yeah."

"You wan' see Mercedes?" Julio knew that his kid brother was soft on Mercedes, that he had a seven-year-old's daydreaming crush on Mercedes. "All right, we goin' see Mercedes and dem—we goin' see Top Cat and dem."

Julio knelt down to lace up Kevin's construction boots, a matching, miniature version of his own. And then for the final touch . . . from the closet Julio took a black fedora, snatched off the head of some young Jew, and carefully adjusted it at a jaunty angle on Kev's head. Julio and his gang, the Tomahawks, had this habit of snatching expensive hats from the heads of Jews—beaver hats, fox-trimmed hats and the black felt fedoras that made Julito and his boys look *bad,* like they were down with Louie Lepke and Albert Anastasia and the old-time hit men of Murder Incorporated.

At the time the Brooklyn Tomahawks were one of the deepest gangs in Brooklyn; Julio headed up his own division. They were all wearing matching knee-length Quarterfield jackets with fur collars and stolen black fedoras that morning when they met down on President Street, between Nostrand and New York.

Julio told Mercedes to take his little brother's hand and not let go. "Hold him right here-so," he said. "Soon come back."

Mercedes was a gang girl herself, down with the Crazy Outlaws. Kev could feel the warm pulsing of her hand, smelled her sweet flowery skin lotion, heard the funky riffs of the Ohio Players' "Fire" blaring from a passing Grand Prix. He watched Julio and six other Tomahawks cross the street and enter the Carvel ice cream parlor.

What was Julio *doing?* Mercedes only shrugged at him.

Julio and his boys entered the Carvel; through the window Kev could see his older brother talking softly for a few minutes, and then the white man opened the swinging counter door, letting Julio come inside. It was almost like Julio and the white man were *homeys.* Julio wasn't yelling or waving his hands; he was talking to the man with a friendly smile as he stood there counting the money, then he lifted the register's tray to where the big bills were stashed, gesturing for the Carvel man to take a seat.

Then the other Tomahawks opened the freezers, started pulling out these big cardboard barrels of ice cream, boxes of Flying Saucers, sprinkles, rainbow pops, everything the Carvel man had in the store.

Then they all walked calmly out of the store. Julio was holding a fat coil of money; his boys had the ice cream under their arms. They gangster-strolled back to Mercedes as if nothing had happened. "Keep walkin'," Julio said. "C'mon, walk in front."

Then they went upstairs to some girl's apartment around the corner, on Carroll Street, and they started divvying up all the ice cream. Kev sat there on the sofa with a Flying Saucer melting in one hand and another one waiting in his lap, watching Julio and Mercedes and the other Tomahawks around him all hugging up their little girlfriends, tongue-kissing, slow-grinding to the music . . .

I'm eighteen
With a bullet . . .

But the truth was he didn't understand *shit* that day. He didn't understand until he was a full-grown man, until one day when he was nearly twenty years old, when he was already knee-deep in the drug game: he was driving by the Carvel shop in his kitted-up Grand Am, and while he was waiting there for the light to change, he suddenly saw everything clearly. *Yes.* That's why Julito had been dressing him up. It was a big day: he was taking his baby brother out on his very first job.

It was only when he was sitting there in his idling Grand Am that he understood: slick-ass Julio had actually stuck up the ice cream store that day—robbed the Carvel man blind without once ever having to raise his voice or pull out his 007 knife.

"Can a muthafucka be born bad? You with them stupid fuckin' questions, boy! Every child is born innocent—of course. But every child is born with bad intentions. Everyone—even judges and DAs—all of them at one time or another have had evil or vindictiveness in them. Everybody's had it in*

---

*The italicized first-person interludes in this chapter come from transcripts of taped interviews with K about his childhood, conducted in Brooklyn and Manhattan, between September '96 and March '97.

them to be a gangster, to be a ruthless muthafucka, to be a killer. It's just a question of who holds it in and who lets it flow free.

"It's what you chose not to do with your bad intentions that makes you what society labels an upright and upstandin' individual. And it's what I chose to do with mine that labels me a menace.

"But at the end of the day—'less you're bugged-the-fuck-out—you got control of your own faculties. You know right from wrong; you know what you're supposed to do and what you're not supposed do. You know what society has set as the standard and the norm of livin'. Then whatever you decide to do is all on you. I think these cats that talk that shit about society-made-me-this and society-made-me-that—I think that's a weak fuckin' cop-out, yo. In the end, you did it because you wanted to do it, because it felt good to you. There's a lot of other things you could've done instead . . .

"When I was a youth I used to think that whatever happened to me was destiny. Now I know that whatever your mental picture is, whatever your mental paradigm is, that's what you're gonna do. Think negative, dwell on the negative, and somethin' negative is surely gonna happen."

But how *not* to dwell on the negative? He'd been cursed, hadn't he? Cursed from the first day. That bitch had put a powerful spell on him when he was still an innocent baby, oblivious to evil, still suckling his mother's breast.

His parents—Miguel and Diana—were both Panamanians living in Brooklyn. But Kevin was actually born, on Halloween night, in Philadelphia, the City of Brotherly Love. And the only reason he was born in Philadelphia—he would come to learn the whole truth, many years later—is that he was not supposed to be born at all.

Miguel hadn't planned to have any kids with Kevin's mother. Miguel didn't need that kind of headache! He was married to another woman—Kevin's mother was just one of his outside flings—and, when he learned of the accidental pregnancy, Miguel did the only thing he could do: he gave Diana the money to have an abortion. But Diana decided that she didn't want to get rid of the child; instead she ran off to Philadelphia to stay with her uncle there. And that's where she gave birth to him.

Miguel heard through the Panamanian grapevine in Brooklyn that Diana didn't have the abortion, that he now had this little baby boy, baptized Kevin Antonio, whom he hadn't even wanted in the first place. He heard that they were living in squalor, that the little boy was sleeping in a dresser drawer instead of a crib. He couldn't allow that— what father could? He sent a Panamanian tough guy called Tito Guerrero to Philadelphia, to fetch the child and the mother and bring them back to Brooklyn.

His legal wife, naturally, was not thrilled to learn that Miguel now had an "outside child." But what could she do about it? Well, for one thing, she could seek out the services of a witch, exact some form of spiritual revenge, put some brujería magic on the infant. Many Panamanians believe in the powers of the orishás, the Saints; they employ santería to bless their homes, to give them personal protection from the unseen—and unforeseen—dangers of the world. Brujería is not protective magic, though: it is the black side of santería, the witchcraft side of the power. Kevin's father's wife went to an old bruja, and had a powerful spell put on the baby boy. It was supposed to cling to him for the rest of his natural life. The brujería magic was meant to ensure that nothing but bad things could ever happen for him and his offspring. It was serious magic, he later learned. It could not be counteracted, the kind of curse that could never be fully broken.

His parents were Panamanian immigrants in Brooklyn—but back in Panama, the families had been Jamaican immigrants. His great-grandparents had left Jamaica to build the Panama Canal back in the early years of the century. They were part of the mass migration of laborers coming from the British West Indies to work on the Canal and the Panamanian railroads. People in Panama often said that the Americans could never have completed the Canal without those arrivals from Jamaica, boats filled with hardened island people conditioned to the backbreaking work of cutting sugarcane in the tropical sun. The islanders took up the Canal-digging challenge and, like the ancient Israelites under the harsh gaze of Pharaoh's taskmasters, they soon mastered the killing task that the Panamanian and American workers hadn't been capable of.

After the Canal was built, his great-grandparents, and then his grandparents, stayed on in Panama as hired hands. Like many of the islanders, they were looking for some way to make it to the *real* promised land, find passage, legal or otherwise, to the U.S.A.

His mother had been born in the Canal Zone itself, which made her what was called a Zonian. Zonians were people caught in limbo: the Americans considered them Panamanians, while the Panamanians derided them as Zonians. In general, there was no love lost between Panamanians and Zonians. Most Zonians were English speakers who didn't bother to learn proper Spanish—they spoke more of a Spanglish—and the Panamanians regarded the Zonians with open contempt.

His father's family came from the bustling port of Colón, Panama's second city, the northern gateway to the Canal. From his earliest days, Kevin had heard tales of Colón's badman districts: Eighth and Central; Fourteenth Street; red-hot barrios that had given birth to many a gold-toothed gunman and murderer.

As he got older, he grew proud of his father's roots in Colón. Because he soon came to learn that most of the Panamanian badmen in Brooklyn—the big-time coke kingpins from East Flatbush and Franklin Avenue—hailed originally from those fast Colón streets.

"I looked just like him: I was the spittin' image of my pops. Except that he's real, real light-skinned and has what we call coolie hair—straight white people's hair. In the early days, I used to bounce back and forth, livin' for a while with my mother, then my father would take me with him for a few weeks. He had set my mother up in an apartment on Buffalo Avenue. He used to pay her rent and the utilities there and everything. He couldn't live

there with her, because he already had his wife and his other family to deal with.

   "And then one time he came by and he found my mother's other man, Shorty, in his bed. My pops flipped. He told my mother, 'I want my son now! Give me my fuckin' son!' After that, I went to live with him for good.

   "My pops had a second wife now—he had divorced the first wife who'd put the brujería curse on me. He was remarried to this short, fat bitch. He was a pretty big deal around town, my pops—you know, he was a player. And you know how a player gets down: nigga's gonna do his thing. So after a while, the same shit he used to be doin' to his first wife with my mother, he started doin' to his second wife with another lady.

   "My stepmother got wind that my father was fuckin' around with another lady and—since I looked just like him—she started takin' that shit out on me. I used to be gettin' into mischief all the time, little-kid mischief, and she used to beat me with an extension cord. Then she used to make me kneel on a cheese grater, strip me butt-naked to kneel on the grater until my knees were bloody. Sometimes she used to burn me in the back of my legs with this hot spoon, and then she'd make me wear long pants all the time so my pops wouldn't see the scabs and pus."

His father, in addition to running some nightclubs in Brooklyn, used to make frequent business trips down to Colón, where he managed the business affairs of several popular Panamanian salsa bands. Being out of town so much, he didn't notice the signs of abuse on his son.

   Until the incident with the pepper sauce.

   Like many Panamanian women, his stepmother used to cook her own hot sauce, a homemade condiment made from fiery Jamaican Scotch-bonnet peppers. She would fill up empty Heinz ketchup bottles with it. He used to love the spicy smell. He would open up the bottle and stand there smelling it in the middle of the kitchen, really inhaling those strong pepper vapors. It smelled so good, it almost made him light-headed.

   This used to annoy his stepmother. "Bwoy, get yuh wutless raatid nose outta dere!" she would shout, slapping at his hand.

But he kept doing it anyway. One morning, she caught him with the pepper sauce, jerked the bottle from him, and some of the pepper sauce splattered into his right eye. Kevin was shrieking and crying. *Hmmmm!* she said: *that* would teach him. Then she became frightened. The boy's eye turned bright red—fiery red like one of the peppers. She tried to flush the eye with tap water, but the redness wouldn't go away.

The eye stayed so bloodshot that she had no choice but to take him to the emergency room at Kings County Hospital. And while the doctors were examining him, they discovered the scabs where he'd been burned, quite recently, on the back of his thighs.

"They sent her to the G-Building, to the psychiatric ward of Kings County for that shit. And I still used to cry after her—like a fuckin' fool!—be there cryin' out: Mommy! Mommy! Don't take my Mommy away!

"I always called her Mommy as if she was my real mother.

"Sometimes I can't believe how soft my thinking was back then. This bitch steady beatin' and abusin' me and I'm cryin' out for her.

"Mommy come home!

"I'll never forget that shit. Never. I used to have fantasies about murderin' her all the time when I was a little kid. But later on, after I was old enough to understand it a bit better, it actually became somethin' useful, somethin' I could focus on, somethin' that could help me harden my heart.

"Later on, whenever it came time for me to do dirt, whenever I had to pick up my gun and step to a muthafucka on some real evil shit—and I'd start havin' second thoughts or qualms not to do it—all I'd have to do is just think about my stepmother, think about what she used to do to me, and then everything would come easy."

His father had always vowed one thing: that if anyone ever did harm to the boy he'd be returned to his mother's care. So after the incident with the pepper sauce, Miguel had no choice but to send Kevin back to his birth mother.

He could remember a few pleasant moments from those days, playing cocoa-leave-yo out in front of the building—the loud *tap-tap-tap* of the coffee can and then *I see fat-ass Puddy hidin' in the bush!*— messing around with his little homey-stromeys, getting into all types of little-kid mischief.

He and his younger brother, Craig, did their best to stay out of serious trouble. They had some good times together, playing sports in the parks and streets. There were only two sports that Panamanians gave a damn about—baseball and boxing—and Kevin and Craig excelled at both of them. Craig was a natural shortstop. The grown-ups all predicted he was going to make it to the pros someday. And boxing came easily to Kevin. He could see himself becoming another Ismael La Guna or Roberto Duran.

Then the phone call came and they learned that their three older brothers, Julio, Pacho and Toño, and their sister, Jean, were coming up from Panama to live with them. Kevin had been hearing about this other family for years—he knew that his mother had already had three sons and a daughter by her other man back home in Panama. Now they were going to have a big reunion; he was very excited to know that the big brothers he'd never met would be relocating to Brooklyn.

Before his roughneck brothers arrived on the scene, he could remember a flight he'd taken down to Panama with his father on an airline called Braniff International. Those Braniff airline people took his heart away. The plane was a bright purple color, and the stewardesses were so nice and friendly to him. They let him come with them up to the cockpit where the pilots were working the instruments. He didn't think his heartbeat would ever slow down after that! From that day on, all he ever wanted to do was go to pilot's school, become an airline pilot for Braniff International, greet people on the plane and make them so happy by flying them home to Panama.

He held on to that dream for a long, long time.

Then for a very short time, he thought he might want to be a scientist. That was when they were studying molecules of water vapor in class.

Then his three older brothers arrived from Panama. And from that day on, it was like a dark red curtain had opened in front of his eyes. Everything was clear to him: all he wanted to be was a gangster-ass tough guy like them.

From their first few days in America, he could see the respect his older brothers commanded—especially Julio, being the oldest. Big men would be shitting on themselves when Julio walked into the room. Sometimes he never even had to say a word—get on his bad side and just the way Julio would *look* at you, you'd feel your bowels clenching up tight. Everyone called him Julio César—El General—out of respect.

"On the other hand, there was a lot of pressure behind that shit. It was almost a father-to-son type of thing. That was the family sport—gangsterism. If Julio was good at gangsterism, then I had to be that much better. If Toño was good with fifty-two hand-blocks,* then I had to be just as good, because I'm Toño's brother and niggas is scared shitless of Toño. How would it reflect on them if I turned out soft? That's how I always saw it. That became my biggest fuckin' thing: uphold my image and uphold the image of my family."

His older brothers had been seriously misinformed about what to expect from life in New York City. Someone back in Panama had evidently crystallized the concept of America in one single image: it was the place where you could eat Oreo cookies every day. That's all they were talking about when they first arrived: eating Oreos. And someone had also told them that New York had palm trees and hot weather and tropical birds just like Panama. Whoever told them that must've seen pictures of Miami and assumed that the whole United States was warm like South Florida.

---

*A style of hand-to-hand combat developed in the New York state penal system and widely practiced among gang members on the streets of Brooklyn in the '70s and '80s.

They were in for a *rude* awakening, boy! Kev could remember how frightened his brothers looked the day they saw that first big Brooklyn snowfall, venturing tentatively out into that mystery blizzard, crazy as a trio of coyotes on skates: slipping—skidding—back-kicking—before busting their asses in the street.

There was something nobody knew about Julio. He was touched, suffered from schizophrenia, heard phantom conversations in his head. No one suspected that's what it was, though; people just thought he was ruthless. They used to say (but only when he was well out of earshot): "*Woy!* Dat bwoy have too much of de devil in him!" And perhaps, Kev sometimes thought, perhaps Julio did have some of the devil in him.

Julio used to be desperately homesick for Panama, and to help him deal with his homesickness he kept many little green birds, parakeets and canaries, in several cages around the apartment. Julio loved all sorts of animals; he had fish tanks filled with goldfish and guppies—to him they were *goopies*—but what he loved more than anything in the world was his birds. It seemed that the birds helped him imagine he was back in Panama. Once a day he'd release the birds from their cages and let them fly all over the apartment; when he was ready, he'd just make a little *pap-pap* sound with his mouth and they'd all fly back around him so he could return them to their cages.

One summer morning his boy Top Cat came by the crib. Top Cat was a tall, skinny, dark-skinned Haitian, famed throughout Crown Heights as a treacherous little rudeboy. All the other Tomahawks called him T.C. for short. When T.C. arrived at the apartment, Julio had let his birds loose; all the chirping and bright fluttering feathers made the apartment look like an aviary. Then Julio went to take a shower and left T.C. alone in the living room. T.C. started messing with one of the birds, grabbing it, playing with it, and, with a stickup kid's heavyhandedness, he inadvertently strangled the little green chirping creature.

Like anyone with sense, T.C. was afraid of Julio. So after killing the bird, instead of telling Julio the truth, the Haitian panicked, shoving the dead bird under one of the couch cushions, sitting back down on it. He and Julio were about to go out on a robbery mission. But before they went on the stickup job Julio took a head count of his precious birds and realized that one was missing. He thought it had flown out the window. That used to happen sometimes; one of the birds would escape from the apartment; but they'd always fly back to him eventually. Julio kept calling out the window to the bird. But the bird wouldn't come. *Pito!* Julio knew each bird by name; he was personally attached to each bird.

Couple of days went by: no bird. And then something started smelling bad in the house. Julio—who did most of the ironing and household chores—was vacuuming the rug and the sofa when, flipping up the seat cushion, he found little dead Pito. The bird was badly crushed, a dry lump of crumbling feathers—murmuring, Julio cradled it, lovingly, in his strong hands. His tongue began to sizzle with rage.

The next day Julio tricked T.C. into coming back to the building. Julio and another Tomahawk named Kurt had T.C. cornered in the hallway by the elevators, Julio hemming him up by his collar, asking him what had happened to his little bird.

"W-w-wha' you talkin' 'bout, Ju-ju-jul—"

Julio said nothing. Stood dissecting the skinny Haitian with his eyes. Finally T.C. cracked, admitted that, yes, he'd killed the bird—but it was an accident—he was just trying to tuck the bird inside his sleeve like a magician he'd seen on TV. He never meant for the fucking thing to die.

Julio wasn't having any apology.

"So you like killin' birds? You like killin' fuckin' birds, huh?"

Kurt knew a magic trick of his own: he had a secret way of opening the elevator doors without the elevator being there, jimmying it on the left side with his knife. So when Julio gave the cue—*presto!*—Kurt opened up the elevator doors.

With terrified saucer eyes, realizing, too late, what was happening, Top Cat tried to break free. Julio, though short, was much stronger than Top Cat. He snatched T.C. up like an empty coat and threw him, without a moment's hesitation, into the open elevator shaft.

"I could hear T.C.'s scream echoing as he fell right down to the basement. When Julito turned around, he saw me and Toño standin' there. He started shoutin': What de fuck you two lookin' at?

"I don't know who called for the ambulance, I didn't think anybody saw it but me and Toño. But the ambulance finally came to get T.C.

"Downstairs, in front of the building, I saw them takin' T.C. out on a stretcher. Instead of his feet bein' straight, they were both twisted to the side, knowmsayin'? His bones juttin' out from the shins. His kneecaps were where they were supposed to be but the feet were both ninety degrees to the right. The fall had fucked up his tailbone and his balls and everything.

"After that day, Julio never talked about what he'd done to T.C. And me and Toño pretended we'd never seen it . . .

"Top Cat was in a wheelchair for the rest of his life. When I got older I used to see him sometimes on President Street. He never said nothin' to me; he never said nothin' to my family. Last time I saw him alive was around '88—when I was sellin' drugs. He was a crackhead, wheelin' himself around in his wheelchair, tryin' to sell a framed picture of Jesus for five dollars."

The stickup kids of Crown Heights were some of the most feared in the borough of Brooklyn. Every night in bed Kev would have a dream that he'd joined a gang, tough-guy posing on the corner, modeling a Quarterfield jacket and black fedora just like Julio. Julio, however, had forbidden any of his younger brothers to join a gang—despite the fact that he was himself proudly heading up a division of the Tomahawks. "Don't let no one tell you different," he'd warn his younger brothers. "Gangs are for fuckin' punks."

"So why you in a gang, Julito?"

"*Shut up!* You axe too much questions!"

Well, if they couldn't join an established gang, like the Tomahawks or Jolly Stompers, the boys would have to form their own crews and cliques.* Julio hadn't said anything about forming *crews* and *cliques,* right? Toño, for one, began running with a small group of unaligned stickup kids based on Washington Avenue. They dubbed themselves the Ave-Ave Crew. Their specialty was sticking up juice and bread trucks. In the late '70s, the drivers of juice and bread trucks made perfect targets, known to keep thousands of dollars in cash on board as they made their delivery rounds. Toño and his crew knocked off so many juice and bread trucks, they quickly gained a reputation as one of the most reckless bands of robbers in a neighborhood famed for brazen banditry.

Of course, they all knew the rules of the game. Getting knocked was just a matter of time. By early '78, Toño had busted his cherry— nabbed on first-degree robbery charges—sent, as a juvenile offender, to the Spofford Juvenile Center in the Bronx. Kevin, who'd been running with the Ave-Ave Crew for a few months—the guys having now dubbed him Little Toño—knew one thing for certain: it wouldn't be long before he joined his brother in Spofford.

They'd moved again (for seemingly the twentieth time in the last two years, the sight of eviction notices being all too familiar to everyone in the family) and were now living in a first-floor apartment on New York Avenue in the East Flatbush section, the notoriously dangerous Vanderveer housing projects. Kevin's mother was now married to a

---

*The word *clique* is often used interchangeably with *posse* or *crew*. Unlike traditional street gangs, cliques, crews and posses generally have no initiation rites, formalized colors, clothing or hand signs; they are loose groupings of like-minded young men and women who live on the same block, hang out on the same street corner, attend the same school.

man named Livingston. Everyone called him Shorty; he stood barely five feet tall. Shorty did his best to be a father figure to Kevin; he spent a lot of time with the boy, helping him improve his English pronunciation and grammar—Kev still spoke with a heavy Panamanian accent—teaching him the basic arithmetic skills he wasn't learning in school. Within a few months' time, Kev began to feel that Shorty was more of a father to him than his biological father.

But he wasn't used to having a father in the house; he wasn't really sure how to act around Shorty. Everything the man did made Kev more curious. He loved to snoop through Shorty's belongings; soon he discovered something irresistible on the top shelf of the hall closet. It was a soft purple Royal Crown whiskey bag. The bag was heavy and, when he took it down, he expected to find a full bottle of Canadian whiskey wrapped up in that creamy purple felt. But, no, he wouldn't be getting drunk today. This was even better. Inside the Crown Royal bag he found Shorty's .22 Ruger pistol with the imitation wood handle. Shorty kept the pistol in immaculate condition; he even had the gun in a leather holster. There was a full box of extra-long shells too. Kev knew he had to sneak the gun out of the apartment that very day. He could already see how the faces of his crew would light up, how all the little Pay-hays would beam when he showed up brandishing a gun.

That day had begun just like any normal Thursday morning except little Eggy was dead. Little Eggy had been his homey-stromey, but now little Eggy was gone: a duppy hovering in the air over East Flatbush. Little Eggy'd been stabbed to death in Vanderveer. Also—another thing that was odd for a Thursday—there was no school tomorrow, not because little Eggy was dead, but because their class had scheduled an overnight camping trip. Everyone was going camping upstate—except little Eggy, being dead, and Kev, being bad, so bad that Mr. Cargell had forbidden him from participating in the camping trip.

So if he couldn't go on the upstate camping trip, he thought, why even bother showing up in class on Thursday? Fuck Mr. Cargell *and* his upstate camping trip. He decided to show up at Smokey's crib instead. Smokey would never be in school. Smokey lived right across the way. Kev was in 1406 New York Avenue; Smokey was in 1404. Kev went up to Smokey's crib, massaging and stroking his stepfather's .22, nestled in the pocket of his navy blue Izod windbreaker, as tenderly as if it was a baby hamster.

When he got upstairs there was already a mob of little hoodlums there: Derrick, Linton, Jermaine, the other Kev, light-skinned Kev . . . *what the fuck?* the whole *clique* was skipping school! In those days, they called themselves the Pay-hays—that was Derrick's name for the crew—but later on the name was changed to V. I.P., the Vanderveer International Posse. Years later that was the name, V.I.P., that got written up in all those newspaper stories about the ruthless criminals terrorizing East Flatbush . . .

As soon as Kev showed the other Pay-hays his stepfather's gun, they all decided to head down to the basement of Smokey's building to bust shots at the wall. Good thing Kev had taken a whole box of the extra-long shells from the Royal Crown bag.

His stepfather had a strip of leather that you were supposed to wrap around your wrist when you busted the gun. Kev wasn't precisely sure how to use it; it just felt good to wrap it around his hand and lick off shots. Soon he and all the other Pay-hays felt like grown gunmen, *authentic rudeboys,* not just little snotnosed twelve- and thirteen-year-olds cutting class. They stood yucking and bullshitting and wrestling the gun away from each other.

"Gimme the burner, K!"

"Naw, it's me next, nigga! Wait ya muthafuckin' turn!"

Guns were still pretty new to Kev, but Smokey was renowned for busting them on a regular basis. Smokey didn't have a gun of his own, but he was good for busting everybody else's tool. Smokey was just one year older than Kev—he'd just turned thirteen that spring—but he sometimes seemed like a big man. He'd been born down in Jamaica, in a deadly ghetto area called Raetown. His father had been a badman from Raetown called Johnny Skanks. Johnny Skanks was a big-time rudeboy, a stone-killer, one of the Untouchables, that murderous Jamaican coke crew that had left a trail of blood and bodies from Kingston to Miami to Brooklyn.

Johnny Skanks had been killed in a Flatbush shootout when Smokey was small. And ever since the day his father died, Smokey stopped caring about everything—going to school, listening to his moms. He was easily the rudest one of their little Vanderveer clique.

Smokey wasn't chubby; Smokey was *fat*. Big and blubbery like a baby walrus. And all that fat made him tire out quickly. When we got tired of busting .22 shells at the wall, he was wheezing—he had bad asthma in addition to being obese; he would always breathe, noisily, through his mouth—and, panting and gasping like he'd just come up from underwater, Smokey came up with a new plan of action. "Fuck it, let's go to the store, right? Get some tomatoes and shit, right? Throw 'em at the bus and shit, right?"

"Smokey! Pass mi rings nuh? Pass mi mi *bumboclaat* rings nuh?"

"Just cool nuh mon—just chill nuh mon," Smokey said, shifting verbal gears, double-clutching—like most of the guys could: seamlessly and unconsciously—between the badman argots of Kingston and Brooklyn. "I got it, knowmsayin'? Let's go and get them tomatoes and shit, throw 'em at the bus and shit, right?"

Smokey's simple scheme was to steal the tomatoes from the little fruit and vegetable store on Nostrand Avenue owned by a family of Koreans. One by one, the Pay-hay crew trickled inside—careful not to arouse instant suspicion—and then, suddenly, each one grabbed two juicy handfuls of ripe tomatoes and made a dash for the door. Kev got stuck behind fat-ass Smokey, the last one trying to get free with his tomatoes—and before he could make it to daylight, the Koreans slammed the door shut on him.

He was a short stocky Korean man whose unblemished shiny moonface Kev had never seen before. He must've been new, Kev thought, just off the boat. Beside him was a bone-thin Korean lady; so thin and fragile she looked like she was made out of see-through tissue paper. It was the paper lady who'd slammed the door shut, locked it, allowing the stocky man to grab Kev in his powerful grip. The man lifted Kev off his feet, threw him over his leg and started to spank him very hard.

"He was spankin' me with a broom handle like I was his own fuckin' kid. He was just beatin' on me, bap-bap-bap, and when I'd get up to run, he'd grab me again and choke me by my collar. He was spankin' the shit out of me. And he was mumblin' some shit in Korean; he wasn't even speakin' that broken English. The woman was lookin' right at me; she looked sad but still had a punish him *kind of expression in her eyes.*

"When I looked up I saw Smokey and the rest of them bangin' on the glass door. Finally, the Korean man stopped hittin' me with the broom and was gettin' ready to lead me out the door to throw me out in the street. But when the lady opened the door, instead of me runnin' out, Smokey runs in.

"When Smokey runs in he had the gun already drawn.

*"And just like dat—*BUCK! BUCK!*—Smokey lick off de two shot. And when Smokey lick off 'im two shot, de lady start fe bawl.*

"The stocky Chineyman had got hit in the head and fell down, face up, lookin' at the ceiling.

"That was the first body I'd ever seen, actually shot down in front of me. The muthafucka didn't kick and writhe. One shot hit him in the throat and one hit him square in the forehead. Smokey just blanked him. At first I couldn't even see straight. I stood there in shock. Smokey was yellin': Come on! Come on! Yo, K! Come on!

"I stood there starin', thinkin', This muthafucka gonna get up and start runnin' like in the cartoons. He not really dead. *I'm lookin' and the lady's screamin', these high soprano notes, and that's got me scared even worse.*

"I didn't see any blood at first. But then I started seein', just his pulse—boo-doop, boo-doop—that's how the blood started pulsin' down the side of his head. It wasn't gushin', spurtin'—just oozin' out slow. And now I'm thinkin', Oh, shit. Duke dead, yo.

"I'm still frozen stiff. Smokey runs over and grabs me by the neck and leads me out of the store. By this time a circle of onlookers has gathered around the scene, tryin' to see what's goin' down.

"By the time Smokey came back and got my dumb ass, the whole crowd must'a been puttin' two and two together. It had to look like I did it. I was the one still inside. Everybody'd seen Smokey comin' from the street, runnin' back inside to get me."

All the Pay-hays knew the drill: split up, shoot off in different directions like a handful of cat's-eye marbles hitting hot summer concrete. Kev and Smokey ran home together, back to the Veer, stride for fucking stride. The whole way Smokey was wheezing so loudly that Kev feared his Jamaican homeboy was going to collapse and die in a heap of his own heaving blubber. They both ran inside the basement of Kev's building, stood staring at each other, speechless. Smokey reached into his pocket and passed the still-warm .22 back to Kev. Smokey knew he couldn't come upstairs to the crib. At that time, Kev was forbidden to bring any company upstairs.

So he left Smokey, wheezing and coughing, and crept back upstairs alone. He knew his first mission was to put Shorty's gun back into the Royal Crown bag. The gun was wet from Smokey's sweaty hands and he tried to dry it and clean it as best he could with the tail of his shirt. He knew that his stepfather was going to notice the missing box of shells, but there was nothing he could do about that now. He'd worry about *that* ass-whipping when it came to him.

It wasn't until the next day that he started feeling scared. Because by then everyone in the Veer was talking about the shooting. His mother, his brothers, his stepfather. They all knew about the shooting but they didn't have a clue who'd done it.

"You hear 'bout de Chineyman dat get shot down the road dereso?" his mother said over dinner. Anybody who was Korean, Vietnamese—they were all *Chineyman* to her.

"*Woy!* Dem shoot him dead, yunno! Dem tek him money an' everything!"

Shit. Everybody was making it out to be a big-time stickup. Kev wanted to explain that it hadn't even been a stickup; he wanted to shout, *Nobody ain't touch the nigga's money! Nobody ain't take no mutha-fuckin' money from the register!* But he was now too scared to talk. He was too scared to eat. Especially when he heard his mother say: "Well, whoever dem catch fe dat goin' *jail!*"

Smokey had warned him that detectives had been canvassing the neighborhood, asking a lot of questions about the crime. How much did they know? If the cops had suspects, wouldn't they have made some arrests? Smokey was already such a ruthless little cat, there was no way he'd ever open his mouth. But with such a big crowd of eye-witnesses, all it would take is *one* do-gooder to step up and say, "Oh yeah, I seen shorty-wop. He live over in the Veer."

Still, the days passed and it began to look as if they'd gotten away with it.

Then one sunny late spring morning, about three weeks after the shooting, Kev was coming out of the basement of 1406 with his Honda Trail motorbike. All the Pay-hays used to ride around on identical Honda Trails; that was their trademark. He'd taken his stepfather's Ruger out again and he had it in the pocket of his green-and-orange Adidas warm-up suit. His stepfather hadn't even checked for the gun yet; he hadn't even missed the box of extra-long shells.

He was wheeling his Honda Trail through the basement and he had his navy blue windbreaker thrown over one arm. The same Izod windbreaker he'd been wearing when Smokey blanked the Korean man.

There was no question that the two white men were detectives. One was a tall red-haired Howdy Doody, the other was shorter with his thick jet-black hair slicked back like an oily helmet. Howdy Doody was wearing an army camouflage jacket with the sleeves cut off, the better to display his bulging reddish white biceps. The oily-haired one had on a tight blue T-shirt with tight new Lee jeans and white Adidas shell toes.

"You! Come *here!"* That was Howdy Doody shouting.

The thought of running never even crossed his mind. The first thing the cops did was search him, pulling Shorty's pistol from the pocket of his track suit.

"Where you live?"

"Right here. 1406."

"Which apartment?"

"We gotta go this way, through the basement."

They knocked on the door for a long time before anyone answered. His mother was doing double shifts at her job at the hospital. Finally there were footsteps and Julio opened the door for them. Badass Julito, unfazed by the flashing of police badges, fixing the cops in the crosshairs of his gangster glare.

"You his father?"

"Naw, his brovva."

The oily-haired detective made a face. He figured Julio certainly looked old enough to be the father. "Well, he's under arrest," said Howdy Doody.

"Fuhwha?"

"We got reason to believe he was involved in a shooting on Nostrand."

They took him down to the 67th Precinct House on Snyder. They logged him in as a juvenile offender. He was handcuffed to the desk. They asked him if he wanted to talk about what had happened on Nostrand Avenue. They said he didn't have to talk if he didn't want to. They asked him where he'd got the .22-caliber Ruger from.

He didn't say shit.

They asked him if he did it.

He didn't say shit.

They asked why did he do it.

He didn't say shit.

They asked him if there were a lot of guys there with him. They asked him to give up the names of the other guys involved. Was it a bunch of those little delinquents from the Vanderveer projects? They kept trying to confuse him with words. He was just a little kid and they were asking him who he was *acting in concert with,* and he just sat there thinking, *We wasn't goin' to no concert—we was just stealin' tomatoes to throw at the fuckin' bus.*

All of a sudden the Howdy Doody detective lost his cool, snatched Kev by the collar, choking him, shouting that he'd better start talking if he knew what was good for him.

And then, finally, for some reason he never fully understood, he said: "Yeah, I did it."

"Why'd you do it?"

"Don't know."

"You were trying to rob him?"

He didn't say anything else. They all just sat there staring at him. "Look, he's either a complete fuckin' retard, or he's the most stand-up little motherfucker I've ever seen."

It was late in the night when they finally notified his mother. They told her it wasn't even worth her time to come down to the precinct house. The crime he was accused of was too serious. They told her he'd be going straight to SJC, to the Spofford Juvenile Center.

He felt like hollering at the top of his lungs: *But I ain't do it! I only stole three tomatoes, it was fuckin' fat-ass Smokey who squeezed off and blanked the old Chineyman and made the Chiney lady wail and the blood bubble out from the forehead! And the moonface muthafucka wasn't even supposed to be dead, was he? Wasn't he supposed to jump up again like the fuckin' Coyote in the Roadrunner cartoons?*

He knew better than to say anything like that. Even though he was afraid of the cops, he was more afraid of Julio and Toño. Because Julio and Toño had already schooled him well in the code.

He could see himself sitting back in his mother's kitchen, back when they were living on St. Marks Place for a few months. It was Kev and his little brother, Craig, sitting at the kitchen table. At the time their older sister, Jean, was pregnant, and she was getting WIC money,* had a fridge full of government meats and cheeses. Craig had stolen some of her baloney to make a sandwich but Jean was very stingy and counted every slice of meat. She discovered the missing meat and she was getting ready to whip their asses and Julio just sat there watching, smirking at them. Julio knew who'd stolen the meat, but he sat still, arms folded, like he was watching an engrossing late-night murder movie.

As she was getting ready to slap Kev, he blurted out: "It was *Craig!* Craig did it! I ain't eat nothin'!"

Jean doled out two separate, stinging ass-whippings that afternoon. Afterward Julio went outside and bought Craig a big coldcut hero with a soda, plus a Snickers bar for dessert. He didn't bring Kev anything.

"Damn, Julio, can't I get some?"

All Julito gave him was the screwface. "You is a fuckin' snitch. Wanna know why I bought him all dis shit? I bought him dis shit 'cause he kept his mout' shut. You squeal't like a little bitch."

And then when he got to be older and he'd go with Toño and the Ave-Ave Crew on a robbery job, Toño used to take it even further. Just before the shit went down—in that quivering, cold, prickly moment when time seemed to freeze—Toño would hem him up by his jacket collar. "Ay yo," he'd say. "Snitches get *stitches.* Don't forget dat shit. Never rat on ya boys no matter *what.* Always keep ya fuckin' mout' shut."

So he kept his fucking mouth shut. And by nine o'clock he was shackled up in a small van driven by a heavyset black man, just Kev and the old man alone in the van, and the old man was mumbling about the traffic problems they were going to hit driving to the Bronx. He knew

---

*Public assistance for Women with Infants and Children.

about Spofford—he'd been waiting for the day he could brag that he'd been to Spofford—but he didn't know he was going to the Bronx. He didn't know anything about the Bronx. He didn't even know they *had* a fucking Bronx.

The old man was driving for a long time and all the darkness and strange scenery was becoming scary and then Kev saw a sign that said *Major Deegan* and then it really hit him for the first time—he was going to *Spofford!* He started sobbing and sniffling, clear salty snot dripping to his lips. He heard himself whimpering "Please!" to the old man (as if the old man could do anything about it now), saying every prayer he ever learned to say to Jesus.

"When you' a youngster, it's not like you go to court, see a judge and get ar-raigned. Due process? None of that shit happens when you' a youngster. Your ass just goes directly to Spofford. Your ass is shackled up and thrown in jail and they do all the paperwork in there.

"Spofford is a big white building on Casanova and Spofford in the South Bronx; the first time I saw it from the van, I thought it was a fuckin' hospi-tal. You walk in the main doors of Spofford and they tell you to kick off your shoes. As you walk in the doors it looks like a little house. You're thinkin', Damn—I'm really in jail.

"As I came in, there was like twenty muthafuckas there, waitin' to be processed through reception, some bigger, some littler than me. There was some shorty nigga named Mag—crazy fuckin' Magnetic: later on he be-came my homey—lookin' wild as hell, runnin' shit in that reception line, talkin' like he was grown people in a grown people's jail: Yo, nigga! Gimme a cigarette, man! Naw, my shit is Newport, not Silkport, muthafucka!"

---

*The boys would be housed in the Spofford Juvenile Center until a hearing before a judge in the Family Court to determine their status. If the judge deemed that they should be re-manded to the Division of Youth, the juvenile offenders would be transferred from Spof-ford to one of the state's "secure centers" upstate.

He felt like a real sissy. He didn't have a clue how he was supposed to act. He knew how to *fight*—he'd been taught well by his brothers—but the whole Spofford scene was awkward to him; he didn't want to start a fight with someone who might have powerful connections in the general population. He didn't even want to bathe in front of the other new inmates, he was so scared one of them would try to take his ass.

Along with all the other new jacks, he was taken directly up to the seventh-floor infirmary to have blood tests done. Kev was so nervous—and not just because he was terrified of needles. He was more afraid of the older inmates, the bigger inmates, passing through the infirmary that night, calling out: "Oh shit! Look at the new jacks! Fresh meat up in this bitch!" These were guys from A-3, B-4, D-5 (D-5 was the worst unit you could be in), boys who were already stocky because they'd been in the house for three or four months already. Seeing them, Kev once again started crying softly, praying, *Please, Lord Jesus, I won't do nothin' bad again. I promise you, Lord Jesus. Please just let me go home.*

But, no, the only place he was going was pop-dog—he quickly learned that's what the veteran kids called general population—where the Spofford staff assigned him to unit B-2; after a few nights, he was transferred to B-3; and then he finally wound up in D-5. His brother Toño was in A-4. Toño had been in Spofford for a while now. Kev kept crossing paths with guys from Brooklyn who knew Toño. But it was weeks before he actually saw Toño face-to-face in the chow line. Toño was vexed with his kid brother for getting himself thrown into Spofford. Toño was just like Julio with the gang stuff—do as I say, not as I do. Tone had been back and forth to Spofford so many times, it was becoming more of his home than any apartment in Brooklyn. This time Toño was in there for pulling an armed robbery of a dry cleaner's on Nostrand Avenue.

*   *   *

He quickly learned the essential Spofford rules, like *never* walk through another unit's tables in the mess hall unless you want war with their unit. He'd made that mistake early on and nearly caused a big brawl with Black Jack's unit. The worst part of Spofford life was the loneliness. No one ever came to visit him. His mother never once came up to the Bronx to see him. Then he started seeing guys like Mack and Black Jack getting sentenced, being sent up north, to the upstate kiddie jails in Brace, Annsville, Goshen. He was thinking, *Damn, with my fucked-up case, I know I'm gettin' served. I know I'm goin' to lockup.*

The counselors had them lining up for a stupid daily drill: you were supposed to stand up straight as a board and not even twitch. Your unit would get some prizes, some extra cookies or extra milk at dinner, if you could all keep that military line. And every unit had one little kiss-ass trusty* working for the counselors, making sure everybody was standing up straight during the inspection.

All the other guys in the D-5 unit—Steve Murray, Rockbone, Gungo Steve, Inch, Diamond—were standing up straight beside him, but Kev was lost in his grueling daydream . . . Miguel hadn't wanted him. Diana hadn't wanted him. Who was there in the wide world who wanted him? And now, just as he'd feared, it had finally happened: he'd forgotten how his mother's face looked. He'd been dreading this day, the day he would ask himself *Yo, how do your moms look, nigga?* and not be able to answer the question . . . Diana's face had now turned to mist and kept shifting shapes like a low-drifting cloud in the sky, and he was so confused he just wanted to sit down on the cold linoleum floor and cry.

Just then, because he was slouching, lost in his daydream, the trusty inmate from the Bronx punched Kev square in the chest, knocking all the wind out of him. On impulse Kev turned, clenched his fists into stone-hard weapons, tagged the trusty up with a nice lit-

---

*Trusted inmate.

tle left-right combination. But then the trusty came back swinging and busted Kev's lip wide open. Tasting his own blood, Kev started crying, hyperventilating; but now the other guys in D-5 were, for the very first time, showing him a little respect. "Yo, this punk-ass Brooklyn nigga got some *heart* after all!"

It was decided that Kev and the trusty from the Bronx would finish the fight up in the dorm. The counselors nodded approvingly; everyone pushed the furniture back, clearing a sparring circle. One of the counselors said, "You got exactly two minutes to scrap."

But Kev had already calmed down, regained his faculties. He didn't want to fight the trusty anymore. "I'm not fuckin' with him," he said, trying to lie down on his bunk with a torn Archie comic.

The trusty from the Bronx snatched Kev from his bed and slammed him to the floor, wrestling style—*boof!*—and then again—*reverse-suplex!*—like he was Gorilla Monsoon. "Man," Kev said, "I'm tellin' you—"

The trusty clocked him in the mouth.

"Yo, man, why don't you—"

Clocked him again. Kev had had enough, he was just trying to get out of the circle, but the rest of the unit kept shoving him back in.

"*Fight* him, nigga!"

He fell to the floor and the trusty started riding his back like a cowboy, hollering *giddyup!* and hitting him in the butt like he was his goddamn barebacked bronco. Everybody was laughing and calling Kev a bitch and then Gungo Steve said, "Break it up! Break it up! This nigga not gonna fight!"

The scrap was over, Kev hadn't even landed a punch, but the trusty kid took it upon himself to step right into Kev's face now and spit the ultimate street taunt.

"Your *mother!*"

What!

After that, Kev blacked out. He couldn't recollect exactly what happened in the fight. The only clear memory he had was taking the trusty's head and banging it on the edge of the counselor's desk, and by then there was blood all over the floor and blood all over the trusty and blood all over Kev. The trusty kid had had a T-shirt on when he said "Your mother!" but now he wasn't wearing a shirt and one of his shoes was off and Kev was in the process of smashing his nose flat on the edge of the counselor's desk. For the first time since he'd come to Spofford he felt good about something. He felt so good smashing and splitting the trusty's nose against the desk, seeing the other D-5 inmates and the horrified counselors dragging them apart, staring at Kev with wide-open eyes like he was some kind of untamed beast.

They dragged him back and forth to Brooklyn Family Court in the Spofford van. His case kept being postponed. The state had assigned him a court-appointed counsel; she was a white lady called Jane. He didn't like her at all; he didn't trust her. She had crooked teeth and a strange smell, like a school desk that's had a piece of rotting fruit trapped inside it. He got the impression that she wasn't even trying to defend him; she was trying to get him sent up north from day one.

They were speaking in tongues. A stream of legal jargon he couldn't understand. The Boy needed to go to such-and-such diagnostic unit to see if he was suffering from symptoms of this-or-that. They had him see the psychiatrist lady named Dr. Monk. They put plaster on his head and wires and tested his brain waves. He was afraid of that. He'd seen that movie called *One Flew Over the Cuckoo's Nest,* and those wires made him think they were trying to turn his brain to jelly. Then, on a quieter day, they asked him a series of vocabulary words and made him figure out a bunch of stupid puzzles. On the phone, he overheard them saying that The Boy's IQ was extraordinary; the tests showed The Boy had a very high IQ. But also The Boy had a serious authority problem. The Boy might be manic-depressive. Aggressive outbursts when provoked.

But the thing that had him messed up the most was when they determined that The Boy didn't have any supervision back at the ranch.

They sent caseworkers to The Boy's apartment and learned that his
mother hadn't returned home for over three days—she was working
double shifts at the hospital and not coming home to sleep those
nights—and this sealed The Boy's case for them.

The judge's chambers were in the back of the Brooklyn Family Court
building. It was really only one single small room, like a bedroom,
with several large windows facing outside. On the day of the final dis-
position hearing, the judge began to utter some more of those strange
legal terms that sounded to Kev a little bit like Spanish, but not exactly like Spanish, and while the judge was talking, he kept gesturing
to the sunny window.

"Son, you see that little tree out there?"

Kev was shaking his head, sniffling, trying to hold in the tears and
the snot. He knew that the judge was getting ready to send him upstate.

"That one right there, son."

"I don't see no tree."

Then he looked close through the glass. Yes, he could see a tree,
just a little sapling, with the thick wooden stake planted deep in the
soil, and the thin wires holding the tree in place, forcing the tree to
grow up straight and strong. Kev knew that without the support of the
stiff metal wires and that thick wooden stake, the skinny little baby
tree would surely snap over in a heavy wind and die.

Kev had no idea why the old white man was making him look at
a skinny little baby tree.

"Son, that'll be a full-grown tree by the time you come home to
Brooklyn."

And, with that, The Boy's case was closed. "Remand to SJC for
transportation upstate," said the judge.

*"Now when I rolled back to Spofford, all them muthafuckas seen me cryin'
and carryin' on, so they knew I had got served. All the older heads, niggas
like Bo and Gator, they're shoutin' out to me, and they're proud as hell: 'Oh,*

you hangin' with me, nigga? You hangin' with me, nigga? I'm gettin' ready to go up north my-muthafuckin'-self!'

"'Man, I don't wanna be hangin' with y'all muthafuckas! I wanna go the fuck home!'

"'Chill out, nigga! You gonna hang with me, nigga! Shit's gonna be all right!'

"There's a fourteen-day period after you get served before they transfer you upstate. And those fourteen days is a long fuckin' time, yo. Those fourteen days feel like months.

"In those dead days after you get served you're just kickin' around Spofford, and you know you better start showin' and provin'. You gotta start mappin' out your strategy in those fourteen days; you gotta start makin' a name for yourself, lettin' niggas know you ain't nobody to be fucked with."

He had no rep. That was his biggest problem. The fight with the trusty kid didn't count for shit. He'd been too barbaric; he'd been banging the trusty's face into the desk out of pure rage. Now he would need to make them all fear—if not respect—his hand skills. He waited for his chance, biding his time, knowing that whoever he selected should have an established reputation as a streetfighter. He had his sights set on one jailyard bully named Peter Chaplain. Peter Chaplain was about sixteen years old, tall and rangy. He wasn't *diesel*, like Toño and his boys, but his lean frame was filled in with muscles and sinews everywhere. When Peter Chaplain took off his shirt, he looked like one of those anatomy drawings: all his abdominal muscles puckered and the striations spread across his broad back. He had all the younger kids petrified. In addition to being a bully, Peter Chaplain was a pervert, got his kicks sticking his finger up littler kids' asses in the shower.

It all kicked off over some stolen pineapple juice. Kev had a little Puerto Rican homey named Frankie who was working the mess hall detail and he hit Kev off with some nice cold Dole pineapple juice. Kev drank it all up, sharing a few cans with his homeys in D-5. Peter

Chaplain came over, screwfaced, saying, "Yo, why you ain't save me one?"

"Nigga, I don't even *know* you. What the fuck you talkin' 'bout?"

"*Bet!* We gon' handle this in the *yard.*"

"Whatevah whatevah."

They met out in the yard. Toño was outside, chilling with his crimies Ant and Greg. Peter Chaplain charged straight over to Kev. "Yo, let's do this, nigga. You ready? Let's shoot some joints! Throw up ya dickbeaters, nigga!"

They both threw up their dickbeaters. Peter Chaplain tried two pitiful moves, then Kev locked up, spun back, touched the ground and—*Thwack!*—back-slapped Peter Chaplain something terrible. The big pervert stood there in shock. Peter Chaplain knew how to street-fight, but he wasn't schooled in the art of the fifty-two.

"See, as far as fightin' goes, I'd come up under the tutelage of Toño and his boys. They all prided themselves on their fifty-two skills. Now one thing you've got to understand about the fifty-two hand-blocks: that shit was developed in the baddest jails up north. That shit was perfected for being in a jail-fight mode, havin' your back against the wall, gettin' stepped to by five or six niggas at once. The moves even have names that come from the jails: like the Comstock Roll, or the El-maow—from Elmira—or the Nap-knock, which came from Napinock. The fifty-two is an art, but it's a lost art. The real heads who was schooled in that shit came up in the late '70s; in them days, all real bad muthafuckas in Brooklyn prided themselves on havin' fifty-two skills. The most ruthless niggas from Nostrand Avenue, from Washington Avenue—they was the undisputed masters of the art. Eric Tweedy, Mother Dear, Mother Nature, Derrick Idi, La La Phil, Cadet Prince, Little John, One-Armed Charlie—them cats was the most feared fifty-two masters in the borough of Brooklyn.

"A trained eye could see a lot of the fifty-two blocks in Mike Tyson, back when he was in the prime of his boxing career. In subtle ways, Mike incorporated that shit into his boxing style: the way he'd stalk his opponent with that flat-footed walk; the way he'd kick up his heels coming out of the cor-

*ner to start a round; the way he'd wobble his head back and forth on his
neck—that all comes from knowin' the fifty-two hand-blocks."*

Kev took Peter Chaplain to school that day, put on a wicked exhibi-
tion of his fledgling fifty-two hand-blocks. Toño and his crimies were
jumping around, shouting, egging him on. "That's *my* little brovva!
What! Nigga learnt from *me*, boy! You *crazy?*"

He put some stain on Peter Chaplain's ass that would not soon be
forgotten in the Spofford yard. He was doing backhands, windmills,
blocking the pervert's punches between two clenched forearms, kissing the useless fist and throwing it back at him like a pair of soiled
drawers. And as he was tagging him up, shuffling, dancing backward,
he started to taunt his beaten opponent, "Break the glass, nigga! Break
the glass!" because that's how Toño used to do it, sticking out his chin,
tempting the other guy to hit you in the face. Kev didn't knock Peter
Chaplain out cold. But he swelled the bigger boy's eye shut, bloodied
his lip, and as Peter Chaplain was trying to back away from the fight,
Kev scooped him up, chopping out the back of his knees, dropping
him on the ground, standing over him, growling, "Nigga *what!* You
crazy? You betta go back to *school*, boy!"

But there was one inmate in Spofford whom Kev wanted no part of—
fifty-two hand-block skills notwithstanding. Everyone called him
Money Mike, owing to his reputation as a wicked stickup kid in
Brownsville. It would be a few more years before he'd acquire his
more famous nickname, Iron Mike—that wouldn't come until the old
Italian man named Cus D'Amato got wind of him in Tryon and began
to groom Mike for his meteoric rise to the heavyweight championship
of the world.

In his Spofford days, Money Mike was so diesel, so renowned a
streetfighter, Kev could remember thinking, *Only a fool or a crazy
nigga would go lookin' to throw down with that badboy!* Money Mike just
didn't give a fuck. No one who'd been in Spofford alongside him
would ever forget the day that Money Mike broke out of the juve-

nile jail, walking right out the front door after receiving a visit from his family.

The funny thing was, any one of them could have done it. In those days, the inmates in Spofford were allowed to keep their street clothes; they weren't issued an institutional uniform like they are today.

"Even though most of us hated bein' in Spofford, none of us really wanted to break out of there too bad. It's hard to explain. You may find this a little bit disturbin' but back then—to us—it was somethin' like a muthafucka gettin' into Princeton. How's it feel when you open up your mailbox and you find that letter sayin' they accepted you to an Ivy League college? You're elated, right? How do your friends feel when you tell them? They're elated for you, right?

"That's how it was for us juveniles goin' to jail. That was our ghetto status symbol, man. Goin' to Spofford, goin' to Brace, goin' to Goshen. We had this warped perception that while we're away all the girls and our homeboys out in the world was braggin' about us: Damn, my nigga in jail right now! When my nigga come home he gonna be diesel! *It was a big thing to be in Spofford. It was an even bigger thing to be up north in Goshen."*

You start convincing yourself: damn, jail is the *bomb*. Maybe your mother didn't have too much food at her disposal back in the crib; she was scraping by with a lot of Hamburger Helper, with a lot of government meat and government cheese. But in jail you can eat all day long. You can get seconds, thirds *and* fourths. Sure, the food is nasty; they're stuffing you full of a lot of horsemeat and powdered mashed potatoes; but keep eating those seconds and thirds, keep doing your push-ups and dips, and soon you'll notice the difference: you're getting kind of big. All your little homeboys are noticing it too: you're looking cock-diesel.

You already know the jailhouse code. Need a new pair of sneakers? Just find a punk and take *his* sneakers. Need a gold chain? Find a punk and take *his* gold chain. Need your dirty drawers washed? Send a punk to the sink to wash them for you.

Raw-dog. That's the only way to go. Glance around the place and you'll see: any guy wearing the latest gear—Fila sweat suit, spanking-new Adidas Gazelles, two-finger gold ring—you know that boy is running the house raw-dog style.

When he was transferred up north, to the Annsville Youth Camp in Oneida County, he got his first cold dose of reality. It seemed like everybody Kev had messed with in Spofford, everybody he'd messed with in the Brentwood juvenile facility, was right there in Annsville waiting for him. During all those months in Spofford, none of the guys who were repeat offenders had really told him what to expect from life up north. So he came in there thinking, *Fuck it, this is just another Spofford. Watch me flip script in this muthafucka.*

He'd handled his brief stay in Brentwood like it was nothing. He was stealing everyone's sneakers, snatching chains, acting ignorant. Certain cats had warned him: *Yo, them niggas'll fuck you up when you get to Goshen—they'll kill you.* He knew that those were the two worst juvenile jails in New York State: Goshen and Elmira.

They called them Gladiator Schools. You made your mark in those juvenile jails. He knew that the reputation you developed there would carry you over to the adult prison system. Because once they'd transferred you to Goshen or Elmira, the only place left for them to send you was adult prison. He heard so many rumors about Goshen. He heard that once you got to Goshen, you started seeing jail shanks, guys sleeping with razor blades in their teeth, guys getting slashed up and gouged and needing hundreds of stitches to close the wounds.

He arrived in Annsville, facing not just everybody whose ass he had whipped, but everybody whose ass Toño had whipped—of course Big Tone had left his own bloody trail behind him through the juvenile system. And now all his enemies were there whispering things about him, worried that he was going to try to run their house, steal everyone's clothes and jewelry, punk them for their commissary.

Annsville was set up dormitory style, with all the bunk beds arranged in one huge room. You couldn't keep too many secrets in there. When Christmastime came, Kev was feeling depressed because he wasn't home with his family; and then New Year's Eve came, and as soon as the ball dropped in Times Square and 1980 flashed on the screen—*Happy fucking New Year!*—all his enemies had planned to bust him up good.

Kev knew the whole plot in advance. Luckily, two little white kids had warned him. One was named Douglas and the other was Mikey— Mikey who later committed suicide, hanged himself in jail—they came to him in secret and Douglas whispered, "Watch your back, man. These guys are gonna fuckin' move on you."

The New Year's celebrations died down. One o'clock came and Kev was tucked in bed and through half-opened eyes he saw this guy named Dolphus from Syracuse moving, suspiciously, around the bunk. What Dolphus didn't know was that Kev had all his clothes on under the covers and that he had a sharpened toothbrush and a tube sock with three bars of Lifebuoy in it. He was just lying there under the covers, playing possum, waiting for them to make their move. He heard Dolphus whispering, "Yeah, he asleep . . ."

"I knew these niggas didn't know nothin' about makin' no jail shanks. When I was younger I used to hear Julio and his crimies talkin' about how they used to be stabbin' muthafuckas up on Rikers. 'Oh yeah, I seen that mutha- fucka, he was in C-74—' '—Yes mon, I just sharpen up me toothbrush and jook him up nice!' I'd close my eyes tight and I'd be right there in jail with them, and I could feel what it would feel like to stab someone up with my shank. I knew how to make it on instinct. Just sneak into the bathroom, pour a little bit of water on the concrete, scrub the end of your toothbrush down to a razor-sharp point."

*   *   *

They were all massing around his bunk with their lock-in-a-socks and their soap-in-a-socks. The silence was broken by a shriek like an Apache war cry and someone came out swinging his lock-in-a-sock. Kev rolled off the top bunk and let out his own shrieking war cry. He was outnumbered twelve to one but he managed to hold his own for a moment, tagging a few of the guys up with his soap-in-a-sock and stabbing at them with his sharpened toothbrush. He knew he was going to go down, but at least he would go down swinging.

The counselors must've wanted him to learn a lesson, because even with all the noise, they didn't come break it up for a long time. More and more guys were charging at him, from all directions, and they really looked like they wanted to kill him. He was doubled up on the floor, trying to shield his face from their blows—he was taking so many shots in the kidneys he knew he was going to piss blood tomorrow—and finally one of the counselors came running, yelling, "Stop!" As they were leading him to seclusion, though, one guy came out of nowhere and coldcocked him with his lock-in-a-sock. Kev felt himself crumpling to the floor, losing consciousness. The white boys, Douglas and Mikey, later told him that the counselors had dragged him by his feet into the front office.

They made him sleep in the front office for three days. He was too scared to set foot back inside the dormitory.

"After Annsville, they moved me someplace else and then someplace else again: the jails all seemed to blur together. I thought I was goin' crazy. It was all white. It was snowing every fuckin' day. I wasn't used to this. Everything was coming down on me at once: the sense of being rejected by my moms and them; the realization that I'm a million miles away from home; that I don't have a friend in the fuckin' world. That's the frame of mind I was in when I came to Goshen."

He arrived at the Goshen Secure Center for the first time in the spring of 1980. Located in Orange County, seventy-five miles from New York City, Goshen was one of four top-level secure centers for juveniles in the state. At the time, the center housed some eighty juvenile offenders, the majority of whom had been convicted of violent felonies before their sixteenth birthdays. The inmates at Goshen were among the most incorrigible cases in the care of the Division of Youth, repeat offenders, kids convicted of crimes like murder, rape, armed robbery, arson.

At first glance, the Goshen Secure Center looked like a boarding school for rich kids, a two-story red-brick building dropped down in the middle of rolling dairy farms, complete with a scenic view of the nearby Shawangunk mountains. But then you noticed the eighteen-foot fence, topped by spiraling coils of steel razor-ribbon, preventing any easy escape from the grounds.

Kev stood in the cold Goshen yard, stamping his feet to keep warm, staring at the coils of razor-ribbon, out at that endless snow-blanketed dairyland. Had the state purposely put these juvenile jails—filled with black kids from the inner city—smack in the middle of all these white people's farms? It had been like that at Camp Brace too. Was that their plan, he wondered, to make them so conspicuous that they could never escape? From time to time an inmate used to try leaping the fence and when the farm owners got word that one of the Goshen kids was missing, you'd see them coming to the gate with their wagons and their little shotguns. They'd tell one of the counselors: "You better find that boy before sundown. If you don't find him before sundown, and he happens to cross *my* field, I'm shooting him."

Goshen was different from any other juvenile jail he'd been to. There was so much studying, so many chores to complete, the kids didn't have any spare time to themselves. If you weren't studying, you had assigned activities, and if you didn't have any activities, you were down there in the kitchen, cooking and cleaning and mopping the floor. The only time they had to themselves was when *Dynasty* came on. *Dynasty* used to stop everybody dead in his tracks. Kev and all the other Goshen inmates were addicted to Blake Carrington like he was heroin.

He was assigned to Unit One. The guys of Unit One were the rejects from all the other units, the fuck-ups, the problem cases. But they all bonded together like a big family. Most of the guys were from Brooklyn, a few from the Bronx, a couple from Manhattan and Queens. Rockbone, Gator, Wonderful, Porter, Rob, Tango, Just, Stinks. They had one radio to the block and they all used to sing along to it, doing harmonies, taking turns at the lead vocal. They'd make up their own words to whatever song came on the radio, then marching down to the chow line, they'd sing in unison, like soldiers on a boot camp drill. The Go Go's had their song "We Got the Beat" on the charts and as Unit One was marching past Keith—this very ugly counselor from Unit Four—Gator called out "Sound off!" and then, out of the blue, Tango started up singing new words to the Go Go's tune—

Keith got no teeth
Keith got no teeth
He got no teeeeeeeeth

—because Keith was missing three teeth and had a nasty-looking dope fiend's mouth. That was Unit One's style: breaking fool on all the counselors. There was one counselor named Shane Kermack—they all called him Spermsack. They used to shout out, "Ay yo, Spermsack!" just to watch him get red in the face. Spermsack ran the gym with this other counselor, Ivan, whom they used to call Yogi. He used to hate when they'd holler, "Hey Yogi!" because Yogi was quite sensitive about being on the fat side.

*   *   *

It was in Goshen that he first learned what it meant to be Righteous. Most of the guys in his unit were members of the Five Percent Nation. Wonderful was the main organizer and enlightener. In the beginning, Kev didn't give a damn about them. They used to go into the bathroom to form their ciphers—manifest their names and study their lessons—and Kev would burst in to bumrush the cipher. Stepping into the circle, he'd shout: "My name is Mastermind Divine, the Maker and Creator of all swine!" Then he'd throw back his head, laugh, point a mocking finger. "Fuck y'all! Fake-ass pork-eatin' muthafuckas! Y'all know you was eatin' bacon and eggs when you was out in the world!"

Back in the dorm Wonderful would stare at him, chiding him with his eyes, like a strict parent. "Yo, why you be disrespectin' us, little K? What's up with that?"

He didn't even know what to tell Wonderful. He just enjoyed breaking fool. It was the loneliness again, lonely thoughts grabbing at his throat, taking his breath, like a very deep dive into black unknown waters. He'd think about being home in Brooklyn with his mother and she'd be in the kitchen, fixing him his favorite dish, a thick slice of her meat lasagna—*Stop, nigga! Don't let them muthafuckas see you cry!* No, better to focus his mind on the bad thoughts—think about his first stepmother and her brujería curse, think about his second stepmother, making him kneel on the cheese grater, taking that hot spoon and burning him on the soft downy brown skin of his thighs . . . *Good, good,* now he could hear himself, back in the innocent days, hear his little boy's voice howling with pain . . .

And that's when he would be ready, ready to find someone, anyone—another inmate, an unsuspecting counselor—creep up on them and hurt them, make *them* howl with the pain he was hearing in his head.

He was behaving so ignorantly, hurting other kids at will, knocking counselors unconscious, that at least once a week they would throw him in the hole—put him in solitary lockdown—as a punishment. Words would come to him in seclusion. *Branded a beast as I sit at the feast.*

He felt so alone every day. Wonderful saw how lonely he looked and he took Kev under his wing. He showed Kev a copy of the Five Percent Nation lessons.* "Look, K, just study this right here." Wonderful was his enlightener. Wonderful taught him that he was not a black boy—he was the Blackman, the Original Man, the living embodiment of the Supreme Being. Wonderful taught him that all Blackmen were Gods. And K, even K, *wild-ass* K, he was a Godbody too: K-God trapped in the belly of the beast.

Wonderful taught him the Supreme Mathematics and Supreme Alphabets that had been developed by Father Allah. Wonderful gave him his Righteous name: Knowledge Born.

The Knowledge of the Cipher is to enlighten you, to let you know that God is right amongst you. Through Wonderful, he gradually began to attain Knowledge of Self. He learned that the Blackman was the Supreme form of life, the vehicle through which Allah's will was made manifest. There was no substance in the universe that the Original Man's body did not consist of. He learned from Wonderful that eighty-five percent of the black nation were mentally blind, deaf and dumb; while ten percent were bloodsuckers who kept the eighty-five percent ignorant and profited from that ignorance. It was

---

*The Five Percent Nation, an offshoot of the Nation of Islam, arose on the Harlem streets in the mid-'60s under the leadership of Clarence 13X Smith (1928–1969). A Korean War veteran and former member of the NOI's elite Fruit of Islam security force, Smith (aka Puddin') was expelled from the NOI's Harlem Mosque Number 7 in 1963 by Malcom X, reputedly because he refused to forgo his fondness for dice games.

Smith, who began referring to himself as Allah, took the NOI's "Lost-Found Lessons" out of the temple and directly to the troubled youth of Harlem. His charismatic leadership attracted the attention of both police and politicians: arrested for assault in 1965, he refused to acknowledge the authority of the court and, diagnosed a paranoid schizophrenic, was committed to the Mattewan State Hospital for the Criminally Insane; after his release, Mayor John Lindsay put him on the New York City payroll, hoping Smith might use his growing influence to keep the streets cool during the long riotous summer of 1968. Allah had often boasted that he could not be killed, but he was gunned down execution-style in the elevator of a Harlem apartment building on June 13, 1969. The murder was never solved.

left for the five percent—the Poor Righteous Teachers of the earth—
to save the black nation from certain destruction.

And following the Five Percent teachings, he began to act more
civilized. He'd still get into trouble with the counselors from time to
time, but he started to think more collectively, think about how his actions would affect the other Gods in his unit.

He had to give Goshen credit for one thing: they did study a lot of
black history there. Mixed in with the Constitution and stories of the
Founding Fathers, there was a lot of black-oriented material in the
curriculum. He didn't know the first thing about those people: Andrew Young, W. E. B. Du Bois; Ralph Bunche; Shirley Chisholm; Mary
McLeod Bethune. He hadn't even heard their names until he was sent
upstate to Goshen.

But as interested as he was in the black history classes, he
couldn't relate much of it to his everyday life. It was all well and
good to call himself a Five Percenter, to know that the Blackman
was a living God, but where were his role models in the *real* world?
The only black people he felt he could look up to were gangsters
and outlaws and thugs. Bumpy Johnson. Nicky Barnes. The real
ruthless black cats.

But regardless of race—white devil or no—there was one thug
who stood out in his eyes, one gunman he admired more than any
other.

"For me—for the criminal mentality—John Dillinger was the MAN. *I loved
readin' about his style, his mannerisms, his whole way of doin' shit. John
grew up in an era when most of the people were poor, and John was the people's man, even though he was an outlaw. All I wanted to do was emulate
him. That muthafucka had so much heart. The way he broke out of jail that
time with the gun carved from soap and covered in shoe polish. Word to
mother! Muthafuckas was so scared of him that when he brandished the
soap gun they opened the cell doors and let him walk out of jail. Bein' in jail*

myself when I read that made me really appreciate how much heart Dillinger had.*

"I studied everything I could about Dillinger, the things he did and said. The way the bitches was all faintin' and dippin' their handkerchiefs in his blood when the feds gunned him down. Of course, it was that bitch in the red dress that set him up.

"Never trust a woman or an automatic pistol.

"That was one of Dillinger's sayings that I always remembered."

When he wasn't buried under schoolwork, he would read all the criminal books he could get his hands on. He read *The Valachi Papers* in Goshen; that was one of the few Mafia books he could find in there. Mostly, the Goshen library used to be filled with do-gooder reading material. Reading those Mafia books, he saw that Brooklyn had its own criminal tapestry, a blood-red collage of gangsterism. It seemed like all the *real* gangsters came from Brooklyn. Not just Murder Incorporated. Even Al Capone was a Brooklynite at heart. Capone first made his name in Brooklyn. Brooklyn was where he picked up the scar *and* the Scarface. Being incarcerated in a backwoods place like Goshen made him even more proud to be from Brooklyn, to know that Brooklynites had long been wreaking havoc wherever they went.

All the years he spent up north, all the years he spent supposedly being rehabilitated by the Division of Youth—being turned into a young man who could function by the rules and regulations of society—Kev actually felt more criminal-minded than when he went in. Most of the guys in Unit One would go on to become stickup

---

*Most accounts of Dillinger's breakout from the "escape proof" county jail in Crown Point, Indiana, describe his bluff gun as having been carved from wood, not soap. According to John Toland's biography *The Dillinger Days*, the inmate had been smuggled a real pistol, but upon his escape, Dillinger instantly self-mythologized the weapon as having been a fake, further enhancing his growing renown as the nation's most cunning and daring outlaw.

men, drug dealers, murderers. What else could you expect? Goshen had been like a crime tutorial program: for years they'd been surrounded by guys with more hands-on knowledge and criminal savvy.

The state authorities couldn't wait until Kev hit sixteen so they could transfer him out of Goshen and into the adult prison system. On his sixteenth birthday they moved him to Oneida, and after a few months in Oneida, he was sent to the big pen at Elmira. He was housed in the reception area of Elmira, which is where they put the juveniles. After a few months in Elmira he was sent back downstate to Camp Brace.

It was in Brace that he finally got the word. They were going to be sending him down to a halfway house, the Youth Detention Center in Bushwick. He would be back on the streets of Brooklyn—*free!*—in time for Christmas.

THREE

original crooks

Straight from Crooklyn
Better known as Brooklyn . . .
        —**Buckshot**

Q : How can a gangster say goodbye to a long life of
     gangsterism?
A : *Find an honest day's work.*

JANUARY '93. K, to my considerable astonishment, has managed to land not one straight job but two. (Yes, I *know* his baptismal name is Kevin; I even *think* of him as Kevin sometimes. But he prefers to be called Big K or Dread or AD—that's how he variously identifies himself when leaving his long freestyle rhymes on my answering machine—and why would I, or anyone, disrespect the man's wishes? Kevin exposes too much, I suppose, and not just in the sense of a couple of Brooklyn detectives, tapping his phone line, eager to break open some cold case on him. The name makes him sound vulnerable. A little tenderhearted boy behind the thick impenetrable scar tissue.)

Around Christmastime, tired of the insecurity and sleeplessness of his gangster life, K went out looking for work. It wasn't a sudden change of heart, some goody-goody epiphany (*Good God! Crime really doesn't pay!*). No, the immediate impetus was a simple obstetrical exam, indicating Faith's pregnancy, that she's expecting their first child by late summer. How're they going to get by? K won't hear talk of an abortion. You crazy? Kill *his* baby?*

"What else *can* I do?" he told me after hearing the news. "Walk these dogs, man. Find a muthafuckin' job."

And so he went out pounding the icy pavement in the dead of December. His wasn't the kind of job search that required a suit and tie, clean-shaven chin and splash of Aqua Velva, computerized résumé lasered on watermarked bond. His résumé was written in the scars on his face. K was looking to hire himself out as security muscle, your friendly neighborhood Intimidator.

And now he's found that legal gig. Working seven days a week. Spends all day Saturday and all day Sunday guarding a sneaker store in the bustling 149th Street shopping area of the South Bronx. The shop is owned by some Nigerians who've been repeatedly robbed at gunpoint; they've hired K to stand in the doorway and put a stop to that. So far, he has.

His weekday job is a little more sedate. Monday to Friday, he takes the D train into midtown Manhattan, to a boutique on Fifth Avenue and 44th Street called Raspberry Sport USA, owned by several Israeli brothers. At Raspberry, the problem isn't stickups as much as shoplifting. Raspberry stocks all the brand names so in demand on the street these days. Timberland. Nautica, Polo. Tommy Hilfiger. Champion. Nike. Just enter any city high school and see it for yourself. You're *nothing* if you don't have one of those brand names branded across your chest or ankle or ass. And to the kids in the street, it's simply the law of supply and demand. Why buy when you

---

*By this time, K had already told me about two other, school-aged children he'd had by women in Brooklyn: a daughter Carla by Yolanda; and a son Tino by Candice. There were, he said, several other young women who claimed to have given birth to his children over the years, but he would only acknowledge that he was the father of Carla and Tino.

can boost? Or (for those without the heart for the chase) why pay retail when you can buy discount from a booster?

For years, I'm told, the entire Fifth Avenue business district has been besieged by boosters. Many of the businesses already employ a number of blue-uniformed security men, but the boosters regard these rent-a-cops with contempt. They laugh in their faces and deride them as "fake-jakes" behind their backs. They know that no fat-ass rent-a-cop, armed only with a billy club and walkie-talkie, can outrun them in a footrace to the subway entrance. Hence the need for deterrents, for muscle, for *real* security, for Big K.

The irony isn't lost on K, that a man of his criminal pedigree should be employed by legitimate businessmen to halt and prevent robberies and larcenies. Doesn't it make perfect sense when you consider it? Who better understands the mind of a thief than a former thief—the scheming of a stickup kid than an ex–stickup kid?

Every few days, after lunch, I'd drop by Raspberry to surprise K on the job. He spent most of the day on his feet, watching the street traffic, listening to his Walkman, writing rhymes and ideas on the backs of Raspberry Sport inventory sheets. Since we first met back in June, he'd gotten much bigger—at least thirty pounds more muscular—bulked up all over his frame. That was the natural consequence of having a regular place to sleep—Faith having found them an apartment on Echo Place in the Tremont section of the Bronx—and eating regular meals of home-cooked soul food.

He liked the working life. That was one thing about K: he wasn't lazy. Sure, he had his bad moods, his sullen days, when you knew it was best not to bother him with trivial details. But in general he came to work with an amiable and professional outlook.

The strangest thing to witness was the easy camaraderie he'd developed with Raspberry's owners and managers, a gaggle of Israelis and Russian-born Jews who tended to make frequent wisecracks without smiling. Before long K had picked up a few Hebrew phrases like *Baruch ha-Shem* ("Blessed be His Name"); and—his facility with languages was quite extraordinary—he'd also mastered a pitch-perfect imitation of the Israelis' expletive of choice, a guttural Arabic phrase which I've since been told is a vulgar reference to the vaginal region of someone's mother.

I could never master it myself. It sounded like he was gargling with gravel. He was forever growling that Arabic curse at the Israelis, causing their cardboard faces to, finally, fold up into smiles. The Israelis would shake their heads and tell me that, armed with just that one Arabic phrase, K could handle himself perfectly well in a Tel Aviv traffic jam.

The only tense moment of his day came at closing time, after he'd activated the rolling metal security grate—stopping the gate's descent just above the six-foot mark—and then, three minutes later, an average-looking Lincoln would pull up to the curb and, from the passenger side, out would step one of Raspberry's owners. K would meet him at the curb and bodyguard him, hip to hip, from the street to the store entrance, glancing furtively down the sidewalk the whole time. Only later did I realize the reason for the extra vigilance: the owner was a prime stickup target, carrying, on his person, thousands of dollars in cash receipts from various Raspberry branches around Manhattan. That was the only time on the job when K wasn't willing to smile and joke. The risk of being gunned down was too great.

Like some wily old baseball manager in the dugout—bubblegum churning, eyes darting, trying to decipher the other team's intricate hand signals—K stands to the left of the doorway, deriving great pleasure from this daily challenge of outsmarting potential thieves. He even sports a Yankees cap today; but his cap is spun backward, the rectangular Major League Baseball logo dead-center in his forehead, staring out at the world like his third eye.

He rubs his bearded chin, awaiting the appearance of some fool-hardy crooks. It strokes his ego to pit his criminal-mindedness against theirs. As a crime-fighter, though, his technique is not what you'd call subtle.

From time to time, a young black high-school-aged kid with a nearly empty backpack slung over one shoulder tries to enter Rasp-berry but—instantly filling the doorway like Frankenstein's mon-ster—K stops him with a powerful straight-arm to the chest.

"Naw, shorty. Not *my* store."

The kid doesn't even argue. Just shrugs his shoulders and slinks away down the block.

Talk about presumption of guilt. The first time I witnessed it, I couldn't help but feel sorry for the kid. Why didn't K do that when a bunch of white kids, in their skulking ballcaps, Airwalks and skate-board baggies, came into the store? How did he know that the black kid wasn't a hardworking paperboy, or sweating over the McDonald's fryer after school, or saving up his Christmas money just to come down to Fifth Avenue to buy the latest Air Jordans?

"The *eyes*," he said. "I can see it in their eyes. I can tell when they come to shop and when they come to boost."

Didn't he find this all a bit arbitrary? Judging what someone might do just by their appearance?

Now he had to laugh at me. I was so naive. First of all, he ex-plained, as patiently as possible, if that kid had really wanted to spend his *hard-earned* money, why wasn't he up there on 125th Street where—as any idiot knows—sneakers and sweat suits are so much cheaper? Why come down to Fifth Avenue to pay jacked-up tourist prices? And secondly, he continued (now sounding more than a little offended by my ignorance), didn't I realize that he *knew* the rules of this game already, that he'd been around little boosters like that his whole life? It seemed like I didn't know a damned thing about the Franklin Avenue Posse after all. *What?* I'd never heard him talking about the Original Crooks?

*   *   *

He talked about the heyday of the F.A.P., the heyday of crack selling in New York City, that bloodiest of epochs—corresponding, roughly, to my own college years—between '84 and '88. In that Wild West era, the younger generation on Franklin—little grade-schoolers alongside slightly older shorties from Prospect Heights High School—were out there in their rubberized rain suits, mobbing in the streets, boosting with abandon. Kids like Little Red and Dieso and Midi and Kenyatta— Kenyatta was now that up-and-coming rapper called Buckshot, the leader of the group Black Moon—they'd perfected the art of boosting, made it their virtual after-school profession. They were all putting Brooklyn on the map. The big Posse men called themselves the Original Heads; the boosting crew called themselves the Original Crooks.

The F.A.P. boosters worked the Fulton Mall in downtown Brooklyn and Pitkin Avenue in East New York. On rare occasions they'd hit midtown Manhattan. They'd come back from their boosting missions and sell their stolen sneakers and sweat suits and jewelry to the bigger Posse men like K and Shabazz and True for half the retail value. Sometimes the Posse members would even send the boosters on specific missions, filling special orders: *Yo, get me them Timbo chukkas in a ten and that blue-and-black Fila shit in a XXL.*

But there was a girl out there who put the Original Crooks to shame, K told me. Her name was Tasha. If street legend was to be believed, Tasha was the baddest booster who ever lived. She was from Roosevelt Projects. She was the best, K said, bar none. Everybody who boosted wanted to be like Tasha.

Tasha used to go into stores like Macy's and Bloomingdale's and steal Sony VCRs and tape decks between her legs, held in place by the tight girdles she used to have on. She would wear a long prairie skirt and come out with Versace and Donna Karan outfits and $1,200 mink coats hidden in there.

"I don't know how the fuck she did it," K said, shaking his head at the girl's uncanny shoplifting ability as if ruminating on the secret of Houdini's milk can escape. "Tasha was *good*, boy. I used to buy all my shit from her at half price. The place I used to have on Rutland

Road, damn near all the shit I had up in that crib I bought from Boostin' Tasha. The only thing that fucked Tasha up was when Tasha started smokin' that crack. That was her big downfall. Ask any Brooklyn muthafucka if he remembers Tasha, though. The bitch was a legend. There'll never be another Tash."

He had no worries about boosters making a dent at Raspberry. The few times a booster was stupid enough to try to steal something under his watch, K would grab him, lump him up a little bit—but not enough to do any real damage—then set him free to spread the good word on the streets. *Yo! Do not fuck with that nigga's store!*

The real worry for K and his fellow security men were the steamers. Steamers were young bands of shoplifters who attacked and dismantled stores with insectlike teamwork. Where a booster would come into a shop on a solo mission, to get a particular size of Nike Airs or Sergio Tacchini sweat suit, steamers were indiscriminate in their thievery, grabbing handfuls of anything they could carry away at a full getaway gallop. And if one or two of them got nabbed, so what? The rest of the crew had made a good day's haul.

That's why K was so adamant about stopping suspicious-looking kids before they even entered the store. "They're like cockroaches. You fuck around and let one of them in, turn your back, a minute later you got seventeen little greedy muthafuckas snatchin' everything off the racks."

One day while I was standing with K in front of Raspberry Sport a report came over one of the rent-a-cop's radios that the Foot Locker on 42nd Street had been blitzed by steamers. They'd come in there forty-deep and managed to get away with half the store's inventory, thousands of dollars in athletic footware. K and the rest of the midtown security guys tried to rush to the rescue, sprinting down to 42nd Street together—scaring the shit out of all the white pedestrians who saw them coming, of course—looking like a cross between the Wu-Tang Clan and the U.S. Cavalry on angel dust. But it was too late for their heroics. The steamers had vanished with all the stolen sneakers, lost forever in the rush-hour mobs of Grand Central Station.

Just because he was working a day job (or two) didn't mean that K had given up on his dream of becoming a famous rap star. Rap was his nighttime thing, after all. Over the Christmas season, he'd done a few hip-hop shows around town, dueting with a reggae artist named Papa Cuma at Fez under the Time Café and with a female rapper called Moet at Café Society on 21st Street. He rapped "Hustler" solo at the Café Society show and had the hard-core audience shouting along to the chorus and pumping their fists in the air.

One day in early February he asked me if I was free to come to a recording studio called D&D located on a lonely block just to the west of the garment district. "What's the matter?" I said. "You don't trust these guys anymore?"

"It's not that I don't trust 'em, it's just that . . . well, yeah, maybe I don't trust 'em."

He asked me to ride shotgun during his session that night, to be a neutral observer, a second set of eyes and ears. "Don't sweat it," he said. "It'll be good. You'll vibe him. You and him got so much in common." *Him* was the producer K was working with; another short stocky Jewish guy named Doug. Surely, K felt, two short stocky Jewish guys named Doug would be broadcasting on the same wavelength.

I came by the studio to meet this alter ego. If the gold records lining the hallways and the frenzied hip-hop activity in the studio were reliable indicators, Doug was the real deal—a man on the move. As we sat on the sofa in his preproduction studio, he leaned back in his black leather executive's chair, eating takeout General Tso's chicken from a wilting paper plate, juggling constant phone calls and clicking at a remote control, hitting play and fast-forward on a DAT machine loaded up with a series of sinister, grimy, fresh-from-the-lab hip-hop beats. "Hear anything you like?" he asked K cheerily.

It took me only a few minutes to see that K had been dead wrong in his theory of the two Dougs. This was *not* good; we were *not* vibing; one of us was transmitting FM and the other shortwave. Perhaps this Doug and I had *too* much in common. We sat smiling at each other, playing cat-and-mouse, each trying to catch sight of the other's true motives, surreptitiously glimpsed from the unsettled corners of our eyes. We had no trouble with the perfunctory small talk. ("Your folks make a big Seder?" "No, actually, we're not too religious." K listening, leaning back, smiling his contented matchmaker's smile.)

But when the conversation shifted to that music business argot, that staccato patter about artist's royalties and producer's points and rate of recoupment, I felt I was bluffing my way through an in-class essay question for which I had done none of the required reading. We were speaking the same language—roughly—but two very different dialects . . . I kept latching on to a few familiar words in the lightning-quick babble, but did any of them even have the same meaning as previously thought?

It had begun as a case of love at first sight. K had wandered into D&D Studios a few months earlier, looking to see if they could give him "some studio time on spec." Doug's partner at D&D, the business end of the operation, was another Jewish guy named Dave; he pulled off his ballcap and rubbed his shaved head and told K that, unfortunately, D&D wasn't the kind of company that offered speculative deals. But they would be willing to hear what he had, give him an honest assessment of his skills. K stood up in their office and began to rhyme, dropping some inspired freestyles, inadvertently knocking stacks of paper to the floor through sheer vocal power and kinetic energy.

Doug and Dave looked at each other, conferred in private for a minute; then they told K that they loved the way he could flip his rhymes in American and Jamaican and even in Spanish. He had an original flow. Charisma. Didn't sound like anybody they'd ever heard before and they'd been in the business for some time now.

Within days they had some papers drawn up for K, a comprehensive twenty-two-page agreement covering both management and production services. They advised K not to sign it right away; he should definitely find a good lawyer first.

Instead of finding a good lawyer, K found me.

"What the hell do *I* know about some music business contract?" I stood there in front of Raspberry Sport in a howling winter wind, thumbing through the agreement, eyes quickly blurring with that boilerplate legal jargon.

"A hell of a lot more than me."

We walked to a Barnes & Noble together and I fumbled through a few music industry how-to books, trying to give myself a half-hour course on music contract law. Most of the contract remained impenetrable—but did it really take a lawyer to recognize that there was some dicey language buried in those paragraphs and riders that could not possibly be to the artist's advantage? Heaving a sigh of exhaustion, I confessed that I wasn't up to the task; he'd have to find a music attorney to dissect the agreement.

K let out a frustrated sigh to echo my own. It looked like he would have to call his father—a man he hadn't spoken to in many years. If ever there was a time to contact Miguel, he said, this was the time. His father was an attorney, he said. (*What?* Could that be true? He'd never mentioned *that* bit of information before.) Yes, and his father knew a lot of the top black entertainment attorneys in New York. They used to have an annual barbecue out at his father's place in New Jersey and sometimes take boat cruises together around Long Island Sound.

Within the week he had reached his father in New Jersey and his father had given him the name of an esteemed music lawyer named Kendall Minter working at the firm of Phillips, Nizer, Benjamin, Krim & Ballon on West 52nd. K gave me Kendall Minter's office number and asked me to please put in the call. When I phoned, Kendall Minter told me that he'd already heard from K's father and would gladly represent him and make whatever mark-ups were required in the contracts with D&D.

*   *   *

In the meantime, Doug said, there was no point letting the lawyers slow down the momentum. The big guy might as well get to work writing new lyrics to their new beats.

K wasn't too pleased with this arrangement, but he didn't want to rock the boat just yet. That's why he asked me to accompany him to all the studio sessions. He didn't like the idea of D&D recording his voice without all the contracts being signed first. He'd heard horror stories about other rappers who stupidly began recording sessions without signing contracts and, next thing they knew, their material had been released someplace in Europe and they hadn't been paid dime one for it. Rappers were always being jerked like that. *Idiots.* So desperate to "get put on" at any cost. But that wasn't going to happen here, he assured me. If anybody ever tried to fuck him like that, he wouldn't waste any breath. He'd let his baby girl Scobey do all the talking.

By our second after-work excursion to the studio, Doug stood warmly greeting us in the lobby, brimming with excitement about K. He said that he and David had been telling all their contacts in the industry about the American Dread concept already. They sensed Dread was going to be *big;* they were looking forward to a long and lucrative relationship together. Doug had even cut K his own key to the building so he wouldn't have to wait downstairs in the dark, deserted street, thumb pressed to that after-hours buzzer.

But before K could let all this praise go to his head, Doug did foresee a few potential obstacles to his success. The biggest problem was that American Dread didn't sound like any other rapper out there in the marketplace. This remark confused me. "But didn't you tell him he had an original-sounding voice?" In carefully measured tones, Doug explained that, while it was always a positive for an artist to have an original-sounding voice, the rap business, like most other segments of the music industry, was populated by frightened A&R executives who weren't looking for creativity or originality; they were simply chasing down carbon copies of whatever was selling for rival record labels.

The lyrics K rapped were dense, complex, multilayered narratives—when you studied the verses, really listened, you couldn't miss the depressing, painfully self-revelatory references. This certainly wasn't *pop*.

"I don't *wanna* be fuckin' pop," K grumbled.

"You don't have to be pop, Dread," Doug said.

But, he maintained, even an underground rap artist's material needed accessible hooks. The music industry, he said, thrived on accessible hooks. K would have to learn to start writing a good hook or they were going to run into big problems.

Right or wrong, Doug's opinion carried a deservedly authoritative weight. By the spring of '93, D&D was fast becoming the premier recording studio for New York's underground hip-hop scene, the favored sound laboratory for critically acclaimed artists like Gang Starr and KRS-One. The studio complex had a funky, unpretentious atmosphere: the little microwave oven in which rappers and producers could reheat their leftover Chinese food; the beat-up pool table ideal for killing idle hours between sessions; the bathroom collage of Magic Marker tags left behind by all the rap crews who had dropped shit— quite literally—within these studio walls.

Every recording studio, I soon learned, has its own sound, and the studios at D&D were reputed to capture the *real* New York hip-hop flavor, the gritty sound of rhyme-ciphers sparked under dim-burning street lamps, the sound of a million maxed-out Walkmans bleating on head-nodding dream-excursions through the midnight subway tunnels of the mind . . .

Perhaps. But it always seemed to me that the biggest attraction to working at D&D was that, stepping out of the elevator, a visitor found himself immediately sniffing and coughing, inhaling thick clouds of skunky weed smoke. No one was ever hassled for lighting up their sticks of Chocolate Thai or sensimillia while they were recording in D&D. Convenient—considering that a large percentage of rappers (K being the exception to the rule) feel that smoking weed lifts them to a higher creative and improvisational level when they write and record their rhymes.

K was one hip-hop head who hated the very smell of weed. He always maintained that it took a fool to willingly introduce that choking *Cannabis sativa* smoke into his healthy lungs, to allow that dumbing and disorienting delta-9-tetrahydrocannabinol to course, free as some parasitic worm, through his gray matter. He'd learned the hard way. Back when he was about seventeen. He'd smoked some *serious* shit one night on Franklin Avenue and then jolted *beyond* paranoia, thought that Comanche Indians had come to Brooklyn to murder him. He had his gun actually pulled out of his waist, running wildly down the Ave, seeing red-faced killers in all the crevices and corners around him.

Unfortunately, I wasn't as quick a study. The third or fourth time we went up to D&D together, we were waiting for studio number two to become available, hanging around the pool table, K acting like he was some big-time pool shark, challenging me to a game for a dollar a ball. I told him I couldn't shoot pool worth a damn but, when we racked up the balls, I realized that neither could he. He shot pool like a boxer: gracefully lining up an easy shot into the corner pocket, then muscling the stick so hard that the cueball would rocket off the table and leave a diamond-shaped dent mark in the wall.

New York rappers never take off their winter clothes indoors. They fill up a poolroom, puffy as a posse of Pillsbury Doughboys, wearing triple-thick goosedown ski coats with Carhartt work vests underneath and the ubiquitous stickup kid's wool ski cap pulled down, ominously, past their eyebrows.

Shooting pool, K and I were surrounded by a bunch of those Timberland-boot-stomping rappers, all of them gaping and snickering at how pathetically we shot pool. They thought we were playing this badly on purpose, as an amusement, like some rehearsed Abbott and Costello routine. Baldheaded Guru from Gang Starr was smiling, sitting there rolling up a blunt—razoring open a fifty-cent cigar, replacing the cheap tobacco with several sticky pinches of high-grade ganja, nodding, resealing the cigar with copious amounts of saliva—all the while never losing track of the lyrics he was composing for his latest album.

When we were done shooting pool—as I recall the match came down to which competitor could *not* scratch the cueball last—one of those puffy abominable snowmen passed me his nearly spent roach, a peanut-sized spliff which I then sparked up and managed to squeeze a tiny buzz from. K frowned at me. Little wonder. I promptly went into idiot mode and proceeded to misplace those precious copies of his newest lyric ("Run Dem Red") somewhere in the studio. I started searching the complex frantically. Could I have left them inside the microwave? K stood glaring at me, then quietly, reprovingly, he told me that it was very unprofessional of me to smoke weed in the recording studio. What was the point of my coming here if I wasn't planning to stay alert, keep my faculties about me at all times? What good was I—to him or anyone else—if I was going to act as ignorant as all the other weeded-out knuckle-heads? I poured myself a cup of day-old hyper-concentrated coffee to perk up. Like drinking bitter black glue. We went into the pre-production studio to wait for Doug to finish with his previous session. Then, a little more quietly, K told me that he had too much respect for me to see me sitting on the sofa with my eyes all blood-shot and a dopey grin pinned to my face. I nodded in agreement. We shook hands and I made him a solemn vow that I would never again smoke weed up in D&D Studios.

It was taking its toll on him, all these day shifts on his feet in Raspberry Sport and night shifts hollering into a Shure microphone at the studio. He was irritable, functioning on four or five hours of sleep, staying at the studio until after one in the morning, taking the slow-ass D train all the way back to the Bronx, up again by seven to make it back down to midtown Manhattan to start the whole cycle again. But no matter how miserable he looked, he always put on a smile when I surprised him on the job. One day when I stopped by, he disappeared into the back, then handed me a folded iron-gray plastic bag from Dave's Army & Navy. A gift, he said. He wanted us to start dressing more like a *team*. I opened the bag and saw one of those quilted navy blue hunting vests that K was always sporting. He had them in black and brown and beige as well. He led me into the back of Raspberry so I could slip the thing on and model it in front of the bank of full-length mirrors. It was ridiculously big. Coming out of the stockroom, one of the Israelis flashed me an okay sign which—knowing the Israelis by now—I took to be wholly facetious.

"I can't wear this. I look like an idiot."

"Naw, duke, the shit is *tight*." (By which he meant, of course, not tight but billowingly, fashionably loose.)

Why, I wondered, was he so intent on having us dress like the Bobbsey Twins? Had it never occurred to him that when he wore these oversized quilted hunting vests he looked like a gangsta rapper—or was it rappin' gangster?—but when I donned one (*now how to take it off without offending him?*) I resembled Chico Marx on a trout-fishing excursion in the frozen Yukon?

"That's 'cause you ain't got no *bop,* man. You need to start walkin' with a bop."

Lowering one shoulder, affecting a slight limp in his left leg, he strode past the displays of hiking boots and sneakers, trying to give me a lesson in the art of the Cool Walk. Suddenly, his smile vanished. Something more urgent had caught his eye.

An enormous blur of camouflage fatigues had entered the store behind us. K instantly stopped doing his lazy bop-walk, shifting, without interruption, into a resolute forward stride, like a heavyweight prizefighter stalking his backward-dancing opponent. I could see why this new arrival required his immediate attention.

"Help you out there, duke?" said K.

"Naw'm good, bruh."

The customer was tall and light-skinned, wearing matching fatigue pants and jacket, with a blood-red Tommy Hilfiger T-shirt underneath. His look was pure Brooklyn badboy—single gold tooth and multiple rows of slightly frizzy braids—but what really gave K pause was the man's size. Not simply big; he was rock-hard—with the thickened neck, shoulders and arms of someone who'd no doubt spent a good portion of his adult years doing preacher curls and military presses under the eyes of upstate corrections officers.

K backed away to his usual corner, feigning disinterest. His boxing training had sharpened his peripheral vision, and he could keep his focus on this camouflaged customer while pretending to be straightening the mauve display of Lady Air Pegasus sneakers.

It was inevitable—everyone in the store knew what was about to happen but no one could prevent it. In a flash the big man grabbed an entire rackful of Champion sweatshirts (retail value $49.99 each) and—clutching seven or eight hangers in one massive hand—he sprinted to the door. K very nearly made it to the door to cut him off but the crook had just enough of a head start to bolt into the street.

Ghost.

K could have shrugged—like many other security guys—turned to the Israelis and said, "Hey, shit happens." But this was K, after all, and he did not appreciate being *punked* in any way. Which is why he wasted no time in giving chase, bolting after the big crook in the busy street.

By the time I got outside, they were a full block further up Fifth Avenue, two huge men sprinting to the corner of 45th Street. All those flapping stolen sweatshirts were spoiling the aerodynamics of the thief's getaway, and K managed to catch up just as he reached the 45th Street intersection. K made a sudden grab for the sweatshirts and then, turning, off balance, the thief—shocked and outraged that he'd even been pursued—took a dangerous but well-telegraphed right-hand swing at K.

With a sudden graceful neck extension, K leaned his head out of range of the looping punch. *Nigga please.* He released his grip on the sweatshirts and so did the thief. The stolen booty fell in a dark blue heap, lumped up like a collapsed body right in the middle of 45th Street.

The fight commenced in earnest. K, squaring up with the crook, landed the first salvo, a crisp one-two combination, glancing off his adversary's jaw and smashing his temple. How bizarre, I thought. The crook barely budged. From a distance he appeared almost to be smiling.

The crook had K outweighed by about twenty pounds; but I sensed that all his weight-lifting power would prove a disadvantage against K's hand speed. As they began to circle each other, slowly, still keeping a respectful distance, K would dance forward periodically on his lead leg and tattoo the crook's face with those strobe light combinations. But even when he landed his best punch—a blinding left hook to the eye socket—the thief gave no visible indication that he'd even felt the weight of the fist.

By now at least thirty people had converged on the corner. And more pedestrians kept crowding in, gawking, pushing, blocking the crosstown traffic on 45th Street as they tried to catch a glimpse of this free-for-view heavyweight rumble.

People are sick, I remember thinking, even as I struggled not to lose my own clear line of sight on the action. Like the seething crowds in the Colosseum, or that swelling mob in *The Day of the Locust,* half of Fifth Avenue's workforce had stopped whatever it was doing, Orthodox Jewish diamond-men next to lanky Haitian bike messengers, eagerly crowding the intersection, grinning lasciviously, awaiting the flow of blood.

And, seeing as he had an audience, K began to showboat, ducking and feinting, coming out of his crouch to connect with a clean right cross to the sweet spot of the crook's chin. But again the crook defied him. Barely blinked.

I'd never imagined this could happen. On the previous occasions when I'd seen K land such clean chin shots, the recipient was always staggered—if not always out. But this gold-toothed bandit had a jaw made of granite.

He wasn't fast enough to hit K in the head, but as they came close together, sparring toe to toe, the crook did manage to connect with heavy body shots to the ribs and kidneys. You couldn't hear the blows. There were too many cars honking, too many frustrated taxi drivers shouting in anger. Behind me, I realized, Fifth Avenue was now grid-locked.

"What the fuck!"

"Part it! Part it!"

"Y'all better break that shit up!"

"Naw! Them muthafuckas is from *up nawffff!* They gonna go at it!"

Yes, this was probably the nearest most of us would ever get to witnessing a prison-yard fight, the type of no-surrender hand battle that could only have been fought between two graduates of those up-state Gladiator Schools.

The only way K would lose the fight, I thought, was if the crook got close enough to grapple him to the ground, pin him to the pave-ment, where he could put his size and strength to advantage. But K wasn't about to let that happen.

He threw another murderous left hook. The crook ducked, and I ducked as well, catching a glimpse through the jumbled mass of by-standers straight into the thief's panting mouth, painted bright red in-side, like a kid's after drinking cherry Kool-Aid. With the crook now bent forward—head offered invitingly, like a cabbage on a stake—K landed a flush right uppercut that made the bright red Kool-Aid thicken suddenly to setting Jell-O, a viscous swishing as the crook stumbled forward, a long globchunk of Jell-O slipping from his lips, and imbedded in that not-quite-liquid drip I spotted—*finally?*—an ivory-and-gold chunk of broken tooth.

For the first time in the fight, it looked like the crook might go down, but he simply staggered backward, regaining his balance, turn-ing, taunting K: "That all you fuckin' got for me? That all you *got*, nigga?"

The crook was actually enjoying this. And K was in danger of punching himself out. You could tell it had been years since he'd had such a marathon fight. When K slowed his punching pace, catching his wind, dropping his fists momentarily to his hips, the crook pounced. With lowered shoulders he charged K, screaming madly, like a crazed outside linebacker unafraid of catching a spearing penalty while making the open-field tackle. He locked K in a bear hug and, still somehow possessing the strength to lift K off his feet, he body-slammed him to the pavement.

K hit the street with the flat of his back. There was a sickening thud and for a moment I worried that he might have shattered his spine. The crook tried to stomp K in the face with one of his thick-soled Timberlands, but K snapped his head quickly to the left, then rolling just as quickly to his right, he leapt back up on his feet.

Eyes luminous with rage, he now gave up all pretense of using orthodox boxing technique. He launched a savage forward assault, using those windmilling fifty-two hand-blocks: a stunning, inexorable whirl of fists and forearms and elbows. And this time, when he landed a clean chin shot, the fist-followed-closely-by-forearm did its intended damage. Finally, the crook's head shivered on his thick neck and his eyes rolled up momentarily and his strong knee joints were replaced by wobbling Slinky toys. But before the crook could buckle fully to the ground, K circled him, skillful as a matador, grabbing him by the head and then twisting his arm back, disabling him in a painful half nelson.

They went down to the pavement together, frozen in a brutal street tableau, the crook dazed and sprawled forward on his belly, K sitting upright, holding that half nelson. And now that K had his right hand free, I watched his face flash a dark and terrifying smile. All the power of his right fist was channeled into beating the crook's unguarded face. *Bring the pain.* The mallet of his fist pounded away with a metronomic rhythm.

Behind me, I heard someone groan.

K kept punching until the crook's face no longer resembled a human face: it was pink and pulpy, bone-white, bright red and gelatinous.

K was wearing the expensive DKNY shirt that Faith had bought him for Christmas. The rich blue of the fabric had turned purple in the spots where it was wet with the crook's splattering blood.

"Had enough yet, nigga?" I heard K say. There was almost a note of tenderness in his voice. The crook kept struggling and wrestling and trying to bite K on the arm with his mangled mouth. And after each attempted bite, even more enraged, K would land two, three, four more short sharp blows to the crook's disintegrating face.

At last, with the loud shrieking of sirens, several midtown squad cars arrived and forced the crowd to disperse from the intersection. Three cops pulled K and the crook apart and, as the crowd backed away, you could fully see the damage K had done: both the crook's eyes swollen shut, his nose smashed flat. But the worst damage was to his lower lip; the entire lower lip had detached from his face; it swung to his chin in a loose red flap, pulsing, desperately clinging, dangling by an elastic strand of twitching tissue. Someone next to me said that it looked like the man's mouth had been smashed with a hatchet. Had the other guy been wearing *brass knuckles?*

No, but he was now wearing bracelets.

The cops handcuffed K and took him to the Midtown South Precinct House on West 35th Street; he stayed there for a few hours until one of the managers of Raspberry, the skinny and bespectacled Israeli named Shmulek, came down and explained that K was indeed a Raspberry security employee, that he was only trying to halt an act of larceny and recover the stolen merchandise.

The crook didn't go to the precinct house; he went straight to the hospital on a gurney. We later learned that his jaw was shattered and his mouth had been wired shut. K had no marks on his face but he had some deep body bruises and an extremely painful lower back. And punching the crook's teeth like that had shredded his knuckles badly. One of the cuts was so deep and wide that I told him he really should go to the hospital for stitches.

That was his biggest worry. He kept cleaning the knuckle cuts with foaming hydrogen peroxide and loudly cursing—*bumboclaat!*— and asking me if I thought he could contract HIV through cuts in his knuckles.

"You never know what a crab-life nigga like that's got."

The next day the strangest news came in via one of the Israelis. Even though the thief admitted robbing the store, he was trying to press assault charges against K. The cops were going to come by Raspberry in the morning to interview K again. They wanted to know if he'd ever been a professional boxer. In the crook's statement he had said that K must have been a boxer to have fought like that.

I had an old friend from Canada staying at my apartment. Philip was a lawyer on vacation from his job in England and I tricked him into coming by Raspberry, ostensibly to shop for sneakers, but actually so he could give K some free legal advice. K was standing there outside the store looking sullen; he was nervous about having to testify in court the next day; he knew that if the cops found out he had boxed professionally, he could be charged with aggravated assault.

Taking a break from sizing up a pair of Aasics Gel Keyanos, Philip offered his legal counsel, pro bono. "Don't volunteer to the DA you were ever paid money to fight. In fact, don't volunteer any information they don't ask for. Say you were just doing your job, trying to recover the stolen merchandise when the guy swung on you. You had to defend yourself."

That's exactly what K said in court. The DA laughed. He already knew K had been a boxer, but he didn't give a damn. It turned out the guy was a career thief with a long string of previous robbery convictions dating back to his childhood. He arrived in court with his jaw wired shut and was convicted one more time.

Their fight was not soon forgotten on Fifth Avenue. Years later, the other security men who worked the block were still murmuring about

it, proudly boasting about the savageness of the beating K had in-
flicted. Of course, like most street legends, it grew with each retelling.
Some claimed that the fight had lasted a full twenty minutes, that it
had veered out into the middle of Fifth Avenue, causing traffic to
screech to a halt. Others said it had taken twenty cops with nightsticks to pull K away from the crook.

But anyone who'd actually been there knew that the tale scarcely
needed embellishment. "I never seen *nothin'* like it," recalled Big Gene,
a massive but mild-mannered 370-pounder who was the longtime in-
store security at the Cosmetics Plus boutique on 43rd Street. "God
knows, I musta seen a hundred streetfights in my life, but that wasn't
fightin'. I don't know *what* it was."

The glow was off. The working relationship with D&D had turned
irrevocably tense. By now K had voiced a handful of master recordings for Doug, but Doug wasn't crazy about any of them. They'd
recorded one of his favorite lyrics, a frenetic party song called "Hilltop Madness," about life in the Harlem neighborhood called the Hill,
on 129th Street and Convent Avenue, where K had first met Faith. For
"Hilltop Madness" K had insisted on creating a new beat from scratch.
He wanted to rap to the backing track that he heard in his own head;
he said that his words needed to flow along to the bass line from Yellowman's reggae classic "Who Can Make the Dance Ram?"

> *Loud and clear boy*
> *Yo, you heard this!*
> *Rudeboy steppin'*
> *We nuh like lip-service*
> *No backtalk*
> *Fi we de gun-hawk*
> *Clean out a Tec inna badboy heart*

Doug couldn't get a clean sample of the bass line from my Yellowman CD, so instead he played the "Three Blind Mice" riff live on his bass. (Doug was an experienced bass player; he'd played in a rock band before he became a rap producer.) But somehow, the lyrics didn't mesh with the new beat and no matter how Doug worked the mixing board, dropping out sounds here and there, he was left feeling unsettled about "Hilltop Madness." (It probably didn't help matters when K insisted that *I* should go into the vocal booth, slip on the headphones and shout his song's chorus into the overhead mike: *It's Hilltop Madness! It's Hilltop Madness!* Lowering my voice an octave, I tried to bring an authentic rapper's growl up from the soles of my Viking work boots. But my enunciation was too precise, I couldn't fake a street snarl; even when Doug, using all his studio wizardry, doubled my voice, tripled it, quadrupled it, the studio's soundproof walls reverberated with a yelping crew of—what was Crystal's mocking remark?—white, middle-class Jewish boys from the wilds of Canada.) In the end, Doug decided to scrap "Hilltop Madness," moving on to a new tune entirely.

It had been nearly a month since Kendall Minter had returned the marked-up contracts to D&D's attorney, but now D&D had started to hedge a little bit on their commitment to K. "Let's see how the music comes out before we sign the agreements," Doug said. "Let's see what we've really got on tape before we put any more money in these lawyers' pockets."

No one with an artistic temperament takes rejection well; K took it worse than most. He kept grumbling about the fact that Kendall Minter had spent all this time making changes to the contracts and now D&D was taking a wait-and-see attitude with him and his confidence was so messed up he'd even started to question his own rapping abilities for the first time since he'd started rhyming. We would spend hours on the phone at night talking through his confused and unsettled feelings. He kept asking me if I thought he should just give up on this rap bullshit entirely, leave this shady music business alone, if he should just stick to his boring-ass nine-to-five life and at least have peace of mind.

Then other times he would grow very, very angry. He'd begin shouting into the phone, furious, frustrated, baffled by the situation at the studio, and I would try to play devil's advocate, explaining things from D&D's perspective. Weren't they just doing their jobs as producers, trying to get him to write the most saleable material? Didn't he agree that they wouldn't want to start knocking on doors at various record labels without having the strongest possible package in their hands?

Taking this tone was a mistake; it caused K to redirect his rage at me. "Why you always takin' up for them muthafuckas? Why you always doin' that shit, man? How come *they* always in the fuckin' right and *I'm* always in the fuckin' wrong?"

By now I knew that once he'd gotten himself to the state of shouting, I had to let him shout himself hoarse—there was no point trying to argue with him. Finally, when he'd finished shouting, when he'd nearly lost his voice and was back to sounding sad, mumbling, "I don't know," over and over, I said the only thing I had to say: "You asked me for my honest opinion and I'm giving it to you. If you want someone who's going to agree with you all the time, I'm not the right guy."

After two full months of recording at D&D, the only fruitful session K had done was a guest spot on a record by the veteran Jamaican singer Edi Fitzroy. The song was called "Revolution on Mi Mind"—its producer, Henry Karyo, had brought the master tape up from his studio in Kingston looking for some verses by an up-and-coming New York rapper and heard Doug and Dave singing the praises of their American Dread. Henry was a young Jewish record producer from Long Island who'd moved down to Jamaica and completely immersed himself in the Kingston reggae scene. Ever since Heavy D dueted with Supercat, Henry told us, fans down in Jamaica couldn't get enough of the reggae–hip-hop combination.

After hearing the Edi Fitzroy song twice, it took American Dread all of ten minutes to disappear into the poolroom and write two hip-hop verses and a singsongy Jamaican-style riff that went: "Praises to Jah inna di revolu*shun*, Marcus Garvey inna di revolu*shun* . . ."

They did the session in one take. Henry said he really loved the flavor American Dread had brought to the track. The album was going to be released on Bob Marley's old Jamaican record company, the Tuff Gong label. Henry said he'd make sure and send up some copies as soon as Tuff Gong pressed up the vinyl down in Kingston.

Meanwhile, as far as his solo recording went, D&D had begun to make some surprising requests. Doug told K he wanted him to write all his lyrics in English hip-hop and Spanish hip-hop versions. "But I don't really speak proper Spanish," K told him. "I only know some bits and pieces of Spanish. *Dame une beso,* you know. Shit like that. My moms only had me speakin' that broken ghetto Spanish."

Doug looked disappointed. He'd been counting on the Spanish thing. He said that the Spanish thing was one of the big guy's biggest selling points. Did Dread have any idea how big the Latin music market was? Down there in South America and Mexico and those places? It was huge. It was fucking massive. He advised Dread never to underestimate the Spanish-speaking market.

K kept grumbling; but he said he'd try. Maybe Yolanda, his Panamanian baby-mother, could help him rewrite all his lyrics. But when Doug left the preproduction room to order some takeout for dinner, K turned to me with a scowl.

"Yo, I ain't writing *shit* for this muthafucka in Spanish! What kind of cornball shit is this? What I look like to you—Julio fuckin' Iglesias?"

The following week it was Snow. Snow, my compatriot—a white Canadian reggae artist—was topping the pop charts in the U.S. with his song "Informer." And now Doug told K that's exactly what he'd need from him: something catchy, something hooky, something with international crossover pop appeal—just like Snow's single. He wanted K to study the Snow record very carefully and come up with something just as catchy as Snow.

One problem: K couldn't stand Snow. He told Doug that no real Jamaican could even follow what Snow was saying in his lyrics. "I been talkin' Jamaican my whole life and *I* don't know what the fuck he's sayin'! It ain't real Jamaican, man—it's just some gibberish that sounds like Jamaican. He don't really make no sense."

Doug said it didn't make any difference if the lyrics made sense. He said few Americans could understand what Jamaicans were saying in any of those reggae records anyway. It was all about a vibe. K strongly disagreed. "And then corny-ass MC Shan comes on the shit, talkin' about how he's sittin' 'round chillin' with his *dibi-dibi* girl—like a real idiot! He don't even know what *dibi-dibi* means—he don't even know he just dissed his own girl!* I'm tellin' you, man, that shit is mad corny."

Doug gave a little shrug and said that the record was selling, that it was moving big units. There was no arguing with dollars and cents. He advised K never to forget that this was the *music business;* there was no point getting intellectual about it.

When we left D&D Studios that night it was nearly one in the morning. At that hour, traveling on foot, there are few places in Manhattan as unsavory as the side streets of the garment district. There's no flicker of residential life: merely shuttered-up wholesale stores and overflowing commercial dumpsters, litter-strewn gutters and underpowered streetlights. On one block alone three massive garbage trucks were backing up simultaneously, their high-shrieking *beep-beep-beeps* competing for airspace like the mating calls of some prehistoric beasts. The sidewalk before us was dotted with malevolent cockroaches the size of Swiss Army knives. Walking down those dark

---

*K was right, of course; in the context of dancehall patois, *dibi-dibi* means "a small or insignificant person or thing; stupid; worthless."

blocks with K, I felt like we'd suddenly stepped into a primeval netherworld.

We strolled up Eighth Avenue, past the twenty-four-hour porn shops and the homeless men sleeping in cardboard boxes and the cracked-out hookers eating greasy McDonald's french fries with their dirty fingers. I could sense K was in such a foul mood, it would only take one gap-toothed crackhead or hooker to hold an insolent stare, and K'd start flipping out, knocking people across Eighth Avenue.

In front of the cab stand at the Port Authority bus terminal he stopped walking suddenly. He looked at the ground and started laughing. He laughed so long and hard that there were tears in his eyes.

I finally had to ask him what was so funny.

"I was just thinkin' about the first day I came home from up north," he said. "Right here on 42nd Street. I was just thinkin' about how Melanie tried to kiss me and when she stuck her tongue in my mouth I was so confused I smacked the shit out of her."

He remembered the day so vividly. When he first came home from up north, his brother Craig was there waiting to pick him up from the bus station. He was coming down from Camp Brace on the Short Line bus and Craig was there waiting to greet him with Melanie, his old childhood girlfriend, whom he'd been scribbling letters to every few months from up north. All his homeys in Goshen used to tease him because he was one of the only guys inside who was still a virgin. Some of the other guys had gone home on little eight-hour visits and gotten laid with their little girlfriends. And a lot of the guys had come to jail at the age of twelve or thirteen already having a full year's sexual experience behind them.

*   *   *

"But I used to be followin' the way Toño handled his shit.* Tone was strictly about money, boy. Bitches were always secondary to him. Rarely did we ever see Toño up in a bitch. Toño had one little girl named Dolla, and he would have Dolla—actually her name was Darla, but we used to call her Dolla, like 'gimme one dolla'—waitin' for him all day and all night and sometimes he wouldn't even show up. Money was always the first and foremost thing on Big Tone's mind."

It was the day before Christmas when he came home. There was a freezing wind whistling through the glass and stone canyons of Manhattan and when he stepped off the bus he saw Craig, wearing a dope-ass sheepskin coat and—*could it be?*—yes, there in the shopping bag, he was carrying another new sheepskin coat. That was an early Christmas present from their mother.

Then he spotted Melanie coming out of the crowd behind Craig with her big bouncing breasts. She rushed up to him and she hugged him so tight. She put her hot tongue in his mouth.

He smacked her. *Bowww!* He didn't know what she was doing. When he'd left the streets, they'd just been pecking each other on the lips, playing spin-the-bottle, little-kid kissing. What was this French kiss business? He thought she was trying to spit in his mouth. And he smacked her, on instinct, like she was a guy who'd fouled him on the basketball court, mushed her mouth back with the palm of his hand.

"The fuck you *doin'*, yo?"

Melanie stood there rubbing her mouth, but he hadn't really hurt her, she was just laughing at him, and his brother was hugging him. "Yo, man! It's good to have you home!"

Then he looked over and saw his parole officer, ready to pounce, like an owl on an unsuspecting mouse. She was a small lady named Miss Cheeseborough. She came forward to tell him that he had to re-

---

*All italicized first-person interludes in this chapter come from a taped interview with K conducted in Manhattan on December 18, 1996.

port to the Youth Detention Center Number 3 on Carroll Street. YDC-3 was for less-classified cases, she said, but they were putting him there on an overload. He was really supposed to be in YDC-1—the most secure kiddie halfway house—down on Howard Avenue in Bushwick. Miss Cheeseborough told him he was free to spend the Christmas holiday with his family, but he had better report to YDC-3 on Carroll Street by the third of January.

That was not to be. He wasn't even home four days before he got into more trouble and found himself celebrating New Year's Eve on Rikers Island. His mother had been waiting for him with his little welcome-home party. The family was living on Eastern Parkway in Crown Heights now and his mother had cooked up some strong Panamanian food, and some of her delicious thick lasagna—that homemade lasagna he'd been daydreaming about all the time up in Goshen—and some of the guys from Washington Avenue came through to pay their respects.

Back in those days, coming home from a long juvenile bid up north, you were treated like a returning war hero. All the Washington Avenue guys were riding him, peppering him with questions about his bid, treating him like The Man. He wasn't running with any of the kids on Franklin Avenue in those times; he was running with all of Tone's old crimies: Rockhead, Stinks, Tyrone, Herb, Ant, the whole Ave-Ave Crew. Toño couldn't be there, of course. By this time, Big Tone was starting to serve his armed robbery time in the adult system.

They had that little welcome-home party, then a big family Christmas, and he didn't leave the house—not one time. Then by the twenty-ninth of December he decided, what the hell, he'd go down to Washington Avenue to check on Rockhead and Stinks and the guys from the Ave-Ave Crew. One of the crew had left him in possession of a little bullshit .22 pistol and he was carrying it in his pocket—for protection, because, as even the inmates up north knew, guys in Brooklyn were being stuck up every single day, sometimes even murdered, for the kind of expensive "sheepdog" coat he was now proudly sporting.

He came down to Washington Avenue, spotted Rockhead, started hanging on the corner of St. John's. But what he didn't know was that the Ave-Ave Crew had robbed a white man on Grand Army Plaza a couple of hours earlier. They had robbed the white man and divvied up the profits, went and bought new clothes and beer and smokes.

"All of a sudden some of them auxiliary police—them thrill-seekin' mutha-fuckas with no guns—showed up and they chased us all over the fuckin' place, chased us all down the block with the white man in the back of the car. We were walkin' and suddenly we hear: Freeze! *And niggas just jetted in all directions. And I got my gun in my pocket and I'm runnin' with Rock-head. Rockhead's talkin' 'bout: 'Gimme the gun, yo! Gimme the gun!' 'Cause he could run faster than me. But I said, no, no.*

"While we was runnin', I zigged, and the car came up the hill, so I turned and started runnin' back down the hill, then finally I reached over and gave Rockhead the gun. Rockhead knew we were gonna get caught and he didn't want me to get caught with no gun when I was on parole. Rock-head just went and melded in with the people outside the store, and I was too stupid, I just kept runnin' like a fuckin' idiot. I didn't know that those auxiliary cops didn't carry no pieces on them or else I wouldn't've stopped. Now I'm arrested again and sent to Rikers Island. But I knew they couldn't hold me for shit 'cause they didn't have no case against me."

He was on Rikers Island until January 8, and the next thing he knew the state came and got him and hauled him in shackles down to YDC-3 on Carroll Street. He felt like cheering out loud when he saw the place, because coming from the Island, that little-kid halfway house was a joke. When you were housed in YDC-3, you could go and come as you pleased during the daylight hours.

It was only a few days before one of the officers realized the mistake. "He's not supposed to be here. He's a Title-3, restricted classified case, he's not supposed to leave. He needs to be in the lockup at YDC-1 in Bushwick."

So he was transferred and lived in YDC-1 on Howard Avenue

throughout that spring. Every month he would qualify for an eight-hour home visit. And it was on one of those eight-hour visits that he finally became a man.

Melanie and his mother used to be so cool with each other. His mother used to love for her sons to bring their girlfriends upstairs to the apartment. She knew what they were up to in the bedroom, of course, but she simply smiled at it. She said as long as they didn't try to bring home any boys—then they'd *really* have problems with her!

The Division of Youth officers would bring him in handcuffs to his mother's. They'd keep the cuffs on him until he was right inside the apartment. He had to travel everywhere with two officers, Davis and Hanes. They were both black guys; he really liked them; Hanes used to open up the gym after-hours and train him with weights; Davis used to slip him the keys to the cafeteria so he could sneak down there and make midnight sandwiches. They had a boring-ass job, sitting up in some stranger's apartment for a full eight hours. His mother used to cook Davis and Hanes dinner and give them lemonade and coffee. She'd let them take naps on the sofa; watch football games on TV; call their girlfriends on the phone and tell them to come over.

Technically, he wasn't supposed to leave their sight; he wasn't supposed to leave the room without Davis and Hanes going with him. But Davis and Hanes used to look the other way, let him go downstairs to talk to his homeys. And they practically flashed him the thumbs-up when he disappeared into the bedroom with Melanie.

"Davis brings me in the door that day and Melanie had her hand over her mouth, sayin', 'Oh shit—he really here!' She'd been sittin' with my mother in the dining room. She hugged me and said, 'Shit, you look good, baby!'

"This was my third home visit. My homeboys were there, Stinks and Tyrone, and my cousin Angel. I went into the bedroom to look for something to give Stinks. Then Melanie came into the bedroom and there was no preamble or nothing: we just started fuckin'. I was fuckin' her for a long time

too 'cause I didn't even know what come *meant. We was on some rough sex shit and by the time we finished my dick was hurtin' me.*

"*Melanie was just a young girl, but Melanie was built like a woman: she had a big round ass, big round titties, real long Indian-like hair. Even Davis and Hanes were diggin' her body. They were like, 'I can't believe that's your girlfriend, man,' 'cause she was only sixteen but she looked about twenty-four. And when they drove me back to YDC-1 in the van, they just kept askin' me, 'So, was the pussy the bomb?'*

"*And I was just lampin' back in the van. 'Yeah, it was all right, man.' Actin' like I knew what I was talkin' 'bout, when I ain't never had no pussy before to compare it to.*

"*But two weeks after, when I went to pee, it just started burning. Melanie had given me some real fucked-up shit. I went to see the old lady named Alberta who worked in the intake, and she was like, 'You caught something bad, boy. I gotta take you to the doctor.'*

"*They took me to a clinic in Long Island and the white doctors and nurses were lookin' at me funny. 'But you're so young. You're having sex?'*

"'*What? I can't have sex now?'*

"'*But you're a baby!'*

"*They gave me a shot in my ass and a whole bunch of pills. I was so fuckin' vexed. I punched that bitch in the eye when I saw her. Then she tried to visit me one time in the YDC and I was like* fuck you! *and I just refused the visit.*"

Wonderful way to lose your virginity, I thought.

"What ever happened to her?"

"Melanie? She moved to Texas. I never really saw her again until later on when I was a drug dealer; then we used to kick it a bit. Once in a while I used to have her carry some of my compressed coke in her pussy down to D.C. Melanie was a real good worker that way: her pussy was built good for that kind of work."

The tense working relationship with D&D came finally—noisily, publicly—to an end. It happened in front of several hundred music industry executives, record producers and radio programmers who were gathered in the Sheraton Hotel in midtown Manhattan for the annual three-day convention called the New Music Seminar. K was there to perform in a popular seminar event called the MC Battle for World Supremacy held on the stage of the Sheraton's Grand Ballroom. Back in June, D&D had submitted an audition tape of K rhyming a cappella; shortly thereafter, for reasons not apparent at the time, Doug abruptly stopped calling K. K called the studio asking for Doug a few times, but Doug was never available. Then K, feeling offended, instructed me never to call D&D again. We stopped dropping by the studio altogether and, as the weeks passed, K grew more and more enraged.

Every day he would call me from his job and ask me if I'd heard from D&D. I kept telling him no. Instead I called the New Music Seminar organizers and found out that K (or, more properly, American Dread) had been selected as one of the sixteen finalists to perform in the MC Battle for World Supremacy. And as one of the perks of competing in the MC Battle, I was told, K would be receiving a laminated artist's badge. The badge gave the wearer full access to all industry panel discussions and concerts and after-hours parties, something for which all the other seminar registrants had paid $370.

On the day of the MC Battle we showed up at the Sheraton a few hours early, and I went to the press table to get my laminated press badge. K went to get his artist's badge but the registration girl told him, sorry, but his badge had already been picked up by the guys from D&D.

K nearly flipped right there; he said they had no right picking up something with his name on it. He demanded a duplicate badge. She gave him one. Upstairs in front of the Grand Ballroom, we finally ran into Doug. He was wearing the laminated badge with the little hologram in the corner and K's government name emblazoned in bold black computerized letters; it was dangling around his neck from a fluorescent green Tommy Boy Records strap. Seeing Doug wearing his name made K even more enraged.

Through the dense mob of people waiting to gain entrance to the ballroom, Doug approached K with a smile and outstretched hand—"Dread!"—but K began to shout angrily at Doug. Doug turned to me, baffled, wondering why K was so upset with him. Now K began to shout louder, waving his arms wildly, and I put myself between K and Doug, and then four hotel security guards in two-button blazers rushed over, ready to get physical with K. K glared at the security and announced in his heavy Jamaican accent that anyone who was fool enough to put a hand on him would feel the wrath.

Nobody put a hand on him.

I looked at Doug's smiling, confused, clean-shaven face; and then I thought of what K had done to that hapless crook's face, turning it to a dripping, pulpy mass of bone and bright red jelly; and then, fortunately for everyone concerned, some beefy hip-hop security guys in tight black T-shirts came over and, unlike the buttoned-up hotel security, they knew how to talk to K. They advised him to come for a walk outside the hotel, to get some air, to cool his fucking heels. They advised him to stop shouting like that in front of all these white people: someone would *definitely* call the cops. Faith was smiling and shrugging at me throughout this whole episode. She'd seen K act like this so many times, she didn't stop to consider his behavior unusual or inappropriate in a place as tony as the plush-carpeted Sheraton Hotel.

We all went outside together. It was a hot, dry mid-July afternoon. K had to walk the midtown streets for thirty minutes growling and muttering *I'm not a fuckin' little kid* to himself before he'd calmed down enough to return to the Sheraton.

We promptly saw Dave in the lobby. K wasn't as mad at Dave as he was at Doug. K always got along better with Dave. Dave and K sat down and had a long heart-to-heart talk, during which Dave told K that this was all just some colossal misunderstanding; both he and his partner held K and his rapping ability in the highest regard.

Inside the cavernous Grand Ballroom, I spotted Doug on the far side of the room. I went over to talk to him in private. It was strange— all my previous antipathy for the man seemed to have vanished now. We sat in two ballroom chairs next to each other and then Doug calmly explained that he had lost his Wizard electronic organizer with all his business numbers in it and that's why he hadn't called K for nearly a month.

I told him that of course I could see his point of view. I could see why he was offended to arrive at the New Music Seminar and find K shouting and cursing at him; but I was more curious to know if he thought it was a wise idea to be walking around the seminar wearing the laminated badge with K's government name on it. Doug said he had paid the twenty-dollar MC Battle entrance fee for K—why shouldn't he wear the badge?

What's the point in us arguing? I said finally.

Precisely, he said.

Then Doug said he could promise me one thing: this was the end of the line. It was over between them. How could he ever work with American Dread after this? Here he was, trying to give the guy a break, giving him free studio time, entering him in the MC Battle for World Supremacy, trying to land him a deal with a major label—and the guy's screaming and carrying on in public like he doesn't know the difference between his friends and his enemies. What kind of person in his right mind would put up with that kind of bullshit?

I nodded, shook Doug's hand goodbye, then I went back outside to the Sheraton lobby to look for K and Faith.

THE FINAL SESSION. More than three years later, in the fall of '96, K and I rode the elevator back up to the D&D Studios complex, K having decided that it was time to bury the hatchet, "squash any beef" lingering between himself and Doug.

In the years since the ugly episode at the Sheraton, business had been good to D&D. More gold records lined the walls; the studio complex had been expanded, walls had been torn down, recording equipment upgraded. K and I took a brief tour of the new facility, the new game room, populated by a new breed of grim-faced pool-shooting rappers.

Doug and Dave's proudest souvenir was the poster of their 1995 album *The D&D Project,* a big-budget release on Clive Davis's Arista Records, well received by the hip-hop press if not a big seller, featuring such established stars as KRS-One, Jeru the Damaja, DJ Premier and Guru, but also highlighting the wealth of undiscovered Young Turks working at the studio. It was an album on which K and his lyrics would no doubt have appeared, had he kept his cool, stuck it out, been a little more patient with Doug's production style.

In the hallway of the new expansion, K and Doug caught sight of each other for the first time since the Sheraton debacle. K made a direct, smiling approach. "Yo, it takes a big man to admit his mistakes," he said. Shaking Doug's hand heartily, K said that he'd learned the hard way, that he'd been too arrogant, too wild, too hotheaded to understand anything about the music industry back in the spring and summer of '93. Doug listened, nodding, but he looked uncomfortable: he didn't want to hear any apology—shit just happens in this industry, he said. Shit happens and you move on.

After all those years he still seemed mystified as to why K had flipped on him in the Sheraton before the MC Battle—but he did acknowledge that there were two sides to every misunderstanding, that something in their chemistry, in their innate communication styles, had obviously been off from the beginning.

We sat bullshitting in their office for a half hour or so, K swiveling in his leather chair, chewing Wrigley's, talking about a screenplay he and I had written together, Dave and Doug telling us about the new company they'd founded, Bulldog Records, an underground label on which they hoped to "put out the real raw street shit" that the major labels didn't know how to market and distribute.

Outside their offices, as we turned to leave, promising to keep in touch, I stood staring at the graffiti mural Doug and Dave had commissioned as their office decor, a riotous collage of spray-painted tags, the names of all the hip-hop artists who'd recorded albums in the D&D studio complex. Slanting up toward the ceiling, nestled between the graffiti monikers of established soloists and rap crews, the words AMERICAN DREAD burst out at me, emblazoned in dripping red Krylon, a bold, bubble-lettered reminder of what might have been.

FOUR

kick the
ballistics

"He liked guns."

—Meyer Lansky, on his boyhood
pal Bugsy Siegel

Double Agent. Deep Cover. The Not-so-Secret Relationship Between Blacks and Jews. I'd heard them all. Living with Crystal in a tiny one-bedroom walk-up on West 21st Street, barely scraping by as a Jewish journalist, writing cultural stories for *The Forward*—the newly founded English-language offspring of the venerable Yiddish daily—where I'd been lucky enough to wrangle a staff title and the use of a phone and half a desk. Coming into the office on East 33rd Street, sifting through the messages on my chair, I'd try to make sense of the chicken scratches one of the other staffers had left on those pink sheets of paper. "Translation?"

"Special K. Danny Kaye . . . *Somebody* K . . . Who's that? A *source?*"

"What'd he say?"

"He said he was calling to kick you—or kick *something*—don't ask me, it was all very strange . . . By the way, where's your necktie? Why are you wearing that village-idiot hunting vest? Are you going back to Canada to track the migration of caribou?"

What was happening here? Was I becoming more like him than I realized?

Indeed, there was something liberating—if not appealing—about the way in which K never made the slightest pretense of conforming to anyone else's standard of professional etiquette. One afternoon I was doing a phone interview with Leonard Nimoy for a feature which my editor had demanded to see on her desk the previous morning; at last, having crossed three frustrating hurdles of publicists and assistants, I now had the actor-director on the line, somewhere in Beverly Hills, happily reminiscing about his Orthodox Jewish upbringing in Boston, talking about *Star Trek* as a metaphor for our people's Diaspora and how his split-fingered Vulcan hand greeting had been inspired by boyhood trips to the synagogue on Yom Kippur—but halfway through the interview I couldn't concentrate on my note taking because the other line kept beeping so insistently. Why wouldn't the person just call back? What kind of deranged soul would be so intent on disrupting my lifelong dream of melding minds with Mr. Spock? I had no choice; I had to click over. Who else? Sounding breathless, wanting my instantaneous feedback on a new reggae rhyme he was writing. "—Look, I can't talk. I'm interviewing Leonard Nimoy on the other line."

"Oh shit! For *real?* I love that pointy-eared muthafucka. Do me a favor now? Tell him I said *live long and prosper . . .*"

The barrage of jokes from my young wisecracking colleagues came as quick and unrelenting as the patter of Uzis. Didn't I see how absurdly funny this all was? Didn't I see that, between my live-in relationship with Crystal and this bizarro double life with the Brooklyn badboys, my world was a sitcom-in-the-making? Call it *Boychik in da Hood.* No, it really could be a sitcom, they assured me. They began spontaneously to compose a TV treatment one day over a platter of tunafish sandwiches and stale Wise potato chips.

PREMISE: Jewish rap fan runs around Brooklyn with gun-toting gangstas while, halfway across town, his African-American girlfriend is busy trying out a new rhumba move in Roseland with her European ballroom dancing buddies. Later that night, back at their apartment, she's trying to study for her graduate school comprehensive exams, but he keeps breaking her concentration by goof-stepping around to the strains of Snoop Doggy Dogg.

One afternoon Jeffrey Goldberg, the head writer of this never-to-be-seen situation comedy, called me over to his tiny cluttered corner of the office—next to the fire exit, reeking of Xerox toner and fire-escape pigeon droppings, behind bent-up file cabinets crammed with photos of long-deceased Yiddish poets and labor organizers shaking hands with L.B.J.—a pungent disaster area which was dubbed (in all seriousness) the National Affairs Bureau. Jeff was now straight-faced. He'd recently started writing some freelance features for *New York* magazine and said he had a quick but important question for me. (A funny rule-of-thumb with journalists: always take freelance assignments more seriously than staff work.)

"You ever heard of the Desert Eagle?" he whispered. In addition to being a small, cluttered, strange-smelling office, it was an insanely *nosy* office, and Jeff, like most of us, was understandably protective of his outside story ideas.

"The pistol?"

"Yeah."

He showed me a glossy brochure that came from the gun's manufacturer, Israeli Defense Industries. Wasn't this a seriously perverse weapon? In terms of muzzle energy, he said, the Desert Eagle was easily the most powerful handgun available on the streets. And it was fast becoming a favorite of Hollywood's propmasters—especially the new .50-caliber Eagle. It was Schwarzenegger's chrome piece in the posters for *Last Action Hero;* guest-starring in other action flicks like *Cliffhanger* and *Red Heat;* the gun that the psycho kid O-Dog had employed to blow the brains out of the Korean store clerk in *Menace II Society.* Also, he said, wondering aloud, hadn't the Eagle recently become a favorite subject of adoration in all those lovely gangsta-rap street serenades?

Was that his question?

Not quite. "—About these felonious friends of yours—"

"'Friends' is okay."

"These friends of yours—any of them know about the Desert Eagle?"

"What do you need them to know?"

"If any of them have any hands-on experience with one. And if they do, would they want to go on the record for a magazine piece?"

I called K on his job to find out. It took a while for the store manager to locate him downstairs and bring him to the phone. "This better be important," K barked. He'd been enjoying his single moment of solitude in the entire day's routine—on the toilet moving his bowels.

I couldn't ask him straight out if he'd like to be interviewed; that would make him suspicious; that was a little *too* close to cop language. I first asked if he knew of the Desert Eagle. His response was to laugh. Loudly and for a very long time. Then, when the laughter petered, he said we could go to his crib right now and he'd let me look at one.

That wouldn't be necessary, I said. By now I was used to seeing him traveling around with Scobey, his number-one girlfriend, that most loyal of Colt .45s. But I was a little curious to know what the hell he was doing in possession of a Desert Eagle.

"What?" he said. "Now you expect me to tell you every *bit* of my muthafuckin' business?"

I told Jeff that I would set up a meeting for the next day. But it would have to be in the early evening, after K got off from work. I met K on 42nd Street and then we stopped at our favorite midtown hangout, the Pronto Pizza shop on Sixth Avenue. Before I knew it, we were eating slices, sipping root beer, and I was laughing—along with half the pizzeria—as K did his best Beavis and Butt-head impersonation. He was in a silly frame of mind and his silliness had prevented me from explaining to him (not that I knew precisely) what Jeff was interested in gleaning from him about the Desert Eagle pistol. Evidently, I may have neglected to mention the fact that Jeff was coming to meet us at all.

Despite being a working stiff just getting off from his day shift, K still had a gangster's eating habits. Whenever he dined in a restaurant, pizza shop or fast-food establishment, he had to sit with his back pressed to the wall. It was a physical compulsion: he could not touch his food unless he had a clear line of sight to all the exits. That's exactly how he was sitting when, burning the roof of my mouth on an over-hot pepperoni slice, I heard the approaching sound of Jeff's voice. I didn't have to turn; I could tell it was Jeff from the tone of playful sarcasm, simultaneously making eye contact with K and a joke at my expense. "Hey, what the hell are you doing hanging out with *this* shady character?"

The incandescent light glowing again in those eyes. He rose slowly from his chair, mouth clenched tight, offering Jeff the kind of homicidal glare few sane people would ever want to see face-to-face. "Do I *know* you?"

I whirled around in time to see Jeff, looking quite flushed, forcing a smile as he backed away from the table. "What?" he said. "You didn't even tell him I was *coming?*"

Belated introductions were made and we all sat down, three tense, awkward faces staring at the empty Parmesan shaker in the center of a wobbly Formica table. Jeff broke the tension with something approximating an apology. "Listen, I was just messing around."

"I don't too much appreciate that shit," said K, making no effort to hide his annoyance. "Muthafuckas get *hurt* messin' around with shit like that." He wiped the pizza grease from his fingers on a small stack of napkins. "For all I know, you and him could be enemies, knowmsayin'? How the fuck do I know you wasn't comin' over here lookin' for beef?"

"I assure you," Jeff said, "I wasn't coming over here looking for beef."

Jeff was not the kind of journalist who scared easily. It was a quality K instantly admired in him. K later told me that—despite the initial chill between them—he really had to respect anyone who could walk into a pizzeria with such an I-don't-give-a-fuck attitude.

Jeff had been a crime reporter for the *Washington Post* straight out of college, covered murders in D.C. at the height of the late '80s crack epidemic. Then he'd gone to Israel, enlisted in the army and been sent to patrol the West Bank during the *intifada*. Among his other soldiering duties, he told me, he'd once done a stint as a jailer, guarding a camp filled with wild-eyed Hamas terrorists.

K liked the idea of being quoted in Jeff's article about guns. To add color to the story, he suggested, Jeff should travel with him out to Franklin Avenue and the Vanderveer projects. The Veer was real Desert Eagle country, K said. Jeff didn't even flinch at the prospect. Sitting sheepishly between them in the pizzeria, feeling as irrelevant as the referee in a pro wrestling bout, I explained that I had to go away to Canada for the week and that they'd have to spend the day running around Brooklyn without me. *Yeah, so?* their eyes tag-teamed. I shrugged away their now unified sarcasm, and said I hoped they would both remain on their best behavior.

I called them both from Canada later in the week to hear how it had gone. Another *Rashomon* slant to each retelling. K recounted, matter-of-factly, how Jeff had picked him up in a nice mid-sized rent-a-car, how he'd taken Jeff out to the Veer and to Franklin to get quotes from some of the Posse. But there'd been one problem, he said. Quite early in the drive, as they were crossing the Brooklyn Bridge, still getting to know each other, Jeff had asked a question about his upbringing and family life and K had been talking about his brother Julio getting murdered following his deportation to Panama and Jeff then said something offhanded, flippant: *Oh, was he down with that Noriega business?* K didn't want to show it at the time, but he'd been very offended by that remark. No, he'd been more than offended; he'd been angry. But he was trying to keep his sense of professionalism and he didn't say anything to Jeff about being upset.

I tried to explain to K that he simply wasn't used to Jeff's manner of speaking. I was sure that Jeff hadn't knowingly meant to cause any offense. "Well, then his sense of humor's a little too tart for my taste," K said. "He's gotta watch that sarcastic bullshit with me."

Then I called Jeff's apartment on the Upper West Side. He said the interview had been fine; he felt he could put K and the guys from the Franklin Avenue Posse in the story's lead. The Vanderveer part of the excursion had been a dead-end; they hadn't seen anybody who'd wanted to talk. But he was very impressed by the respect K had been shown by all the guys on Franklin Avenue. Even the old Sicilian guy in the pizzeria treated him with such deference. The old Sicilian guy had given everyone who was sitting with K free pizzas and sodas.

I asked Jeff if anything unusual had transpired during the day. No, he said. Then, after a moment, rerunning all the events in his mind, he said that while they were crossing the Brooklyn Bridge they'd been talking a little bit about Panama and his brother's deportation and murder and suddenly K was in a very bad mood and sullen-looking and it was a bit scary to see. But within minutes he seemed to snap out of it and the rest of the day went fine.

Before the issue of *New York* magazine hit the newsstands, Jeff got a call from one of the producers of the *CBS This Morning* program; they were interested in doing a midweek segment that would be a tie-in to his Desert Eagle article. They had booked John Risdall, the president of Magnum Research, Inc., the Minnesota company that invented the Desert Eagle, who was flying in for a studio interview with Paula Zahn. They asked if it would be possible to do a live studio interview with K as well. K said, yes, under one condition.

"What condition?"

"The same thing that I told Jeff for the article—the thing about guns not being fuckin' toys—not to glorify them to the shorties. If I'm on TV I wanna let the shorties know that there's some dire fuckin' consequences to carrying one of these things."

The night before the interview was to take place, I was on the phone with him for over an hour running through potential interview questions. Now, I said, it was conceivable that Paula Zahn might ask him something that completely pissed him off—

"—My friend," he cut me short. "Lemme ask *you* one question: Do you take me for a fuckin' barbarian?"

I had to click over to the call waiting. It was the producer from CBS, saying that there was a problem—they were going to have to bump K and the entire Desert Eagle segment. A hurricane named Emily was wreaking havoc along the eastern seaboard and, unfortunately, that was much bigger news. Welcome to the world of live television.

I clicked back to K. He didn't take the news well. How the fuck could they do that? he kept asking. How the fuck could they *renege?* It wasn't just his own disappointment talking; he'd called everybody he knew and told them to tune in. Faith had called everybody she knew too. Now everybody was going to think he was a big bullshit artist. I told him that the interview was still likely to take place before Friday and I'd call him as soon as I heard any news.

"Don't call me at all unless it's a go," he said.

"It's a go." CBS News sent a black Town Car to my place before sunrise Friday morning; as arranged, I called K from the car phone to make sure he was awake. Yawning, stretching, he said he was just waiting for Faith to do his hair. He took great pride in the subtle variations of braids she could weave into his hair.

The driver of the Town Car was a swarthy square-jawed Israeli named Ari. He wore aviator sunglasses and a stony expression that made me wonder if he did freelance work as a Mossad operative. In the predawn traffic, Ari made it up to the Bronx in record time. But then he got lost, and even with a detailed map of the Bronx in our hands, neither one of us could figure our way around the crazy sloping streets of Tremont. I called K again from the car phone and, like some air traffic controller, he talked the driver onto Burnside and eventually down to Echo Place.

His neighborhood at that hour had a hellish glow: the only eyes in the street belonged to the most desperate of crackheads and junkies and hookers. After a few minutes, K strolled out of his building with his hardrock glare, sporting a baby-blue denim shortsleeve shirt with a patch of red-and-white embroidery on the pocket. He hadn't shaved in over a week. And those fussed-over braids were wholly hidden beneath a black-and-red St. John's University ballcap.

He clearly loved getting this star treatment, beaming when he swung his legs inside the spacious baby limo. "Yo, this shit is the *butters*," he said, nodding admiringly at the interior of the Lincoln, complimenting the Israeli on the immaculate condition in which he kept his car. He said he was always impressed by a man who knew how to take proper care of his vehicle.

"Could I call my wife on your phone please?" he asked.

She must be missing you terribly these last three minutes, I thought. K took the phone from Ari and then smiled mischievously.

"*Baruch ha-Shem*," he said, thanking the driver in a Hebrew inflection so perfect that the stone-faced Israeli was forced to do a double take, thinking that I, like some ventriloquist prankster, must have thrown my voice to the opposite end of his Lincoln. Now K said it a second time, very clearly, nodding, and Ari shot me a confused glance in his rounded, elongated rearview mirror.

"How he *knows* this?"

The sprawling CBS Broadcast Center on West 57th Street, headquarters of the Tiffany Network's august news division, once the haunt of white-haired Uncle Walter himself, seems to shiver slightly on its foundation at the sight of the big man in baby-blue passing through the security check. Traveling upstairs by sleek, wooshing elevator, beaming now with the unrestrained glee of a boy contemplating the prospect of a catered birthday party, he enters the greenroom, making a fast flanking move for the breakfast buffet, sampling the array of muffins, bagels and croissants. He downs two bowls of oatmeal, gives a glowing critique—"Yo, check it! This shit is the bomb-*diggity!*"—before pouncing on the fruit platter on the opposite side of the room. Without hesitation, he eats every piece of fruit on display, leaving only several melon rinds and the sprigs of leafy garnish which have been found to leave an unpleasant and bitter aftertaste.

"Some guests get nervous stomachs before they go on the air live," mutters the young curly-haired CBS news producer with whom I've been brokering the on-and-off-and-on-again arrangements these past few days.

"Man, fuck that," replies the guest, chewing, smiling and cheerfully popping his mouth full of those miraculously uniform cantaloupe balls. "I ain't have time to eat breakfast this morning—a nigga *gots* to get his grub on."

With the greenroom now devoid of anything edible, with the guest still grumbling about having been shortchanged on his share of the breakfast provisions, I head down to the commissary to buy (CBS-subsidized, I am told, and therefore heavily discounted) platters of scrambled eggs and french toast. "Take care that shit don't touch no *swine!*" I hear barked after me, in dire warning, as I proceed down the hallway to the elevator.

He is still barking when I return from the commissary, juggling several Styrofoam breakfast containers, but, even stepping from the elevator, I immediately recognize that his shouting is no longer playful. Rushing into the dressing room, I find a frightened makeup artist backing away from the guest with a plastic bib and a tiny fan-brush in one hand. The guest has been speaking (or, rather, shouting) in his Jamaican patois—though to the makeup artist it might as well have been some variant of Mongolian—proudly declaiming that he is not Boy George or Michael Jackson, that he will not allow his face to be decorated in lipstick and eyeliner and rouge.

He is not, he says with a wave of his powerful arm, partial to such *maama-man** business.

I manage to block the doorway with my timely breakfast delivery, preventing the makeup man from fleeing the room.

"He's not entirely comfortable with the idea of wearing makeup on his face," I explain. The makeup artist mumbles softly that this guest, like most guests, has somewhat shiny skin, that the human face tends to radiate brightly under the unnaturally strong lighting of broadcast television. At the very least, he says, not quite insisting, the guest should be dusted with some kind of anti-glare powder.

The guest stares at me before reaching for his Styrofoam container filled, somewhat disappointingly, with soggy and lukewarm french toast. Popping open the lid, he shrugs, relenting, sitting back down in the makeup chair.

"Dig, a little powder's cool, I guess."

The interview opens with the words HOT GUNS superimposed under Paula Zahn's face. "Can this be true?" is the rhetorical gambit. "Can a gun featured in the movies become *hot?* Well, after Clint Eastwood's *Dirty Harry* was released in 1971, sales of the .44 Magnum skyrocketed. This summer it's *Cliffhanger* and *Last Action Hero,* which showcase the Desert Eagle. It's a gun that *New York* magazine calls the weapon of choice on the streets."

The camera angle now pulls back to reveal, in extreme foreground, a small table decorated with an array of massive, virginal Desert Eagles, chrome-plated and pearl-handled, .44 caliber as well as .50. It also reveals Paula Zahn welcoming her two in-studio guests. "Joining us this morning are John Risdall, whose company invented the gun and imports it, and aspiring rapper American Dread, who has seen the gun up close in his Bronx neighborhood."

---

*Jamaican slang for a homosexual or effeminate man. Considered extremely offensive.

Even slouching in his interview chair, the aspiring rapper is dwarfing the gun importer. Mr. Risdall is a soft-spoken man with a bushy gray-brown mustache who bears a passing resemblance to paleontologist Stephen Jay Gould. Whether it's the heat of the studio lights, or the prospect of being grilled on national television about the dubious necessity for putting such a powerful handgun on America's streets, or the simple fact that he is now seated next to a hulking unshaven rapper (aspiring or otherwise) who shows no intention of leaving the studio anytime soon, Mr. Risdall does not look well. As the interview proceeds, he begins to squirm in his chair; his mustache twitches nervously. Fortunately for him, the rapper is first on the live-TV hot seat.

PAULA ZAHN   Where have you encountered this gun, American Dread?

DREAD   Vanderveer Projects in Brooklyn. Gowanus Projects. The Bronx. All over Brooklyn. All over New York you see them.

ZAHN   You actually own one yourself.

DREAD   Yessir.

ZAHN   Why?

DREAD   It's like this—if you don't own a gun in New York, it's *over*. You can just count it off.

ZAHN   This is a very powerful weapon. There are a lot of less powerful weapons out on the street. Why this particular weapon? Is it the allure of seeing it in these movies? Is it in fact—

DREAD   It's not that. The Desert Eagle in itself means status. Once you have the Desert Eagle you're the king of the mountain. The power of this Desert Eagle is awesome. I've seen times where guys got shot in the arm and the arm totally came off. The Desert Eagle puts a little hole like this [indicates pencil-sized diameter] entering and a big hole like this [indicates melon-sized diameter] exiting. So . . .

ZAHN   But you object to the fact that you feel that these guns are glorified in movies, and you still own one. Help me understand the dichotomy here.

DREAD   My thing is this—I don't *object*. I'm *pro*-gun. I'm glad he put the Desert Eagle out on the market.

ZAHN   What is it that you're opposed to?

DREAD   I'm opposed to *some* movies—where you're showin' it to the little kids—that's so graphic, knowmsayin'? An adult is gonna do what they gonna do regardless. Regardless to the movie, regardless to the videos—you have your own mind. Whatever you're gonna do, you're gonna do regardless. But don't glorify it to the kids. I'm talkin' about little *kids*. Little kids see this gun and they want it.

Mr. Risdall's turn to weigh in now. Speaking slowly, without emotion, the Minnesota-based gun importer says that he must agree with the rapper's free enterprise worldview. "He's exactly right. In America you get to buy what you want to buy—if you've got money, you can buy anything." But what about the glorified portrayal of his gun in so many recent action movies? Does this not trouble him? Does he not perceive any moral dilemma here?

Not at all. "I've been a movie fan forever and the movies of the '30s, '40s, '50s, '60s, '70s all have guns. It's something America has been in love with forever."

Paula Zahn, for her part, no longer seems to be in love with her two guests. Visibly frustrated by their unanimity on these issues, she turns back to the hulking rapper, detecting a gaping hole in his logic:

ZAHN   You say you object to this whole thing on the basis of children, children seeing these weapons. What about the glorification of guns and violence in the rap music these kids are listening to? Aren't we talking about the same thing?

DREAD   See, in rap it's different. I can't speak for every rapper, but I know this rapper has *lived* it. Most of the other rappers also, Onyx, Tupac. It's reality for us: the streets, the guns, the drugs, violence—it's *reality*. So therefore we only rap about what we see, we only speak about what we've seen.

Her impatience is now palpable. Where's the debate here? One guest imports the world's most fearsome handgun; the other enjoys using it. She glances furiously at her clipboard. *Who was responsible for booking this segment?* (Hearing, perhaps, the deafening click of a million or more channel-surfing remotes. Another riveting breakfast-time feature brought to you by this, the lowest-rated of the three network morning shows.)

She's aiming for the semblance of a graceful wrap-up when the rapper interrupts. He's been waiting for an opportunity to launch into his riff about how every era in American history has its own fashionable firearm, a gun that, for one reason or another, registers in the public consciousness. "You figure in the '30s there was the Tommy gun. Then there was the Saturday night special in the early '70s, the latter part of the '60s. Now it's the Desert Eagle. I mean, there's nothin' you can do to deter it. The Desert Eagle is in the *house,* so to speak."

The interviewer thanks the aspiring rapper and the gun importer for their time and weapons expertise and then, offering one more forced smile for the camera, she cuts to the 8:16 commercial break.

Everyone loves a good gun story, and Jeff's was no exception. Before long the Desert Eagle hype had even spread to England. A few weeks after his article ran Jeff received a fax at *New York* from a pop-music-and-youth-culture program in London called *The Word.* The producers of *The Word*—intrigued by all things violent and American and, in particular, by the synergy of the two in this Desert Eagle phenomenon—wanted to send a camera crew to New York to interview "a gangsta, reformed or otherwise," regarding the street status of the handheld howitzer now so beloved by Hollywood's dreammakers.

Hopefully, they said, Jeff would be able to put them in touch with his contact American Dread.

Jeff showed me the fax with considerable embarrassment. He now saw his little two-page Desert Eagle story as a golem run amok. Anyone who'd actually read the article would have realized that, unlike American Dread, Jeff was *not* pro-gun. His story had contained a tacit criticism of both American gun culture and the mercenary element in Israel's military economy that could produce and market a .50-caliber man-mangler and claim, with a straight face, that it was a firearm expressly designed for target practice and the hunting of wild boars. Unfortunately, the criticism had been cloaked in his tone of irony and understatement, literary commodities which had not traveled well— if the buoyant, bubbly tone of this latest transatlantic fax was any indication.

But if Jeff was chagrined by the vagaries of his story's afterlife, K was simply bemused. "Y'all some funny muthafuckas, you know that? The Desert Eagle been out on the street since '84 and nobody ain't say shit about it. But then Jeffrey Goldberg goes and writes one article and turns it into a muthafuckin' *phenomenon.*"

It was a sunny day in mid-October when the crew from *The Word* arrived to shoot their on-the-street segment with K and the Franklin Avenue Posse. I'd made arrangements to meet up with K on Franklin Avenue and Eastern Parkway, a full two hours before we were supposed to rendezvous with the English TV crew. All week, K had been worried about the English crew's safety, asking me if the sort of camera equipment they were bringing was worth more than a thousand dollars. It was worth considerably more, I informed him.

He said that out here in Crooklyn, capital of the daytime stickup, it wouldn't take more than the blink of an eye for the Englishmen to be robbed of their camera equipment and their Jeep and be left standing on the sidewalk in their fruity little Euro briefs. But he had taken every precaution to ensure that wouldn't happen today, providing his own security for the shoot, arriving on Eastern Parkway in the company of three fellow bruisers from the Fifth Avenue business district.

It was a collection of men so gigantic that, when I first caught sight of them emerging from the subway station, I half expected to see a gaggle of NFL offensive line scouts trailing after them waving Parker ballpoints and cellular phones. There was Big Joe and his partner Kwane, both working security at branches of Raspberry Sport, each wide as a house and weighing in excess of 320 pounds. There was Big Troy, with the six-inch flattop haircut rising like a reddish wheatfield above his six-foot-six frame; a baby-faced bulldozer who, in his weekend job as a hip-hop bouncer at the Tunnel, was known to derive inordinate pleasure from the nightly task of tossing loudmouthed bullies headlong into the street.

K, though the least massive of them, remained the most menacing. Perhaps it was that extra-large bulge on his hip today. The producers of *The Word* had been explicit in that one request: they wanted K to be packing his Desert Eagle throughout the interview.

Having over an hour to kill, K decided to take a walk over to the other side of Franklin to see if he could find Justice and his brother Life. He said he'd like them to be in the TV segment, if possible. If anybody from F.A.P. was a gun specialist, K said, it was Life. Life had been a big-time gunrunner, done fed time for it already.

But crossing over to the other side of Eastern Parkway posed a potential problem. K explained that there had always been beef with the guys from the other side of Franklin Avenue, bad blood dating back to their teenage years. It was on this side of the Parkway that his girlfriend Monique had been murdered in 1989. The gunmen had really been looking to murder K and rob him of his money and coke; Monique, with her big mouth, had been bragging for weeks about how K was coming up from D.C., carrying thousands in drug profits. But before he could even arrive at her apartment on St. John's Place, the gunmen murdered Monique in the vestibule of her building. MOM SLAIN WHILE TOT SLEEPS, said the next day's headline. K said he could never prove it, but he'd always suspected that the guys on this side of Franklin, though not the actual triggermen, had had something to do with setting up Monique's murder.

We were walking down St. John's Place in the warm October sunshine and Big Troy, who was thirsty, said he wanted to stop at the bodega to get a bottle of Mystic iced tea.

It began so innocuously. There was a single pay phone on the corner across from us. A muscular guy in a black leather jacket was talking on it. We were all standing in front of the bodega. When Big Troy came back outside with his iced tea he looked at the muscular guy on the phone and said, "Don't the nigga look like Mike Tyson?"

"Word is bond." K nodded. "Nigga looks just like Mikey T."

One brief glance. But as soon as we moved off the corner, the guy in the black leather jacket hung up the phone and began to follow us. To me it seemed an innocent coincidence; but to K and everyone else, the Mike Tyson look-alike was approaching with obvious menace in his stride. True, he did have his hand tucked ominously inside the pocket of his leather jacket. And now a second leather-clad figure had fallen in step beside him.

K knew exactly how he wanted to respond to these two pursuers.

"Keep walkin'," he instructed the four of us. "Get the fuck outta here. I got this shit."

He began to slow his walking gait, stopping momentarily, then proceeding a few steps, then stopping again. He had his hand clearly positioned on the bulge in his waist.

I kept glancing back nervously. "See, what it is," Troy calmly explained to me as we walked, "this nigga's talkin' on the phone and he sees a bunch of wild-lookin' muthafuckas on his block he ain't never seen before. So naturally he gonna think we's some heavy-hittin' muthafuckas out here to take care of some business."

K was now a half block behind us, standing there with his gun in hand, waiting to confront the pursuers. But they didn't want any part of K. He'd called their bluff. The Mike Tyson look-alike stopped his approach suddenly; he and his partner veered up another street.

Once again, the threat of a deadly shootout had passed as quickly and capriciously as it had arisen. I had an irritable throbbing in the side of my head and the bitter taste of bile on my tongue. How, I wondered, could anyone live in this constant state of stress? By now K, smiling, walking quickly, had rejoined us.

"That's just how shit goes down," Troy said with a laugh.

But before I even had time to cleanse my system of fear, I felt K walking too close behind me, fidgeting with his waist, telling me to slow down.

"What the hell are you doing?"

"Keep steppin'."

I heard my track bag unzipping behind me, and K fidgeting a little more with his waistband, and then I felt the sudden heavy weight on my shoulder. We walked on for a long time in silence before I spoke.

"I came out here with you to do this TV thing for England—*not* nearly get caught in a shootout or mule your fucking gun all over Brooklyn."

When I looked up at him I saw that he was smiling. As usual, he found my anger quite amusing.

"What if some cop stops me and asks to see—"

"Shut up, muthafucka. You sound stupid. Take a glance in the mirror sometime—you *white*. Ain't no beast out here stoppin' you for a muthafuckin' thing."

"You're saying it couldn't happen?"

"I'm sayin' it *won't* happen. Keep steppin'."

So I kept stepping with the illegal Eagle now swinging heavily in my track bag. As we came up toward Eastern Parkway, a police car came cruising slowly up Washington Avenue, and K told me to cross the Parkway and walk down to Franklin alone. No one would look at me suspiciously if I was walking alone on the other side of the Parkway. So we parted company and I waited for the light to change and then I crossed to the other side of Eastern Parkway. They continued walking on as if we'd never been together.

I knew, thanks to Jeff's statistics-packed *New York* article, that most Desert Eagle models weigh, without magazines, approximately four pounds; but as I crossed Eastern Parkway this particular Desert Eagle model in my track bag felt like a twenty-pound dumbbell, doing a slow pendulum swing before smacking hard against my hip.

I began to wonder if K had remembered to put it on safety. Then, knowing absolutely nothing about the mechanics of handguns, I began to wonder if the safety switch could somehow, with repeated jostling, drift into a *non*safety position.

I recalled his words on *CBS This Morning* about the Desert Eagle's destructive capacity—"I've seen times where guys got shot in the arm and the arm totally came off"—and all the while the pistol kept slamming against my hip and then I began to imagine how my ridiculous life would be reduced to a postage-stamp Metro item in tomorrow's *Post:*

MYSTERY DEATH OF 'VILLAGE IDIOT'

A Canadian-born journalist bled to death on Eastern Parkway in Brooklyn yesterday, the apparent victim of an accidental and self-inflicted gunshot wound to the buttocks.

Police sources said it was not immediately apparent why the unnamed journalist, a 29-year-old Manhattan resident, was in possession of the high-powered pistol—an unregistered .44-caliber Desert Eagle—which took his life.

But, miraculously, I managed to mule the gun all the way down to Franklin Avenue without shooting myself in the ass. We'd said we would all rendezvous inside Pop's pizzeria on Franklin, and when I got inside Pop's they were already sitting in the two back booths. I walked over and angrily dropped the track bag on the seat beside K.

"Don't *ever* do that shit to me again."

They were all laughing at me, pointing out how pale my face was, how the front of my Champion T-shirt was drenched in sweat. K beamed as if welcoming me, after a rigorous interview process, into the confines of a select and secretive club.

"Ay yo, Pop! Give Doogzilla here an extra-cold Mystic to calm his fuckin' nerves!"

"I don't want a Mystic. I just want you to get that thing out of my bag."

"Don't getcha drawers all in a bunch! Relax, sit down, have a slice of pie. You ain't heard Pop makes the best fuckin' pie in Brooklyn?"

He took his time opening my track bag. Under cover of the orange Formica booth, on which Pop had just now set down a tin platter holding one of his steaming twelve-slice pies, K rustled inside the bag, hoisted his sweatshirt, then tucked the obscenely large pistol back into his waistband where it belonged.

Still slightly queasy, I scanned the vintage black-and-white photographs of Ebbets Field and Coney Island in the '20s and '30s—the same crowded Boardwalk my mother'd walked as a four-year-old girl—then went over to the counter to talk to Pop. He was a tiny, squatly muscled man with impassive features and a silvery black sweep of strong Mediterranean hair. He'd been in business here on Franklin Avenue for some fifteen years, but he still spoke with a nearly incomprehensible, straight-from-Palermo accent.

Standing there in his tomato-stained white apron, working his hands into a lump of floured pizza dough, Pop gave me his tough-guy once-over.

"Siciliano?" he asked.

I shook my head. "Jewish."

He nodded and winked one of his heavy hooded eyes. Then, with one stubby index finger next to his ear, he mimed the looping twirls of Orthodox sidelocks. Either that, or he was making the universal hand gesture for *mentally deranged*.

"Sicilians . . . Jews," I heard myself muttering now, though I didn't have the slightest idea what concept I might be trying to communicate.

Pop seemed to understand. He winked at me again, then smiled, then tapped that sausage index finger twice to his right temple. "Money," he said, kneading his powerful hands back into the lump of pizza dough.

Seeing as this was the day for kicking ballistics, said K, seeing as how we were still waiting for the English TV crew to arrive (and where were those fucking dickheads anyway?), seeing as how my face was still bent out of shape from muling his Eagle a few simple yards down Eastern Parkway, he thought he would break the tension between us by recounting a nice little gun-related yarn of his youth. It was something that had happened right here at Pop's pizzeria, something that had irrevocably altered the direction of his young life.

We were now facing each other alone over the empty tin pizza platter. The rest of the guys were outside in the sunny street, under orders from K, keeping their eyes peeled for the Jeep Cherokee filled with clueless, camera-toting Englishmen.

There was one thing K could honestly say about that man Pop. There'd never been any white-versus-black bullshit in his establishment. There was none of that *Suck my dick, you moulie!* stuff you see in the movies. True, that might've been going on behind their backs, when Pop and his guys were all talking in Italian. But then, K reasoned, if somebody really hates you because you're black, why would he have you eating all kinds of free pizzas and drinking up free sodas in his pizzeria?

Few of the original Franklin Avenue clique paid for anything here in Pop's. And nobody's mother paid. Pop showed everyone love that way. He made a point of remembering everyone's mother. And back in the old days, Pop's son Angelo used to call the Franklin Avenue Posse his "little militants." He'd always smile and say, "Dose are my little fuckin' militants right dare." Sometimes they'd see those big-time guys stopping by from Sheepshead Bay, straight-up John-Travolta-looking cats with the silk shirts and the gold chains, driving the old two-door Cadillacs. And you knew *they* were prejudiced; they'd look at Pop and Angelo and then they'd look at the F.A.P. clique sitting in the booths. "Who are dose fuckin' ruffians?" But Angelo would always say, "Relax, Sal, dose are jus' my little militants."

K was just seventeen, had just come home from his time in the halfway house, the Youth Detention Center Number 1, out in Bushwick. He was so glad to come back to his mother's place. One of the first (non-sex-related) things he wanted to do with his freedom was order a big pizza pie from Pop's. They were all sitting in the living room that afternoon, his kid brother, Craig, and Craig's little girlfriend and their little man Jetta. Since everyone was hungry, they sent Craig and his girlfriend down to Pop's to pick up a large pie.

In those days, the guys on Franklin Avenue used to hide their drugs underneath the Space Invaders machine inside Pop's. They used to sell dimes of coke in foil paper, folded up in square packets. One of the guys on the Ave had left a Sucrets can packed full of dimes, roughly $400 worth of powder, secreted under the Space Invaders machine.

Craig returned with the pizza pie and everything was as it should be; they were divvying up slices and getting ready to chomp into Pop's famous drooping-crust-and-mozzarella masterpiece when—*boom! boom! boom!*—the door starts banging like it's the police. And someone's shouting, angrily, "Open the fuckin' door!" Craig went to the door alone. They heard a gravelly voice saying, very softly, "Yo man, we got a problem—you better come with us."

From his position on the sofa, through the crack in the door, he could see that it was two young guys, roughly his own age, who he knew as Dante and True. Then behind them, he spotted the outline of a grown man, a tall man known on the Avenue as Doc.

Doc was a lean-faced man with gray in his temples. He was feared all over Brooklyn as an enforcer, a stone-cold hit man. He was one of Franklin Avenue's original badmen, the straight-from-Colón gangsters. Men who had their own factories processing the perico down in Panama. Men who'd had Franklin Avenue under pressure for years.

*"Craig was gettin' ready to go with them because Craig didn't want no type of problems.**

"I tells him: 'Craig, don't go nowhere till I put on my shoes!'

"Then Doc looks me up and down.

" 'Oh, so you is a badman now?'

" 'Yo Craig! Don't go nowhere till I put on my shoes!' I looked at Doc and said, 'Yo, my brother ain't goin' no-fuckin'-where unless I go with him. Y'all muthafuckas best ta slow down with that bullshit.'

"When I said that, Doc slowly opened his coat and showed me the Uzi. 'Lemme tell you sumting, bwoy. All de real badmen are dead.' "

He stepped into his Filas and raced outside behind them. They were heading down to Franklin Avenue where—as he now saw, with considerable disbelief—there were at least forty people lined up in front of the pizzeria. Guys and girls and even a few little kids. The whole block from Pop's to the corner was one big lineup of suspects. A Sucrets can had gone missing from under the Space Invaders machine and nobody was leaving the block until they found out who had taken it.

Snake and Fuquan were patrolling the line; they had everybody standing still, waiting for Doc to come back with Craig. And now True was also patrolling down the line, saying, "Every five minutes somebody gonna get snatched outta this line and get they ass whipped—

---

*These italicized interludes are from a taped interview with K, conducted in Brooklyn on January 14, 1997.

until we find this muthafuckin' thing. And if we don't find this mutha-fuckin' thing—then we gonna start blazin'.'"

"See, these niggas was showin' me somethin' new in the game. They was showin' me that they really did not give a fuck. I was scared—but I was also mad. These niggas was gettin' ready to fuck up my brother Craig, along with the thirty-nine other muthafuckas waitin' in line for they ass-whippings. And every few minutes they would take somebody into Pop's and the muthafucka would come back out into the street with his nose and lip bleedin'."

All of a sudden a squad car came squealing around the corner—but nobody ran off. Doc, even with his big Uzi on him, didn't panic, didn't even walk fast. He just stared at the cops and then calmly disappeared around the corner. Now all the people who'd been lined up could eas-ily have jetted in all directions: but no one left. They knew that any-one who ran off would instantly become the *prime* suspect; so they gathered right back in front of the pizzeria as soon as the police were out of sight.

With the coast now clear, Doc and True moved everybody to a more secluded location, the park in the back of Prospect Heights High School. Everybody was standing up against a wall like it was going to be the St. Valentine's Day Massacre all over again.

How could he stand idly by and let True and these guys beat the shit out of his little brother Craig? "Yo, my little brother don't got nothin' to do with this shit," he said. "My brother just came to Pop's to get a pizza."

He was scared. He was thinking, *Damn, I'm outta my league. These niggas is sophisticated.* They had everybody lined up like real mobsters.

"Shuttuuuup! Don't fuckin' taaaaalk! You wanna be next?"

No, he told True, he did not want to be next. He felt like a little punk for backing down so fast, but what could he do? Actually, he wasn't even afraid of True and Dante and Snake. He was only afraid of that man Doc. Doc wasn't a kid—Doc was old enough to be his father.

And though he knew he possessed the hand skills to knock Doc out in a fistfight, Doc was packing an *Uzi*; he was blatantly disrespecting the police. Doc, it was obvious to even a casual onlooker, was a man playing by his own set of rules.

But he was still talking to True, trying to save his kid brother from catching that ass-whipping. "Fuck you yappin' so much for?" True snapped. "You wanna take the licks for him?" Then a girl said something in the line and Doc, turning suddenly, butted the girl in the eye with his Uzi. That *hurt* him: and he wanted to hurt that man Doc. By now they had pulled three people from the line and beat them badly. The fourth person they were going to fuck up was his little man Jetta.

But then Craig stepped up, looked at Doc, and said, "You not gonna fuck Jetta up 'cause he wasn't even there. He didn't have nothin' to do with nothin'. If anything, fuck *me* up. I was there."

Doc cocked his head to one side. "So you tough? You is a tough man?"

"*Please*, man, don't do it!"

"Shutdafuckuuup!" said True. "If you say it one more time, I'm a shoot you in ya muthafuckin' face, knowmsayin? Why you actin' so stupid? This ain't personal, muthafucka—this is *beeznisss*."

He'd never forget the sound of that word: the way True spat it at him. Years later, without even thinking about it, he found himself saying the same thing when shit got thick in the drug game: *This ain't personal, muthafucka—this is beeznisss.*

By now they'd started tearing into his brother Craig, four or five of them, beating and slugging and stomping; but Craig was showing his heart, standing upright, falling down, getting back up again, taking the beating like a man. Now he finally understood why Craig had stepped forward so willingly. Craig knew how these F.A. gangsters were running the block. Craig knew it was better to take the ass-whipping than to get himself shot.

"Watchin' that, watchin' them whip Craig's ass and me bein' powerless to stop it, had the tears streamin' down my face. You see, up to this point in

*time I had never been shot before; I'd never even been shot at. I was real
scared of guns. My time in the juvenile jails had conditioned me to think
about some get-away-with-it type shit—but also to know when to fold 'em.
And this was a time to say I definitely gotta fold 'em: this muthafucka Doc's
packin' an Uzi and I don't especially wanna die today.*

*"See, I had come out of Goshen and Elmira with the best of intentions.
I was still thinkin' maybe I could go to college and become a legit muthafucka.*

*"But now I was seein' that these niggas was gettin' ready to bring me
down—because in order for me to live out here, I gotta act like a savage just
like them. And the thing was, I knew that I could do that. I knew at any
point I could harness the wildness, the ability to just fuckin' flip script. No
question."*

"So who did take the Sucrets can?"

"What happened was, they were still fuckin' Craig up, and at one
point Craig fell down and they were kickin' him and stompin' him so
bad that finally one guy jumped in and said, *Stop! I know who got it!* He
pointed his finger and said this guy J.D. from Park Place had the Sucrets can with the dimes in it.

"Oh my God! Craig lost his fuckin' mind—because at this point
he was all bruised and bloody. Sure enough, they found the Sucrets
can on J.D. Craig picks up a garbage can and starts beatin' this muthafucka J.D. with it. We all teamed up on him, beat him into submission. Had him bawlin' for Jesus, boy."

From the moment the English TV crew cruised to a stop in front of
Pop's pizzeria there were problems. The Englishmen were driving a
borrowed forest-green Jeep Grand Cherokee, the license plates of
which were labeled with the letters NYP. This seemingly trivial information reached our ears inside the pizzeria; K shot up from his seat,

dashing, breathless, into the street. Angrily pointing at the plates, he hissed: "Who *are* these muthafuckas? Are these muthafuckas *police?*"

No, I said, trying to get him to calm down, those letters NYP were stamped on the license plates of members of the working press. Press plates? No one had heard of such a thing. I asked K if he'd ever (in his long history of ducking and avoiding the police) seen an unmarked detective's car with NYP stamped on the plates. Wouldn't it be somewhat foolish for undercover detectives to announce their arrival with specially labeled tags? K nodded now, acknowledging the logic of what I was saying if not actually buying my explanation, then went over to warmly welcome the four Englishmen to Brooklyn.

By now there were several dozen Posse members gathered in the street in front of Pop's pizzeria, word having spread through the neighborhood that a television crew from England was here to make everyone famous. It was a smattering of the old F.A.P. men, along with the members of the closely affiliated crew known as Partners-in-Crime (P.I.C.), based on Franklin and President Street. The most conspicuous absence today was Shabazz. But Shabazz would not be showing his face on Franklin Avenue for many years to come.

Against the advice of K and other Posse members, Shabazz had taken his case to trial. His court-appointed lawyer had tried to punch holes in the official accounts of Shabazz's alleged assault on the police officers back in '89. But the cops themselves had taken the stand and recounted how Shabazz—who was rail-thin and weighed approximately 147 pounds—had been fighting and kicking with superhuman strength.

All day long, while K and the rest of the Posse were out here on Franklin Avenue, gesticulating, laughing, talking into the English TV cameras, I kept picturing Shabazz doing his time, alone in his cell, somewhere behind the old fortress walls of Sing Sing.

Midway through the interview segment, while the cameramen were repositioning their equipment for a different lighting angle, K called me over to whisper in my ear. He asked me if I agreed that the English interviewer in the trendy glasses and the gray suit was an idiot. Here he'd been hoping to have a discourse about the history of gun-play in America, talk about Dillinger and Babyface Nelson and Bonnie and Clyde, but now he could see that the only thing these Englishmen wanted from him was "some rah-rah ghetto bullshit."

His suspicion was confirmed when the aviator-jacket-wearing assistant producer named Carl came over and told me that, although the interview had thus far been fascinating and elucidating, there was a slight problem.

"Problem?"

"He still hasn't shown us the gun."

Why did they need to see him brandishing his gun? Hadn't they already gone to a firing range in Manhattan to shoot a segment of the Desert Eagle in ear-splitting action?

"For purposes of authenticity, you understand," Carl said.

Of course, I nodded. It was important—indeed, it was crucial—that the teenyboppers of the U.K. got some cinema-verité-style video-tape of an enormous black Brooklynite waving his .44 Magnum with a murderous-yet-strangely-sexual gleam in his eye. K, when informed, wanted no part of their charade. This was exactly what he'd been fearing, he told me. He'd long suspected that the English TV crew had intended to make black people look like a bunch of brainless barbarians. His personal ethic, as he told blond-headed Carl, could best be summed up by a phrase uttered by that great hip-hop preacher and pontificator, KRS-One: *Real badboys move in silence.* Translation: a true gunman never pulls out his burner until he's ready to make toast.

Yes, of course, nodded Carl. But now the Englishmen were huddled around the Jeep Cherokee, murmuring, staring sadly at silver-box-clip-boards, clearly disappointed not to have captured the brandishing image they'd wanted. Suddenly, impulsively, K walked over to the Jeep, grabbed one of the cameramen by the shoulder and gave him instructions to follow. He led the cameraman to the entrance of a nondescript Franklin Avenue apartment house. If they wanted to see the gun they could see it; but he wasn't brandishing it out in the street.

*   *   *

The sunlight on Franklin Avenue was now too dim to shoot videotape clearly and someone in the crew had the bright idea of moving over to the other side of Eastern Parkway. "Naw," said K. "That ain't *our* side of Franklin. That's them other niggas' corner over there." But the light was so much better over there. That other corner was bathed in the most spectacular autumn sunlight. Visibly losing his patience with the English TV crew, K nevertheless gathered up the Posse and his massive security guys and led the ragged caravan to the other side of the Parkway. The English crew circled the block in their borrowed Cherokee, double-parking in front of the fried-chicken joint on the opposite corner.

Now they set up the whole Posse, along with ringers like Big Troy, Big Joe and Kwane, positioned just behind K. It began to resemble a swarming dog pile, some human pyramid created by a team of circus acrobats in camouflage fatigues. More and more people kept streaming into the frame, trying to get on camera and flash their hardrock smirks. One of the streaming new faces mumbled something to K, who, snapping to attention, mumbled something right back. Suddenly, many of the newcomers were streaming angrily out of the frame as quickly as they'd streamed in.

I approached K and asked what had happened. Just what he'd predicted would happen, he said. The guys from this side of Eastern Parkway were feeling jealous that the English crew hadn't asked them to be in their shoot. They felt dissed to see these white strangers with expensive cameras occupying their corner. So they'd left? Yes, he said, but they'd vowed to come right back. They were just going to get their biscuits.

"Biscuits?" Carl grinned, eavesdropping on all this.

"Guns," K explained.

Carl and the rest of the English TV crew were still smiling their happy-just-to-be-in-Brooklyn smiles. K was very close to exploding in anger.

Biting his tongue, he instead took Carl gently by the arm and told him that it had been a pleasure and an honor doing business with such seasoned TV professionals. He hoped that his interview had been informative and that they'd captured everything they needed to satisfy their young English viewing audience. But, he said, not meaning to be overly blunt, the time had now come for the Englishmen to buckle up inside their forest-green Jeep Cherokee, take their expensive camera equipment and their New York Press license plates, and depart.

Carl smiled at K, then at me, uncomprehending. K rolled his eyes skyward. "You came out here to find out about gunplay, right? Well, if you stay here another two fuckin' minutes you just might learn a bit more about gunplay than you wanna know."

Heeding his advice, the crew from *The Word* loaded up their Cherokee and drove off, waving bye-bye, once and for all, to Brooklyn and its photogenic Franklin Avenue Posse.

The rest of us crossed back to the—relative—safe haven on the south side of Eastern Parkway. No sight yet of the guys from the rival side returning with their guns. There was much speculation that their words had been a bluff, an idle threat born of envy and late-afternoon boredom. But bluff or not, again I was nauseous, tasting that bitter bile in the back of my throat. K stood boldly under the lamppost, neck craned, gazing over to the other side of the Parkway like a lookout on the prow of a pirate galleon. It had been a long day and everyone else was ready to go home. Big Troy said he had to work the door at the Tunnel that night and wanted to get home in time to take a shower. Kwane and Big Joe had a long journey back to Jersey.

K agreed, finally, to leave Franklin Avenue. But before he stepped off the corner, I saw something that shocked me, a dark haze in his eyes I'd never seen before. There was no mistaking it. A look of abject terror. Under that lamppost, leaning slightly to the left, he stood frozen, unwavering. Staring into his eyes, I saw the void, as if someone had tapped a microscopic hose into the side of his head and siphoned out all consciousness of his current surroundings.

What was he so afraid of? Surely not the boastful threats of those kids from the other side of the Parkway?

He shook his head and was silent. He wouldn't answer me that afternoon, or during the train ride back into Manhattan, or even weeks later when, still baffled by that horrified look, I asked him again what had precipitated his moment of fear.

He kept me waiting. It would be several years before I fully understood the reason for his haunted eyes, several years before he told me the story of the dreadlocked marksman who had nearly, on that very corner, drained his body of life.

K was one gunman who'd stood on both sides of the ballistics equation. He'd looked square into the pale murderous eyes of an old dread as he leveled his rust-flecked Jennings. The thing that frightened him most was the dream. *Why* had he had that dream? The previous night, he hadn't slept in his own bedroom; he'd fallen fast asleep on the living room sofa; and as his mother left for work, waking him early, he stared up at her, feeling groggy, the icy feeling of the dream filtering back to him.

"Ma, you know what? I just had this dream that I got shot."

"Bwoy, don't talk like that. You shouldn't talk like that."

"But damn, Ma. It felt like it was *real*."

In his dream he was gunned down on Park Place, near the Franklin Avenue Shuttle. He saw himself as if from above, wearing a baby-blue short-sleeve shirt. He couldn't see the face of the shooter, simply heard the report of automatics, then felt himself dying, felt his blood leaking out from various holes, draining out of him, making him melt like a piece of ice in the sun. Feeling himself dying, he woke up gasping for breath.

Then he fell back asleep and when he woke up it was almost noon and *Gilligan's Island* was on the TV. He was still so groggy that it took him a while to remember where he was. For a time he felt like he was back upstate in Goshen, a juvenile remanded into the custody of the state of New York. But no, he was a free man, home in his mother's apartment in Brooklyn; he was nineteen years old, getting married in two days' time. His Panamanian girlfriend Yolanda had just become pregnant with his baby; he'd agreed to marry her if she'd arrange everything for the wedding. As he was getting dressed—throwing on a white T-shirt and a Guess? jeans jacket with some AJ pants, draping his neck in his heavy Turkish rope chains—Yolanda called, reminding him that he had to take her downtown to finalize the wedding arrangements.

Before picking Yolanda up, he decided to drive down to Franklin to see what was what. He had Jazz and Markie and True riding with him in his Audi. He also had a big .357 Magnum in the glove compartment. He parked the Audi right on the corner of Franklin and Eastern Parkway. Immediately, they saw Shabazz walking toward them, being followed and hassled by a young guy on a Honda motorbike. Then Shabazz started shouting and arguing with two light-skinned twin sisters who were standing on the corner.

He got out of his Audi, slipped off his Guess? jacket and draped it on the hot hood of the car. "Yo Bazz! What's up?"

"Naw, ain't nuttin', K. This nigga tryin' to sweat me over some bullshit!"

Now the young guy with the motorbike turned to face him. He was wearing a brown-and-black leather front with a nice diamond pattern in it; he had a wary look in his eye, but still stood there muttering his threatening badman words to Shabazz.

There was no mistaking the bulge of the gun, stretching out his brown-and-black leather.

"Yo, son! What the fuck you gonna do with that gun?" K reached out to try to touch the bulge, but the young guy pulled away. "Yo, why you got a *gun,* nigga? What's the deal? You want some a us? You want some a F.A.P.?"

And with that, little Jazz ducked into the open window of the Audi, reaching into the glove compartment for the big .357.

*   *   *

"Up until that point, we coulda had the whole situation under control.* We coulda clapped this nigga right then and there. The only thing we underestimated was the old man. I had seen the old man standin' right there with his ten-speed bike in the vestibule. I knew he wasn't from Franklin but I didn't know that the old man was involved. I thought it was just the young guy and the two twin girls.

"Then my brother Craig runs across the street with his big-ass mouth. 'What! Y'all niggas got beef? What y'all niggas want? What! What!'

"Now the whole rest of the Posse, Dante and Snake and True and them, was across the street just lookin' at us. It was a school day and there was mad schoolkids just gettin' outta class down at Prospect Heights.

"Now the old man—he was an old dreadlocks man with salt-and-pepper dreads and a salt-and-pepper beard, wearin' one of them long off-white Muslim smocks—steps out of the vestibule. And the young guy in the leather front was even more scared. I looked towards the kid: 'Yo, man—dig, you besta just turn the fuck around with your gun and g'head, man. 'Cause you gonna fuck around and get your ass into some real trouble here.' Actually, I didn't want no real trouble: all I'm thinkin' is that I'm gettin' married to Yolanda in two days. I didn't need no more fuckin' beef."

As soon as he finished speaking he saw the old dreadlocked man stepping fully out of the vestibule. The dread's gaze was piercing. He showed absolutely no fear.

"Your name Knowledge Born?"

He heard his voice, echoed by his brother Craig's, answering in unison. "Yeah—why?"

"Look, son. Today you gonna get hurt," the old dread said. "No, let me rephrase that. Today, you might even *die.*"

He knew he had to lunge at the old dread now, because he could see that the old dread *definitely* had heart. But before he could even

---

*These first-person recollections come from a taped interview with K conducted on December 21, 1996.

charge, the old dread flipped up his Muslim smock, revealing the semiautomatic he had kept hidden so successfully from view. He flipped up the smock and wasted no time in firing from the hip.

BLUCK-BLUCK-BLUCK-BLUCK.

He felt the first two rounds hit him and he was thrown back like a wrestler drop-kicked in the chest. Indeed, eyewitnesses on the block later said it looked as if he'd been shot in the chest, from the angle and the force with which the bullets flung him down. In reality, the first two bullets had torn into the flesh of his hip and his side. And as he was crawling back to his feet, getting ready to run, he saw that his kid brother, Craig, was now right in the old dread's line of fire. And all he could hear was his mother's voice in his head, telling him, "Don't you never let that bwoy get hurt. *Y'hear?* Craig is my *baby!*"

So even as he was scrambling up from the ground, he couldn't move anywhere until he saw which way Craig was running. And, in that moment of hesitation, the old dread clapped him again, and again, and then he took a bullet from the young guy in brown-and-black leather who'd been blazing away at Shabazz with his pistol.

Falling, Shabazz pushed Craig out of the way, and then Shabazz took the glancing bullet in the top of his forehead. Shabazz was bleeding heavily, having already been shot in the arm and the hand. With Shabazz and Craig stumbling, running, he tried to run too. But he couldn't run. His body would not let him run. The best his legs could manage was a stiff-legged hobble, zigzagging uncontrollably into the middle of the street.

He felt the old dread coming close behind him with the gun leveled at his back—it must've been an old bullshit Jennings, he remembered thinking, because if it had been a new Tec-9 he would most definitely have been dead—and now he heard the tick-tick-turning sprockets in pursuit, the dread now mounted on his ten-speed, pedaling fast to catch him. He stumbled spastically right out into the middle of Eastern Parkway, the dread pedaling hard, dollying, weaving from side to side on the bike.

He tried one more time to get his body to run but now his body said *sorry* and he fell down flat in the middle of Eastern Parkway. When he looked up, he saw the old dread standing right on top of him. Tears were leaking down his cheeks when he screamed at the dread. "Yo, fuck it! You got it, nigga! I'm a *die!*"

The old dread glared and there were shards of ice in those pale eyes and he remembered thinking *this nigga really is the Grim Reaper come to life.* Lowering the rusty black gun, the dread tried to fire again, right into his face, but the gun was now either out of bullets or jammed. *That's a bullshit Jennings for you.* K stared up into the gun barrel, heard the old dread kiss his teeth very loudly before dollying off on the ten-speed, making his zigzagging getaway down the block.

"The thing about gettin' shot is it doesn't really hurt until the next day. The first feelin' you feel is like somethin' is in your body that's not supposed to be there, like gettin' a piece a meat caught between your teeth: real agitatin'. You have that feelin' combined with—you ever eat one of those real, real good Wint-o-Green Life Savers and then breathed in, sucked up air, felt that icy mint sensation on your tongue? That's how your body feels in the place you got shot, all cool, like winter air is whistlin' through you."

He had been shot four times, picked up three 9-mm bullets from the dreadlocks's gun, and then another .32 slug from the young guy in the brown-and-black leather front. He was feeling that icy-yet-burning feeling in his hip, upper side, lower stomach and lower back. The only one that had him worried was the lower stomach. He was holding that tightly with his cupped hand, but the hot blood kept bubbling out between his fingers. He started stumbling and staggering down across the Parkway, but now he was on the other side of Franklin where his enemies all lived. No one would help. Everyone he looked at just started running away.

"Oh *shit!* That nigga Knowledge Born got shot!"

Now he was remembering that dream from the morning, and he kept thinking that all his blood was going to drain out of his body—

yes, he was going to die before his twentieth birthday, before he could see his baby born, before he could slide the gold band on Yolanda's wedding finger . . . But he told his body to keep moving, just keep walking to Brooklyn Jewish, to die in the hospital or in some doorway or vestibule. Because the one thing he knew was that his mother didn't want him to die out in the street.

He could hear her voice clearly again. "Bwoy, I don't want you to die like a dawg in de street." So he kept repeating those words over and over in his mind, *At least get to the fuckin' hospital to die if you gonna die, nigga.*

He was halfway to Brooklyn Jewish on Franklin and Prospect, drenched and sticky in his own hot blood, when he spotted his brothers Pacho and Craig come running back on the scene, ready for retaliation. They spotted him just as he was about to turn the corner on Prospect and, in relief, he felt himself smiling. Then he blacked out and his brothers picked him up and carried him the rest of the way down to Brooklyn Jewish Hospital.

When he woke up he was in a bright room in Brooklyn Jewish surrounded by detectives. He'd never seen a room so deep with plainclothes beast.

"Is he all right? Is he all right?"

"K. Who did it, K? Tell us and we'll get the fucker for you."

"Who's that? That's Knowledge Bomb or Shazzam?"

Coming out of the haze, he remembered grimacing at the way the cops were intentionally fucking up their Five Percent names.

"Is he all right? Can he talk?" That was Johnson, the only black DT there.

"Knowledge, who shot you?"

"I don't know."

And he really didn't know. Only later did he learn the truth: that the old dread was some heavy-hitter from East New York. They heard rumors about him being a trained killer, some crazy fucking war hero over in Vietnam.

* * *

"I was in Brooklyn Jewish for two and a half weeks, but Shabazz stayed in Kings County a lot longer than that. I came out in the wheelchair and went and visited Bazz in Kings County. I spent two months fuckin' around in that wheelchair. I was drivin' around with that wheelchair; goin' to dances and park jams, doin' everything cripple-style.

"All Yolanda cared about was the fuckin' wedding. She came the next day to the hospital, cryin': 'We did all of that work and now we ain't gonna get married? I'll bring the minister and everything to you here in the hospital!'

" 'Naw, fuck that. I ain't gonna get married now.'

"The only thought in my mind was revenge."

Of all the stupid things to nearly die over, Shabazz later told him that the whole beef had started over a cheap silver nameplate. Shabazz had let one of the light-skinned twin sisters hold the silver nameplate and she'd given it to her man to hold—some ridiculous bullshit like that. Supposedly, the old dreadlocks was the twin girls' uncle. The twin girls had told him, "We can't start no shit with Shabazz 'cause he fucks with Knowledge Born and Knowledge Born will *tear* shit up."

"But really it was the old dread who tore shit up. You could tell the old dread was a marksman. Lyin' in the hospital bed, I kept on replayin' that shit in my head. Seein' every second of it in freeze-frame. The whole block was so crowded with kids, but every shot this muthafucka busted off hit either me or Shabazz. Every fuckin' shot.

"Do you know how hard that is—when a bunch of people are all around, runnin' and screamin'—and the gunman keeps hittin' his intended target? Muthafuckas was runnin' all around me and I was lookin' dead in the nigga's face and he just kept bustin' steady from his hip. Lookin' real calm all the time.

*"*Bluck-bluck-bluck-bluck-bluck.*

"To this day I still got fear in my heart for that old man. Whoever the fuck he is."

FIVE

flippin' script

Take ye heed every one of his neighbor, and trust ye not in
any brother; for every brother will utterly supplant, and
every neighbor will walk with slanders.
—Jeremiah 9:4

Villains. I was in London to learn about
"villains": unassuming, ruddy-faced, semiretired criminals, denizens
of a small homey pub in Notting Hill Gate, a loose-knit conglomerate
of seemingly mild-mannered Englishmen who'd spent the bulk of
their lives engaged in careers of armed robbery, hijacking, smuggling
and swindling. Never an organized "firm," like the famous Krays of
the East End or the Richardsons of South London, the villains of Notting Hill Gate had always prided themselves on their free-spiritedness
and independent-contractor status.

The most open and affable of the villains was Donald, a fiftyish
West Londoner who'd done fifteen years in prison on various
stickup and smuggling convictions. He was now a garage attendant
on a tony block in nearby Kensington. When he wasn't playing
parking lot hopscotch with the Jags and Rovers of younger men,
Donald could dream an emperor's dreams in his little dimly lit corner of the pub. After stripping off his blue overalls and scrubbing off

the knuckle grease, he would saunter through the door each night to a chorus of profane cheers, modeling his hand-tailored houndstooth blazer and a paisley silk ascot, looking more the retired banker than bank robber.

The dead giveaway with Donald—before hearing him speak, of course—was a four-inch scar that began under his left eye, like an internal teardrop, and continued its cruel beveled line down to his jaw. I'd assumed it was a knife wound. But one night after we'd been drinking together for a few weeks, Donald explained that his scar was the result of a boyhood "glassing"; back when he was seventeen, just before he'd gone into the merchant marine, some "cunt" he'd been arguing with had, without a moment's notice, shattered a pint glass in his face.

Perhaps because of this traumatic boyhood experience, Donald was a barroom iconoclast. He never drank pints like the rest of the villains. He always threw back small glasses of gin without ice. He seemed to have traded in his liver for a carburetor; no matter how much gin he consumed, perched high on his bar stool, Donald was never the slightest bit tipsy. He rolled his own lumpy cigarettes with recently smuggled duty-free Drum tobacco, smiling constantly and flirting with Irish bar girls half his age.

He was a born storyteller with a lively and self-deprecating sense of humor. He was also the most unabashed bigot I'd ever met. He murmured freely of Pakis and wogs and their conspiratorial role in the demise of his once-illustrious island nation. But Donald's greatest obsession—as a man who'd long made his living on the wrong side of the law—was how the influx of Caribbean immigrants into Great Britain had ruined the criminal trade for the English. The Jamaicans in particular had brought such an unprecedented level of violence and gunplay—especially since the advent of crack cocaine. Human life meant nothing to those people, Donald said. They'd as soon shoot you as spit on your shoe.

He never used the word *black* during his complaints. He and the villains preferred *Luke* as a general descriptive for Britain's darker populace. Was this their own creative coinage? I wondered. No, it was a bit of Cockney rhyming slang. Began with Lucozade, a barley-based sports drink popular in Great Britain and a brand name which, conveniently, rhymed with another good old-fashioned epithet—come on, you know, as in *Black as the Ace of?* "Snip off the tail, leapfrog back and, QED," said Donald, offering nothing more than a heavy-lidded wink and the none-too-graceful hand flourish befitting a scar-faced man in an elegant paisley ascot.

Yes, that was one thing Donald and the villains could justly boast about. It was still *their* manor. No Luke had ever been served so much as a half-pint of lager in this pub.

If there was a more vocal Luke hater among the villains than Donald, it was Robbie, tall and pimply and only slightly older than me. Robbie had many opinions about the Lukes of America which he had picked up from movies and videos and magazines. He considered himself quite well informed about the racial crisis in America. (Being as I was a harmless Canadian, Robbie felt he could take me into his confidence on these delicate matters.) I nodded and listened as Robbie recounted sitting at home on a Friday evening to watch that "shite" music show *The Word:* how shocking and amazing to see these hulking Lukes in New York City running around with the biggest automatic weapons known to man, some kind of .50-caliber handcannon! Had I heard of this? What hope did the white man have in a world like that? Mark these words, Robbie assured us all with a grave nod, that's what London would look like in five years' time: an occupied territory, a war zone, a city in which the rule of law had been replaced by the rule of Lukes with .50-caliber automatics.

Later that same night, under the influence of one too many pints, I decided to locate the man whose brief but controversial appearance on *The Word,* Channel Four's now-canceled pop-music-and-current-affairs program, had so shocked and terrified the pimple-faced racist. With a heavy handful of pound coins laid out in front of me, I stood in a red phone box decorated with yellow, pink and orange construction paper advertisements (stuck to the glass with a curiously gummy blue plasticene) which offered a visitor to London the chance to indulge in all manner of sexual recreation and perversion. I dialed the number in the Bronx and let it ring. It gave me my own perverse twinge, the thought of bringing his presence to the same block as a public house—filled with loudly singing red-cheeked villains—so proud of its unblemished record of never having served a glass of beer to a black man. At last the connecting hiss, and the *kerchunk* of the pound coin dropping, and drizzling night-time Notting Hill Gate was linked—via transatlantic fiber-optic handshake—to a sunny afternoon on Echo Place in the Tremont Section of the Bronx.

He began by yelling at me and laughingly telling me that I was a real piece of shit for not having called him earlier. I'd been away from New York for nearly a month. A lot had changed in that time, he explained.

What had changed? I asked.

His little man, for one thing. His little man was changing every day. He told me he was so proud of his little man. He wished I could see the way Little K was growing and learning and taking charge of the world. Not a day went by when he didn't marvel at the miracle of infancy. He held the phone close to Little K's mouth so the nine-month-old infant could gurgle in my ear. Did I hear that? That was his little man trying to bust a rhyme for me. He kissed his son's forehead and told me he loved his little man so much.

Then his tone changed. In a somber voice he said that things with his brother Toño were not looking so good. Tone had come home from prison in the months before I'd left for England. He'd been in a halfway house in Queens for a while, then he'd come to live with K and Faith on Echo Place. I'd met him at last one snowy day in the winter. Toño was nothing like I'd expected from his younger brother's many stories about him. Big Tone, as he was often called, was in fact rather small—no taller than me. He walked with a pronounced limp and spoke with a heavy Panamanian accent.

Something mysterious and horrible had happened to him during his decade-long stretch in the Clinton State Correction Facility—Toño had not seen the streets of New York for thirteen years—that was causing his body to waste away. Toño had always been muscle-bound and disproportionately strong for his height but now he was starting to lose weight and look frail. He was stumbling when he walked and his eyesight was failing and he was complaining of frequent debilitating headaches.

K was initially depressed about this; but pretty soon he began to lose patience with his brother's complaints. He thought his brother was loafing and feeling sorry for himself. But when Toño's weight loss became more obvious, sometime in February, K began screaming at his brother: *Was you fuckin' with them homos up north?* Because he thought Toño had contracted HIV in jail. Toño was adamant in his denial, but K persisted. *If you was fuckin' with them homos,* he shouted, *I don't want you even breathin' the air around my baby!*

But now, as I stood inside the phone box on a misty block in Notting Hill Gate, slipping pound coins into the slot every few minutes, he was telling me that all the tests for the HIV virus had come back negative. And it wasn't sickle-cell anemia either. For a time they had thought Toño might have the sickle-cell. The doctors still didn't know what was wrong with Toño, but the latest theory was that he had sustained some sort of violent traumatic injury to his brain stem while in prison. This was a theory that sounded plausible enough to K, it being common knowledge, he said, the way those redneck guards in Clinton liked to fuck up the black inmates for sport.

I told him that I was sorry to hear about the way Toño was deteriorating. He said he was sorry too—it pained his heart to see the once-invincible Toño hobbling around like a cripple—but what the hell could he do about it?

Then, reaching under the Atlantic Ocean with that massive malletlike fist, he whalloped my head so hard that it remained ringing for days. "Oh shit! I forgot to tell you—I'm with this new clique of real *thorough* muthafuckas. You remember me tellin' you about them Crip mutha-fuckas I got with when I was out in Cali boxing?"

What? *Crips?* Yes, I supposed, vaguely, yes.

Oh, they were in New York now, this clique of Crips. They'd formed an independent Crip set based in Harlem. He was rolling with them, and whenever they rolled, wherever they rolled, they were rolling *deep.*

Rolling deep doing *what?*

A number of creative enterprises. Lately they'd been providing se-curity services for Khallid Muhammad.

Khallid *Abdul* Muhammad? The former Nation of Islam spokesman whose anti-white and anti-Jewish ravings had been con-sidered too rabid even for Minister Louis Farrakhan? A transatlantic squelch—ghostly echoes—stuttered repetition of his prior phrase. Could I have heard this correctly? Could he really be running around New York with the man who'd recently gained national notoriety by proclaiming, in a speech—before a loudly cheering undergraduate mob at a small and heretofore-unheard-of New Jersey college—that Jews were the "bloodsuckers" of the black community, that "the old no-good Pope" was nothing but a "cracker" who should have his "dress" lifted over his head, exposing, once and for all, the criminal-ity of the Roman Catholic Church?

Yes, K said. I'd heard him right. Big old baldheaded Khallid.

Of course his involvement with Minister Muhammad was strictly a mercenary thing, K said. Surely I realized that he did not subscribe to the Nation of Islam's views on race relations. He did not believe that, like all people of my complexion, my ancestors had been eu-genically grafted by a mad black scientist named Yacub some six thousand years ago. Nor did he believe that the Jews, as Minister Far-rakhan had once opined, were responsible for the majority of the world's wickedness. If he did believe such things, how on earth could he and I remain friends?

"What kind of security services?"

"Just personal bodyguarding-type shit."

"What's in it for you?"

Studio time. He said that Khallid Muhammad was going to be arranging studio time for the Crips to record their album. Oh, so these Crips were also rappers? Yes, he assured me, they were all quite *nice* with the microphone.

But back to those security services for a minute—

Well, he said, they had escorted him to the Phil Donahue show the other day, down to Rockefeller Center, where they were forced to put the smack down on some cornball NBC security guards who did not want Khallid to enter the studio with his full entourage of admirers and supporters.

Put the smack down?

He sighed. Why was I so dense? Why did I always have such trouble following the *simplest* of stories? Khallid had asked them to accompany him to NBC Studios in Rockefeller Center, where he was scheduled to tape an appearance on the *Donahue* show. The NBC security staff tried to block their entrance, tried to tell the fiery-eyed Muslim minister that he could have only ten invited guests with him. That's when Khallid smiled, gave the cue, and the uptown Crips (along with their newfound friend) strong-armed their way past the security to occupy the elevator. Khallid had given them clear instructions: fill up the first two rows of the television studio, loudly voice their approval of his opinions and shout down those who might try to dominate—no, distort—the proceedings with their shameful lies.

Leaning against the rain-streaked glass in that little red phone box, I found myself running short of pound coins and coherent responses. Across the street now I saw Donald, trying not to let the rain spoil his houndstooth blazer and silk ascot, rushing, leaping puddles, almost prancing down the pavement like some scar-faced ballroom dancer. A cloud of confusion came down heavy as a swarm of hornets. Villains. Crips. Khallid Muhammad and Phil Donahue and lukewarm lager and boxes of smuggled tobacco. I still had more than a minute left on the phone, but I told him that my time was up. I'd have to call him when I got back to New York.

Arriving back in New York, I jumped—without even a day to decompress—from one circle of villains to the next. The first night I met the Crips they were driving around aimlessly in a white Ford van, eating pizza and drinking forty-ounce bottles of St. Ides malt liquor. There were no seats in the back of the van and we were all piled in together on the cold metal next to some enormous box speakers that were blasting the sinister organ vamp of Snoop Doggy Dogg's "Gin & Juice."

All the Crips had neatly pressed blue bandannas tucked into their back pockets and they were all wearing navy-blue-and-black clothing topped off by Chicago White Sox and Seattle Mariners ballcaps. A handful of them were originally from South Central L.A. and a handful more were New York guys who'd been recruited in. It hadn't hit the newspapers yet—it wouldn't be reported in the press for another three years—but factions of the Crips and Bloods were beginning to make serious inroads in the New York City jail system and on the streets of Harlem and Brooklyn.

K wasn't a full-fledged Crip, of course—he was considered some kind of associate—but he was nonetheless dressed all in blue and had a pressed blue bandanna tucked into the back pocket of his sagging navy blue chinos. As we drove around Manhattan, the Crips were singing along to Snoop and changing their hands into the sign of their particular set. Even K had that contorted hand sign down pat. The Crips, to this point, didn't seem to have noticed me. I was silent—I think they regarded me as a needless, but inoffensive, appendage to the big man they called K-Lōc.

We had to stop on Tenth Avenue to fill the van with gas. That's when I spoke, for the first time all night, asking to hear the full story of how K-Lōc had come to know the Crips. It began back in '90, I was told, when K had first come out to L.A. to box. He was staying in the hotel in Inglewood across from the Great Western Forum and training at the gym down on Hoover Street. Every morning his jogging route would take him down Figueroa to Manchester, then he'd run up Manchester and turn onto Hoover. Taking that route, he was forced to run right past Hoover Manor, smack in the middle of Crip hood.

He'd only been in L.A. for about a week when he set out jogging, early one morning, in his cherry-red Fila sweat suit. As he came running down Manchester, four guys pulled up in a white Impala with its top down. In a few weeks' time he would learn their names: Tariq, Malik, Spice, Deuce. In a few weeks' time they would all be cool with each other, going to parties, driving around L.A. But that morning, they were just four unsmiling faces in sunglasses and jheri-curls, slowing their Impala to a crawl, studying his cherry-red Fila sweat suit.

"Yo, where you from, mark?"*

"The fuck you mean where I'm from? I'm from *New York*."

"Naw, where you *from*, fool?"

Fortunately for K, he was jogging that morning with his trainer, Thel, who now jumped into the fray. Thel yelled: "No! no! no! He from New York—he ain't from here! He don't know nothing 'bout no colors!"

"Man, fuck these niggas!" K started to shout, but Thel drowned him out with some shouting of his own. He asked K to *please* shut the fuck up—*please*—because he knew that these Crips were not playing any games.

K kept looking at them like they were suckers, riding around in an old convertible with that played-out jheri-curl juice dripping from

---

*State your gang affiliation or neighborhood; an extremely confrontational query, unique to L.A.'s territorial gang culture, *never* used as such in New York.

their heads. He was smirking and saying to himself, *These muthafuckas can't be no real murderers.*

But later on at the gym, Thel and a heavyweight in the stable named Dangerous Dave Dixon took K aside and began to school him to the rules of life in L.A.

"Yo, dog! You can't be wearin' them loud-ass colors, dog!"

"They *will* do it to you, dog!"

"Yo, I'm from *Brooklyn*—a muthafucka ain't gonna do me *shit*."

But then in the hotel room he was watching the local L.A. news and he started seeing the way these Crips and Bloods were murdering each other, the way different sets of Crips were murdering each other. This shit was even wilder than Brooklyn. One day he saw a news report on how some Crips had discovered that an FBI agent had infiltrated their set. They not only beat the FBI agent into submission, they left him handcuffed to the steering wheel of his own car wearing nothing but his boxer shorts.

Around midnight we came to a nightclub on West 20th Street whose name had changed three or four times in the past year. I followed the Crips and K inside without waiting on line or paying any cover charge. What could the bouncers do to stop them? Three steroid-inflated goons stared at each other sheepishly: grammar school bullies overawed by the prospect of taking their first steps down high school halls.

The Crips didn't need girls in order to dance. Swaggering through the crowd, waving their arms overhead, they occupied the dance floor like German colonels in Paris. They were masters of a sideways shufflestep called the C-Walk. They called each other *cuz,* shouted *Fuck Slobs!* repeatedly—meaning, of course, their hated rivals: the Bloods—raised foaming bottles of Heineken in the air and C-Walked in a tight inward-facing circle. It seemed rather harmless, a private boys party, until the DJ began spinning the Frankie Cutlass record whose chorus had the crowd chanting "Puerto Rico! *Ho-o-o!*" After a few seconds I realized that the Crips weren't chanting "Puerto Rico! *Ho-o-o!*" They'd ad-libbed their own catchy chorus.

> *Kill the white people!*
> *Kill the white people!*

Left the Crips C-Walking, was on my way out of the club, when K caught me from behind. "Ay yo," he said. "Them niggas don't mean nothin' by that shit. They just actin' stupid." He didn't look like himself—or at least the person I thought I knew—dressed all in navy blue with a Seattle Mariners cap and that sharply pressed blue bandanna tucked in his pants. I'd only been in London for five weeks but, as he'd warned me that rainy night in the red phone box, a lot of things had changed. I went to shake his hand goodbye. He grabbed me by the forearm, pulled me to him, hugged me tight. When I got out into the cool night air of West 20th Street I had the odd feeling I might not see him again for some time.

I was wrong. It was only a few days before I saw him again. He was on television with Khallid Abdul Muhammad.* NBC was finally airing the *Donahue* episode that had been taped while I was away in Notting Hill Gate: Khallid Muhammad sitting onstage, facing his white-haired host across a small square table, smiling, wearing a collarless white dress shirt and a splendid single-breasted blazer cut from brightly colored kente cloth. When he gestured with his

---

*Born Harold Moore Vann, in Houston, Texas, Khallid Abdul Muhammad was an honor student and quarterback on Houston's Wheatley High School football team before meeting Louis Farrakhan and joining the Nation of Islam in '67. In the '70s Muhammad rose to the position of supreme captain of the Fruit of Islam and was later appointed the NOI's minister of defense and national spokesman. His career was interrupted briefly in 1987, when he was convicted in an Atlanta court of using a false Social Security number to apply for a $175,000 home mortgage loan. He was sentenced to three years in federal prison and served nine months.

hands, as he often did when speaking, the camera caught the brilliant flash of his jewelry: a large pinky ring inset with the Muslim crescent moon and star, and, on the index finger of the other hand, an even larger gold ring in the shape of an ankh, the ancient Egyptian symbol of life.

He was a handsome brown-skinned man with a cleanly shaved chin and a cleanly shaved head. For some reason—perhaps he'd expressed the same aversion K had that day at the CBS News studios— Khallid had not been properly made up or even dusted with anti-glare powder, and under the bright broadcast lights his shaved head gleamed like it had been rubbed with baby oil.

He spoke in a mellifluous preacher's cadence peppered with references to rap lyrics and the latest street slang. He had a charming smile and an uncanny ability to spout statistics and figures which bore no obvious relation to reality, but which caused his supporters—many of whom were strategically placed throughout the studio audience— to whoop loudly and clap their hands in agreement.

He wasn't easily snared. Early on Donahue tried to catch his guest off guard by playing a recent tape recording of Khallid making a breathless, seething reference to "the hook-nosed-bagel-eatin'-lox-eatin'-imposter-perpetratin'-a-fraud-Johnny-come-lately-just-crawled-out-of-the-caves-and-hills-of-Europe-wannabe Jew." Khallid skillfully sidestepped the issue of anti-Semitism, spinning quickly, counterpunching, describing himself as "one of the Holocaust's *victims*—of the *African* Holocaust." Then Donahue made a somewhat bizarre request; he urged Khallid to publicly address the families of Andrew Goodman and Michael Schwerner, "two white Jews" murdered down South during the summer of '64, while on an expressed mission of "trying to promote the civil liberties of *your* people."

KHALLID MUHAMMAD   I don't know why they were there, and *you* don't know why they were there.

PHIL DONAHUE   Really? So you're wondering whether they were there at
all for your people?

KHALLID MUHAMMAD   I'm not wondering at all about them. I'm concerned
with the suffering and the pain of the masses of black people. No one
wants to pay reparations. The Jews received over a hundred billion
dollars in reparations, and get four billion annually. A Holocaust
museum was set up for them on *this* soil for over two hundred million
dollars, and they get twenty-one million annually just for operating
expenses. But the Catholic Church, the Pope, the Jews, the Arabs,
white people in general—no one wants to pay reparations to these,
the sons and daughters of Africa. So I speak to them—I don't speak to
the families of those two *Jews*. There are too, too many of us.

The Sons of Africa he was gesturing to—the burly blue-clad men filling the first two rows of the studio, now loudly voicing their approval—were none other than K and the uptown Crips.

K was, typically, at the center of all activity. Every few minutes he
and the Crips would jump out of their chairs, cheering loudly and
throwing up that gang sign I'd seen them doing in the white Ford van.
Perhaps because he was the biggest person in the studio audience, the
cameramen seemed to be focusing on K for many of the reaction
shots. He was positioned in the middle of the front row, snapping his
gum, wearing a light blue denim short-sleeve shirt with his oversized
navy blue hunting vest on top. Faith had separated his long hair into
two puffy West Coast–style braids which were adorned with the sort
of glass bobbles normally worn by small girls. He'd grown his goatee
very long and twisted it into a bayonet-sharp point. I could tell that
he loved the contradiction of his new look: baby-girl bobbles in his
hair and satyr's beard on his chin.

Now came a few pitifully earnest questions and statements from a
contingent of Jewish war veterans who, stepping up to the microphone, stammering with rage, tried to tell Khallid Muhammad that
fifty thousand Jewish-American soldiers had lost their lives in the Sec-

ond World War fighting for the very right to freedom of speech he was now exercising. ("You make me sick to my stomach with that," Khallid angrily rebutted.)

Thanks to the clever preparatory work of K and the Crips, the debate was dominated by dreadlocked college kids and old men in kufis and dashikis and the nattily attired Fruit of Islam, all of whom invariably deferred to the program's guest as "Dr. Khallid." There was the young woman in teardrop-shaped glasses who took the microphone, fidgeting with her right earring, and asked Phil Donahue: "Why don't we talk about how the merchant Jews come into our black neighborhoods and suck the life and the money out of our neighborhoods and put it back into *their* neighborhoods?" There was the young man in a Chicago Bulls ballcap (official hologrammed NBA tag still dangling fashionably in back) who rose from his chair, called out "Peace to all the Gods and the Earths!"—the standard Five Percent Nation greeting—before pointing out that, as far as the Jewish people were concerned, "in the Bible it says that ye are of the synagogue of Satan."

Donahue kept running up the steps and wading through his audience, still trying—had he now made five separate attempts?—to force Khallid Muhammad to look into the camera and express "some love" for the families of those martyred Jews, Schwerner and Goodman. (As if the righteously angry minister would suddenly rethink his position, bow his head and humbly utter: *Yes, Phil, we are sincerely grateful for the heroism and altruism of our Jewish brothers.*) Khallid took a theatrical pause, smiling at his host's perfect straight-man delivery. "You cannot get me to look into the camera and show love for two Jews. I don't even know them. I live with *this* pain and suffering every day among our own people."

The whole spectacle was a publicity coup for Dr. Khallid, as slick and well orchestrated as any street corner three-card monte hustle.

"What's the name of this book, brother?" one young woman innocently asks.

"*The Secret Relationship Between Blacks and Jews.*"

"Okay then."

In no time, at least twenty audience members are proudly holding up their own copies of that lilac-covered tome.

I knew a little something about *The Secret Relationship Between Blacks and Jews.** In the annals of anti-Semitic slander, it was a worthy successor to *The Protocols of the Learned Elders of Zion,* that infamous czarist forgery once embraced by Henry Ford and still happily peddled by the Nation of Islam in its bookstores.

If the book lacked any semblance of reputable scholarship, it was still a wonderful prop for the NOI's shills in the audience to hold up and wave urgently over their heads, like bidding paddles at a crowded auction. Clutching copies of *The Secret Relationship,* several audience members rose to ask why, if Dr. Khallid's teachings were false, no scholar, Jewish or otherwise, would come forward to debate him or dispute his facts. Donahue might have responded that he'd be similarly hard-pressed to find a reputable anthropologist willing to sit down to debate the position of Sasquatch on the tree of human evolution, but instead he kept running through the audience mumbling the names of those two murdered civil rights workers as his only mantra.

He didn't dare venture into the front section where K and the Crips sat. Nor did they ask to take his microphone to voice their opinions. That wasn't their task for the day. Their task, as best I could determine it, was to do for Dr. Khallid what you see the Brownshirts doing in the old Weimar-era newsreel footage: growling and smirking and threatening to break the bones of anyone foolish enough to detract from the Leader's infallible aura.

---

*Compiled by an anonymous editorial staff at the NOI's "Historical Research Department," *The Secret Relationship* is 334 pages (complete with some 1,275 footnotes) of pseudo-scholarship purporting to document the "Jewish domination" of the West African slave trade, commencing in the Middle Ages and ending with the American Civil War. ("Jews have been conclusively linked to the greatest criminal endeavor ever undertaken against an entire race of people—the Black African Holocaust," reads one line in the introduction. Apparently—according to the Nation of Islam's version of history—there would be no black population in the United States, the Caribbean or Latin America today had it not been for the long-standing and nefarious schemes of European Jewry.)

Well, at least they seemed to be having fun on the goon-squad assignment. From time to time, when Donahue or one of the white audience members would walk face-first into one of Dr. Khallid's prerehearsed barbs, K and the Crips would pipe up, cupping hands to their mouths, and chant the call-and-response of the latest party anthem from down South:

Whoomp! There it is!
Whoomp! There it is!

I sat on the floor, shaking my head in disbelief: who knew that Jew-baiting could be set to such a danceable beat?

We hadn't talked since the night in the club on West 20th Street when the Crips had been chanting *Kill the white people,* words which took on a new meaning now that I'd heard them in the context of Khallid's TV appearance and all the talk of a coming racial Armageddon. (At one heated moment in the taping, a man in a light brown business suit had risen from his seat to say that "with respect to the race war, there *will* be a conflict between black and white, and I fast and pray [for] the day that God, Allah, in his good time, removes all white folks from the planet earth.")

Shortly after *Donahue* went off the air K called me at my apartment. He didn't ask me if I'd seen him on TV. He didn't have to. Why was I so out of breath? Well, no, no, no, I was just running out the door on some pressing business. But K wouldn't let me off the phone so quickly.

Been kind of busy.

That's good.

What's been going on?

Ain't nuttin'.

Yeah?

Yeah.

That's good.

Yeah.

And on it went like that another few minutes, neither of us really saying what was on our minds. Then I said, sorry, but I had something rather important to take care of, and we said goodbye.

When K called back, after dinner, he was shouting angrily in my ear. What was he so upset about? Oh, of course. He felt I was being childish. No, childish wasn't the word: I was behaving like a real little bitch. Well, he said, I could keep on behaving like a real little bitch if I wanted to. But *he* wasn't about to let the baldheaded Muslim fuck up our friendship.

It might be a little late for that, I told him.

Too late? Too fucking late?

Then he began shouting even more furiously and, for the first time that I could remember, I heard myself shouting back at him. Two phones clogged with a primal crisscrossing roar about race, hate, history, hypocrisy—and K, having the much more powerful voice, being considerably more adept at shouting, soon got the better of the battle.

What about Ed Koch? What about Howard Stern? What about all the Jews who said racist things every single day and never once took them back? But let a black man say one thing about Jews—and that's the first thing you'll hear: *Retraction! Apology!*

And?

And what about all the personal slights he'd endured in my company, all the foolish but offensive remarks he'd swallowed, biting his tongue, turning the other way? What about that time we were at that party on the rooftop in Chinatown and one of my friends, the Jewish pop music critic, had been trying to demonstrate some stupid tai-chi self-defense move using another of my friends, the Jewish entertainment attorney, as his pretend knife-wielding attacker, and the entertainment attorney, not wanting any part of the demonstration, turned to K and said: *You're the big black guy. I'm the little Jewish guy. C'mon, you be the mugger.* What about that? What about the thousands of times in his life that people—white people—Jewish people—had said things like that? Smiling the whole time, of course, because to them it was just a big fucking joke! And he wasn't supposed to say anything—no, he was just supposed to shuffle and smile, right? Supposed to swallow it, right? Swallow those words like so many tiny grains of cyanide. And sure, maybe one or two won't kill you, maybe you'll live, but the poison builds up over time, don't you think? don't you think the poison breeds its own poison? And when that poison is spit back in *your* face it stings tell the truth now it fucking stings DON'T IT?

He called me back two hours later and said he didn't want to argue with me anymore. I told him I didn't especially want to argue with him either. We were both silent for a long time. We had our TVs on the same channel, the sound of the same painfully unfunny sitcom, the same canned laughter, droning in the background on both lines. He spoke first, asking me if I wanted to know the truth about Khallid Abdul Muhammad.

"What truth?"

"The truth about him being a real piece of shit."

There were so many things to tell me that he didn't even know where to start. He'd been holding so much inside. Just the other day something had happened to one of the Crips named Malik—Malik was the guy with the long braids who'd been sitting right next to K throughout the *Donahue* taping. The other day Malik had been arrested up in Harlem on a gun charge. Malik had been one of the main guys organizing all the "security work" they were doing for Khallid so they figured they would all go down to see Khallid about Malik's situation. Tariq knew where Khallid was and they found him eating in a restaurant and approached him about raising the bail money for Malik. Khallid just calmly finished his meal—without even offering them something to eat—then his aide-de-camp reached into his pocket and pulled out a crisp five dollar bill. He handed over the five dollars and said he sincerely hoped that the young brother would keep his head up.

You believe that shit? Five bucks for his commissary* and keep his fucking head up?

And what had ever happened to the studio time the Crips had been waiting for? That was turning out to be a big pipe dream. But that was Khallid's style. He was strictly about selling pipe dreams.

He was sick of them all—Khallid, the uptown Crips. He should've listened to Faith in the first place. She'd been telling him all along that he needed to leave them alone. Be his own fucking man. Stop following the crowd. Faith said none of the Crips were even his friends. They were just using him for his wildness. They just wanted him around when it came time to flip the script.

All week long at my office, I'd heard my colleagues murmuring about Khallid Abdul Muhammad's appearance on the *Donahue* show. Nothing he'd said had been that new or surprising; it was the same old rabble-rousing invective we'd heard in his past speeches. What no one could understand was why Phil Donahue had just let him spew on like that, rarely challenging Khallid's kooky view of history or pointing out his most egregious flaws of logic. No one could understand why Donahue had allowed the show to be taped in front of an audience heavily stacked with Khallid's wildly whooping supporters, half of whom seemed to be waving copies of *The Secret Relationship Between Blacks and Jews*. No one could understand why Donahue had been so pathetic and ineffectual.

Passing the fax machine I made an offhanded comment. I said that it wasn't hard to understand why Phil Donahue had been so pathetic and ineffectual. Phil Donahue had simply been scared shitless.

Scared of what?

---

*Jailhouse account books from which an inmate must buy all his supplies: snacks, toiletries, stationery.

Then, dragged into the office of my editor-in-chief, I told the story of how Khallid's Crips had come down to Rockefeller Center and bullied their way onto the set of the *Donahue* show. Those were gang guys, I explained, Khallid's personal bodyguards, jumping up and shouting in the front row. Moments before the taping they'd just finished strong-arming the NBC security guards in order to overload the audience with Khallid's supporters. My editor-in-chief sat staring at the table in silence, spinning his fountain pen, looking bored by my information. Then, looking up, squinting, he told me that I should be sitting in the corner of his office wearing a fucking dunce cap. How could I be so myopic? Didn't I realize that I was sitting on top of a scoop? He told me to take off my dunce cap *tout de suite* and get to work writing up my scoop for that week's paper.

Flip the script. Well, he'd used the phrase himself, hadn't he? I called K at home, asked him how he felt about the idea of doing just that, turning the tables on Dr. Khallid, teaching Minister Muhammad about a *real* Secret Relationship. He sounded baffled and tired and a little annoyed by my vagueness. So I made it more clear, asked him if he wanted to be my source, cooperate in a story I was writing about how the Crips had strong-armed their way onto the *Donahue* set.

He wasn't crazy about the idea. But, he said, since I was my own man, I should follow whatever was in my own heart. If I wanted to write about all that "rougher-than-Rambo-shit," I should go ahead and write about it. Just so long as I didn't mention him by name. He saw through Khallid now, regretted ever having rolled with him, ever having bodyguarded him. But he still wouldn't want anyone to think he was a snitch.

I promised I wouldn't mention him by government name, rap moniker or any of his established criminal aliases. Then, noticing that the hour was getting late, I told him that if I was going to write the story, I would have to get off the phone and start writing. Before I could hang up, though, he said he had one last thing to ask me.

What was that?

I waited, fidgeting, flipping a gnawed No. 2 pencil in the air. K broke his silence with a string of questions. *Did I honestly think this was gonna change things? Did I honestly think this was gonna make everything right between us again? Did I honestly think that writing some fucking newspaper article about Khallid was gonna push everything back to the way it had been before?*

I hung up the phone and wrote up the small news story about how the *Donahue* audience had been stacked with a set of New York–based Crips who were doing informal security work for Khallid Abdul Muhammad; how at least one of the guys—I gave K a new Crip-style alias—who'd been there bodyguarding Khallid now felt disgruntled about the experience. Scoop? Anyone who'd been watching the program closely could have discerned the gang affiliation of all those angry young men with blue bandannas and braids, jumping up, grinning, flashing hand signs. *Steady Crippin', cuz!* Indeed, Khallid Muhammad had been publicly linked to various factions of L.A. gangs since the early '90s when he'd helped broker a truce between warring sets of Crips and Bloods.

After I'd landed the story, one of the editors at *The Forward* faxed an advance copy to an editor at *New York Newsday,* and when I awoke the next morning, Thursday, May 26, I saw that *Newsday* had mentioned the story in a gossip and media column called "Inside New York."

When the *Newsday* item hit the newsstands everything turned very hot, very fast. By that afternoon Khallid and the Crips had all seen or heard about *Newsday* and some of the Crips had called K. They were rather upset with him. Why had he stabbed Dr. Khallid in the back? Why had he turned traitor? One of the Crips said he knew why. Perhaps, cuz speculated, K had never really been down for the cause; perhaps he'd always been secretly down with the Jews. Yes, it was just like Dr. Khallid had warned them: the Other Man always schemes to *divide and conquer.*

K recounted this conversation, barking angrily in my ear. Look at the bullshit I'd dragged him into! Now he wasn't sure *what* was going to happen. It might come to war. Then again, it might not come to war. Who knew what the fuck they were scheming?

Well, he sighed, let 'em come to 219 Echo Place if they wanted some drama. He and Scobey were making their own preparations. He sat cleaning the Colt .45 on the kitchen table as he shouted at me, and then, loading up his clip, he started shouting at Faith too. *Where were the rest of his fuckin' bullets? Why could he never find all his fuckin' bullets?*

When K finished shouting at me on the phone, Crystal began shouting at me in person. She was getting fed up with all of it: Nation of Islam, Crips, Big K. She was, in fact, getting fed up with me.

She hated this taste of fear in her mouth. She'd tasted fear too many nights back in the Bronx, heard the shouting and threats and talk of violence. She did not want this feeling in her life anymore. If she'd wanted a life like this she would never have left Crotona Avenue. She could have stayed with someone like Tommy.

She kept shouting at me and I started shouting back at her and finally I left the apartment and went for a walk down the street, down to the decaying little Sephardic cemetery in the middle of the next block. A tiny sliver of land, overrun with weeds, the riotously lush neighbor to an empty graffiti-streaked parking lot. No one seemed to notice it. I'd often seen rowdy kids, drunk from a night partying at the nearby Limelight cathedral, double-parking their cars in the street and pissing through the bars of the graveyard fence. Litter cluttered the cemetery corners: a rusty abandoned rake; a single sheet of a year-old *Daily News* sports section; a soiled balled-up diaper shoved between the black wrought iron spears. Interred in those narrow centuries-old graves were members of Congregation Shearith Israel, New York's early Spanish and Portuguese Jewish synagogue, the oldest congregation in the city. I stood staring at the crooked headstones, squinting through the black bars, trying to make out their Hebrew and Spanish names in the darkness. I wasn't sure what kept drawing me back there, but whenever I walked past the old Sephardic cemetery I always felt very peaceful and alone.

When K called me again, later that night, he sounded sedate, almost sleepy, like there'd never been a problem in the first place. He was eating a very late dinner, chewing mouthfuls of Faith's baked chicken and collard greens noisily in my ear, half talking to me, half complimenting his wife on her always-up-to-par culinary skills.

"What happened?"

"It's all peace."

"Peace."

"Spoke to Khallid."

"You called him?"

"He called me."

"What'd he say?"

"Just wanted to say he ain't vexed with me or nothin'. Said, *Don't worry about it, brother. Ain't no such thing as bad publicity. You didn't do me a bit of harm.*"

I was hoping never to hear the name Khallid Abdul Muhammad again. Three days later I was working on my story about Donald and the villains in Notting Hill Gate, listening to the hours of tape-recorded interviews I'd done in that too-noisy pub. The background noise was so thick and fuzzy that I had to listen to the tapes on headphones with the volume maxed-out in order to hear anyone speaking clearly. But after a while, I was able to block out the annoying hum and could feel myself being transported back to that smokey pub: the clinking of half-empty pint glasses, Roy Orbison bleating on the jukebox, the smell of Donald's Drum tobacco and gin-soaked coughing, the wheezy laughter of Donald's latest drinking mates, a trio of South Africans supposedly in the business of fencing stolen firearms.

Then coming through the noisy tape-recorded cheer of the London pub, like fast-approaching headlights through a blizzard, I thought I heard that name again. I pulled off the headphones and ran to the TV.

No, I wasn't losing my mind. Every station I flipped to was covering the same late-breaking news story. The shooting of Khallid Abdul Muhammad.

Khallid had just finished a speaking engagement at the University of California at Riverside, some fifty-five miles east of Los Angeles; crossing the parking lot, bodyguarded by a bipartisan contingent of Crips and Bloods, he'd been approached by a lone black gunman who began firing a 9-mm handgun at close range. Khallid was wounded in the leg. Three members of his entourage were also gunned down.

The next morning's papers reported that the assailant had been identified as James Edward Bess, forty-nine, a disgruntled and defrocked Nation of Islam minister from Seattle. In the moments after the shooting, Bess was apprehended by a mob of some seventy bystanders who proceeded to badly stomp and beat him. According to eyewitness accounts at the scene, many in that mob were heard chanting, "He works for the Jews!"

SIX

mad love

the hood gave me my breath
the hood became my fam
they [f.a.p.] raised me to what I am
   and what I always will be
so to you I owe nothing
        —Big K, "Owed to My Father"

K had a tinge of madness in his eyes whenever he spoke of Dante. Dante the cunning. Dante the treacherous. Dante the second-wildest motherfucker to ever walk the cracked and blood-flecked pavement of Franklin Avenue. They'd begun their adolescent lives as partners-in-crime and ended them trying to perforate each other's bodies with .45-caliber slugs.

Of all his enemies (and by now I'd realized that there were more than a handful), K feared this Dante more than any other. While many of his rivals from the drug days were either dead or doing long jail bids, K remained terrified of Dante precisely because he had no idea where Dante was, who he was running with or what sort of nefarious illegal enterprises he was currently mixed up in.

They'd first gone to war in the summer of '85. After that, Dante and his faction stayed down in D.C. and Virginia, making money in the crack hustle, rarely returning to Brooklyn; once K and his faction set up their own drug operation down in Washington, they engaged in many a running gun battle with Dante's crew in the bombed-out ghetto streets and murderous reggae after-hours clubs of the nation's capital. By the winter of '88, Dante was reputed to have taken out a contract on K's life; and though several hit men made attempts to fill it (once in N.E. Washington, once in Virginia, once on Rutland Road in Brooklyn), K was not—as the multiple bullet holes in his torso testified—an easy target to bring down for good.

What had set off this series of internecine shootouts? The often conflicting and contradictory street legends agreed on one point: it was the murder of Little Steebo that had torn the Franklin Avenue Posse in two.

According to K, the feud had begun as just another case of gold fever, a routine dispute over a Turkish rope chain and jewel-encrusted medallion. Little Steebo had been seen flaunting the expensive rope chain on Franklin Avenue, but another young F.A.P. member named Puma came forward claiming that Steebo had stolen the chain from him. Puma, with Dante at his side, confronted Steebo on the street, demanding the chain back. To settle the beef (as all internal beefs were then settled), the entire Posse gathered up in Shabazz's mother's apartment on Eastern Parkway to hold court. There was heated arguing on both sides. Little Steebo was one of K's protégés (one of the young boosters who used to sell stolen merchandise on the Ave), and out of gratitude K had recently bought them all matching Ninja motorbikes.

Dante, meanwhile, stood arguing vehemently on behalf of fourteen-year-old Puma. Puma had always been under Dante's wing. There was no doubt that Dante was grooming Puma as his little criminal disciple. Finally, after a good deal of shouting, it was resolved: Steebo and Puma would throw joints for the chain. The fight took place on Franklin Avenue between Park Place and Prospect Place. Steebo was a stocky seventeen-year-old with more upper-body strength, hand speed and fighting experience. Not surprisingly, Steebo tore Puma up.

As Puma lay there on the concrete, bleeding from his lip and nose, they all shook their heads in admiration. Just a fourteen-year-old shorty, but he'd taken his beat-down like a man. They helped the boy to his feet. Steebo and Puma shook hands. The beef was squashed. Steebo swaggered off modeling his glittering Turkish rope.

It was later that same week that K found himself standing at a pay phone on Franklin, crying like a little bitch. The reason he was crying was that he'd just received word that his cousin Nesto had died in prison. A girl had come to see him on a visit, muling some coke for him to sell on the inside. Nesto had swallowed the balloon filled with seven grams and made it past the scrutiny of the guards, back to his cell; but then he went into sudden convulsions (the balloon having ruptured in his belly) and was dead of an overdose within minutes.

While K was learning this news, crying and cursing into the phone, he saw two shadows in his peripheral vision, little scab-mouthed Puma and shifty-eyed Dante slinking up the block dressed in matching forest-green rain suits. Even in his state of anger and dis-orientation, K could see that they were holding heat, moving as if on a murder mission. He reached out from the pay phone to clothesline Dante as they came past.

"Yo Tay! What the fuck is goin' on?"

"Ain't nuttin'. We just gotta handle this shit."

K let the receiver dangle and grabbed Dante roughly by his slip-pery rain suit. "Tay! We held fuckin' court! That shit is *squashed*. I'm telling you—don't make the youth shoot Steebo!"

"Yeah, all right!" Dante shrugged, wriggling away from K's clutches, and then he and Puma continued on foot up Franklin Avenue.

Despite the direct warning, Dante and Puma went straight up to St. Marks Place and found Steebo hanging out in front of his building. No words were exchanged. Puma reached into his rain suit, drew out his .38 and put two bullets in Steebo's brain while Dante and a half dozen other witnesses watched.

Within days Puma was arrested for the murder. He pleaded guilty to manslaughter and was sentenced as a juvenile offender. He did nearly five years in prison and, upon his release, he immediately went to work for Dante down in D.C. (By this time, Dante had established himself as one of the biggest Brooklyn drug dealers in Washington.) Within weeks of his arrival in D.C., Puma was himself murdered in a turf war with a rival Jamaican crack crew.

K always held Dante responsible for Steebo's murder; he couldn't understand how Dante could've violated the Posse's unanimous ruling that Steebo and Puma should fight for the chain. It wasn't until years later that he learned the true reason for Dante's treachery. He'd had no choice in the matter: it was the old-time Panamanians on the block who'd ordered the hit. Steebo had messed up some of their drug money and had to die for it. The beef over the gold chain was just their excuse; they would've found any pretext to kill him.

What's more, K later realized, the bad blood between him and Dante had been festering so long, it was like a hardened, throbbing boil—bound to burst eventually. They were too much alike, K and Dante, too headstrong and vain to share control of the Posse.

Dante could never have challenged K in a one-on-one fight. But he had all the old-timers in his corner. While K had spent his adolescent years locked up in the juvenile jail system, Dante had been reared right on Franklin Avenue, starting out in childhood as a mule and a worker for the block's original Panamanian drug dealers. Dante's bloodlines were wholly American, but he adopted the identity of an honorary Panamanian. The old-timers always called him Dantino, and from an early age they taught him to spit out thick Spanish slang like he'd been born down in Colón.

"Dante was always a feared muthafucka," K would later tell me. "Dante was low and slow with his shit. He was very calm and very easy, and he wouldn't let you know he was coming. Dante would wait eight, nine, ten months and then do shit to you. Me, I wouldn't wait ten fuckin' minutes.

"To be honest, I did more dirt than Dante. But Dante had a lot more credibility with them older Panamanian heads than I had. He was the only one that could talk to them. All the younger heads would give me mad props,* but the older heads was like, 'Naw, we can't fuck with that nigga K-God—he too fuckin' wild.'

"They'd only talk to me when it came time to tear shit up. They'd say: 'Yo, let's deal with K now,' but they didn't wanna deal with me if they didn't have to 'cause I was mad arrogant, I didn't give a fuck, I was ready to set it on *them* if I had to.

"Dante was more of a soldier, a team player—I'll give that to him. I was a team player, but only for my Posse. I didn't give a fuck about them old-timers 'cause they didn't really give a fuck about us. If we wasn't being their mules, if we wasn't runnin' up in spots and tearin' shit up for them, they wouldn'ta even fucked with us."

As long as I'd known K, even back when he was lean, ashy-skinned, calling himself American Dread, with those dark circles under his eyes from riding the subway all night, I'd heard him mumbling strange things about Dante. Sometimes he would speak the name, apropos nothing, as we were walking in the Village or waiting on 42nd Street to get a slice of pizza. "Fuckin' Dante, boy. Ya wanna know why Dante got all the money? Dante got all the money 'cause he stole everyone else's shit."

It was common on Franklin Avenue to hear these stories of Dante—he was at once cruel and magnanimous, revered and despised. Where was Dante today? I often wondered. No one had seen him in Brooklyn for years. There were reports that he had been murdered down in Virginia, but these were supplanted by rumors that he'd been locked up by the feds on kingpin charges.

According to K, Dante was too wily to get himself locked up; since their juvenile days, Dante had never spent a single day in jail. K

---

*Much respect.

had no doubt that his archrival was still one step ahead of the cops, that he was still getting "mad drug loot" down in D.C.

Then there were those eerie occasions when K would assume his rival's name. I'd be pressed up beside him at a hip-hop show, deep in the three A.M. head-nodding mob inside the Muse or the Lyricist Lounge, and K, meeting some guys from Brooklyn or Harlem whom he didn't fully trust, guys he thought might turn out to be potential enemies, would murmur—without a hint of self-consciousness—that they should call him Dante.

This confused me a little bit, and even though K privately told me that it had long been his habit to "put shit" on Dante (just as Dante was reported to have shot up spots in Washington, shouting, "Yeah! Tell 'em K-God did it!"), I didn't fully buy his explanation. After a time, I began to question the existence of Dante. It was easy enough to imagine Dante as just another of K's schizophrenic aliases, another of his crazy cast of criminal alter-egos.

Easy enough, that is, until K and I made our late-winter excursion to a storefront mosque in downtown Brooklyn, when the archnemesis popped up before us like a jack-in-the-box (a dreadlocked, bugeyed, karate-kicking madman), when I saw with my own eyes that Dante was not simply a figment of K's imagination.

The subway doors were snapping shut but I made a dash for it—so lost in my reading that I nearly missed my stop. I'd been book shopping at the Strand that afternoon and, riding the F train uptown, had my nose buried deep in a used copy of *The Gangs of New York*, Herbert Asbury's 1927 account of early New York gangsterism, tales of Irish and Italian and Jewish thugs organized into such colorfully named crews as the Plug Uglies, Dead Rabbits, Frog Hollows, Forty Thieves, Hudson Dusters, Bridge Twisters and Dock Rats. Names which the book's previous owner had had the annoying habit of highlighting in thick fluorescent yellow or green swabs or underlining in the jagged blue ink of an overexcited hand.

The crazily defaced pages of Asbury's text were in my mind that afternoon when I stepped out into the hazy late afternoon light of 42nd Street. I'd promised to swing by the Swatch boutique on Fifth Avenue where K was now doing work as the in-store enforcer. Swatch was his newest midtown anti-theft posting; he'd found work there a few months after quitting his job at Raspberry Sport. (*Quitting:* a rather grotesque euphemism . . . I'd been there, after all, an eyewitness to the wild dispute triggered by a snitty Russian-Jewish cashier named Tanya who'd snapped, "Mind your own business!"—K having stepped into the midst of a confrontation she was having with a loudly complaining customer who was trying to return a pair of Nikes after having obviously worn them for at least one muddy romp through Central Park—and by five minutes to six, when they were finally locking up the shop, the many months of perceived disrespect from Tanya boiled to the surface, and K was pacing and sulking and suddenly shouting, "Shmulek, ya better tell the bitch to apologize!" and when Tanya refused to apologize, K went on his rampage, knocked over all the racks of sweatshirts and jogging suits before turning, whirling, decapitating the store's computer terminal and then hurling the wire-dangling monitor across the store and square into the rib cage of dumbfounded Shmulek . . . Now *that's* how you make an exit, I remember thinking, as I watched K dashing out the glass doors of his former employer without a second thought or a single backward glance . . .)

But there was another rampage in my mind as I walked up West 42nd Street toward Fifth Avenue, one I'd been reading about in Asbury's text during my subway ride. An account of the Draft Riots of 1863, the most bloody nights of streetfighting New York City had ever seen; riding the F train I'd come to a passage about how the largely Irish mob had besieged the Colored Orphan Asylum, which had been located on Fifth Avenue between 43rd and 44th Streets, right up the block from where K now worked; how the orphanage's superintendent had managed to rescue some two hundred black children from the lynch mob by sneaking them out the back way to Madison Avenue—but finally the rioters burst through the locked doors with their hatchets and axes and killed a little black girl who'd been left behind and was trying to save herself by hiding under a bed.

I stood there on the corner of Fifth Avenue, visualizing the freckled faces and green eyes and leering mouths of the mob massing in the middle of the street, raging out of ignorance, refracting hatred, desperate to mutilate and burn the only souls lower on the social ladder than themselves. I wanted to tell K about the little black girl they'd hacked to death; I wanted to point out that the shops down the block had once been the Colored Orphan Asylum; but when I saw him out in front of the Swatch boutique, deep in a flirtation with the two young Dominican salesgirls, I lost my train of thought and soon we were gone, striding back down windy West 42nd Street, rumbling downtown on a crowded Number 2 train, final destination (he informs me only in passing): Planet Brooklyn and a place (not a time) called When Worlds Collide.

Over the grinding din of the 2 train, I asked K about his odd choice of words—*Whose* worlds were colliding? Where were we headed? Not a screening of that 1951 B-movie about a team of scientists trying to stave off the impending destruction of life on earth? He kissed his teeth long and loud; my interrogation was truly pissing him off. Leaning forward, he snatched the *Gangs of New York* from my hands; grimacing, flipping backward through the book, he stopped at the folded-back page in the chapter on the Draft Riots, studying a small illustration captioned *Hanging and Burning a Negro in Clarkson Street*. He gazed at the ugly image, then at me, looking angry enough to spit. He abruptly snapped the book shut.

When Worlds Collide, he explained at last, was a mosque on Flatbush Avenue in downtown Brooklyn. When Worlds Collide was where True was waiting to meet us.

"True?"

"You don't remember hearin' 'bout True?"

True . . . I thought . . . Yes, from the story about the Sucrets can filled with cocaine that had gone missing from under the Space Invaders machine inside Pop's pizzeria on Franklin. True had been the one patrolling down the lineup with his gun, the one who had threatened to shoot K in the face, saying, *This ain't personal, muthafucka—this is beeznisss . . .*

It was growing dark and lightly drizzling when we reached Brooklyn. I'd never walked this stretch of Flatbush Avenue before; I noticed that a crew of city workers had spray-painted a series of yellow arrows and hieroglyphs on the sidewalk, as if laying down a secret trail for us to decipher as we traveled. Judging from the sign hanging over the Flatbush Avenue entrance, When Worlds Collide was a storefront community center that doubled as the office for a company called X-Men Security. We entered the little lobby, sidestepping three young kids in oversized karate robes. K didn't utter the name True; he asked the young grim-faced bow-tie-wearing gentleman at the door to locate a certain Brother Terrence for him.

"Don't never call him *Terrence* to his face," K privately advised me while we waited. "Always call him True. True's mad sensitive about his government name."

After a brief wait, Brother (True) Terrence came barefoot to the door, looking like a diminutive Ninja in his all-black martial arts outfit. He had a thick black mustache and heavy hooded eyes. He spoke slowly and deliberately, carrying himself in a gentle, childlike manner that I couldn't reconcile with the descriptions I'd heard of him as one of the Posse's most vicious and indomitable streetfighters. He shook my hand soul-style and hugged me close to his chest.

Standing there in the small lobby, inhaling the too-sweet scent of Blue Nile incense hovering around True, I glanced at the stacks of *The Final Call* newspaper and the pictures of Farrakhan and Elijah Muhammad on the walls and the stream of young boys in their karate outfits coming out of the hall snacking on cellophane-wrapped bean pies and I suddenly realized—why hadn't it occurred to me earlier?—

that I was setting foot for the first time inside a Nation of Islam mosque.

K caught the discomfort in my eyes. "What's up?"

"You sure about this?"

"What?"

"You sure this is cool?"

"Why not?" he announced with a theatrical boom in his voice, and then—considering all that had happened with Khallid and the Crips—he decided to let True in on our little secret. Leaning in close, muttering in his clenched-teeth brand of pig Latin, he said: "Dig, you know he a Oojay, right?"

"Word?" True said, glancing at me in confusion. "I thought he was a *German*. It's cool, dun . . . ain't got no problem with that . . ."

This exchange left me even more discomfited and confused. Much later that night, walking back down Flatbush Avenue with K, I asked why True had referred to me as a German.

"Puerto Rican. He thought you was Puerto Rican."

"So why'd he say German?"

"You be *killin'* me with them muthafuckin' questions, know that?" He let out a heavy exhale which then down-shifted into a long low whistle. He was overtired and hungry and I didn't risk asking him anything more. He watched me walking beside him and his impatience gradually dissipated; he wrapped his arm tight around my shoulder as we jaywalked through the Flatbush traffic. *German* was just Rikers Island slang, he said. It was the way black inmates referred to the Puerto Ricans. The blacks and Boricuas were often at war with each other on the Island, so the brothers referred to the Puerto Ricans as an enemy nation: Germans.

"Why German, though?" I persisted.

He started shaking his head and muttering to himself: "Princeton, right? Now I know they don't be givin' out them Ivy League diplomas to complete fuckin' retards . . ."

"Forget I said anything."

"Read between the lines, muthafucka! Shit! You ain't never seen a fuckin' World War II movie? *The Dirty Dozen? Guns of Navarone?* Who's fightin' who? It's us against them—the good guys versus the Germans."

German or Jew (or simply white devil), I found myself deep in the belly of a black Muslim mosque, surrounded by hissing steam pipes and high-cheeked schoolchildren hunched over Maya Angelou homework assignments and off-duty Fruit of Islam security guards striding around tall and bold as Masai warriors. True had us camped in a semicircle of square wooden armchairs on the little stage in the main hall of the mosque. At first it was only K and True and another guy from Franklin Avenue—never a full-fledged Posse member, I was informed, just a hanger-on—whom K and True referred to as Fartbreath. Fartbreath was a small, unassuming Muslim guy in thick glasses who never raised his voice above a whisper and who had (at least from where I was sitting) no discernible problem with halitosis; he seemed intelligent, well spoken—someone who preferred reading encyclopedia entries to hanging out with ruffians. Fartbreath, Fartbreath, Fartbreath—I couldn't understand why he sat there allowing himself to be abused that way . . . had he shut his ears to the incessant teasing? had he been answering to Fartbreath his whole life?

Now a beautiful little girl in a pink parka pranced on the stage. This was True's daughter, Medina, batting her large bright eyes, begging her father if she could please please *please* eat some jujubes outside with Lashonda and Kenya and Toni. True sternly told Medina that she could not have jujubes because, he explained, those little bright-colored candies, innocent-seeming though they were, contained a filthy gelatinous substance extracted from the fibrous connective tissues of swine.

"And what we learned from Sister Kallilah?"

"The swine is the devil of the animal kingdom," singsonged Medina.

I ruminated on this exchange for a while, wondering if True's information was accurate, if millions of Muslims and Jews worldwide were unwittingly breaking their rigid dietary laws by indulging in handfuls of chewy candies contaminated by hidden pork by-products. Medina accepted her father's admonishing kiss on the forehead and then, sticking her tongue out rudely at Fartbreath, she ran off to play with her candy-chomping girlfriends.

Enough with the fun and games, True announced with a loud handclap and a batlike flourish of his black karate robe. Yes, K agreed. Down to *beeznisss*. What business? I wondered. It soon became apparent; the purpose of this meeting was the upcoming talent show True was promoting here in When Worlds Collide. He'd recently got the green light from his superiors in the mosque to start hosting a talent show the first Wednesday of every month. Each show would feature up-and-coming hip-hop acts and R&B singers and African dancers and raunchy stand-up comedians from all over Brooklyn. The profits wouldn't be great at first; it was more important to build word-of-mouth, most Brooklynites being prejudiced against their own borough, True claimed, convinced that you could only party properly (and safely) uptown. Since he had the use of the hall for free, since the X-Men could provide the security for free, he'd make most of his money selling beer at the show, and could get away sticking people for a mere five-dollar cover.

Selling alcohol in a *mosque?* I wondered aloud, but True, so adamant in his opposition to swine-contaminated sweets, brushed aside my objection with a libertine laugh. (Later, when I asked K about this seeming hypocrisy, he stared at me, solemn-eyed, annoyed by the smugness he detected at the corners of my mouth. He had only one question to ask me—"Doug, are *you* a good Jew?" I thought it over, trying to interpret those words in any number of ways, trying to deny his obvious meaning. Where were the Laws of Moses in my life? I'd had no bar mitzvah; there was no miniature scroll of the ancient *Sh'ma Yisroel* tacked diagonally in my parents' doorway; as a kid, the only dietary ritual my family observed was my mother's feast of crisp

Canadian bacon and scrambled eggs stirred up every Sunday morning. No, I told K. I was no one's idea of a *good* Jew. "All right then," he said with a satisfied nod.)

True had big plans for his monthly talent shows and, as he began to outline them for us, his deep voice droned in a hypnotic monotone. My thoughts drifted away on an arcane tangent, listening to the headphone-bleeding of Mary J. Blige somewhere nearby, a disturbing image settling in my mind like a thunderhead . . . Could it be true, as Fartbreath had casually mentioned moments earlier, that pouring a can of Coca-Cola on a raw pork chop would, after a time, cause hundreds of tiny worms to wriggle out of their hiding places in the vile hog meat? If so, *who* had arrived at this loathsome discovery? I imagined a team of Chicago-based Nation of Islam scientists, in lab coats and bow ties, standing patiently over their slabs of foaming swine flesh, taking meticulous notes as they tipped out the dripping contents of their cola cans and waited for the wriggling hordes of vermin . . . I heard my name being intoned by True now and, as everyone turned to stare at me, refocusing my thoughts, I learned that my services had been volunteered (by K, of course) as the perfect person to design the talent show flyer on my personal computer. True had access to a computer but no idea how to use it. He was not, he explained with an embarrassed cough, fully up to speed in the computer literacy department. A tutorial? Well, sure, I supposed I *could* give him a brief lesson in using WordPerfect sometime . . . his thick eyebrows drooping in disappointment when I confessed that I really didn't know the first thing about designing spreadsheets and alphabetized databases for mailing lists . . .

Before I could get sucked too deeply into True's party-planning vortex, I excused myself from the semicircle and left them murmuring excitedly about the First Official True-Allah Productions Talent Show Extravaganza, at which American Dread would be the featured performer and the entire Franklin Avenue Posse would be reunited and in *full effect* for the first time in years . . .

Venturing downstairs to locate the bathroom, I passed through the lower-level gymnasium and watched a class of various-aged boys engaged in their after-school martial arts training. The instructor had them doing brutal sets of knuckle-push-ups; even the littlest ones weren't flinching, merely grunting and bravely chanting out the count in perfect unison. Dozens of little shining eyes trained on me like searchlights as I passed. It frightened me to realize that any one of these grade school fighters could, on a whim, render me unconscious with one swift roundhouse kick to the temple. In the bathroom, zipping up my fly, I came under the surveillance of an obese nine-year-old straggler, rushing to join his training companions, huffing asthmatically as he kicked off his banged-up Air Jordans, round belly taxing his brown karate belt to its limit; he studied me suspiciously as I stood at the sink, sizing me up for combat, and in my state of gnawing paranoia I began to wonder how I would explain to K and True and Fartbreath that, no, actually, I hadn't *fallen* down the stairs, a fat little fourth-grader had karate-chopped me into submission in the mosque's men's room . . .

We returned to the mosque later in the week to let True inspect the mock-up of the flyer. He scanned it, nodding and humming, said that he'd have to make some late additions—more acts wanted to perform on the bill. There was a group called Da Hardroxxx from Washington Avenue and another group called the Bushmasterz from East Flatbush and a couple of Crime Heights comedians like J.D. and Mighty who wanted to get up and do their stand-up routines. True jotted these names on the back of the flyer in his florid left-handed script. Behind us, K stood doing a freestyle rap which had True and Fartbreath nodding their heads in unison. The rapping stopped suddenly and when I glanced back at K, his eyes had gone hazy, that familiar film of madness settling in place again.

"Oh *shit!* Tay! I *know* that ain't you, nigga!"

A compact white blur leapt suddenly onstage, bobbing and gyrat-

ing with the boundless energy of a genie just released from his lamp.
A knotted stocky body swimming inside oversized white karate robes.
K stood shouting the name over and over. So this was the treacherous
one? The most-feared enemy? His powerful bobbing shoulder
brushed against mine; I studied the tight cluster of Cantonese characters, tattooed in bluish black ink, which formed a menacing down-
turned dagger on the smooth meaty trunk of his neck. On his head he
wore a knitted Rastafarian tam packed tight with the compressed mass
of his dreadlocks; as he bounced the tam drooped down past his
shoulders like a soggy gray mushroom.

"My nigga!" called K.

"*My* nigga!" came the smokey baritone response.

Hollering, they clenched each other, swinging around the stage in
a crazed sumo wrestlers' waltz. And when that long clench finally
eased K kept pronouncing, softly at first, then at greater volume:
"Word, I got *mad* love for this nigga! Fuck what ya heard—I got *mad*
love!" True and Fartbreath were gaping at each other, slackjawed;
never in their wildest dreams had they thought they'd see the feud
come to such a happy conclusion; for years, everyone had been assuming that the next time the two rivals came face-to-face, they'd let
their automatic pistols do all the talking.

I was most confused by the sight of all this tough-guy hugging. How
could two sworn enemies greet each other with such unabashed tenderness? Was this some bizarre con game—the lull before the storm—
or were badboy bygones really badboy bygones? Nine years of
animosity and gunplay instantly forgiven—if not forgotten? Well, I reflected, hadn't Malcolm X, after his release from prison, returned to
seek out his old enemy West Indian Archie, found Archie, once one
of Dutch Schultz's feared strong-arm men, wasting away in a rented
room in the Bronx, barefoot, wearing rumpled pajamas—and there
they stood, the two former hustlers who'd come so close to murdering each other, gunning each other down over a disputed $300 pay-
off, the now "righteous" Minister Malcolm (no longer known as Red)

wanting nothing more than a cleaning of the slate with his old numbers-running foe?

Perhaps it was the same with Big K and Dante here in When Worlds Collide; all the malicious street rumors and hateful invective swallowed up—washed clean—in the vastness of the Brooklyn night . . . K and Dante still hugging each other like opposing quarter-backs after a hard-fought Rose Bowl, intoning each other's names with an intensity that bordered on disbelief.

Hours later, I studied the flicker in K's eyes as he conversed with this boyhood rival, eyes wide with the possibilities of a reborn friend-ship. There was so much ground to cover, so many stories to recount, so many plans and schemes to run past each other. K blurted out an impulsive notion—incorporate Dante into his rap stage show. Word, why the fuck not? Wouldn't Dante make a dope hype man? Every rap-per needs a sidekick onstage with him, K maintained, someone to shout the ad-libs, punctuate the choruses, get the heads bobbing and the arms waving—and *who* in the whole of Brooklyn would make a better hype man than crazy-ass Dante?

Dante stood mute, expressionless, scratching his goatee, running one wizened and darkly creased finger along the line of his shimmer-ing gold chain.

"Just me and you, nigga?"

"Naw, Just and Life gon' be up there with us."

"Justice? Stop frontin'!" Dante's frown curled slowly upward and opened into a broad smile. "Word, I ain't seen that nigga in *uhdeen* . . . since we was all down in D.C., right?"

Dante was fidgety, stroking his bearded chin, glancing furtively at his Rolex, fingering his neck chain. He rubbed his nose vigorously with the flat of his palm, trying to alleviate, or provoke, the nagging torment of a long-threatening sneeze. *Mmmmmm . . . hype man.* He sampled those words on his tongue as if slipping on a new pair of lizard-skin loafers. Then in a whirling feline flash he pulled off his tam and let his thick dreadlocks spill out in a wild gorgon's mane. He piv-oted around the stage in his bare feet, executing his crisp snapping karate kicks, stirring up wind currents with his calloused heel, stopping just short of my unprotected chin. The guy was coming unhinged, I thought, and I banished myself to a seat in the corner. K stood egging Dante on, cheering every lunatic leap and kick—but I doubted that, when the night of the talent show came, he could coax Dante into repeating such a hyperkinetic performance onstage.

He was still a drug dealer and lived by the drug dealer's oft-cited credo: *If it don't make dollars it don't make sense.* For Dante, I'd come to learn, these days in the mosque were just his laying-low period, free time, a chance to hone his karate skills and read the Qur'an and catch a brief vacation from the rigors of the crack game. He was on the lam: wanted for questioning in the District of Columbia and in several states south of the Mason-Dixon. He'd crept back into Brooklyn one night—an invisible man. But the moment he got word from his lieutenants, Dante would race down South again to oversee his lucrative hustler's empire.

"C'mon, break the glass, nigga! Think you got skills now? Sheeeit, you ain't got nuttin' for me, Tay! *What!* You ain't said a muthafuckin' thing!"

I watched the two former enemies playfully sparring, fifty-two hand-blocking, K parrying Dante's fists with his loglike forearms and cupped hands. "Yo, dun—" True approached me now, leaning in close, forcing me to smell again that heavy Blue Nile incense which had permeated all his clothes and seemed to cling to him like an overripe cloud. "Tell the truth, dun—ain't it some crazy shit to see them two niggas puttin' they heads together? Word 'em up, dun, that's some *dangerous* shit . . . some atomic *fusion*-type shit . . ."

The tracks K was planning to rap to had been prepared by another pair of white devils, a couple of long-haired New Jersey rock musicians named Nick and Rob. K had been traveling out to their basement home studio in Hoboken for weeks now, at first skeptical about whether two AC-DC–loving rockers from Jersey could capture the urban crackle of hip-hop; but over the weeks their sessions in that basement on Bloomfield Street began to gel; and K was soon telling me, as we rode the PATH train together to Hoboken, that Nob—his time-saving amalgam for the production team—were the first guys, black or white, who'd been able to translate the sounds he heard in his head into music.

They'd recorded a sinister-sounding track called "Have You Ever Been to Hell and Back?"—an account of one of the times K had been gunned down and felt himself dying, slipping away on the gurney as he was wheeled into the Kings County emergency room. They also recorded "Born Loser," his dark, depressing autobiographical lyric set to an incongruously bouncy R&B beat, a girlish Michael Jackson sample punctuating every chorus; and "Don Baron," a frenetic romp which opened with the echoing sound of K hollering the Franklin Avenue Posse's signature battle cry:

The Mountain Men are all he-e-e-ere!

The week before the show we stayed all night in Hoboken with Rob and Nick and an engineer named Scott, editing the instrumental versions of the songs on Scott's Mac. We made sure we had two clean tapes for the show, and two more just in case of an emergency. I took all the instrumental tapes home with me, K having decided that the safekeeping of the show tapes would be my sole responsibility.

"Check, *check!* Yo, True, gimme some more volume up in this piece!" K was pacing the stage in When Worlds Collide, tapping two fingers noisily on the mesh of the Shure microphone. True adjusted the levels on the mixer, K nodded, and I hit the play button on the tape deck. The synthesized backing track began its sinister gallop and K, walking the stage with the mike pressed to his month, unfolded his intense saga of being gunned down and nearly bleeding to death—one minute he's in the Kings County emergency ward and the next he's in hell, assigned a shovel and a hard hat, has to work seven days a week for no paycheck and eat "murderer's stew" and sleep on the jagged bones of murder victims—and when he finally can't take it anymore he tells two of Lucifer's underlings they'd better take him to see the big dog himself—

—down this hallway, the door it was hot on touch; stench caught my nose as I prepared for the bumrush. These two nigs, if we was on the street, woulda got they fuckin' caps peeled, 'cuz I can't be beat. Looky here— "ENTER! ENTER!"—*the room full of flames, in this bottomless pit laid niggas' souls and they names. With his back turned, chair blockin' my view, You-know-who had my records in front of him—and my case on review.*

"Picture this, punk-bitch!" I says to him with a hiss. "You besta free me up outta this bitch—or shit's gon' get thick!"

With a puff of smoke, flash of light, he appeared: half man, half beast: it was that nigga with the beard.

Says he: "My name's Sam, son of ram, from the damned—ain't no nig ever dis me—I don't think a mere mortal can! Step to me with that five-and-dime bullshit! I'm a pack and a half, punk-bitch, and you's a loose cigarette!

"I'm disguise: pullin' wool over eyes—when a nig murders a nig, I'm the cause and the alibi. State ya claim, Mr. K, start spittin' game and if ya shit's not wack, I'll send you back from whence you came."

As I start to, like, flippin' and flowin', this punk-bitch grabbed his head 'cuz my shit was mind-blowin'; start to spittin'—nig jumped all on my rod; his flunkies dropped to they knees and started screaming 'bout they praisin' God. Shots of light burst through from every angle as I commence to rip shit, leavin' shit bent up and mangled.

"It's all good, nig—all's fair in love and war—"

I left that place: they'll never see me anymore . . .

With K free from Satan's clutches, with True's sound check successfully completed, the far-flung members of the Franklin Avenue Posse began to congregate in the hall of the mosque. I spotted Life and Justice, the pair of powerhouse brothers whom K had lately recruited to be his security team; neither one as tall as K, but as densely mus-cled, bull-necked, broad across the back, with neatly trimmed goatees and single gold-tooth caps, sporting the clean, pressed camouflage fa-tigues and spotless leather work boots that were the requisite uniform of the '90s Brooklyn badboy. There was bearded DJ Buggs, confined to a wheelchair these last few years owing to his Uzi-induced status as a quadriplegic, wheeling himself around the party, smoking Newports and somehow dancing gracefully in his rolling chair. Others I'd met briefly, nodding to them in passing: Daquan, Black Todd, Shatique, Nitti-Don, Barry Dread, Jah-Know, Sticks. Here came Melquan and Flaco and Junior and Junebug. Then Shammgod, unkempt and un-washed, with the hollowed-out cheeks and yellowed teeth of a crack-fiend—which, reportedly, he had once again become, much to K's chagrin and embarrassment.

There were cold bottles of Heineken that True was selling for three bucks apiece; forty-ounce bottles of malt liquor smuggled in from the outside in brown paper bags; there were even a few blunts being rolled and smoked right there in the hall of the mosque.

I sat on the edge of the stage, sipping my Heineken, eavesdrop-ping on several conversations at once, listening to the laughter and hooting and barking of Posse war stories, the Ave's most memorable shootouts and throwdowns and knockout punches—by consensus, it seemed, everyone's favorite knockout being the time K hit Fuquan so clean that Fuquan flew out of his sneakers. I closed my eyes and could see K and Fuquan squaring up on the corner of Franklin and Union, K taunting him ("Good night, Fu! Good night!") before exploding with that right-uppercut, left-hook combination, Fuquan soaring back, back, back, landing on the sidewalk unconscious, a full six feet away from his unlaced green-and-white Pumas.

By the time the show got started—with a sulky performance by the crew called Da Hardroxxx—many of the audience members had downed one too many bottles of True's ice-cold Heineken. From my vantage point in back of the hall a zooish cacophony kept drowning out the sound onstage. Of the fifty-odd bodies in the seats I figured only half had paid the cover charge—all the Posse members were getting in free, after all—but True still seemed pleased as he sauntered around the mosque, shaking hands and calculating the night's take in his head.

Behind me, in the little lobby, K pierced my eardrum with his sudden holler: "Jeffrey G in the muthafuckin' hizzouse!"

Jeff's was the second white face to appear in the mosque that night—I was frankly glad for his devilish company in this home of Original Men. He stood grimacing in the doorway, arms raised in a crucifixion pose; while he was being frisked by a pair of the X-Men, Fartbreath and another security guy were rifling through the black vinyl computer bag he used as a briefcase.

"What? No body cavity check?"

But even Jeffrey Goldberg could not make the X-Men smile. K gave him a long handshake and hug, turning, introducing him to Dante as that "wicked-ass journalist that did that Desert Eagle joint I was tellin' you 'bout."

Dante stared hard at Jeff, sniffing up his nose.

"Smell like Babylon," he said.

"What?" Jeff said, looking to me and K for translation.

"You a fuckin' cop?" Dante sniffed.

"I'm not a cop," Jeff said.

K vouched for Jeff's journalistic credentials again and Dante nodded uneasily. But for several more minutes the compactly muscled, tam-wearing hustler kept muttering his half-intelligible remarks about Jeff—saying that he looked just like some Nosey MacFuckerson, that burly Irish detective who'd been asking too many questions down in Maryland last month.

I'd hoped that the comedy phase of the talent show might lighten the sour, unruly atmosphere brewing inside the mosque—but then I saw

Faith coming back into the lobby looking very upset, telling K he'd better hurry up and do something; the situation in the hall was getting out of control.

"The fuck you talkin' 'bout, boo?"

She said that she and her friends didn't feel like sitting there and being disrespected by that drunken fool onstage.

We all looked into the hall to see the skinny guy called Mighty roaming the stage. He was naked from the waist up, striding off balance, kissing the mike loudly and murmuring in a boozy slur. There was a screech of feedback and when I looked down I saw that Mighty's fly was open, thumb and forefinger pinching his dark brown hose, waving it and making it talk like a profane squeaky-voiced hand puppet. At least two of the women in the audience—the Dominican sales girls from the Swatch store on Fifth Avenue—rose from their seats, grabbing their leather jackets and purses, angrily telling K that they'd had enough of this nonsense: they were jetting back to Queens.

"Good luck, papi—see you at the shop, right?"

Kiss-kiss on both cheeks, K mumbling a distracted goodbye, then staring hard at Mighty, the rage in his eyes burning white hot. Big Life stood at his flank, trying to reign in the impending violence. "Naw, duke, let that muthafucka g'head with his punk ass . . ."

K turned to me and snapped: "You got them tapes ready, D? We gotta do this shit *now*."

He wasn't scheduled to go on for another hour. Two other hip-hop groups were waiting to perform first. But he was afraid that with Mighty acting the fool onstage, there wouldn't be anyone left in the mosque in a few minutes.

True ran forward in a version of the Groucho crouch, waving his arms and chasing Mighty off the stage. Mighty wouldn't let go of the Shure microphone, and as they wrestled for it, the would-be comedian's baggy jeans and striped boxer shorts fell unceremoniously to his ankles. For a long moment Mighty stood there with outstretched arms, a tall naked idiot, soaking up the hoots and cheers of his boys as if he'd just broken a long run down the sidelines for the go-ahead touchdown.

I told K I would give him a hand signal when I got a level on the monitor; but when I put the first instrumental tape in the tape deck, the only sound I could get was a thick fuzzy hum. Strange. The level in the headphones was fine, but whoever'd set the mixer up for the comedians had repatched the cables in back and we couldn't get any sound from the deck.

True and Fartbreath stood over me, trying to offer assistance, flicking random buttons on the mixer, confusing the situation even more; suddenly I heard a *woof-woof-woofing* and looked up to see Life and Justice and K coming down the aisle doing their grim-faced stomp.

Leaping onstage, K grabbed the microphone, Life and Justice pacing just behind him, set for a hip-hop battle royal. Still no sound from the deck. The soundless delay got longer and longer, the impatient shouting louder and louder, catcalls from the Posse raining in heavy Crime Heights patois—"Paloff, rudeboy, paloff!"—and at last K turned to me with a hiss:

"*Yo!* What the fuck is the *problem?* Hit that muthafucka!"

But I couldn't hit it because we still couldn't squeeze anything more than a pitiful buzz from the mixer.

They'd stopped pacing the stage like caged panthers. K threw the mike down with a disgusted growl and then stormed off the stage, followed by his fatigue-clad security force. I spent a few more minutes with True and Fartbreath trying to rewire the sound system—but with the departure of K and Life and Justice, the audience began to disperse, disgruntled and disorderly, making their way back to the lobby.

The party was dead and there would be no reviving it. I left True and Fartbreath still trying to jump-start the mixer, came up to the lobby to find K, ready to mumble some excuse about our abysmal failure. The lobby was cramped and ugly. People were filing out the doors, K leaning against the wall doing a slow burn, still flanked by Life and Justice.

From where I stood I could overhear some of Da Hardroxxx and the Washington Avenue mob making disparaging remarks as they milled around by the exit. I wasn't sure if K could hear them clearly, humming about the Franklin Avenue Posse, about True's bogus-ass show, about how everyone should get their admission money back.

I heard one loud voice—drunken Mighty—rising above the murmur:

"They prawbly wanted the money to smoke some fuckin' crack . . . all them F.A. niggas is muhfuckin' crackheads . . ."

With that K burst from the wall like a flaring bottle rocket. He'd been frozen in his statuesque pose, brooding, glaring off into space as if lost in the maze of his own angry thoughts; but now I saw that the blank stare had masked his intense concentration—his mind filtering out all the extraneous background noise and homing in on the words of Mighty and the Washington Avenue mob.

"The fuck you just said, nigga?"

As he was lunging at Mighty I caught the chrome flash of Scobey clutched tight in his hand, cocked and leveled; and everyone else must've glimpsed the massive Colt .45 because a simultaneous gasp of panic echoed in the lobby and dozens of confused bodies began pushing and ducking and fleeing through the glass doors.

Justice and Life didn't flee; legs planted wide, they threw themselves in front of K in a cold immovable wall of muscle. "Not in the *mosque*, nigga!" Life was shouting, grabbing at the gun arm with both hands, icy and impassive, like he'd done this a thousand times before. He put all his upper-body strength into keeping K from raising his pistol, and for the first time I realized how powerful Life really was, watching him muscle the furiously shaking gun arm gradually down; and there was his brother Justice standing chest to chest with K, veins and sinews bulging from his chocolate neck, grunting, "Not in the *mosque!*" over and over as he held on tight to K's furiously quivering left arm.

And then in the corner of my eye I saw crazy Dante shooting past me—had he sprung up from some hidden trapdoor in the floor of the mosque?—his karate robes spreading and flapping like white angel's wings. And in a stutter-stepped blur I saw that Dante had his gun drawn too, the sheenless blue-black plastic of a Glock .9, a gold-toothed smile splitting his face like a dark gash—dark glee indicating that he was ready, more than ready, to start blazing: *whoever, whatever, whenever.*

Where was Jeff? What had happened to Jeff? I'd momentarily lost sight of his shock of dirty-blond hair and his dark blue cloth windbreaker and wondered if he'd managed to flee outside into the street . . . but no, there in the frantic every-man-for-himself turmoil I spotted a sliver of his pink clean-shaven cheek again and then his pale blue eyes searching frantically for mine and when our glances met finally it was unmistakable—the long-distance handshake, the moment of tribal solidarity, as if, through it all, we'd sealed our silent pact, each acknowledging responsibility for the other's safety. Couldn't ask for a better guardian, I thought—a guy who'd volunteered for combat duty in the Israeli army, patrolled the rock-raining chaos of the West Bank with a stony grimace on his face and a jet-black Uzi on his shoulder.

But at present Jeff was no slate-eyed IDF vet, glancing back in confusion, lips parted soundlessly . . . and I could feel my own mouth dumbly gaping and the blood draining from my face like murky water whirlpooling out of a lukewarm bath. Turning, sidestepping, we careered toward each other through the confused crush of bodies, standing arm to arm, a pair of misplaced pillars in the midst of the Philistines' fray. I could feel the warmth of Jeff's breathing next to me and heard myself breathing out a sigh of relief and contrition—until that night, until that very second, I suspected, we'd both secretly disliked each other . . .

Through the stampede now I saw the Washington Avenue mob ducking out into the street, then K rushing outside with Faith right at his side. In the midst of the commotion I heard a loud plastic crunch and looked down to see the inexpensive Walkman I'd given K for his last birthday falling to the floor, flipping and skittering and cracking as it was crushed underfoot.

Out in the street the commotion surged in separate streams, dividing into two camps, inching further apart down the sidewalk of Flatbush Avenue.

And then: silence.

Jeff and I were alone.

Where?

WHENWORLDSCOLLIDE

My arms were pinned to my side as if I'd been mummified in duct tape. A warm drip hit me—my own piss trickling down my right leg? In my immobile trance I scanned the glass display case beside me with its pictures of a charming beaming smiling Louis Farrakhan and neatly stacked copies of this week's *Final Call* and crookedly stacked copies of *Message to the Blackman* and *The Secret Relationship Between Blacks and Jews* and, yes, of course, *The Protocols of the Learned Elders of Zion*. I felt the heat of the young Zionist breathing beside me and, looking into his pale blue eyes, searching behind the confusion, I could already hear him constructing the trapped-behind-enemy-lines wisecracks to lob at me like live grenades, later, much later, when we were alone in the safe haven of the little Jewish newspaper.

Still no gunfire sounding outside. The only noise was the sporadic late-night traffic on Flatbush, whooshing and wheezing like a chorus of muffled laughter. Something told me that the thin gauze of laughter would soon be punctured by the echoing reports of automatic weapons.

"What the fuck are you doing *now?*" Jeff followed me back into the empty hall. A disaster for poor Brother Terrence. Chairs kicked over. Empty bottles of Heineken and St. Ides malt liquor scattered like bowling pins on the puddled floor.

I went back to the abandoned mixer to retrieve the instrumental tapes I'd left behind. The cases were lost; one was crushed on the ground. I snatched up the labeled Maxells and threw them in the crumpled-up Barnes & Noble plastic bag with a picture of Langston Hughes on one side and Gertrude Stein on the other.

Back in the lobby we ran into True. He was speechless, so angry at K that he couldn't even look me in the eye. How could the motherfucker have pulled out his strap in a *mosque*? Now Dante walked in with his mischievous, murderous grin, Glock safely tucked away, swaddled in the loose folds of his karate outfit. Glancing timidly through the door I saw a long stretch of empty sidewalk. Ghost town.

Jeff was mumbling something directly in my ear. Should we make a break for the subway station? Wiser to wait and be sure that the coast was clear?

The decision was made for us. The door of the mosque flew open and camouflaged Justice, out of breath, grabbed me by the arm, telling me to hurry up and move.

Yes, move. Movement was good. The night air cool and invigorating as we fast-walked up Flatbush Avenue to the intersection where K and Faith and the others were waiting. They'd made their getaway a full two blocks up Flatbush, Justice explained, ready to disappear into the dark side streets, when they'd realized that we'd been trapped behind in the mosque.

K rushed forward to greet me. But it wasn't a look of relief on his face—the hideous flash of rage once again. Roaring, waving both arms wildly, asking me what was the matter with me—how could I have spent so much time around him and still not have a fucking *clue* about the code? I heard myself stammering something senseless—tapes, the tapes, needing to go back for those tapes—

"Listen, muthafucka!—and *don't* make me tell you this again: when I step—*you* step! You don't go back and get *shit!*"

He was pacing in front of me, still madly gesticulating. He couldn't understand it. Could not fucking understand it. This wasn't his responsibility, that was *my* responsibility: move as one with the crew. Was I blind? Didn't I see the way Just and Life had been there at his side when he stepped? Didn't I see the way Faith had been right beside him when the time came to break the fuck out?

I glanced at Jeff but his eyes offered nothing, focused tight in that impassive squint. This was *my* personal golem. Standing on the curb of Flatbush Avenue with the traffic whizzing close behind me, I had a strange premonition—yes, there *would* be bloodshed tonight: the sheer force of K's voice was going to propel me backward into the path of a speeding car . . .

"—and then if somethin' *does* fuckin' happen to you, then I gotta hear Crystal on the phone tellin' me it's *my* fuckin' fault! How the fuck you expect me to deal with that shit, huh? *Huh?* Answer me, mutha-fucka!"

He whirled around at the approach of sneakers. There stood Rob and Nick, straight from Hoboken, all faded Levi's and leather jackets and shoulder-length hair, lost and forlorn in the ink-black Brooklyn night. They'd had an earlier gig in Manhattan and were racing to catch the end of True's show, hoping to hear K perform, and coming down Flatbush on foot, trying to find the address of When Worlds Collide, they'd stumbled on the bizarre sight of K, towering over me, waving both arms, savagely chewing me out in front of a dozen bystanders.

"What's going on? How'd it go?"

The snarl morphing into a wide sarcastic smirk.

"Guess what, Nob? Show's over! Show never fuckin' happened!"

Justice broke in with some somber advice: best to get off the street before beast rolls up. K nodded in agreement and made a beeline for the nearby fried-chicken joint.

I wanted to veer away from them, head to the Nevins Street station alone with my token, never set foot in Brooklyn again. Life was trying to light up his cigarette with his back to the wind. He had a contemplative air about him; I'd noticed that he tended to think long and hard before speaking. Sure, he had a reputation for heavy violence—in jail he'd been known as an accomplished razor-fighter—but so little of K's hotheadedness.

"Shit," he said, showing me his gold-toothed grin, wheezing with laughter. "You was like, Fuck *that!* I'm makin' a run for the border! These muthafuckin' niggas is *crazy!*" His loud throaty laugh echoed in the clear Brooklyn night; we straggled on slowly behind the rest. Elbowing me in the arm, his voice dropped down to a solemn whisper. "See, it's fucked up when somebody gets caught up in a spot and everybody—I mean every-*fuckin'*-body is there. All the real niggas from the original clique"—a rhythmic, emphatic nod now—"that's some heavy shit, duke."

He was pulling hard on his Newport and I walked into a ribbon of mentholated smoke. He asked me if I understood why Knowledge Born was so vexed, why he'd gone off on me like that.

No, I told Life, I understood nothing about Knowledge Born.

Anything could have happened back there in the mosque, Life said. The Washington Avenue mob might have come back with burners, looking for K, and just shot up anybody unlucky enough to be standing there.

I watched a white delivery van rumbling past us—one of the back tires looked flat, blood-red bumper sticker reading HUMPTY DUMPTY WAS PUSHED.

They were inside the Kansas Fried Chicken, sitting at the Formica tables, waiting for us to join them. I watched Life swaggering in front of me, a red neon glow flickering over the green-and-brown swirls of his camouflaged back. Solid as a Sherman tank rolling slowly through the shadows. He lingered in the darkness with his glowing Newport. "Fuck y'all. Let a nigga finish his muhfuckin' cigarette in peace."

I sat sipping bitter black coffee, dreaming I was home in Chelsea, lying next to Crystal, rereading my favorite sections in *The Gangs of New York* while she rustled through pages of public health research, a world away from ghostly midnight Brooklyn and its Franklin Avenue Posse. K had spotted a solitary patrol car cruising down Flatbush and decided it was best that we stay put for a few more minutes. I looked at Jeff sitting silently across from me, bored and unhappy, eager to get back to his wife and his Upper West Side apartment, bookended securely on a bench between Justice and Life; at Nick and Rob, staring blankly at each other like a couple of poker players; at K, sitting next to smiling Faith, muttering about his lost Walkman, his *birthday* Walkman, the disconnected headphones of which were still dangling, useless and pathetic, around his neck.

K blamed Mighty for everything that had happened tonight. It was Mighty who had made him lose his faculties, dropping his drawers on-stage like that, disrespecting all the young ladies. The Dominican girls from Swatch had been so pissed—how was he going to face them to-morrow?—they'd come all the way from Queens to hear some nice hip-hop only to be confronted by Mighty doing that ventriloquist's act with his big gnarled dick. But K would catch up to Mighty one of these days and, when he did, *word to mother*—he kissed two fingers to the sky—he was going to step to Mighty's mustache about this.

Life said: "I pass by that muthafucka every day on my block. Never even conversate with his punk ass. Next time I see him I'm a rock his knot—said speed."

I rustled around in my Barnes & Noble bag, realized that I'd left something back inside the mosque—seemed like *years* ago—thoughts I'd been jotting down after K did his sound check. A pocket-sized black notebook crammed with my indecipherable scrawl. I tried to re-construct some of the words in my mind—hopeless. K, watching me rustling in the bag, asked, very softly: "What up, D? Left somethin' back there?"

I shrugged. Just a notebook. Just another little thing that got lost in the madness.

SEVEN

point blank

Full-time hustlers can never relax to appraise what they are
doing and where they are bound. As is the case in any
jungle, the hustler's every waking hour is lived with both the
practical and the subconscious knowledge that if he ever
relaxes, if he ever slows down, the other hungry, restless
foxes, ferrets, wolves and vultures out there with him won't
hesitate to make him their prey.

—The Autobiography of Malcolm X

JULY 20, '94. *Two times for your mind.*

Battle-scarred but battle-ready, K paces the plush carpeting of the
Sheraton Grand Ballroom, trying to mask his nervousness, impatient
for the contest to commence. "This nigga had better keep his cool,"
Life's muttering in my ear. "Starts breakin' fool today, I ain't doin' a
muthafuckin' thing to stop his ass." Once again K is scheduled to
compete in a freestyle free-for-all—the MC Battle for World Supremacy; in last year's battle he'd let his anger take hold, never regained his composure after his loud public confrontation with Doug
from D&D Studios, found himself soundly beaten in the first round

by a lanky rapper from Virginia called Mad Skillz.* K'd opened the battle with a salvo of his gruff Jamaican gunman lyrics, realizing too late that the crowd, comprised of rap purists, wasn't interested in hearing anything but unadulterated hip-hop. Barely a smattering of applause when K finished rhyming. "American Dread—that's a big nigga right there!" quipped Doctor Dré, the obese MTV comedian who was acting as the battle's host. "Y'all *betta* give it up for him—he could jump in the front row and take out 'bout fifty of you niggas!"

But for this year's MC Battle K is subdued, clear-eyed. With the audience still filing into the ballroom, he drops himself heavily on two empty seats next to Jeffrey Goldberg. The official MC Battle for World Supremacy T-shirt tossed loosely over his shoulder, even the XXL too small to fit his frame. No, he doesn't want to talk about the battle; he wants to hear more about Jeff's recent trip to Africa. Details, he's hungry for details—what about the children and the rivers and the wildlife? Says it's always been his dream to visit the Motherland one day. Jeff shrugs and tells K, quite frankly, that he wouldn't have cared for the side of Africa he'd seen.

Jeff just returned from the killing fields of Liberia, covering the country's civil war for the *Times Sunday Magazine.* K and Life listen with blank faces as Jeff relates snippets of his strange Liberian days and nights, running through the rain forest with the guerrilla fighters, loosely organized gangs of teenage mass murderers, eyes crazed from drinking cane juice and smoking bush weed, bony kids with names like General Rambo and General Murder, dressed in hand-me-down American high school wrestling T-shirts, toting hand-me-down AK-47s and rocket launchers and machetes, clutching juju amulets they believe will make their bodies impervious to their enemies' bullets . . .

K nods at the war zone anecdotes, frowning, doesn't seem especially impressed. He suspects Jeff is exaggerating the cold-blooded-

---

*Mad Skillz ultimately lost a memorable, marathon final to the goggle-wearing freestylist extraordinaire called Supernatural. The decision was hotly disputed by those in attendance; many in the Sheraton ballroom felt Mad Skillz had been robbed of the title.

ness of these Liberian child killers. Let 'em swing their jungle asses through Medina some Saturday night—let 'em try and bring the ruckus to Crime Heights! He and Life bump badman fists. BOO-YAAKAAH!

While I'm picturing that ludicrous scene, a running gun battle in the Brooklyn streets between the Franklin Avenue Posse and those AK-toting guerrillas, K shoots suddenly to his feet—there's been an announcement calling all the MCs to the side of the stage. K is one of sixteen contestants from across the country selected to compete today. DJ Clark Kent, the battle's promoter, begins briefing them on the rules and regulations of the competition. The ballroom now humming expectantly; every year, the MC and DJ battles are among the most popular events in the New Music Seminar. I scan the hall, filled to capacity with a who's who of record executives, rappers, singers and radio personalities, hip-hop journalists and music video directors, posing in the latest in Versace and Donna Karan, retro-trendy Kangol caps and Adidas jogging suits. Onstage, Doctor Dré is introducing the celebrity panel of judges—producers, artists and twenty-something millionaires like the brash hip-hop impressario Sean "Puffy" Combs.

Picture Muhammad Ali, in the heyday of his poetic braggadocio, showing up for a press conference and facing an opponent just as quick-tongued and vainglorious, someone who can grab the microphone and match Ali insult for insult and rhyme for rhyme. Set the verbal sparring to beats, a thumping bed of "Funky Drummer," and you'd have the world's first official freestyle battle.

To many afficionados, a battle is the truest expression of hip-hop culture: two MCs, alone with a microphone, improvising lyrics a cappella or to the backing of a beatbox or randomly selected instrumental track. Unlike studio recording, in which most lyrics are carefully written and revised, a battle is all about spontaneity and verbal inventiveness; the winner is invariably the MC who can string together the most facile metaphors and personal insults, incorporating rude references to his opponent's physiognomy, shabby taste in clothing, indeterminate parentage, anything to prove that he is rapping "off the dome"—from the top of his head—not simply reciting verses of previously memorized material. The audience at an MC battle doesn't crave the skills of a storyteller, wordsmith or abstract poet. They want disses. Snaps. Quips about *ya broke-ass mama and her fridge fulla guhvmint cheese.*

K is fortunate in his first-round draw, pitted against a red-haired whiteboy named Necrophiliac whose rhymes, for some nauseating reason, involve vivid descriptions of himself in the act of defecation. K swaggers to the mike stand, unholsters his weapon and dispatches Necrophiliac without breaking a sweat.

It looks as if he may make it to the final showdown; but in the semifinals, K finds himself facing King Sun, a towering, charismatic Five Percenter from the Bronx. Life is perplexed by King Sun's presence. "Yo!" he hollers in my ear. "What the fuck is Sun doin' in this shit?"

Good question. The battle is supposedly for unsigned artists—in addition to a silk bomber jacket and boxing-style championship belt, the winner is to receive a major-label recording contract—but King Sun's been an established, if underrated, rap star since releasing his first hit record ("Hey Love") in 1987. Cupping his megaphone palms to his mouth, Life begins to wonder loudly if the fix is in, if the battle has been rigged from the start.

K and King Sun have known each other for years. They were reminiscing about the old hustling days out in the hotel lobby before the battle.

The first round ends in a standoff. Sun has a fearsome reputation as a freestylist, but K comes back with some solid lyrics, a couple of clever hooks and jabs. King Sun has his finger on the pulse of the crowd. By the second round he's striding across the stage with the relaxed air of a street corner champion, has the audience bobbing in unison and hooting as he ridicules the West Coast–style braids K is sporting in his hair:

Then I dip—and I duck—
And I'm creepin' through the alley
My man chillin' in the Bronx—
But he front like he from Cali

The buzzer sounds, the panel of judges does a perfunctory tally, then sends King Sun into the finals against an unknown kid from Chicago called Judgemental, who ultimately bests King Sun in a dramatic upset.

I stand waiting at the side of the stage for K. Smiling, he hugs Sun and congratulates him on the victory, makes his way through the crowd of rappers gathered to the right of the stage: Jeru the Damaja, KRS-One, C-Knowledge from Digable Planets. Whatup, yeah, peace, God, one love. Off to the side, standing alone, I spot Kool Herc, the Jamaican-born DJ with the aviator sunglasses and the bodybuilder's physique—the man credited with single-handedly birthing hip-hop back in the Bronx circa '71–'72. It was Herc who first took Jamaican sound system culture and made it something distinctly American, spinning disco and R&B records at his parties, picking up the mike to rock *yes-yes-y'alls* and dropping impromptu rhymes about his gangster friends and fellow graffiti-bombers as he saw them entering the Hevalo, his packed-to-the-rafters Jerome Avenue nightclub.

Turning sideways, K muscles through the crowd—Kool Herc reaches out and offers a loud slapping pound. "Big man!" says Herc. "I like what I'm hearin' from you!" K bends his head in silent deference, like a child receiving a blessing from a strict parent. He hugs Herc and then we make our way together back through the crowded ballroom. Grimacing, upset about losing the battle, he takes some solace from the Father's words of praise. "That shit meant somethin' comin' from Herc," he says.

He's in an edgy mood later that night, in the Palladium on 14th Street, well after one A.M. We're in the basement of the sprawling nightclub, at the base of the carpeted staircase, talking to a ballcap-wearing radio team from Ontario—a black-and-white duo who host a popular university hip-hop show, the white Canadian very bland but knowledgeable, the black Canadian a flamboyant breakdancer—when up stumbles some stoned blond bimbo in tight white jeans, training her ridiculously dilated pupils on me before swinging her gaze to K.

"S-s-scuse me, dude—you look like the man to talk to—you know where we could, like, score some coke?"

"The fuck you mean I look like the man to talk to? Because I'm *black?* What, every black man looks like a fuckin' *drug dealer* to you?"

"N-n-naw . . ."

"How the fuck ya gonna ask me some shit like that? Stupid *bitch!*"

"Chill *out,* man—alls I was—"

"Dig, get out my *face* 'fore I smack the *shit* outcha!"

He chases the stoned white girl and her long-haired boyfriend up the stairs in a panic, leaves the biracial Canadian hip-hop duo doubled over, holding a long, finger-snapping handshake, gasping with laughter.

Two nights later, we take a long walk across the Brooklyn Bridge, through the tree-lined streets of Brooklyn Heights and Prospect Heights and Park Slope, down Eastern Parkway into Crown Heights. Crossing the bridge his dark mood returns. His self-esteem is ebbing, confusion cresting—as we walk he lays all his insecurities bare before me. Why is he even *trying?* What's his life ever going to amount to now? Should've ended back in the hustler days—out in a blaze of gangster glory. Not this. Rags to riches, riches to rags. Too old to be doing this now, getting up onstage in a corny-ass freestyle battle, still trying to make a name for himself as an MC.

Strange, though: as much as he hates depression, it seems like he does all his clearest thinking when the darkness takes hold.

Starts talking about the curse again, about the brujería spell his father's first wife slapped on him at birth. How else explain all the shitty luck he's been experiencing? He's spent two years trying to get somewhere as a rapper, but everything that can possibly go wrong for him has gone wrong. Everyone he's ever met in the music business has lied to him, smiled in his face, promised him one thing and then done another. Take that situation with Frontin' Felix, he says.

Felix was the president of a small independent record label called E-Legal that had offered him a multiple-album contract in the fall of '93; but as soon as K called his lawyer, Kendall Minter, to negotiate the royalty and advance terms, Felix began to stall, hedge, then abruptly stopped accepting phone calls or returning messages. "Be patient," I told K. And he was. But the weeks became months; and the only thing that came in the mail was a $300 invoice from the firm of Phillips, Nizer, Benjamin, Krim & Ballon for services rendered . . . Soon K learned that E-Legal Records had shut down their Broadway offices and Felix himself had disappeared without even calling to say goodbye.

A business? Try the lying game. More honesty—if not honor—among hustlers. At least a hustler looks another hustler in the eye, speaks the truth once in a while. *Try sellin' ya shit on my block I'm a murder ya.*

The former hustler clears his throat and spits a tight wad of phlegm in a long swirling arc. I watch it falling, twisting, disappearing in the darkness.

He finds a new way to vent his frustrated energy: begins to slapbox me, bouncing on his toes, snapping body shots which glance off my ribs and back. Playful or not, the body shots hurt more than he realizes; I have to sprint away to avoid internal injury.

Running fast I look down at the Brooklyn-bound traffic racing beneath me, thinking about the Depression days on the waterfront, about Velvl, the Little Wolf, my stevedore grandfather, brawling on those docks to fend off the anti-Semitic slurs. K laughing out into the wind behind me: "Stop frontin', muthafucka! I wasn't even *hittin'* you!" But I don't want to stop, keep jogging my way across the Brooklyn Bridge, head filled with dreams of my tough-guy grandpa.

A little later, thoughts of another immigrant tough guy touch K, on the Parkway, in the eerie darkness of Crown Heights. He begins to talk about Orito, his long-lost compadre, his early mentor in the drug game. Orito—now there was a hustler's hustler. Orito's been coming to K a lot lately. Bad dreams? More like visitations. Panamanian duppies going bump in the night.

It's always the same. Orito will come right into the bedroom, stirring him from his sleep, dripping blood on the edge of the bed. Hands still bound by the gray telephone cable, mouth leering as if ready to speak—but every time he starts to say something, there's just an empty gasp—no words will ever pass his bloody lips . . .

the hustler
A FABLE OF BROOKLYN

He was K's compadre, godfather to K's firstborn daughter, Carla, and between Panas, that's a lifelong bond, as strong and unbreakable as any bond between brothers. His government name was George, but only a select few were trusted with that information. On the Flatbush streets everyone called him Orito—the Panamanian version of Goldie. He was tall and dark-skinned, with long wavy hair, born down in the town of Paraíso—smack in the middle of the Canal Zone, between Colón and Panamá City.

Orito'd first got word of K through K's cousin Jorge. Heard that there was this new crazy motherfucker, just home from juvenile jail, tearing shit up on Franklin Avenue. Orito sent Jorge to fetch his primo and bring the boy into the operation. Strictly on the strong-arm side, of course.

It was all a new game to K. When he first got home from juvenile jail, crack hadn't made its debut. People'd been freebasing for years, taking licks off the chalice; some of the older Panamanian heads were smoking a potent cocaine paste called bazuko. But that sexy white witch—*the rock*—hadn't come into effect. Powder? K'd seen plenty of it; his older brothers and cousins had been running a small coke operation from the crib; he used to watch with boyish fascination as they cut the pure gray-brown shit with the lactose, packaging it up in tinfoil to be sold in their ten-dollar increments. But they weren't true hustlers. Violating the cardinal rule of hustling—*never get high on your own supply*—constantly snorting up more than they were selling.

No, K later realized, his brothers and cousins were strictly party-time motherfuckers. Never into the longevity of the game, the money-making and collectivizing. Never down with the re-up—like most small-timers, living for today. Just to say, *Yeah! We sellin' drugs!* and have the bitches riding their dicks.

It was in Orito's crib that K first saw the alchemy. Springtime '86. He'd just started rolling with Orito, just started to see the day-to-day operations. Orito's crib was a lavish apartment complex on Clarkson, between Nostrand and Rogers. He had the whole seventh floor hooked up. Knocked down the walls and made every apartment on the seventh floor into one mazelike crib. It was an emperor's palace hidden behind nondescript brick walls.

Unlike most hustlers, Orito liked keeping the drugs in his own place. He was so paranoid, he didn't trust anybody to get him a safe house, had to have the blow right under his nose. And his crib was so big, a visitor could be at one end of the apartment and never know someone was cooking crack up in the kitchen.

Never had any trouble with neighbors turning snitch on him. People on the block showed Orito mad love. He acted like some kind of Flatbush Robin Hood, used to pay old people's rent for the year, feed people's grandmothers, buy little kids' school clothes. Plus he was having sex with every other girl on the block—so nobody used to *think* of messing with him.

K's cousin Jorge was cooking up the rock that morning. Two big pots on the stove. Four family-sized mayonnaise jars in each pot bubbling away.

Jorge was the alchemist—the way that his wrists'd turn the mayonnaise jars, with a deft flick here, a sharper turn there—binding those simple ingredients magically into ghetto gold.

He'd start by measuring out the ounces, take the vitamin B_{12} and add it to the coke, then the baking powder, put all that mixture in the mayonnaise jars. The B_{12} was Jorge's secret ingredient. Nobody else knew to put B_{12} in their shit. Made the blow *boof* up real nice and big.

Now in the pots he's got just a little bit of water, barely enough to cover the bottom of the mayonnaise jars, right above the mixture line. Then once the water comes to a boil, you start to see some oil in the mixture—that's the cocaine transforming, changing, releasing its greasy poison. That's why Jorge was so good. Think it's easy to have your hands in big oven mitts, knowing just when to turn the mayonnaise jars on time? Twirl, twirl, twirl. And while he's twirling, he's adding a little sprinkle of cold water to make the mixture solidify into the rock.

Takes the rocks out of the jars once they're hard, puts them in a towel, a clean white towel, blots the rocks dry. Two hours later he'll start cutting it up and packaging it for sale on the street.

The rock always scared K shitless. Wouldn't touch it with his bare hands. He was scared to even breathe the coke-dusted air around the kitchen. K had a girlfriend who was a nurse—she'd get him the medical face masks and hair covers used in the Kings County operating rooms, real surgeon's gloves and the whole nine. And K'd just sit there at Orito's table with the mask and gloves on, watching Jorge the alchemist at work.

Just the smell used to make his stomach hurt. The only time in his life he ever handled it—Jorge was away in Panama—K had to measure the coke out and by mistake he touched it with his bare hand, forgot to wash up afterward. In the living room he started talking to one of his homeboys, must've touched his lip or his cheek—and suddenly his whole face was numb and cold like he'd been to the dentist. Stayed frozen and rubbery for the rest of the day.

He'd been with Orito a few months now, but Orito was still treating him like a punk, taking K's loyalty for granted—using him as his flunky and his enforcer. He'd say, "Bwoy, I waan you to go to Newkirk and pick up dat fuckin' money from my raatid sister-in-law. Then I waan you to take dat ounce down to fuckin' Nando on Nostrand, y'hear?"

In July '86 Orito and Jorge went to Panama for Jorge's wedding. Orito was picking up the tab for the wedding, shelling out thirty-five grand just for the reception. While they were down there, it was K and Orito's cousin Danillo—K used to call the clown Woody Woodpecker—K and Danillo who were running the whole operation in Flatbush. Orito and Jorge chilled in Panama the whole summer. Orito loved it back there; K heard stories about Orito being a living god in Paraíso; the people down there worshipped the ground he walked on.

K and Danillo were supposedly splitting up the drug duties, but in reality, Dani didn't do shit that whole summer. Dani was just into his bitches and driving too fast in Orito's cars. Orito knew that his cousin was a piece of shit; he'd told K distinctly the morning he left: "Stay on top of de business—and *watch* fuckin' Dani!"

Think the Colombians weren't watching? Think they weren't observing everything that was going down in that lavish crib on Clarkson? Pablo and Fabiana kept coming around, noticing, nodding. Yeah, Orito's never home, Jorge's never home, Danillo's never home—it's just K, some nineteen-year-old Panamerican boy, running the whole goddamn drug operation. K's the only motherfucker giving them their money like clockwork; K's the only motherfucker home when the bricks get dropped.

Finally, one August day Pablo took him aside, whispering in Spanish, a conspiratorial hiss. "You want your own shit? Looks like you're ready for it."

"No," K told him. "I wanna see what Orito talkin' 'bout when he comes home."

He was still a little unsure of himself. Thought he needed Orito. Never imagined he could run a big-time hustling operation on his own. But now that Orito's gone back to Panama, staying in Paraíso for months, K realizes that he *is* doing it. He's just doing it with Orito's money.

By now, K understood all Orito's economics. Testing the waters, he'd started to flip a few side deals on his own. Orito'd left K a price for everything. A kilo that summer was selling for $28,000; K would turn around and sell it for $35,000. There was a bad drought in July and August and they were some of the only cats in Brooklyn who had a steady supply from the 'Lombians. K had no problem telling Orito's regular customers: "Look, Orito's gone—ain't shit out here—you gotta deal with *me* now."

Orito was paying the 'Lombians $10,000 a key—and charging his customers 28 on the street. In Orito's absence, due to the drought, K could get 35 for that same key, still giving Orito thirty grand—two thousand more than he was expecting. Put his own extra profits to the side, using those extras to buy himself an eighth of a key for $1,700, knowing he could flip that eighth of a key for over $4,000 on Franklin Ave. Never mixing up his own money with Orito's, still flipping that shit and making a little profit for himself on the side.

When Orito landed at the airport, there was K, still the loyal soldier, waiting to pick him up. Not driving Orito's Cougar—the Cougar he'd left K with. K came to the airport in his own car, the brand-new blue LeBaron he'd bought.

"Oh raas! So wh'appen? You have a new car! Wha' de fuck goin' on here? Is a rental?"

"Naw, Orito, it ain't no rental. I bought this, yo."

Through a sidelong glance K could see Orito holding his face tight. Screwfacing him the whole drive back to Brooklyn, thinking K'd flipped on him, that he'd stayed in Panama too long and now K was trying to take his *puesto*.

Back at the crib, Orito wanted to see his papers—K went into the back and got all his money out and they sat down for a good two hours counting all the singles and fives and tens and twenties on his bedspread. This wasn't some Hollywood shit; they never used counting machines. All the bundles had to be counted by hand.

K noticed something out of order, but it wasn't the money. Orito began grumbling now about some falling-out he'd had with Jorge down in Panama. He snapped two pink rubber bands angrily around the fat thousand-dollar bundle.

"Y'know your fuckin' cousin is a *dawg*."

"That ain't got nuttin' to do with me, Orito. I'm still with *you*, duke. We got money to make here."

"Oh raas! Look like while I was gone you got serious, eh?" Orito was spread out on his bed, resting his chin on one knuckle, taking in all of K's jewelry. While he was in Panama K'd started wearing all the crazy rope jewelry; now he was sporting more jewelry than his boss. "What you was doin' while I was away?"

"Just makin' a move here and there, man. But I never turned on you. I always made sure your money was tight first."

"You was makin' moves with *my* connections?"

Why the fuck was Orito getting so heated? Did he really think K'd be stupid enough to start pushing up on the 'Lombian motherfuckers?

"Naw, I was just makin' moves on my own, duke."

"Who the fuck are *you* to make moves on your own?"

"Orito, it ain't what you think. I ain't tryin' to dis you or nuttin'. I just saw an opportunity and I capitalized on it."

"You the same ting like your fuckin' cousin! Y'all man-dem is like *dawg!*"

And with Orito getting so heated, now K was starting to get heated. "Yo, lemme tell you somethin', Orito! I always been on your fuckin' side—I ain't never fuckin' turned on you. But *don't* play me like I'm a fuckin' sucka! How many times you coulda put me at your fuckin' right hand—how much shit I done did for you and you got me over here being *Dani's* right hand? A muthafucka that didn't even do a lick of work since you been gone! It's been me and my muthafuckin' clique—it's been me and my niggas from Franklin Avenue—young-ass niggas that you don't even fuckin' *know* been makin' moves for you!

"Dig, all your money is here, *all* your money is here—and then some! How the fuck you gonna justify flippin' on me when I'm just tryin' to make mines—same way you tryin' to make yours?"

They kept arguing like that for a few more minutes, and then finally Orito gave in with a sigh. "Bwoy, yunno, you givin' me a real fuckin' headache."

Laughing, they bumped fists. Everything was peace. They went out and hit a few of the spots, the Dynamite, the Villa, all the Panamanian rudeboy clubs where Orito and K used to chill.

But Friday night of Labor Day weekend K was on Franklin with his homeboys. Orito, taking one of his girls out for the night, double-parked his Benz at the corner store to get some cigarettes.

K happened to have a fat coil of money in his pocket, profits from the ounce he'd bought and was flipping on the street. Coming out of the store with his pack of smokes, Orito grabbed K suddenly and checked his pocket. Pulled out the coil of money, stared at it, slapped K's face. Not hard—just like the Italian wiseguys, tapping their flunkies a couple of times on the cheek. "Bwoy, you makin' moves on your own?"

"I told you, Orito. I'm not makin' no moves on my own. This is just a little ounce that I bought."

There was about $1,200 in the coil; Orito peeled off half the cash, shoved it in his pocket. K stared hard at his boss. "Orito, that ain't your money, duke. That money don't got nuttin' to do with you."

"Yeah, ahright. I jus' need some money to go to the Parrot."

Chumped him. Chumped him in front of his homeys, made him look like a punk right on Franklin Ave.

"Yo, I'll see you tomorrow," he says, getting back in his car.

From that moment on K knew he had to break out, start making his own moves, take Pablo and Fabiana up on that offer.

In the beginning he needed his baby-mother Yolanda with him all the time. There was the language problem: K only knew Spanglish—that pig Latin Spanish from the Canal Zone—but the Colombians spoke proper Spanish, which Yolanda could understand and speak fluently. He damn sure didn't want any misunderstandings with those 'Lombians over a couple of sloppy words.

Fabiana and Pablo drove a brand-new Oldsmobile station wagon. They'd ring the buzzer of K's apartment building and he'd come downstairs to talk in the car. Fabiana was fat, middle-aged, *plenty* ugly. Pablo used to wear the same pair of white painter's pants with blood-red latex-paint stains on them. They both wore cheap, cheap shoes. It was embarrassing. For drug dealers, they looked dirt poor.

They'd come and tell K when the meet was set. Always the same place: Kings Plaza shopping center, in the Marine Park section. They'd always meet during crowded shopping afternoons in the Burger King. K and Yolanda'd carry several big bags, looking like they'd been shopping for sneakers. But these Nike and Fila boxes were packed with bundles of cash, set down under the table while they were happily munching Whoppers and sipping Cokes. When they finished eating, getting up to leave, Pablo would be the one carrying the bags with the heavy sneaker boxes.

Forty-five minutes later another car of 'Lombians would come by K's crib to make the drop.

*   *   *

Getting consi—slang for consignment—every young hustler's dream. Getting consi from the 'Lombians is the highest level you can reach as a young street hustler. What? No young black Brooklyn cat's flying his own planes into Florida. No nineteen-year-old cat's driving tractor-trailers up from Mexico.

But all the wannabes and bullshitters, they don't understand the pressure; they don't realize that getting consi is a devil's bargain.

Plenty of times K'd find himself sitting on ten keys, eleven keys, twelve keys—and didn't have a dime to his name. Rent's due, phone bill's due, Con Ed's getting ready to cut off the lights—because nothing's moving on the street. Nothing's selling in New York and you've got shit in D.C. that's selling and your lieutenants haven't come back from D.C. yet so you're stuck sitting on keys.

Just like restaurants or real estate, the rock trade is seasonal. Certain times of the month nothing moves. Certain times of the year nothing moves. Some years, right after the Christmas splurge, nothing moves again until March. The only time you can really count on some steady sales figures is the summer months. Other times it'll move slow, you'll be making money, but what you get, you've got to pay the 'Lombians, and they're coming every two weeks, serious as cancer, don't want to hear any sob stories or lame excuses—"Yo, man, it's slow out there—"

FUCK YOU! PAY ME!

That's one thing K learned fast about the 'Lombians: better have that money tight, son, 'cause those Medellín motherfuckers value a dollar bill more than they value a human life.

After you've got your quota with the 'Lombians, you're always searching for more spots. Preferably spots out of state. Spots out of state always turn a higher profit than spots in New York. In Crime Heights, Love People One was the main source of information for spots out of state.

Love People One was the rudest Jamaican disco in the history of New York. An old funeral home on Washington Avenue and Sullivan, converted into a reggae club. Nothing but rudeboys and drug dealers and murderers up in that joint. Every weekend, another wild shootout in Love People. So many motherfuckers got murdered inside Love People that K and his boys started calling it Dead People.

They'd be chilling in Dead People on a hot Saturday night, rub-a-dubbing with some nice big-butt honeys, might overhear a couple of Jamaican hustlers, some Spanglers or Showers* who'd just rolled in from D.C., pockets fat with their profits.

"Yes mon! Nort'-Eas' a *bubble* right now!"

"Yes star, me hear seh Montana a *bubble,* yunnoseeit?"

So Montana Place was bubbling hot, huh? First move: soon as K got back to D.C., he'd send one of his workers down to Montana Place, bummed out like a homeless crackhead, with orders to buy some of the Jamaican's rocks. Back at their own spot, they'd examine the crack, see how big and potent the rocks were. Then they'd give it to a basehead from their own territory, let him light it up, get his feedback on the buzz. "Nigga, how you like that shit?"

And if the Jamaican's rocks are no bigger, no more powerful than K's own, then it's simple logic: why can't K get money where the Jamaican's getting it?

Second move: send three cats down to the Jamaican's territory to start selling right out in the open. You need heavy-hitting motherfuckers for this move: one of your lieutenants and two chieftains. Head down there and start selling rocks downstairs, right outside the Jamaican's spot. Barricade the entrance and stop the other cat's customers from going in.

Now the motherfucker comes running out to see what's going on, and if he wants a shootout, then you shoot it out with him. Normally,

*The two principal Jamaican organized-crime groups born in the bloody political turf wars of Kingston's ghetto districts. The Spangler Posse supported Michael Manley's People's National Party; members of the rival Shower Posse backed Edward Seaga's Jamaica Labor Party.

they'd want to talk first. "Yo nigga, you can't sell here!" Your lieutenant tries bargaining with him: "I need a piece, nigga—*please*. Y'all makin' a lot of cheese here. There's enough money here for all of us."

Sometimes they'd settle it by dividing up the week: "Y'all can sell Mondays and Wednesdays, we'll sell on Tuesdays and Thursdays, and we'll both try to sell on Friday and Saturday." (Sell rocks on a *Sunday?* You crazy? The Lord's Day? Who needs that kind of bad luck? K ever caught one of his workers selling rocks on Sunday, they'd never work for him again . . .)

But if they decide to give you a play, split up the week with you— if they don't rush out with guns blazing from the jump—then you know they're suckers, and eventually you're gonna take the whole block from them. A real hustler's always going to let his gun do the talking. Most of the murders you see in the crack hustle happen right then: motherfucker's moving onto the next man's block, taking money from his kids' mouths. Share? Share *what?* Doesn't matter how much money's out there, the pie is never big enough.

Finding virgin territory was simpler—driving down a desolate block, light bulb goes off: "Shit! We could do something here!" Next day, start with the advance advertising, print up some little cards saying *Kurtis Blow!* or *The Iceman Cometh to a Block Near You!* Hand them out to the local fiends.

Shit would move slow for the first week, shit'd be slow for the second week—by the third week shit's *booming*. Now you start writing in a log. Memorize the figures. Once you've got them locked in your mind, burn the logbook. Never keep *any* papers around you. That's why hustlers are always good with numbers; any drug dealer making money is real fast with his mental arithmetic.

After a while K never saw cocaine as a physical substance, never saw it as the dirty gray powder—pure perico is *never* white: it only turns white as you cut it—that could leave half your face frostbitten and rubbery. It was a lot easier to see that key over there as a Benz, this key right here as a Cherokee, that half a key as some spending money for his baby-mother and some new clothes for his little daughter . . .

To K and his crew, any motherfucker who chose to suck the glass dick was a fool. Soft. Weak-minded. But if they wanted to smoke it, somebody had to cook it up for them, and it might as well be K and his little clique, right? "Yeah, smoke your fuckin' brains out, nigga. We gonna get *paid*."

And all the preachers talking about, *Black man, wake up! You're poisoning the blood of your own brothers!* What a fucking crock of shit that was! Ever heard of free will? Somebody put a gun to your head and *ordered* you to smoke that shit?

Wasn't even a black-white issue to K. Certain of his spots he had white cats coming through like *dirt*. White cats who'd beg you to come to their crib with daily deliveries. You'd be amazed by all the yuppies—silk-tie, nine-to-five, Wall Street motherfuckers—who can't stop smoking that shit.

K had a saying about it, used to tell his workers how he saw the whiteboys' vicious circle. "What these yuppie fiends do is work more hours, so they can get paid, so they can buy more of our shit—then they smoke our shit, so they can stay up longer, so they work more hours, so they can get paid, so they can buy more of our shit . . ."

In the end, they're not even putting in the overtime for IBM or AT&T or Merrill Lynch; in the end, they're just slaving for the white rock.

Funny thing—you're too caught up in the daily drama to realize it—but the hustler is just as hooked as the crackhead. Say your operation is taking in $75,000 every two weeks. You don't see that type of money in a lump sum. You're taking it in, dribs and drabs, fives, tens, twenties—partying it away, spending it as fast as it comes your way. The only type of money that you see in a lump sum is the money you're bundling up for the 'Lombians every two weeks. But all your own money, you're just spending-spending-spending . . . Save? *For what?... You ain't livin' to see twenty-three, nigga!* Your first thought when you wake up every morning: *Mmm-hmmm ... today is a good muthafuckin' day to die ...*

Your brain's racing 210 miles a minute. One of your workers gets busted, one of your packages gets lost down South, the back of your brain telling you something ain't right here, somebody's ripping me off—but you don't have *time* to suspect, you don't have *time* to find out what happened. You just have to leave room for it. Boggle your mind with how that money got missing, you're only gonna lose more money tomorrow. Just gotta tell yourself—*fuck it!*—it's missing— move on to the next thing. Hurry up and sell this next key so you can get this next money together for these 'Lombians so you can get that next batch on consignment ...

Some days you're crying and beating your head against the bedroom wall because the Colombians are coming in ten minutes and you don't have all their money straight. You're a few Gs short and you're giving them the keys to your car, giving them all your jewelry, giving them anything you've got on hand.

It's not out of them wanting to hurt you *themselves;* it's out of fear of *their* bosses. A chain of fear moving up the line. They know if they don't have their money straight every two weeks, the main motherfucker over there in Medellín is sending a hit squad for *their* ass. Quick-fast.

If K was on the top rung of the ghetto operation, then Pablo and Fabiana were the bottom rung of the 'Lombian operation. Any half-ass Brooklyn hustler was making five times the money they were. They were just little mules. Living like peasants in a half-ass crib in Rego Park, Queens.

Never could figure out how his luck held so long. In all those years, he never once got busted with drugs. Closest he ever came was in Pemberton. Pemberton, boy! They could've put K away for two lifetimes!

Pemberton had been a fuck-up from the start. This little quiet-ass town in South Jersey and K and his crew show up with their barbaric Brooklyn style, modeling all the rope gold chains, profiling in kitted-up cars with the booming Bose stereos making little babies shriek in the night. Just a handful of houses in Pemberton, families working day jobs at nearby Fort Dix and the air force base.

K'd first come to Pemberton to see his sister Jean. But as soon as K showed up, she started smoking that rock. He caught her smoking it one day and gave her a real nasty ass-whipping. Out of spite, she tried to set him up with the police. Got everybody involved, state troopers, feds, the MPs from Fort Dix. She even gave them photos of K.

Luckily, K's right-hand man, Twin, had someone inside the precinct who gave them a tip-off about thirty minutes before the raid. They had to ditch the van and sprint down to the bus stop. But when they got to the bus, a bunch of MPs were surrounding the area—looking at everybody's face real close. They ran across a huge lawn the size of two football fields, on the edge of Fort Dix. There was this one little shed where the gardeners kept their lawnmowers, a little hut in the middle of this sprawling field. K and Twin pressed themselves tight against the shed.

"We busted for sure, yo."

"I can't go back to jail," Twin said—he was still on parole.

"Naw, all right," K said. "This is what we gon' do—you hang back and I'll turn myself in." He reached into his pocket and tried to hand Twin his coil of cash.

Twin wouldn't take the money. "Naw, muthafucka! You ain't goin' to jail! If we gon' do this, we goin' all out! We gon' *die* if we gotta die—but we *ain't* goin' to jail!"

The MPs were driving around on the edge of the big field; Twin and K started inching around the side of the little shed to keep out of sight. More MPs circled; Twin and K kept hugging the side of the shed. They stayed hidden behind the shed until night came and all the MPs were gone from the bus stop.

*   *   *

K still thought they'd have him busted for all those keys that were in the apartment. But his girl Candy saved his ass. Before the cops showed up with the search warrants, she went in the bathroom and got all the drugs together. She started stuffing the drugs into a gigantic teddy bear K'd given her. She took some stuffing out of the teddy bear and put the drugs inside, sewed it all back up in the bathroom.

Cops came banging on the door, and she's crying, making like Tina Turner: "Help me! I'm *afraid* of him! He beats me up! He might even *kill* me!" And she had the cops so bamboozled that they asked her if she wanted to get an order of protection against K. "No," she said, "I just wanna go home to Brooklyn."

Candy even had the cops escort her teddy-bear-carrying-ass in their squad car down to the bus stop. Got on the next bus and muled the teddy bear back to Brooklyn. Back in Crown Heights, she was laughing, ripping open the teddy bear seams to show K the drugs.

K kept shaking his head in disbelief. That bitch had ice running through her veins—imagine how much *time* she would've got for that stunt!

No, they never nailed him for drugs. Guns—now that was another story. He was always having trouble with guns. The most serious charge was the two bodies. Delroy left him holding that weight, giving him his nine-shot .22.

K was holding the .22 rings, riding in a gypsy cab, trying to get up to Franklin Ave. He knew the cops were stopping the traffic ahead—searching for people drunk-driving—so he started yelling at the gypsy cab driver. "Don't go up this block! Don't go on Hawthorne!"

What does the motherfucker do? Panics, thinks K's trying to rob him or something, tells him to get out of the cab. Soon as K steps out of the car, the driver turns down Hawthorne and tells the cops that he was nearly stuck up by a suspicious-looking dude. By now K's flagged down another gypsy cab, a dark skinny Haitian, but he won't move the car, no matter how loud K's barking at him—*Just drive the mutha-fucka, yo!*—and then the police cars pull up with sirens wailing. K gets out of the cab, tries mumbling to the cops: "I don't know what's wrong with him—he's *crazy* or something." He'd slipped the rings under the man's car seat. But as he's trying to walk away, one cop starts yelling, "Yeah, Harry, I got the gun!"

Fucking Delroy! Cops did the ballistics on the .22, boom, found two bodies on it. So now K's on Rikers Island, locked up in C-95, charged with two counts of Man-1. He'd wiped the gun with his shirt before shoving it under the seat—so he knew his prints weren't on it.

Did sixteen months on Rikers Island, going back and forth to trial for the two bodies. Finally, K beat trial, came off the Island in the dead of winter. First day back in Brooklyn he runs into Orito. They're hugging each other, laughing about the old days; soon as Orito learns K's just come off the Island, he tells his compadre to come get some money, come check him in two days, pick up $500 so he can get himself back on his feet.

Two days later, K swings by Orito's crib. Somebody's just coming out of the building so K walks right in, takes the elevator to the seventh floor. Rings the bell two or three times. No answer. Starts banging on the door, sees it isn't even locked, goes inside and starts calling out:

"Orito! Orito! Where the fuck you at, duke?"

Coming into the bedroom, he sees his compadre waiting for him.

Orito's bedroom was done in various shades of dark red and shiny black, thick red carpeting, nice lacquer bedroom set. Orito was kneeling down in his praying position, leaning on his bed, with all his money spread out in front of him.

For a second, K thought he was talking on the phone. Orito used to relax like that—he'd be on the phone, leaning down by his bed, laying his head and upper body flat, and stay kneeling down like he's praying while he's talking.

But if that was the case, then why the fuck was he doing it *naked?* K took another step closer before seeing the gray telephone cords tied tight around his legs and his arms.

Then the blood-soaked circles in the carpet. Watery blood, pissy, clear. They'd clapped him near his bladder and the draining blood had mixed with urine.

K knew exactly who'd done it and why. Didn't touch the money on his bed. There was at least thirty Gs in cash; bundles spread all over. A telltale sign that the 'Lombians had blanked him, not just some rival Brooklyn hustlers.

The 'Lombians are deep into santería and brujería, just like Panas, and to touch Orito's money, to take *anything* from the dead, would be to bring some real evil spirits down on your ass. Even though Orito'd fucked up their money—it'd happened so long ago that he thought he'd got over—the 'Lombian hit squad would never touch those bundles on his bed.

That was the 'Lombian way. Wait for years and years, make you think you got over, make you think they've forgotten all about what you did to them. Three years, four years pass. And then, just like that, they're in your apartment. 'Cause when the 'Lombians come for you, they're not coming to spray up your Jeep or your vestibule; they're not blazing from the safety of a screeching getaway car. When they come for you, they come in *stealth*—and they don't leave the scene until they've seen you good and dead.

Now K's thinking of doing something he's never done in his life: pick up the phone and call the cops. He knew they could never pin the murder on him. There was no residue—if you clap somebody there's always gun residue, no matter what precautions you take, microscopic residue gets on your face, on your hands, on your clothes. All the cops would do was take K's clothes to forensics, flash some infrared light, see that there were no gunpowder traces.

But what would've happened, once they saw K's rap sheet, there would've been a whole lot of questions: "How'd you know the deceased?" and "What were you doing in his apartment?" And coming straight off Rikers Island two days earlier, K was in no condition to handle the handcuffing and heavy interrogation. *Lemme just step. Let some next muthafucka find Orito's body.*

He went into the bathroom, took one of Orito's nice maroon hand towels, went around wiping down all the doorknobs and countertops, getting everything clean of his prints. Then he closed the door to Orito's crib quietly behind him.

Didn't even hit him, till the elevator stopped at the ground floor, walking out of the building, he felt the cold stinging air on his face, felt the hot tears dripping down, heard himself crying like a little kid. *Damn, my nigga's dead!*

Revenge? Who could he even go *see* about this shit? The 'Lombians had gotten too strong. Back in the old days, the 'Lombians didn't really know the city too well. They'd mostly been in L.A.; New York was fresh territory for them to pioneer. Back in the old days, if some bad business did happen, you could always lose yourself in the wilds of Brooklyn.

But now the 'Lombians *knew* New York thoroughly. They'd got wise to the game. By '89 they had black cats working for them, Jamaican killers getting down with them, helping them weed your ass out. K knew that if he lifted a finger against those 'Lombians, he was definitely going to die.

Still, should he maybe have called the cops, even just an anonymous tip from a pay phone? After all, it's his compadre up there. It ain't right leaving his body lying naked like that, bound up and bleeding like some slaughtered animal . . .

K's driving and crying, the tears and snot streaming down his face— sees two girls at the light staring at him and laughing. He doesn't even care, keeps mumbling crazily to himself, wondering how the hell can he explain to his daughter that her godfather, the Little Gold One, is gone—

And then all of a sudden Orito's sitting in the car next to K, looking just like he used to look back in the old days. All the eighteen-carat jewelry, red-and-black silk shirt, nice pair of black-and-gray suede Clarks. Sitting there in the passenger seat, staring hard at his compadre, resting his chin on one knuckle.

"Oh raas! What de fuck is wrong wid you, bwoy? Look like you gettin' *soft!* Since when does badman shed so much fuckin' tears?"

EIGHT

pressure
drop

"He was like a pistol when he got mad."

—Lou Weiner,

Bugsy Siegel's Las Vegas attorney,

on his notoriously hot-headed client

G rinning madly, K sits drumming his fists on the tabletop, making his scattered french fries dance and hop across their bed of opened napkins. *Why don't you hit me with your best shot?* All eyes in the midtown McDonald's are on him: but that doesn't stop him singing and grinning and hammering out his own heavy accompaniment. *What the fuck you starin' at, nigga?* K loves Pat Benatar and he doesn't give a fuck who knows it. Brings him back to the dayroom in Goshen—he and Gator and Tango sparring, throwing up their dickbeaters, dancing and slap-boxing whenever Pat Benatar came on the communal radio.

He follows a specific ritual whenever he unwraps his double cheeseburger meal: carefully removing the top bun from each burger, peeling off the lettuce and tomatoes, laying the individual french fries on top of the melted cheese. Arranges the french fries in tightly spaced rows, adding a second tier of french fries at a perpendicular alignment. He uses his teeth to tear a tiny hole in his ketchup packet, squeezing out thin red ribbons on the french fries so meticulously, so delicately, he resembles a baker putting decorative icing on a little birthday cake.

I've wolfed down my Big Mac before he's taken the first bite from the first of his cheeseburgers. He studies me with scolding eyes. "That ain't even *human,* duke. That's how snakes be eatin' mice."

Waiting for him to finish I pull out a black Uniball and begin doodling a face on one of the grease-spotted McDonaldland napkins. I have to move the pen quickly and with a very light hand because if I hold the tip too long in one spot the ink will billow out in wet black clouds.

"Who's that supposed to be, duke? That supposed to be *me?*"

Hardly.

"Muthafucka, it looks just like me." Watching intently, he loudly sucks the remnants of cheeseburger from his teeth, pauses, eyes sparkling with a new notion. "Yo, you think you could draw a heart?"

Finding a clean napkin, I trace two womanly curves, meeting in a sharp point, hold it up for his approval.

"The fuck is wrong with you? *I* can draw a Valentine heart. My fuckin' *one-year-old* can draw a Valentine heart. A human heart, muthafucka—like them anatomy book hearts. You know: ventricles, auricles, veins and arteries, all that ol' good shit?"

Somewhat more complicated than a Valentine heart. He leans across the table, lowers his voice to a whisper, tells me to check this out right here.

Several weeks earlier K had a dream in which he saw his own heart. Written above his heart, in some kind of gold shining letters, he saw the words *Blessed by Orishás.* As the dream progressed he could see his heart changing: the hard black shell of a cocoon opening to reveal a butterfly. The lower half of his heart was dark and hard because the tissue down there was dead: that was his old self, his evil self. The upper half of his heart was light, the muscle becoming red and living and pulsing with fresh blood again.

There were four reasons for this transformation: the four orishás watching over him. In each of the heart's four chambers dwelled one of the orishás. San Miguel, the archangel Michael, doing battle with Lucifer. Christ at Golgotha, crucified between the two thieves. Below them, Babalu-Aye, coming in the guise of Lazarus, awakened from the dead. And then—most important of all—there was Elegua, the orishá who controlled human destiny, the lord of the crossroads, the great trickster god, standing at the threshold of all things human and divine . . .

His four orishás were blessing him with a second life. Yes, it was through the grace of these orishás that his heart was being cleansed of evil.

I took up the challenge, told him I'd do my best to draw his heart's metamorphosis. He wanted to send it to his santería priest down in Puerto Rico—he referred to the man as his "spiritual god-father"—so that it could be properly blessed. The heart wasn't as difficult as I'd imagined; Crystal had *Gray's Anatomy* and several thick medical textbooks and a scientific encyclopedia in our apartment—a wide selection of detailed cross sections of the human cardiovascular system.

For the mysterious orishás, K had gone to a botánica in the Bronx, buying four small laminated cards with those African gods from his dream. Three of these cards were indistinguishable from traditional Catholic images: Christ in the agony of crucifixion; a haloed Lazarus surrounded by happy little dogs; the archangel Michael flying down from heaven, sword unsheathed as he prepared to vanquish Satan. But it was the fourth card that I found most fascinating. The Elegua card. On the back was a small prayer which said:

ORACIÓN AL GLORIOSO
ELEGUA

A Ti, señor de los caminos, guerrero
ilustre, Principe in mortal. Te pido:
Aparta de mi casa el mal, y Protégeme
cuándo esté despierto o dormido.
Acepta mi ruego diario al Gran Olofi

I flipped the card over. An indistinct black-and-white image, the dark shape in the center resembling several different things at once: a medieval knight's helmet with a sharp point jutting from the forehead— a primitive statue chiseled from blue-black granite—a horribly charred skull courtesy of Mistah Kurtz . . .

I was still struggling with Elegua when Crystal came home from her office at Columbia. She found me hunched over in the middle of the floor, surrounded by my many crumpled failures.

She was curious to see me poring over her *Gray's Anatomy*—how long had I been interested in human biology? she wondered. But her smile vanished when she got a closer look at my weekend project. Recognized those laminated cards: some of her Puerto Rican friends back in the Bronx used to frequent the botánicas.

"You're doing that for *him?*"

"I'm doing it for me."

"That's nice—now he's got you practicing voodoo."

No, the only thing I was practicing was the jutting outline of Elegua's jaw.

She let out a loud sigh, said *God bless America,* asked what had possessed me to bring something like that into our home. Said she'd greatly appreciate it if, in the future, I would refrain from bringing such demonic artifacts into our home.

"Look: San Lázaro," I said, holding up his laminated card. "You've got a San Lázaro. No, I forgot—your patron saint is Jude. Look at all his nice puppies. Call him Babalu-Aye. Babalu. Hey, remember Desi Arnaz singing 'Babalu'?"

I didn't need to tell her about Babalu, she snapped. Lena, her Panamanian-born grandmother, knew all about such things. She used to call them demons.

Demons? No, they were orishás, the proud gods of the Yoruba. Centuries ago these gods had survived that murderous Middle Passage—taken cover under the guise of Catholic saints so that their identities would never be discovered by the Spanish slave owners. A remarkable feat of spiritual subterfuge, right? Gods who were also masters of espionage—undercover agents in the New World.

She said she didn't care what I'd read in some damned anthropology book: no one was going to convince her that they weren't evil spirits. She was losing her patience with me and my assumptions, felt she needed to clarify a few things. She'd been born in Jacobi Hospital—in the northeast Bronx—that made her an *American,* okay? Not Panamanian. Not Jamaican. Not African. So Yoruba, Aruba, *whatever* crap I was talking—to her it was voodoo, and it was giving her the creeps.

Good, good. I was finally bringing Elegua to life, seeing some depth in those dark eye sockets, shading in the contours of that inscrutable face with my No. 2 pencil . . .

"Anyway," I told her, "you've got it all wrong—he lives in a *white* house."

"What's that supposed to mean?"

"Means you're only doing it for your own protection. You know, good-luck charms—like a crucifix, or a mezuzah. If you live in a black house, now that's brujería—witchcraft. That means you're putting hexes and curses on your enemies."

She was silent for a while. Coughed into her fist. Told me that I needed to visit the synagogue one of these days, that I was losing my way, turning into a very troubled young man. She disappeared into the bedroom and, when she emerged a few minutes later, she was holding a small plastic bottle. Bronx Holy Water. From the Grotto of

Lourdes. She began to sprinkle the water in droplets, reproaching me with her beautiful dark marble eyes, traversing the small crowded living room of our apartment. As she passed by some of the Holy Water sprinkled my arm.

Now *that* had me reeling back in horror.

"You trying to *baptize* me?" But she was so lost in her Catholic fervor that I had to start waving around the little laminated orishás to keep her at bay. Fanned them out proudly, one card short of a straight flush. Could her liquid superstition match the power of Elegua—the trickster who controls all human destiny?

She kept sprinkling the Holy Water around the apartment—on the kitchen table, on the phone, on the microwave, on the armchair, on her grandmother's antique rocker—until she'd cleansed the area around me several times, de-demonized the premises, left me sitting alone in my own little santería circle.

K stood in front of the Swatch boutique on Fifth Avenue, unscrolling the drawing, staring at my pencil-and-ink rendering of his own heart. Yes, he said finally, it was exactly like his dream. He leaned down and gave me a rib-crushing hug. The next step would be to send it down to Puerto Rico, along with a box of Nat Sherman cigars, so that Tony could perform the blessing.

"Cigars?"

"Word, Elegua likes cigars. Cigars, candy, rum. Tony's gotta smoke the cigars as an offering to him."

He was carrying a jumbo-sized Duane Reade bag filled with a month's supply of Pampers for his baby son, Little K. He put the rolled-up drawing in the bag with the Pampers. We walked down 42nd Street through the crowds of Sunday afternoon shoppers. Soon he was going to be buying twice this supply of diapers; Faith was six months pregnant, expecting their second baby by early winter.

Halfway down the block, a tall young high school kid approached, holding hands and laughing with his chubby-cheeked girl-friend. K put up his hand suddenly to stop their progress. The kid's smile vanished; he stared at K with a look of undisguised terror.

"Youngblood," K told him softly, "don't make your lady walk on the curbside." He touched the girl gently on the arm, switching their positions, moving her away from the busy street. "Check it—that's the way we *black* men supposed to do things."

"Uh huh," nodded the kid, still terrified, then he and the girl continued down 42nd Street.

"Can't understand that shit," K said angrily. "These young-ass niggas don't show no type of respect for they girls. Who the fuck's schoolin' them? That's one of the first things Julio and Toño taught me as a youth. Never make your girl walk next to the street. Basic fuckin' chivalry, yo."

When we came to the Sixth Avenue subway station, I told him that I had a writing assignment that was taking me out of town for a few weeks. He set down the jumbo bag of Pampers, face twisting in an exaggerated look of disappointment. Had I forgotten all about his birthday? I said it wasn't easy to forget his birthday—not with all the black cats and witches and jack-o'-lanterns in the midtown windows to remind me.

Back in Canada on a peaceful frozen late-October night, I tried calling him at his apartment to give him some good news: I'd finally found a professional hockey jersey big enough to fit him. (Official NHL jerseys had recently—inexplicably—become the de rigueur hip-hop fashion statement, but K was frustrated because he couldn't find any in New York that would billow loosely on his frame. At six foot three and 270, I realized he needed the specialized services of the Goalie Shop, catering solely to Canadian goaltenders and their Canadian goaltending needs, figured if the replica Montreal Canadiens jersey could slide over all that ludicrously bulky goalie padding, it could slide over that ludicrously bulky Big K physique . . .)

The phone rang for a long time in the Bronx before Faith answered. Was everything all right with the pregnancy? Yes, she'd just had the sonogram a few days earlier—the fetus looked strong and healthy. They were still anticipating a normal delivery sometime in early January.

But there was something else wrong in that Bronx apartment—why wasn't K barking excitedly for the phone by now?

Faith just laughed quietly into the receiver. Where was he? Locked the fuck up, that's where he was.

I called back the next night when he'd been released, as they say, on his own recognizance. Laughing heartily about everything now. *Want some advice? Don't never spend no fuckin' birthday sittin' in no Central Booking . . .*

Oh, it was a long, long story.

He'd gone to work as usual on Sunday. At the end of the workday, when his brother Craig finished his shift as a personal trainer at the New York Sports Club on 37th Street, he came by the Swatch store to get K and take him out for a nice brotherly pre-birthday meal. They walked over to the Howard Johnson's restaurant on 49th Street and Broadway.

"Why shit popped off was this—the waiter they assigned to wait on us was a real racist dickhead."

He said something racist?

"His face was all scrunched up when we sat down in the booth—you know the look? Like, 'Aw man, why the fuck do *I* get stuck waiting on these two big fuckin' hoodlums?'"

But did he actually *say* something racist?

"He didn't have to! Just the way he was lookin' at us, all leery and shit, like he was thinkin' we didn't even have the money to pay for our muthafuckin' meals—like we was gonna pull a muthafuckin' dine-and-dash on him."

They ordered from the menu without incident. It took a long time before the waiter brought over their meals. K had ordered a cheeseburger with french fries and a large root beer. Before eating, he began that ritual, pulling off the top of the bun, carefully arranging his french fries on top of the hamburger patty. And then Craig saw the ant. All of a sudden Craig was shouting and pointing—he'd spotted a red ant crawling in his brother's french fries. Now K, shouting too, called the waiter over to show him the ant. Said he wasn't paying for this fucking meal; he wanted a fresh cheeseburger and a fresh plate of french fries.

K had nibbled some of his french fries already and was feeling nauseous; wondered if he could possibly have chewed up and swallowed another ant without realizing it. Then as the waiter was taking away the plate, K caught him muttering under his breath: "—don't have time for this fuckin' shit . . ."

He promptly got up and followed the waiter back toward the kitchen.

"The fuck you mean you don't have *time* for this fuckin' shit? There's a fuckin' ant crawling in my fries and *you* don't have *time* for this shit? Faggot-ass muthafucka! You probably stuck the fuckin' ant in there on *purpose!*"

Everyone in the HoJo's was quite afraid of him. White ladies squeezing into the corners of their booths, pressing purses tight to their hips. Then one of the Mexican cooks in the kitchen, hearing the ruckus, got so frightened that he came running out brandishing a Heinz ketchup bottle overhead. *Tryin' to brain a muthafucka with Heinz 57?* On impulse K turned and decked the Mexican cook. The panicking waiter dropped the plates of food he'd been juggling. He threw up his hands to defend himself and then—not on impulse but simply because he *felt* like it—K dropped the waiter with one shot to the chin.

Sometime during this fracas someone called the police. A passing squad car wailed to a stop in front of the HoJo's, K was shackled up and taken to the Midtown North Precinct House.

"Charged with?"

"Misdemeanor assault and theft of services."

"Theft of services?"

"Dickhead tries to tell the cops it was all just a stunt so we could leave without payin' the bill."

The hearing was set for three weeks later, on November 21, at the Midtown Community Court on West 54th Street. K told me it was *imperative* that I be there with him.

"As a character witness?"

"They call it 'ties to the community.'"

I knew a few things about the Midtown Community Court; I'd read the articles in the *Times* and the *Daily News* when it opened the previous year. A new experiment in decentralizing the judicial system, an attempt to alleviate the overload of criminal dockets down at the 100 Centre Street courthouse. The judges at the Midtown Community Court were specifically empowered to deal with so-called nuisance misdemeanors, doling out sentences of community service to vandals, streetwalkers, shoplifters, panhandlers, unlicensed vendors and small-time drug offenders—thereby keeping thousands of petty criminals from clogging up the city's badly congested jail facilities.

A brisk and sunny November morning. I met K at nine A.M. out in front of the courthouse. A line thirty deep stretched down the block, waiting for the courthouse doors to open. K looked anxious, eyes downcast, darting. Asked me what I thought was going to happen today. I told him that he'd probably get sentenced to thirty days of envelope-stuffing in the court's basement or, at worst, assigned to one of those graffiti clean-up crews, have to spend a few weeks whitewashing spray paint from midtown office buildings and storefronts.

"Naw, duke, it ain't gonna go like that." For somebody who'd been arrested so many times he seemed surprisingly apprehensive about his day in court. Stood there without talking for a while, chewing a small wad of peppermint gum. Finally he whispered: "Ay yo, I gotta let you in on a little secret . . ."

Again? It was always like that with K: he'd say he wanted to let you in on a little secret and you felt like you were being invited to fish your hand around in a picnic basket filled with scorpions.

Today's little secret? He was still a fugitive from justice in the state of New Jersey. Stemmed from his being arrested in East Orange on a gun charge back in early '92. The bail had been set at $10,000; Faith had pawned her jewelry and got him out on the ten percent bail bond, but shortly thereafter they'd been evicted from their apartment and kept bouncing from place to place. He called every week to find out about his next court date but all they'd tell him was that he'd receive written notification by mail. Tried to explain to them that he wasn't getting his mail in East Orange anymore; they told him to keep calling back. The weeks passed and he got tired of calling, tired of waiting around. Finally, he and Faith left East Orange and came back to New York.

I did the mental calculations. Spring '92. Just a few months before we'd met down in Alphabet City, in the Nuyorican Poets Cafe.

"Why you think I was fuckin' homeless them times? Why you think I was ridin' the muthafuckin' train all night? I'd just come outta Essex County."

Picked a fine time to tell me.

"I *been* fuckin' tellin' you. Kept sayin' I can't fuckin' go back to Jersey. You never heard me? That's 'cause you never fuckin' listen. 'Member when we was takin' the PATH to Hoboken—'member when them two jakes got on the train? I kept sayin' I hope nothin' don't happen out here—I damn sure can't get arrested again in Jersey."

I listened to him, nodding, but something didn't add up. Hadn't the cops run his fingerprints after the HoJo's fracas?

"Muthafuckas *always* take your fingerprints. But you gotta understand—these fuckin' police computers be doin' some stupid shit sometimes. They mad inconsistent. Sometimes the shit'll come up quick-fast: 'Look, muthafucka, you got outstanding warrants for this,

this and this.' Then other times, nothin' won't come up and you out—ROR."

"Well, they let you walk, right? You probably slipped through the system."

"Know the minute we get inside them doors."

The court officer on duty at the door was in his early forties, dark curly hair, neat mustache. Looked a little like a pudgy version of Barney Miller. The double chin and slight potbelly; clean white uniform short-sleeve shirt. As the line inched forward through the door I found myself staring at his holstered gun and nightstick.

K approached the officer and, very softly, said his government name. The officer looked up from the ledger with the list of that day's cases. He asked K to repeat his government name.

As soon as K spoke those words again, another young court officer who'd been standing off to the side rushed forward. Together they threw K up against the wall, shouting for him to spread his legs. One officer frisked him while another pulled his wrists behind his back and clamped on the handcuffs. K wasn't offering any resistance, but the cops were muscling him hard just the same. Arms wrenched behind his back, he turned, flashed me his *I-told-you-so* glance. Then the cops led him into the courtroom and sat him all alone on a private area just to the left of the judge's bench.

The first row of benches was reserved for defendants and their lawyers. I sat a few rows further back, with a clear line of sight to K. We were too far apart to hear each other whisper. I tried lip-reading for a few minutes without much success. Finally he slumped forward, staring at the floor, with his hands tightly cuffed behind his back.

I opened my briefcase. I had some work to finish for an interview later that day, started to reread the last few pages of a legal thriller called *The Advocate's Devil*, Alan Dershowitz's story of a Harvard law professor who faces the ethical dilemma of defending a client he knows to be guilty of rape. Every few minutes I'd glance up from the novel and K would shrug at me and we'd try reading each other's lips again. He kept scanning the courtroom entrance, waiting for Faith to show up with Little K.

Straining, wriggling, trying to find a way to sit with his hands cuffed behind his back. Staring at the floor with a docile, self-pitying look on his face. I stopped reading and watched the strange scene unfolding. A couple of the courtroom cops had begun playing mind games with K. They got a kick out of baiting him. It was quite subtle—you had to watch closely to notice how they'd taunt him, making contorted faces as they walked past every few minutes, bowlegged as cowboys, paperwork in hand. One young red-haired cop bared his teeth and stuck out his lower lip in what I took to be an imitation of an ape. Minutes later the pudgy cop who looked like Barney Miller passed by, paused, leaned forward and held out his chin until his face was only inches away from K. "Not such a tough guy *now,* huh?"

I got up and went to the little adjacent conference room to talk to the Legal Aid attorney who'd been assigned the case. He handed me one of his business cards; his name was Tom Tracy; a jowly, kindly, avuncular-looking guy, the spitting image of one of my high school social studies teachers. I asked him what were the chances of the judge setting bail today.

"Are you an attorney?"

"Just a friend."

There was no possibility of bail being set today. It wasn't the assault at the Howard Johnson's that would be the problem—that was just a misdemeanor assault. No, it was these three outstanding felony bench warrants from Brooklyn, Queens and Manhattan. There was also a felony warrant here from Essex County, New Jersey; but his client would have to come before three separate judges in Brooklyn, Queens and Manhattan before the Jersey criminal justice system ever got its hand on him.

Three New York warrants? I was trying to look over his shoulder at the rap sheet—it was as thick as a small-town phone book—but Tom pulled it away so I couldn't read it. *No, no, no.* That would be a violation of his client's privacy, he said.

He cleared his throat and said that the three outstanding New York warrants were all for gun felonies dating back to '86 and '87. Brandishing, firing shots from a moving vehicle, that sort of thing. Stared at me, as if I should be taken aback by the gravity of the information he was imparting. But I could only shrug, telling Tom I was certain there was nothing about his client that would surprise me anymore.

Didn't take K long to prove me wrong. A sudden dreadful roar erupted in the courtroom behind us. Tom and I turned quickly to see what had happened.

In the far corner of the room K was on his feet, trying to lunge at the pudgy curly-haired cop who'd been taunting him earlier.

"Take off the fuckin' cuffs, bitch-ass muthafucka! Take off the muthafuckin' cuffs, *then* talk that ol' bullshit! Word to mother—soon's I get *one* hand free, I'm a mash in yo' muthafuckin' grill, *bitch!*"

The bear-baiting strategy had worked. From all corners of the courtroom, cops were rushing to the scene, nightsticks drawn, biceps flexing. K lowered his shoulders and grinned at them: even with his hands shackled he was eager for the battle.

As usual—now that the pin was irrevocably out of the grenade—his voice flipped suddenly into his Jamaican badman howl, the gritty dialect of the Crime Heights streets, the rapid-fire patois that most perfectly captured the intensity of his rage:

"*Yeow! Wha de bomboclaat yuh a deal wit? Yu tink seh me gi a fuck bout yu Babylon? Pussybwoy! Come yah! Mek I-an-I mash out yuh bloodclaat!*"

Poor Tom of the Legal Aid Society. Showed up in court expecting a routine morning's work defending streetwalkers and parking scofflaws and shoplifters—but (luck of the draw) he finds himself representing a crazed gangster wanted on gun warrants in three of the five boroughs (not to mention this pending extradition to New Jersey) . . . and now, coming out of the Legal Aid room, file in hand, hoping to begin briefing his client on the gravity of these three New York bench warrants, Tom hears a deafening and incomprehensible ruckus and realizes (with a visible shudder) that, yes, he is responsible for the legal defense of that violently cursing young fellow, realizes that he has for a client a freewheeling 270-pound West Indian scarface who has not only disrupted the morning's court proceedings but is actively engaged in an attempted assault (and how is that even *possible* given the impediment of handcuffs?) on every single member of the Midtown Community Court's police force . . .

I had seen K so many times in this state of explosive rage that I'd forgotten how terrifying he must appear to strangers. Brought me back to that first night in Medusa when he'd erupted with his West Indian roar and had a clubful of downtown hipsters fleeing for the glowing exit signs. Now he'd upped the ante, had six armed court officers surrounding him with nightsticks raised and ready—but it was the *cops* who stood frozen in fear, uncertain how to get within striking distance.

That was always his ace in the hole: his power to terrorize. He ducked his shoulders, bobbed, shifted his weight, lunging forward in his sudden boxer's feints. The cops couldn't mount any organized attack; his reaction time was much too fast. He raised his right leg and lashed out with a vicious kick that had all the cops dancing backward and futilely swinging their nightsticks at empty space.

Watching him dodge the nightsticks I felt a pang of sweaty delirium, my mind soaring away from me again, wondering if there'd been a similar spectacle in the days of the Roman Colosseum, some early morning matchup featuring a hulking wild-eyed prisoner of war, captured on the fringes of the empire, thrown into battle with his arms shackled behind him—not that he stood a chance of *winning*, of course—just some lopsided preliminary to get the crowd hooting and whistling and taking wagers on how long the raging barbarian could hold out against six cool-headed gladiators armed with sturdy wooden black clubs . . .

In a flash two of the cops managed to sneak behind K—then all those heavy bodies smashed together at once and there was a thundering surge like a rugby scrum at the end of which a door opened and K and all the cops disappeared into the back room. The door slammed shut with an echo of cannon fire. The judge, visibly shaken by this violent disruption, announced a ten-minute recess and disappeared from the bench.

An angry buzzing in the courtroom. All the shoplifters and hookers and scofflaws awaiting their three minutes before the judge were now staring at me—assuming, I suppose, that I'd somehow played an accomplice's role in this strategic outburst.

Behind that door I kept hearing K shouting in Jamaican and metal doors clanging and a lot of unpleasant-sounding thuds. Finally, the door opened and out came a heavyset black court officer. The only black officer I'd seen in the court all morning. Stood at least six foot four with salt-and-pepper hair. For some bizarre reason, this enormous court officer was now calling my name.

"Over here," I said, one hand raised like a second-grader during morning attendance. The black officer gestured for me to get up and join him at the back of the courtroom. Wheezing angrily, he immediately launched into a lecture.

"What the hell is *wrong* with your man?"

"I don't know. Why don't you try asking him?"

"I'll tell you what it is—he likes to fight too goddamn much."

"You're right. He likes to fight too much."

"Better calm himself down before he gets to the Island—they gonna throw his ass in the Bing*—see how *bad* he is then."

---

*Nickname for Rikers Island's Central Punitive Segregation Unit, housing the most violent rule-breakers in the city's eighteen-thousand-inmate jail system.

"What is it you want from me?"

"Keeps sayin' he wants to talk to you."

"You want me to talk to him?"

"Hell naw. I can't let you talk to him." Still wheezing with rage, the cop fished deep into his pants pocket for something. "Is his wife out here? He keeps asking about his wife and his kid."

"They're not here yet."

He pulled out a tremendous mass of keys on several connected key rings. "Here—he wants you to hold these."

I took the handful of keys from the courtroom cop. More confusion—I'd never seen K with such an unwieldy set of key rings—fifty or sixty keys, all dangling and twisted together. Had he secretly become the superintendent of some apartment complex in the Bronx?

Five minutes passed. The judge had not even resumed hearing cases. All the impatient Arab hot dog vendors and hookers in pancake makeup and tight purple miniskirts were still staring irately in my direction. Suddenly, the tall black court officer came stomping back out, started calling my name again.

"Gimme back my keys."

"I thought you said he wanted me to hold them."

"Your man's got my head so damn messed up"—looking sheepish, lowering his voice—"I gave you his keys *and* my keys." I smiled and reached into my overcoat pocket, handed all the keys back to the cop. He began to untangle the rings, gave me back one little set before shoving the remaining jumble deep into his own pants pocket.

Now I understood why he was so embarrassed: in his confusion he'd handed me the keys to the Midtown Community Court and all the holding cells in back. He glared at me, slowly grinding the meat of his palm into the butt of the holstered handgun on his hip.

"Good thing you didn't try to leave," he said.

Faith finally showed up with Little K during the lunch recess. Her mother was double-parked outside the precinct house in her white van. Faith had been through this jail experience with K so many times that she knew exactly what he'd need: at least three new pairs of XXL Fruit of the Loom boxers and some African Pride hair conditioner to keep his hair from turning brittle and some Jergens hand cream to keep his skin from turning ashy and plenty of Right Guard deodorant to keep his armpits from stinking up the jail. We went to the Duane Reade and purchased the boxer shorts and assorted toiletries. But the irritable officers at the Midtown Community Court wouldn't give the bag to K. They said we'd have to go visit him on Rikers Island or down at the Tombs as soon as he was assigned a bed someplace.

After lunch, K was finally brought before the judge in handcuffs, surrounded by four cops. It took less than a minute: Tom Tracy made one brief motion and then the judge decided that the Howard Johnson's misdemeanor assault case would be postponed until the defendant could be sent to Queens to answer to the first of his outstanding felony warrants. K stood there glowering, uncooperative, unrepentant.

As the cops hauled him away, he once again disrupted the silence in court with his violent shouting. This time it wasn't a spontaneous outburst; he wanted to enter the jail system carrying a reputation for craziness, wanted all the other inmates to view him as some untamed monster. He glanced back quickly to say goodbye to Faith and Little K; then, muscling his shoulders against the cops as they led him out of the court, he resumed his maniacal howl. *"What! What! What! F.A.P. in full effect!"*

I was running late for my afternoon interview, had less than fifteen minutes to get all the way over to the East Side. I grabbed a lift with Faith and her mother as far as Third Avenue and during the ride Little K kept trying to bite me on the hand and then we got stuck in gridlock and I jumped out of the van and started jogging toward Tudor City. I was running as fast as I could in my double-breasted suit and heavy cashmere overcoat and by the time I got to Tudor City I was sweating so profusely that the doorman stared at me like I was some deranged assassin who'd just emerged from the dark waters of the

East River. Then I mopped my forehead dry with a tissue and went upstairs to interview Professor Dershowitz about *The Advocate's Devil,* and he was talking a mile a minute about the Von Bulow attempted murder case and the Tyson rape case ("The Mike Tyson case is the easiest I ever couldn't win. Any first-year law student should have been able to win it . . ."). His secretary at Harvard kept calling him on the phone every ten minutes and I'd overhear him whispering about O.J. Simpson but he wouldn't answer any on-the-record questions about O.J.'s upcoming murder trial besides confirming that, yes, he was part of the Simpson defense team, and I was just hoping that the pulsing red light on my tape recorder meant that the damn thing was actually recording because now I wasn't even listening to Dershowitz anymore, I was just thinking about K fighting the cops, dodging the blows of their nightsticks, wondering how many more people he was going to try to physically attack before they dragged him howling into his jail cell . . .

When I got home there were six messages flashing on the answering machine. All of them from K down in the Tombs. Every message ended with him saying, "Yo, call you back in a couple of hours," but then he would wait only ten minutes before calling again. I barely had time to take off my overcoat before the phone rang. He sounded calm and matter-of-fact.

"Yo, what's the deal, homeboy?"

"Ever heard of contempt of court?"

"Fuck 'em! They wanna add another fuckin' ninety days to my sentence, let 'em fuckin' do it. They already got me starin' at a muthafuckin' *ass*hole full a time."

Since we were on the subject, what did he know about those outstanding felony warrants? The '86 case out in Queens was the most serious, he said. In Queens he stood accused of firing a semiautomatic weapon out of the sunroof of an unlicensed vehicle while speeding recklessly down the sidewalk.

Come again?

They were in a long-standing war with a rival crew in Queens. The Dominicans were blazing at him with Tec-9s and he'd been firing shots out the sunroof back at the Dominicans with his own Tec when he lost control of the car and crashed into an abutment. That's when the cops showed up and surrounded him. The only question was whether they still had enough evidence to proceed with the case: '86 was a long fucking time ago.

And the Brooklyn case?

That was also a gun felony. But that one was only for brandishing the weapon—not busting shots. They'd probably have to drop that shit for lack of evidence.

"Why didn't all these old warrants come up when you were arrested back in '88?"

"That's what I been tryin' to tell you, man—the criminal justice system is some completely fucked-up shit. Them computers don't know what they doin' half the fuckin' time."

He came into the system ready to fight everyone: the COs, Latin Kings, Netas, Bloods, Zulu Nation—any gang or posse or clique they could put in front of him. On his first full day in the Tombs one of the COs recognized him as a potential menace to prison safety and brought him down to see the shrink. The shrink diagnosed him as a manic-depressive and promptly pumped him full of lithium and Prozac. The antidepressants soon took hold and he no longer felt like flipping the script. Just sleepy all the time. Wanted to snooze eighteen hours a day. He'd lost his appetite as well. Didn't even have the energy to do his sets of push-ups and dips. Shit, they'd managed to sedate him into submission.

"Can't understand this shit, D. All them fuckin' years I was livin' foul, wakin' up every fuckin' mornin' just to do more dirt, just to sling more shit and clap muthafuckas up, all them fuckin' years pass, and now, now that I'm tryin' to be a boring-ass muthafucka workin' a nine-to-five, stayin' with Faith, tryin' to raise up my little man proper—now we got a second baby on the way—now this bullshit drops down on me. Why now? You know how much shit I done got *away with* back in the days? This shit don't make no type of sense to me. What the fuck is goin' on with my muthafuckin' life?"

He gave me the phone number of his spiritual godfather down in Puerto Rico. Sounded frightened now, worried about the santería magic turning bad. Wanted me to call Tony and find out if all his beads had been contaminated while he was fighting with the cops. Some of the cops had managed to put their hands on the beads around his neck during the scuffle. (Touching those multicolored beads was always a sensitive issue: even Faith was careful not to make contact with them for fear of damaging their mysterious protective powers.)

I called down to the town of Carolina in Puerto Rico and asked Tony the questions exactly as K had said them. (Didn't dare let Crystal know: *now* I'd become a santería conduit.) The soft-spoken santero at the other end answered me in perfect English and only a slight trace of a Spanish accent. "Tell him not to worry. I can always send him more beads. The most important thing is that he keeps his mental composure. He can't keep losing his temper like that. Tell him I said this: the orishás can't help him unless he remains calm at all times."

Yes, Tony was right, K said. The orishás were still strongly blessing him. One by one his outstanding bench warrants were dismissed for lack of evidence. He called me from the Tombs right after they'd brought him before the court in Queens. Said that the judge there had glared at him. "Young man, I would like nothing better than to see you prosecuted to the fullest extent of the law here in Queens County. It pains me greatly to have to dismiss the case against you for lack of evidence. But I see here that you have several other outstanding bench warrants and I can only hope that justice will ultimately be served outside the confines of this courtroom."

On his third day in the Tombs the COs woke him up at four in the morning, shouting strange words in his face, telling him he was lucky to be alive. They dragged him down to the clinic for emergency treatment. His blood tests had come back: he was suffering from diabetes coupled with extreme hypertension. *The fuck you talkin' 'bout?* Told him it was lethal combination, that he could suffer a stroke or a heart attack or go into a diabetic coma at any moment.

Crystal overheard this conversation and picked up the bedroom extension. This was her specific area of public health expertise; her doctoral research dealt with the complications of type 2 diabetes in the African-American community. She began to bombard K with technical questions: How high was his sugar? And his pressure? Any blurriness of vision? Thirstiness? Exactly how much weight had he gained in the last few years?

"Eighty pounds."

"That's much too much weight."

"But you *seen* me, sis. I ain't fat, right? I can still do my hundred push-ups every morning no problem. And my foot speed—just ask them fuckin' cops—my foot speed is *very* much up to par."

She said he would have to bring his weight down if he wanted to control his diabetes without dependence on regular insulin shots.

"Naw, I ain't gonna lose no weight, sis. Soon's I get myself back in the gym, I'm tryin' to bulk up to a nice even three hundred. Three hundred sounds like a good weight for me."

"That's ridiculous."

"What, you want me to be all skinny like some muthafucka with AIDS? You want me to look like a fuckin' crackhead?"

She hung up the extension and stared at me. How could a grown man be so hardheaded?

The Tombs. Formally known as the Manhattan Detention Complex, located on White and Centre Streets, just south of the frenetic, shoulder-to-shoulder, counterfeit-Rolex bustle of Chinatown. A block with Manhattan's longest history of lockups: the current facility, housing roughly eight hundred inmates, is the third-generation jail to stand on the site. The colloquial "Tombs" dates back to the 1830s, the original jailhouse having been modeled, for reasons unknown, after an ancient Egyptian mausoleum. The current complex, resembling a municipal office building more than some Pharaoh's crypt, still clings to that ominous and incongruous nickname.

In old New York, I knew, the Tombs was indeed a palace of death, a killing fortress, place of execution for many of the town's most notorious gangsters and thugs. Charles Dickens, during his American travels of 1842, paid a visit to the jail, appalled by the filthy, overcrowded conditions he witnessed; built to sleep 350 men, the old Tombs routinely housed several thousand. Nineteenth-century London jails were positively humane by comparison. In *American Notes*, the novelist-turned-travel-writer mused on the fate of those inmates who would be leaving the Tombs only by way of pine box:

> Into the prison yard—this narrow, grave-like place—men are brought out to die. The wretched creature stands beneath the gibbet and the ground; the rope about his neck; and when the sign is given, a weight at its other end comes running down and swings him up into the air—a corpse. The law requires that there be present at this dismal spectacle, the judge, the jury and citizens to the amount of 25.

If it's no longer the scene of such "dreadful performances," the new-age Tombs is still a morbid place to visit on a windy winter afternoon. No fear of smallpox or cholera epidemics; today the halls, reeking of

Lysol disinfectant, are paced by hollow-eyed inmates mad with delirium tremens or the quiver of crack withdrawal. Still others wasting away under that viral death sentence. Being a house of detention—rather than incarceration—economic status is the prime factor in determining the demographics; most of the inmates are awaiting trial, no hope of posting bail or bond—or of affording a decent defense attorney to argue on their behalf at the bail-reduction hearing.

The jowly corrections officer on duty at the door is not a happy man. No, I explain, pulling out my passport, I am not an attorney here to confer with my client. No special entrance privileges. I'll have to wait on the bench with the rest of the civilians.

The waiting area is packed with dozens of young black and Latino women—wives and girlfriends for whom these jail visits have become as routine as a trip to the A&P or Duane Reade. It's a familiar crew—today Faith runs into one of her old girlfriends from the Hill in Harlem. *What he in for? Yeah? Again?* They've all been to the beauty parlor to get their hair and fingernails done, all wearing skintight Guess? or Levi's jeans and sexy silk blouses so that their men can snap that mental Polaroid, commit their images to memory before being led back to lockdown—healthy round young body parts to be summoned up again in the brief onanistic solitude of showertime.

You'd be amazed the things people try to bring down here on visiting day, the heavyset CO tells me. Find them hidden all over the yard outside. Glocks, Colts, Tecs. Not to mention the selection of blades and box cutters. Beepers aren't allowed inside the waiting area, can't even be left in the coin-operated lockers, so many of the young ladies scheme ways to bury their pagers in the dirt outside.

K has been complaining that he's starved for reading material—in the midst of Giuliani's budgetary cuts, the upkeep of the prison's library services has been deemed an unnecessary luxury—so I've brought him a couple of paperbacks (Richard Wright, Nicholas Pileggi), the latest issues of *The Source* and *The Ring,* a few of Crystal's educational diabetes pamphlets (*The World Is a Beautiful Place to See*), along with a blank legal pad so he can keep penning his rhymes and self-analytical snippets of poetry.

The only good thing he can say about lockdown: so many lyrics coming to him, day and night, he barely has time to write them all down. He's been catching wreck in the daily freestyle battles they have up in the dayroom. A couple of guys in the Tombs recognized him from the New Music Seminar MC battles and from the Zulu Nation 20th Anniversary Show at the Puck Building (K'd *torn* shit up that day), kept challenging him to show and prove, step into the cipher for the lyrical throwdown.

In Leadbelly's day, I keep thinking, you'd have heard blues-shouting contests echoing across the prison yard. Now the inmates gather in the dayroom for that freestyle rhyme cipher.

K's never heard of Leadbelly. "The Midnight Special"—"Goodnight Irene"? Still drawing a serious blank. Old-time Southern bluesmen are not his area of expertise. Even ones who did hard time for homicide.

"Nigga was actually named Lead*belly*? That's fucked up, duke. Musta got clapped a few times in his gut, huh?"

No, his government name was Huddie Ledbetter. I give him the basic outline of the Leadbelly legend: how he'd shot and killed a man in a fit of passion, ending up on a Texas chain gang; how he'd sung his way to a pardon in front of the governor of Texas; how, rearrested for assault in Louisiana, he'd been "discovered" by John Lomax doing his twelve-string blues compositions in Angola penitentiary; how, when he came North to do his first concerts in New York City in the '30s, the *Herald Tribune* trumpeted his arrival with the infamous head-line:

SWEET SINGER OF THE SWAMPLANDS
HERE TO DO A FEW TUNES
BETWEEN HOMICIDES

"They was usin' that shit as a marketin' gimmick? Even back in them days?"

"He lived up to his image. One night in Harlem he got in a fight, stabbed a guy sixteen times and ended up on Rikers Island for eight months."

But K had no interest in the Leadbelly legend: another stabbing scene was flashing in his mind. His eyes darted around the visiting room, ever vigilant, as he excitedly remembered a made-for-TV movie he'd been watching the previous evening. *Escape from Sobibor.* The true story of several hundred Jewish prisoners who'd staged a revolt in a Nazi extermination camp. That shit had *moved* him. By the end of the movie he was sitting there bawling like a baby in the dayroom.

The sheer cunning and *heart* of it! He loved the way the Jews had carefully waited and planned for the day of the escape. The only thing that had kept them alive all those months was a thirst for revenge. The first person they had to kill was a Jewish traitor called a kapo: murdered him by beating him in the belly so that the Germans wouldn't see any marks. Then when the appointed time came, they began to lure the SS guards one by one into the barracks with clever excuses. Told one guard that his new pair of leather boots was ready, another that they had a beautiful new leather coat for him to try on. When the SS guards would show up in the barracks, the Jews would leap out with their homemade shanks and hatchets and *jook* the Nazis up real nice. Then they'd drag the bodies into hiding spots so they could continue with the day's killings. Everything had to be completed within one hour's time.

His favorite scene took place in the kitchen barracks where this little bald Jewish guy who'd been a plumber before the war was cooking up some slop in a big pot. In walks a fat SS guard with a face like a pig's. A real sadistic son of a bitch, always whipping the Jews with his riding crop. The SS pig lifts the lid on the slop pot and takes a deep whiff.

"How do you do it?" he says. "Only a Jewish plumber could cook up something so obviously delicious!" Walks over to the Jewish plumber and touches him on the nose. Almost looked like he was going to plant a big faggot kiss on him. "What is your Christian name?"

Then the little Jew—who's been hiding an eighteen-inch knife blade behind his back the whole time—looks the German in the eye. "I don't have a Christian name—only a *Jewish* name!" And he plunges the full length of the knife into the pig's belly, slicing him open from the bowels up to the lungs.

K was screaming with pleasure when he saw that. Only a *Jewish* name! He loved that scene more than anything he'd seen in a long time.

On a cold morning in December I returned to the Tombs; I had to meet a young rapper from Harlem named A-Sharp. A few months earlier, he and K had done an impromptu show together at a club in SoHo; K said they were planning to start collaborating on some rhymes. Sharp was a very talented lyricist—like K, he was still looking for a record deal, kept getting the run-around from various managers and production companies. (A typical music business saga; for every rapper who actually gets signed and has a record released, there are thousands more like Sharp and K struggling just to make it through the industry's labyrinth of bullshit and lies.)

A-Sharp had already had some songwriting success; back in '92, he'd been one of the co-writers of Wreckxs-n-Effect's multiplatinum hit "Rump Shaker." K was forever teasing him about it because when Sharp would go by the ASCAP offices to get his royalty checks the white guys working behind the desk would shout out *Rump!* as if that was A-Sharp's rap name. "Hey *Rump!*" K would holler in his teasing white-guy impersonation. *"R-u-u-ump!"* I tried it once myself when we were all in the pizza shop on West 42nd but Sharp just glared at me and advised me never to do it again.

Sharp was already waiting for me outside the Tombs on the corner of White Street. We went inside to visit K, signed in, showed our photo

IDs, but after a long wait the CO on duty told us that K had been transferred, for no apparent reason, in the middle of the night, to Rikers.

I failed to see the logic in the transfer. "Why move him all the way out to Rikers? He has to be right back here in Manhattan court first thing Monday morning."

The CO just shrugged.

"Isn't that a waste of manpower and gasoline?"

"Do I look like I make the fuckin' rules here?"

His hearing had been rescheduled for the morning of December 5 at the 100 Centre Street Criminal Court building. Out in front of the courthouse I met up with Jeffrey Goldberg and then, a few minutes later, we were joined by my friend Bernie Jackson, an entertainment attorney who'd known K for a couple of years. Bernie'd volunteered to come down to the court, not as legal counsel, but simply as another tie to the community. Took a long time for us to get through the security line; a cold sleety rain began to fall on our heads while we waited.

The long delay was caused by a crush of print reporters and TV camera crews waiting to get into the courthouse to see what kind of prison sentence would be meted out to Tupac Shakur today. For weeks, the New York tabloids and local TV stations had been obsessively covering every new development in the Tupac saga.

Several days earlier, the twenty-three-year-old rapper and budding movie star had been convicted of sexually assaulting a female fan (he was acquitted on related charges of sodomy and gun possession). The most bizarre twist in the story came right in the midst of the trial: shortly after midnight on the night of November 30, stopping by Quad Studios in Times Square for a recording session, Tupac had been gunned down and robbed of $45,000 in jewelry, shot five times in the head, hand and groin, losing one of his testicles in the process. Then, barely out of surgery the next day, he'd vanished from his Bellevue Hospital bed—against his doctor's orders—and showed up at the courthouse in a wheelchair and head bandages, flanked by Fruit of Islam security guards, to hear the guilty verdict and then give a press conference in which he unapologetically denounced his accuser. "I didn't sodomize her," he said. *"She's the one who sodomized me."*

(The young woman, a twenty-year-old Brooklynite, admitted in court that she'd willingly had sex with Tupac twice on the night they met; but then during a second rendezvous in his Parker Meridian hotel suite, she testified, the rapper had watched and assisted as three members of his entourage grabbed her, groped her and forced her to perform oral sex as she wept and begged for mercy.)

The child of a former Black Panther, a graduate of Baltimore's High School for Performing Arts, Tupac was a young man whose every action elicited wildly conflicting opinions. To his legions of fans, he was a gifted street poet and thespian, a veritable icon of youthful black rebellion; to his detractors, nothing but a boastful, self-described "thug" who'd been arrested five times for violent crimes in an eighteen-month period.

Like everyone else in the crowd that morning, Jeff and Bernie and I stood there in the cold rain debating the life and times of Mr. Tupac Shakur. Jeff frankly admitted that he couldn't stand most of the rap he heard on the radio or saw on MTV these days; it was pathetic to hear these guys trying to make lives of violence and drug dealing seem so *sexy.* What ever happened to De La Soul and A Tribe Called Quest? Bernie countered by saying that it wasn't an issue of morality so much as one of artistic freedom; if Scorcese and De Palma and Tarantino could make ultra-violent movies, gaining critical acclaim and enriching themselves in the process, why couldn't Tupac and Biggie and Snoop do the same thing with their lyrics?

Waiting outside the courthouse, trying to keep my head dry with a folded copy of the *Times,* I found myself eavesdropping on the dozens of reporters and photographers and cameramen, many of whom weren't even sure how to correctly pronounce Tupac's name, impatiently pushing their way into the courthouse hoping for a

glimpse of the handsome doe-eyed young man in the head ban-
dages—*Does Toe-Puck really have the words* THUG LIFE *tattooed across his
belly?* and *Did Toe-Puck really shoot two white cops down in Georgia?*—
everyone eager to get a face-to-face glimpse of that diminutive but
dangerous rap star, eyes sparkling, smirking, unrepentant to the last.*

Inside the courthouse we managed to break free from the Tupac media
circus, taking the elevator upstairs to the fifth floor. Walking through
the quiet upper halls of the courthouse you were immediately struck
by the contrast: away from the blinding TV lights and the hyperventilating reporters, New York's criminal justice system continued its inexorable grind, processing hundreds of cases without fanfare or
outside scrutiny. I looked over at a young pregnant black woman who
sat alone on a bench, her arm in a sling, hand heavily bandaged: there
were no newspapermen sticking tape recorders in *her* face.

Jeff and Bernie and I went from courtroom to courtroom, trying to
determine which Legal Aid attorney had been assigned K's case. We finally found him. Christopher Pisciotia; a fresh-faced kid straight out of
law school. He knew absolutely nothing about the case yet—Legal Aid
attorneys routinely meet their clients only minutes before the day's
court session—but when we briefed him on the facts he said the best
thing he could do today was ask the judge to dismiss the misdemeanor
assault charges so that the New Jersey detectives could take him away.

"What if the Jersey detectives don't show up in court?"

"Then he'd be free to leave. That's not New York's responsibility—
it's up to New Jersey to come get him."

*   *   *

---

*Tupac's sentencing was postponed that morning owing to the severity of his injuries. On
February 7, 1995, Judge Daniel Fitzpatrick imposed a sentence of one and a half to four
and a half years. Tupac served only eight months of that term behind bars. In October
1995, he was released from the Clinton State Prison on bail of $1.4 million, pending his
appeal of the conviction; the bail had been posted by Marion (Suge) Knight, CEO of Death
Row Records, for whom Tupac immediately began recording a new double album, *All Eyez
on Me*. Less than a year later, on September 8, 1996, Tupac was gunned down in Las Vegas
while riding in the passenger seat of a BMW 750 sedan driven by Suge Knight. He died on
September 13. To date, no one has been arrested for his murder.

The judge didn't call K's case all morning. By lunchtime Jeff and Bernie both needed to go back to work. Returning to the courtroom with Faith, I spotted the two New Jersey detectives sitting in the front row waiting to extradite him to Essex County.

The judge arrived back for the afternoon session and K was led into the prisoner's dock in cuffs and leg shackles. He was wearing the huge gray sweat suit Faith and I'd brought to him in the Tombs. It no longer looked clean. His eyes were tired; his braids had become disheveled and frizzy. Evidently, the nights on Rikers Island hadn't agreed with him. He slumped forward on his bench, quietly waiting for his case to be called.

Faith and I were sitting alone in the back of the court when K's younger brother, Craig, showed up. Entering the quiet courtroom, he started shouting in an angry voice, saying that this whole case was a bunch of bullshit. His brother hadn't punched anybody in the Howard Johnson's—he'd only *mushed* them. If his brother had punched them, really *punched* them, they would've both been taken to the fuckin' hospital! Craig handed me his handwritten account of everything that had happened in the restaurant, how rude and abrasive the waiter had been when they showed him the red ant in the food, how the Mexican cook had tried to rush at his brother with the Heinz ketchup bottle. I read the rambling letter through to the end; then I told Craig that I didn't think the judge would deem it a relevant piece of evidence.

Faith noticed that K was trying to signal something. I squinted but still couldn't read his lips. Craig felt that it had something to do with new sneakers. Sneakers were a very big issue to K in jail.

Craig and Faith were trying to whisper things to K and the volume of the whispering kept getting louder and then the judge whirled furiously around on the bench and pointed at us in the back of the courtroom.

"Look!" she said. "Either *shut up* or leave my court!"

There was a pause and then K leapt to his feet in the prisoner's dock. No one, not even a criminal court judge, was going to shout at his pregnant wife like that.

"Watch ya muthafuckin' mouth! That's my *peeps* you disre-spectin'!"

"What did you just say to me?"

"You heard me! Want me to say it *again?* Check it out—what ya need to do is suck my muthafuckin' *dick*, bitch!"

She no longer looked angry—simply incredulous. Turned to one of her clerks. "Am I *hearing* this person correctly?"

Once again K had brought all the courtroom proceedings to an abrupt halt. Once again a gang of courtroom cops were rushing at him and he was ducking his shoulders, preparing to fight them using just the hulking mass of his body. Once again he was dragged back in shackles, cursing and raging. In the front row, the two New Jersey detectives tensed, stood up in their matching Essex County windbreakers. Evidently, this was not going to be a routine extradition drive back to Newark after all.

Later that night K tried calling me collect three times from the Essex County jail in Newark. I wouldn't accept the charges, let the machine pick up. Finally, on the fourth call, I caved in.

"Yo, I was tryin'—I was really *tryin'*."

"Oh yeah?"

"I *was*—until I seen that bitch pointin' her ugly-ass finger at Faith and shoutin' '*Shut up!*' like that. That shit made me lose my mutha-fuckin' mind."

"She's a *judge*."

"Man, *fuck* that! Whatcha sayin'? My wife ain't worthy of *respect?* The bitch can't be, like, 'Please be quiet' or 'Hold it down'? She's gotta point her fuckin' finger and yell 'Shut up!' at y'all like y'all a pack of fuckin' mangy dogs?"

In a court of law, I tried to point out, a judge has the prerogative to do whatever—

"Yo, check it—I ain't tryin' to *hear* that shit. You can think I'm a fuckin' barbaric nigga for sayin' this, but as long as I'm walkin' this fuckin' earth, if I *ever* see some muthafucka tryin' to disrespect my boo like that, I'm a have somethin' to say about it. *Trust* me! Judge, DA, beast, whatever—I don't care if they gotta lock me up for the rest of my fuckin' life. I ain't lettin' *nobody* disrespect my fam like that!"

I told him he wasn't making too much sense.

"I *never* make no fuckin' sense to you!"

Then he hung up the phone.

When he called back thirty minutes later he was crying. He'd been trying to call Faith but their phone bill wasn't paid up and she couldn't get any collect calls. Sounded like he was hyperventilating. Sobbing and sniffling. I was tired of hearing his bullshit. I told him to stop feeling sorry for himself.

"Yo, I can't fuckin' deal with this shit no more . . ."

"You don't have much choice."

"You don't gotta say it—I *know* I fucked up! . . . Can't fuckin' take doin' this shit to my Baby Boo . . . I love that girl too much . . . she don't deserve the *bullshit* I be puttin' her through—was she upset with me? She looked upset when y'all was leavin'?"

No, I'm sure she was delighted, lugging her swollen body down to the courthouse at nine A.M., eight months pregnant with his child, watching him jump up in shackles to tell a criminal court judge that she should hurry down from her bench to fellate him.

"Yo, please call Faith tonight and make sure she's all right. *Please,* duke. I got this fuckin' premonition that she's gonna lose the baby. If she loses the baby because of me, word is bond, I don't know what's gonna happen—I'm gonna end up killin' some nigga in this muthafucka . . ."

He was facing a minimum of a five-year jail term in Essex County. The charge was aggravated assault with a handgun. In the state of New Jersey, I learned, there's a statute called the Graves Act under which gun-related assaults are punished far more severely than in New York.

He stood accused of pistol-whipping a teenager named Rayshaun in East Orange back in '91 and making "terroristic threats" against the youth. According to K, Rayshaun was one of his drug workers; he didn't deny that he'd hit the kid, but he denied having used his gun to do it. The whole case, he claimed, was bogus. The cops didn't have a gun. They didn't have any eyewitness. No hospital report of injuries. The shit wasn't even about Rayshaun, he said. The whole thing was about some "bitch" called Joyce, some former girlfriend whom K accused of being jealous of Faith.

I didn't trust his version of events, so when I spoke to Faith, I tried to find out what she knew about the case. She said basically the same thing K had. Told me that K had been messing with that girl Joyce out there in East Orange. Faith had warned him about messing with Joyce. Rayshaun was Joyce's little brother. He was working for K, selling that shit. She wasn't sure what had happened, but whatever it was, Rayshaun's mother and Joyce didn't go to the cops to press charges until practically eight months later.

Why had they waited so long?

"'Cause by then they had seen me and him drivin' in East Orange in his Jeep. That's when they went to the police. Joyce got jealous and got her mother to go down to the precinct to press charges and say that he had fucked up that boy Rayshaun. But they didn't have no hospital reports or nothin'—the thing had happened too long before."

Where was this Rayshaun today?

"I couldn't even tell you," she said.

In his first week in Essex County the shrink switched him from Prozac to Zoloft. The antidepressants kept him fairly stable, curbed the constant desire to fight, but he was still swaggering around the joint like a hardrock, stealing food from the other inmates. Jail instincts died hard. He had to be the top-ranking badass—intimidate his fellow tier-mates into giving up their commissary-bought snacks and goodies.

Despite Crystal's warning on the phone about monitoring his diabetes, he was stuffing himself each night with his hoarded cakes and cookies. I didn't get his collect call for a few days, assumed that he'd been fighting again and thrown into the hole.

When he finally called, later in the week, he said he hadn't been in isolation—he'd been in the clinic. Nearly died in there. He'd been gorging himself on pilfered Twinkies and Devil Dogs and swigging back cupfuls of Tang and then he'd blacked out. Collapsed. The doctors said he'd gone into diabetic shock.

Crystal took the phone, indignant, trying to knock some sense into his head. "Why are you such an *idiot?* Do you want to end up in a wheelchair with your legs amputated before you turn *thirty?* Or maybe you want to experience the joys of progressive blindness and dialysis before succumbing to renal failure? Sure, that'll be good—you can be the first blind amputee rapper, wheeling yourself onstage in your Stevie Wonder shades—you can have the microphone in one hand and your dialysis bag in the other . . ."

"I know, sis . . . I'm a stupid fuckin' ass."

"You're not like these old people I deal with every day, some seventy-three-year-old from Mississippi or Guyana who really doesn't know any better—who can't read the literature—I gave you a *pamphlet,* didn't I?"

"You're right, sis. You did, sis. Word up. I'm a complete fuckin' ass . . ."

Faith and I were standing outside the Essex County jail, shielding our faces from the howling winter wind, impatient for the guards to unlock the doors after the lunch break. Up above us, at the open windows of the dayroom, a couple of inmates in black shimmery do-rags were making like jailhouse Romeos, hollering down to the young girls waiting patiently with their bags of clothes and magazines.

"Show me that ass, bitch! Word, you got a nice *big* ass, don'tcha?"

"My man gon' *cut* you for that shit, faggot! Wait an' fuckin' see—
dick-suckin' muthafucka!"

Huddling together in the cold, Faith and I talked and talked, just
to keep our mouths moving and avoid thinking about the subfreezing
temperature. She was telling me, for the first time, about how her father'd been killed—he was a gypsy cab driver who'd been shot in the
back of the head by an off-duty cop on Staten Island when she was
just two years old; she said her mother had all the newspaper clip-
pings about the case at home, how the cop had been acquitted of
manslaughter, how his only punishment was to be kicked off the police force.

Then I was telling her about K's latest, strangest request: now that
his court date was set, he'd begged me to call Tony down in Puerto
Rico again, give him the name of the judge and the exact time of day
when the hearing would take place. (What now? Was the long-distance
santero going to make the judge have a mysterious "accident" on the
way to the courthouse? Was some innocent Puerto Rican rooster
going to lose its life in ritual slaughter so that K could go free?)

Faith's family were originally Southerners, not Panamanians, and
I was curious to know if she shared any of her man's beliefs in all those
mysterious santería gods.

"I don't really know. I only know one thing that was true.
Nazareno—when we used to have the Nazareno—I think that was
true."

It was when they were first living together in East Orange, she
said, when he was still selling drugs out there. He used to have a
golden statue of Jesus he called Nazareno. They had a big apartment
out there in East Orange and he had Nazareno in its own little room—
a walk-in closet. It sat on a table surrounded by candles. He would go
in there alone every day and say his blessings. Leave pieces of jewelry
and twenty-dollar bills around Nazareno. Offer glasses of water and
sometimes pieces of bread and fruit. But mostly he left money. Pretty
soon you couldn't even see Nazareno for all the money piled up there.

He warned her very clearly about one thing. Told her that once you put the money on Nazareno, you could *never* take it away. Said that everything was going to be good for them as long as they walked with Nazareno.

Then when he got arrested—for this same case, for pistol-whipping that kid Rayshaun—and his bail was set at $10,000, Faith had found a bail bondsman who gave her the ten percent deal but she didn't have the full thousand dollars. She pawned off some of her jewelry and was still short and she didn't know what to do. She talked to her mother and her mother said to just take some of the money from Nazareno and sprinkle a little Holy Water where the money was. So she took some money, maybe a few hundred dollars, from Nazareno and went to bail K out. She completely forgot about sprinkling the Holy Water.

He went crazy when he found out she'd touched Nazareno's money. He said she'd ruined everything. Nazareno was going to turn against them now. With a vengeance.

"I had just become pregnant in them times. And the same night I took the money off Nazareno to bail him out, I went to the bathroom and I started to see spotting and little blood clots. When we got to the hospital they said it was too late—I had already lost the baby."

She was squinting at me, and I thought she'd started to cry at the memory of her never-born child. But she wasn't crying. Her eyes were just tearing from the bitter gusts of wind that kept howling through Newark.

"He went to his santería lady and found out that there was only one thing to do. She said he had to take Nazareno to a church and not look back. So he put Nazareno in a Glad bag and we drove to a church and he went and put it out on the front steps of the church. And then we drove away and we never looked back."

We came back to Newark the next day for his hearing, before Judge Thomas Brown, in Essex County Superior Court. The public defender assigned to his case was a young woman with curly reddish hair named Sean Burke. (Maybe I should've bought K the New Jersey Devils jersey, I was thinking, since his court-appointed lawyer, strangely, had the same name as the Devils' former all-star goalie.) Sean said she didn't have much time to talk, had to hurry back into the holding cell to brief her client on the details of the DA's plea bargain offer.

I sat thinking about how much more efficient the New Jersey court system was in comparison with New York City, how the courtrooms here were deathly silent, the floors and benches and bathrooms spotless, the proceedings began promptly, even the courtroom cops had a clean-cut, paramilitary bearing with their knee-high leather boots and chiseled bodybuilder physiques and those tight black leather gloves they wore even indoors while standing at attention like extras in some Schwarzen—

The tranquillity of my daydreaming was shattered by the sound of K roaring somewhere in the holding cell behind that wall. He was shouting at his public defender so loudly that Judge Brown stopped speaking in mid-sentence and the Terminator cops in their tight black leather gloves all ran toward the door—unfastening their pistols and leaving them outside, of course—and once K saw the police coming at him ready to fight he started shouting more angrily, roaring wild rudeboy threats: *Come yah! Wha gwaan? Tink seh a Rodney King dis?*

His hands must have been free this time, because the whole courtroom echoed with the sound of K and the cops beginning to fight. I could hear the heavy footsteps of more cops arriving, more black-gloved storm troopers trying to subdue him and beat him with nightsticks and drag him down to the hole.

Judge Brown announced a recess and disappeared back in his chambers.

Sean Burke came out from the holding cell, cheeks cherry-red, gesturing for Faith and me to come outside to the hall where we could talk in private.

"What is he—Jamaican?"

"Panamanian."

"Couldn't understand everything he was saying. Was he threatening the *judge?*"

"He wasn't threatening the judge."

"I *think* he was threatening the judge." Sean leaned back on the windowsill and let out a long sigh. "It's probably my fault."

"How's that?"

"He was fine at first—he was actually very calm and cogent. We were reviewing the facts of the case and I was telling him about the DA's offer—told him the DA's willing to drop the Graves Act and just have him plead guilty to straight assault. But he was saying, no, he didn't want to take any plea bargain. He said that he never hit the kid with a gun and he wanted to take it to trial.

"That's when I blew it. I said, 'Well, gun or no gun, to be perfectly honest, the judge is going to take one look at your size and figure that you settle everything with your fists.' When I said that, he just *lost* it . . . I should've known better—it wasn't a very prudent thing to say . . ."

We walked down the hall toward the bank of elevators. Sean smoothed down her skirt, trying to regain her composure. What a start to the week, she said. Now she had to rush off and prepare for a homicide case she was taking to trial.

The bottom line, she said, was that her client had now fucked himself. Big time. The judge hated him, and the DA—well, the DA no longer even had to try to establish that the defendant had a violent streak; the defendant had established it himself in front of the entire courtroom. The DA's plea bargain offer was gone with the wind; they might even try to add more charges now: contempt of court, assaulting court officers.

And the worst thing, she said, was now Judge Brown could let him stew in jail for months—Christmas would come and go, spring would come and go, six months could pass and the judge still wouldn't have any obligation to reschedule a new court date . . .

*   *   *

Faith and I walked back together through the desolate freezing Newark streets. I thought of Philip Roth's lost world, looked at the ghostly facades of the old Jewish department stores and once-grand movie palaces that had been bombed out and abandoned and never rebuilt since the riots in the mid-'60s. I kept trying to flag down a taxi but downtown Newark isn't midtown Manhattan; yellow cabs don't circle the streets in overeager flocks. We stopped a few times to sit down; it was hard for Faith to walk so far with the heavy weight of the baby inside her belly. The fetus kept kicking her, she said. She was sitting on an icy bench in the howling wind and I saw her trying to force a smile and then she pulled a crumpled pink tissue from the pocket of her bulky Bear goosedown coat and I noticed that, for the first time since I'd known her, she had actually started to cry.

"Muthafucka, you forget somethin'? I been passin' through this criminal justice system my whole fuckin' life. She ain't really tryin' to defend me in there! She supposed to be talkin' 'bout my presumption of innocence—not takin' up for the DA or tellin' me some shit 'bout how the fuckin' judge is gonna see my *size* and figure I settle every dispute with my fists. What type of bullshit is that? Now the case is decided by my fuckin' *size*?

"And even if that was fuckin' true, it ain't her job to be sayin' it— she supposed to be my legal counsel, safeguardin' my legal rights.

"What? You ain't heard? You was absent that day? *You have the right to a fair trial.* Not, you got the right to be railroaded by your own fuckin' attorney into takin' some muthafuckin' plea bargain just so they can hurry up and process your ass through the fuckin' bogus-ass overcrowded shits-dem!

"That's what it is, you know: a *shits*-dem. Ain't no system. Take a good look over the judge's head sometime—what's it say up there in big bold letters? IN GOD WE TRUST. Now what's it say on the dollar bill? Flip it over and tell me what's it say? They not makin' no secret 'bout it neither. *Step right up, muthafucka. We sellin' as much justice as them dead presidents can buy.*"

*　　*　　*

K came to me in a dream that night. We were standing in front of
the Swatch boutique on Fifth Avenue and he asked me if I wanted to
see his new bulletproof vest. Some newfangled lightweight Teflon.
Couldn't be penetrated by bazooka or rocket launcher. He unzipped
his jacket, then unbuttoned his blue flannel shirt *Peep it, duke!* Smiling proudly. But there was no bulletproof vest. He simply had a sheet
of thick Plexiglas inset into his chest. No skin, no lungs behind the
glass; you could see straight through to his empty chest cavity. And
through the glass I saw the outline of the heart from *his* dream, the
half-light, half-dark heart in which dwelt the four orishás—but it was
no longer half-light and pulsing with blood: now the whole heart was
covered in a hard black shiny shell.

I looked up at his face—and now his face had been replaced by
the inscrutable face of Elegua. He'd changed into the African trickster
god with a heart of shiny black stone.

Stumbling out of the bedroom, I told Crystal about the dream. She listened, smearing margarine on her toast with a white plastic knife,
rushing to prepare for the brutal statistics seminar she had that afternoon up at Columbia. Laughing, she said she doubted I would find a
listing for *bulletproof vests* or *bulletproof hearts* in her Panamanian
grandmother's dream book (an old dog-eared, orange-covered man-
ual, categorizing dream images alphabetically, assigning each a corresponding number, a treasured family heirloom and long-favored
source of inspiration for her grandmother when placing a bet in the
uptown policy game).

I sat sleepy, half delirious, waiting for the fragrant stimulant to
trickle down into the Braun coffeepot. That bad dream had me seeing
things, twitching, jumping at shadows. Crystal's pink-and-green
Alpha Kappa Alpha sorority paddle seemed to move of its own accord,
poised to swing down from the bookshelf and deliver a phantom *pock!*

to the back of my head. I stared at the cordless phone, wondering if the ringer was on, wondering how many more minutes would pass before I got another collect call from K in the Essex County jailhouse, another urgent message for me to relay to Faith.

I went to the window, watched the falling sleet turn West 21st Street into a slick and treacherous thoroughfare; across the street, people were throwing open their windows, shouting: some asshole's car alarm had been wailing for the past fifteen minutes. It took me back to the winter of '90, when Crystal and I still kept separate places, back when she'd first told me about her ex-boyfriend, Tommy, that square-jawed gunman with the weight lifter's build, still calling collect at her mother's Bronx apartment ("Tommy, are you crazy?" Crystal's mother would chide. "She doesn't live here anymore!"), Crotona Avenue Tommy, touched in a game of frozen tag, living out his fantasy life with Crystal's tiny high school picture taped up on the wall of his upstate prison cell.

Back when it was so easy for me to scoff at her, smirking—*What? You know somebody in jail?*—and she snapped at me that I would never understand her confusion, knowing someone behind bars, wanting to cut bait, erase the sneering face from memory—but it's no random thug incarcerated up there in Comstock; it's someone you've shared intimate secrets with, exchanged birthday gifts with, laughed so hard at his ridiculously childish sense of humor that you thought you might actually pee in your pants on the subway ride down from the Bronx . . .

Was that the answering machine clicking? No, just the heating element in the coffee maker giving off its mysterious metallic tick. I poured my first cup, lightened it, sweetened it. My nerves were fried. I thought about a little-known phone company feature I'd discovered: NYNEX could block incoming collect calls from all correctional facilities. Maybe it was better to call Faith, tell her that I wanted out, that I couldn't continue as her man's go-between and sounding board, his only lifeline to the outside world. How long could things go on this way? Who could handle the bullshit—not to mention the bad dreams—for more than a few weeks?

Later that afternoon, when I spoke to K's public defender, Sean Burke, she told me that her client had done something quite remarkable—called her to apologize for his actions. What's more, he'd asked that he be brought before Judge Brown to apologize to him in person. Came very humbly before the judge and asked for forgiveness; explained that he had been feeling distraught about his wife's pregnancy and his inability to be back in New York to help her financially—not to make any excuses, mind you, this was just an *explanation,* he understood that he alone was to blame for the outburst, and he'd now had time to reflect on the error of his ways and to see that it was more than simply inappropriate behavior—it was behavior unbefitting a civilized human being. He realized that he had no right to expect mercy from the court, but he asked if the judge could please make every effort to remain impartial when considering the facts of his case.

Crocodile tears? I asked Sean.

"No, actually, he seemed very sincere. Judge Brown was quite impressed by his candor. He was so well spoken and intelligent. No one could believe it was the same guy who'd been screaming and fighting the cops in the holding cell." She said that she often had clients who start blowing off steam in court; nerves, fear, false bravado, whatever—that was nothing new to her—"but it's kind of rare to have someone who asks if he can come before the judge to apologize and take full responsibility for his actions."

Waiting to come before Judge Brown and apologize, K had been locked in a holding cell next to an eighteen-year-old kid from New York who was bragging about how he'd just received a sentence of forty-to-life.

"Yo! yo! yo! Them muthafuckas just gave me a forty-to-man, kid!" Laughing and bragging like he'd accomplished a very great thing.

"Forty-to-*man,* kid! I'm gon' be hangin' with my brother J.T. and 'em—gon' be in *Rahway*—shit's gon' be *a-ight!*"

K was trying to ignore the howling eighteen-year-old; but finally he could no longer hold his tongue.

"Yo, what the fuck is *wrong* with you, nigga? You think that shit is *funny?*"

And the kid kept laughing and bragging about his life sentence and K kept hoping that they'd open his cell and put them together, just for two minutes, so that at least he'd get a chance to punch the loudmouth eighteen-year-old in his grill.

Toward the end of December they moved him out of Essex County into a much smaller jail unit in Caldwell, New Jersey. Caldwell was an annex facility; only a few dozen inmates, housed in mobile trailers. Now nearing her ninth month, Faith lugged Little K out there to see his daddy on Christmas Day. The jail provided a turkey dinner and they all spent Christmas together as a family in one of the jail trailers.

Call it Christmas spirit. Or perhaps the cigar-loving Yoruba trickster god pulling a few strings. Once again K caught a lucky break. Apology accepted; Judge Brown had forgiven him. He'd agreed to hear the case immediately after the New Year's recess.

On the morning of January 6 I was on my way out to 33rd Street—the usual rendezvous spot; Faith and I would always meet on the corner in front of A&S Plaza to take the PATH train together—but just as I was locking the front door the phone rang. I rushed back inside and answered. She was out of breath, panting, moaning in pain. Calling from her hospital room. "Ain't gonna be in court today. The labor . . . *started* . . . tell him baby's on the way . . ."

When I got to the Essex County courthouse I overheard Sean and the assistant DA playing their game of high-speed plea bargain poker. Sean teasing the DA about the paucity of his evidence: Some Graves Act agg-assault! Where was the gun? There was no gun. Where were the eyewitnesses? There were no eyewitnesses. Where was the complainant? Rumor had it, he couldn't be found. And why had the mother waited eight *months* before pressing charges? Come on. What a waste of taxpayer dollars! A case begging for dismissal.

Outside in the hallway, talking privately, Sean told me that she'd love to take this case to trial; there was no way in hell that the DA could get a conviction based on this evidence. One problem. Since her client couldn't make the $10,000 bail, he'd be stuck sitting in jail for at least six months before he got a trial date. The DA would stall for as much time as he needed to try to drum up evidence, find that kid Rayshaun or his mother and get them deposed.

Of course, there was still the plea bargain option. The DA was still willing to let him plead down to misdemeanor assault. With luck, it would work out to being time served plus probation.

"The only problem is he's going to have to come before the judge and plead guilty—admit that he hit the kid." She was shaking her head at the thought of it. "As his lawyer, I should really advise him against it. There's no way they can convict him in this case—and the DA knows it. But then again *I'm* not the one who has to sit there waiting in Caldwell for a trial date."

When K found out that Faith was in labor that morning, he instructed Sean to take the DA's plea bargain. He was brought before Judge Brown—the first thing he did was offer another apology for his violent outburst back in December. I could hardly believe it: the only time I'd ever seen him maintaining his composure in a courtroom. Polite, softspoken, actually referring to Judge Brown as *Your Honor.*

Yes, Your Honor, he'd agreed to plead guilty to the lesser charge of misdemeanor assault. Yes, Your Honor, he had hit that boy Rayshaun with his fist back in '91. Yes, Your Honor, he regretted doing it.

Sean Burke asked for leniency in sentencing, asked that Judge Brown be mindful of the following facts: that her client had been gainfully employed for several years doing security work in Manhattan retail stores; that he had numerous ties in the New York City community (she gestured to Jeffrey Goldberg and me behind her); that he'd been living with his common-law wife and their little son; that his wife was, at this very moment, in labor, giving birth to their second child.

"Your Honor, please do not deprive two more children of a father."

Judge Brown gave a perfunctory nod. He sentenced the defendant to time served plus probation.

Out in the hall, I checked my answering machine. One message, Faith's mother, calling from Lenox Hill Hospital. Fifteen minutes earlier, at precisely 10:36 A.M., Faith had given birth to a healthy six-pound, six-ounce baby girl.

They had to take him back to the jail in Caldwell to process his release. Sean told us not to wait around, that the checkout process could take all day, maybe even all night. Jeff and I stopped in a Newark coffeeshop for a sandwich, then took the PATH back to Manhattan.

We'd just pulled out of Newark when I noticed the sickly look on Jeff's face. Had the tuna melt and coffee turned sour on him?

He shook his head distractedly. Something deeper than heartburn. A pang of conscience, making him squint, chew the inside of his mouth.

I took his meaning. Shades of Mailer and Jack Henry Abbott, right? Well, this wasn't a *parole* hearing—and I was quite sure *our* presence on those back benches hadn't affected the judge's sentencing one way or the other. Jersey's cells could barely contain its murderers: why would they want to hog another bed for a four-year-old assault case?

That wasn't the point, Jeff said. Sure, K was free now, had another shot in life—but was he capable of changing, curtailing the violence? Was he even making an *effort?*

"He says he is."

"But is he?"

"I think he *thinks* he is."

"You're playing with semantics. You can't give me a straight answer."

I stared out the window at the sooty smokestacks of the passing wasteland. No, I admitted, I didn't have a straight answer.

It was after six P.M. when they finally brought him back to Newark. He called me collect from a pay phone in the street. One of the coldest nights of the winter and he was stuck out there in Newark dressed only in his dirty gray sweat suit. "You got a coat I could wear?"

I laughed at the thought of him trying to squeeze into any of my winter clothes, busting every seam like the mutant Dr. David Banner after the rage takes hold. I jumped on the PATH train back to Newark and met him in the train station with a ski cap and a wool scarf.

"I'll never do this shit to you again, duke."

"Yeah, okay."

"If I ever get arrested again—word to *moms*—you got permission to punch me in the fuckin' face."

"Let's just go find Faith."

There was heavy evening traffic in Manhattan—but we were being chauffeured by a psychotic Sikh cabbie who obeyed no known traffic laws, slicing wildly across three lanes at once, barreling through late-yellows and early reds, tires shrieking like a banshee all the way to the Upper East Side.

"Got a name for her yet?"

"Yeah." He grinned, jostled his shoulder heavily against mine to the rhythm of the joyride.

"Oughta call her Liberty."

"What? You been smokin' that *shit,* dun? *Li*-berty? Naw, we gon' call her Keisha. Keisha Antoinette."

We screeched to a halt in front of Lenox Hill. K was still wearing the neon-orange plastic wristband of the Essex County correctional facility. He held out his arm and the security guard added a pale green plastic wristband which identified him as a father of one of the newborns in the Lenox Hill maternity ward.

It was after visiting hours; I wasn't allowed to accompany him upstairs. K gave me a brief goodbye hug in the hospital lobby. Handed me back the scarf but he kept the black ski cap. I watched him half jogging down the hall in his dirty gray sweat suit, a free man, smiling as he got inside the elevator to go upstairs and meet his newborn daughter.

NINE

no sleep
till Brooklyn

Where Brooklyn at?
Where Brooklyn at?
    —Hip-Hop party chant

"Map or no map," I says, "yuh ain't gonna get to know
Brooklyn wit no map."
    —Thomas Wolfe, *Only the Dead Know Brooklyn*

For the first few months after he got out of Essex County, K kept repeating his mantra—stay strong, stay focused, never go back to the belly of the beast. On his wrist he still wore the now-faded orange jail band, alongside the washed-out green one from Lenox Hill's maternity ward. He'd proudly turned those wristbands into personal jewelry: one was supposed to remind him of the things he had to live for; the other of a place he never wanted to set foot again.

Conscience-cuffs, I called them, nice little mnemonic devices—but would they really remind him to keep those *other*, government-issue bracelets from his wrists?

He still had his day job at Swatch waiting for him; with Fifth Avenue being stuck in its post-Christmas shopping doldrums, his work schedule was scaled back to weekends only. Weekdays he started going up to a studio in the White Plains Road section of the Bronx run by an aspiring rap producer called Terror.

I met Terror a few times. Gravel-voiced and dreadlocked, dressed always in black jeans and a black denim vest, Terror came from a long line of West Indian Pentecostal ministers (his father, grandfather and great-grandfather had all been preachers), but he was now sinking into the abyss of mid-twenties rebellion. Eventually, Terror told me, he would have to return to the church, devote the rest of his life to traveling the earth, preaching the Good News of the Lord. But until he got that Skypage, until Jesus hit him on the hip, Terror would spend his days producing extremely profane rap music and his nights fornicating with nice firm-bodied young ladies in the back room of the studio. His rap name and his studio reflected his slasher film fetish—the walls and ceiling adorned with all manner of knives, from box cutters and switchblades to meat cleavers and yard-long machetes.

Riding the Number 2 train all the way up to 238th Street turned a trip to Terror's studio into an all-day proposition. A long, tiring, wasted day. Terror and the guys in the studio smoked too much weed; there were always a lot of hangers-on and bullshit artists and gold-chained Jamaican rudeboys looking for trouble. After a few sessions I begged off coming to the studio with K.

One Saturday afternoon we were standing just inside the Swatch boutique, sharing a pair of Walkman insert headphones, listening to one of the new reggae-hip-hop tunes he was recording with Terror's crew called "Romp & Gwaan." All of a sudden a guy named Porter rushed into the Swatch store, out of breath, terrified. Porter was one of the 42nd Street business district's blue-uniformed security guards, armed with a nightstick and a walkie-talkie and a pair of pretend-cop handcuffs. He never spoke to me, never even looked me in the eye. "Don't take that shit personal," K once explained. "It ain't you—Porter hates *all* white people." (K wasn't especially fond of Porter himself, was forever complaining that Porter behaved like "a real little bitch.")

"Porter! What the fuck's goin' on?"

Porter explained that he'd just got into a beef with some of the three-card monte hustlers up on 45th Street. These three-card monte men were a constant nuisance on the block. To an untrained eye they seemed a disorganized bunch of con artists. But they actually worked the midtown shopping district in a large well-organized network of forty to fifty hustlers, running numerous games at once, rotating the duties of lookout and hustler and shill.

Like most local businessmen, the owners of the adjacent boutiques K protected despised the three-card monte men. Cardsharp hustles were hardly conducive to a pleasant shopping atmosphere. K had to warn them repeatedly not to set up shop in front of Swatch or the Joseph Edwards luxury watch boutique.

Porter now told K the reason he was so stressed. He'd asked the three-card monte guys to move off the 45th Street corner and then one of the hustlers, an ugly dark-skinned guy he'd never seen around before, called Porter a "punk-bitch," threatened to shoot him dead on the spot.

"Word?" K's eyes opened wide and clear. "Where the nigga at?"

"Muhfucka ain't frontin', duke—you got the four-fifths?"

K patted the heavy half-concealed bulge on his hip.

"Come on up to 45th Street. This cat, he really talkin' 'bout he gon' shoot me, callin' me a punk and all that shit."

I followed them outside, trying to keep pace with K as he and Porter fast-strided up Fifth Avenue.

"You don't gotta come, D. Wait for me back at Swatch."

I slowed down, mulled it over, then kept striding a few steps behind them. Along the way, we picked up a few more of the block's security men, more squelching walkie-talkies and baby-blue uniform shirts; then at Cosmetics Plus on 43rd Street we were joined by big barrel-chested Gene (whom K always called Noonie), at a seriously *diesel* 370 pounds, the most massive of all the block's big men. (Baby-faced Gene, as placid as K was hotheaded; Gene, constantly complaining of hunger, whom I'd once watched ingesting an eight-slice pizza pie like so many minuscule Trisket appetizers; Gene, who, if rumor was to be believed, had a bad habit of falling asleep in bed clutching a half-gnawed double-cheeseburger in one hand. Yes, it felt good to be the ant occupying Gene's Paul Bunyanesque shadow.)

If the three-card monte hustlers acted as a unified team, so did the Fifth Avenue security guys. Uniformed and nonuniformed alike, whenever one had a problem, all would rally around him. Still, I'd noticed that they tended to come straight to K when there was talk of any *serious* gun drama on the street.

K was leading the parade up Fifth Avenue; the rest of us followed in a tight V formation like a gaggle of migrating geese.

We came to 45th Street, spotted seven or eight of the three-card monte guys gathered on the corner. Porter pointed out the ugly guy who'd been calling him a punk and threatening to kill him. This badass was called Black. His skin looked like bumpy bark; he was missing several front teeth, had some conspicuous knife scars, like warpaint lining his cheeks. Looked to be in his late thirties, early forties, hard and mean, that fearless gaze the product of extensive jail time.

K made a direct approach.

"You Black?"

"The fuck you lookin' for, nigga?"

"Dig, what's this shit I hear 'bout you gettin' ready to pop my man or some bullshit? Why you goin' on like that, nigga?"

Black shot back an angry glare, the classic crazy act, flailing his arms, flashing his jack-o'-lantern smirk. "Who the fuck is *you?* You ain't no goe-*rilla!* You ain't no goe-*rilla!* Fuck y'all! Y'all toy-cop-ass muthafuckas—y'all don't know, boyee! Word, I'll fuck around and all ya'll niggas be *gone!*"

At first K was incredulous, looked to Noonie for confirmation that this was not some early April Fool's prank. Who *was* this scrawny old-timer, talking junk, standing only six feet away, well within reach of a well-timed forward lurch, clean overhand right, clearing a few more of those yellowed rotting teeth from his grill?

"Fuck all y'all fake-jake muthafuckas!"

"Who you callin' a fake-jake? I ain't no fuckin' *jake!*" This made K livid—how could anyone possibly mistake *him* for a wannabe cop? Now Gene and a couple of the other security men had to step in to hold K from charging.

"Ain't worth it—let it *go!* Nigga buggin' out!"

Gene waltzed K around the corner. Black stood his ground, flailing, barking threats. K reached out and grabbed the arm of one of the more sedate three-card monte hustlers, a middle-aged guy with a slight paunch. "Yo, Fox. School this nigga. He don't know who the fuck he dealin' with."

"Bring it on then, nigga! What? Think you a goe-*rilla?*"

"Muthafucka, you talkin' like you *bulletproof!*"

Black opened his palms wide like Christ on the cross. "Spray if you gon' spray, big man! Spray if you gon' spray!"

But no, there would be no spraying today. Big Gene and the other guys talked K into walking away from Black. K was laughing and shaking his head the whole way back down Fifth Avenue. Fifteen minutes later, with all the security guys dispersed, back guarding their various stores, he stood up in the window of Swatch looking sullen, brooding about big-mouthed Black.

I asked him if he'd forgotten the meaning of the faded orange wristband.

"Naw, I don't wanna go back to fuckin' jail," he said. "But I ain't gonna let that ugly-ass nigga punk me neither." He was extremely calm now, clear-headed, shooting down all my arguments. "True, it's just words. And words by themselves don't mean a goddamn thing. But when a nigga starts talkin' shit about you and he's got an *audience,* that's a different fuckin' story, yo. If other muthafuckas see that this nigga can talk shit, that he got lip service—he ain't put his *hand* on you, but he got lip service—sometimes his lip service can mean more than him beatin' the shit out of you. Because if a muthafucka disrespects you like that and you just leave it—let it pass—sometimes that shit can prove fatal to your reputation . . ."

He went outside again, breathing deeply, pacing the sidewalk in front of the boutiques.

"Muthafuckas like him make me sick. Think just because we workin' jobs and shit, then we goodie-goodies. They think we scared, that we don't wanna get into no bullshit, don't wanna hurt nobody, wasn't no gangsters before. They don't know *what* the fuck we done before."

His mind was fixed. After Swatch locked up, he walked the midtown streets well after nightfall, searching for Black. Couldn't find him. Then, after work on Sunday, he spotted the three-card monte posse holed up in Tad's Steak House on West 42nd Street. Fifteen of them feasting together after a good day's hustle. K walked in and went straight for Fox.

"Yo, dig, Fox—where your man at? Where Black at?"

"I don't know where he at. Somewhere out there in them streets."

Some of the other three-card monte hustlers, chewing their cheap T-bone steaks, began to toss in unsolicited opinions.

"Black—that nigga don't be playin' though. That nigga be *gettin'* his."

"You don't wanna step to him wrong, knowmsayin'? You need to be *ready* when you step to that cat."

K raised up his sweatshirt so that they could all get a good eyeful of the pearl-handled Colt .45.

"Nigga, I'm always ready. I'm ready *now.* You tell that nigga don't never come on that muthafuckin' block again, duke. Don't never come on the block *period.* Anytime I see him on my block we gonna have problems."

I waited for the news, expected Faith to call me, tell me that he'd been locked up again. But the following weekend, when I spoke to K, he told me that everything on Fifth Avenue was peace—the beef with

Black had been squashed. How'd that happen? The three-card monte players had sent a young lady hustler as a peace emissary to find K at the Swatch store. She told K that Fox and Black wanted to meet him on neutral territory, talk it out in public, in front of the stone lions at the Public Library.

After lunch on Saturday, K crossed the street to the library. Could only see Fox standing there in front of the lion. A setup? No, he saw Black now, looking wary, coming into the frame. Still trying to keep up his badman facade, of course, but he wasn't talking all that murderer junk from before.

"Dig, man," K told him. "You said some real disturbin' shit the other day. I ain't really appreciate it. Matter of fact, I was really thinkin' that when I saw you, I was gonna step to ya mustache—turn the heat on up under ya."

"Man, I can understand that—but I felt that *I* was being disrespected as well."

"Check this out: don't have nothin' disrespectful to say to me or *any* of my peeps—and we cool."

"A'ight, bet." Black stepped up to shake, but K turned away.

"Naw, man. It's all good. We straight. But I ain't shakin' ya fuckin' hand."

While he'd been away for that month-long tour of the Essex County jail facilities, a business opportunity had arisen. I had a meeting at Bernie Jackson's law office in Times Square with a couple of guys who needed a hip-hop screenplay written in a hurry. Julio Caro was a friend of Bernie's, a former music business manager who'd been one of the executive producers of the '87 film *Siesta*. His partner, Marcus Morton, was the vice president of rap promotion at EMI records. Their idea was lightweight but appealing, make a feature comedy about Freaknik, the black college spring-break bacchanal that shuts down the city of Atlanta for an entire weekend every April.

They'd had a treatment written and commissioned a first-draft screenplay from an L.A.-based music video director named Stobaugh. Now, dissatisfied with the first draft, afraid some other production team was going to jack their idea, they were frantic to get a rewrite done in less than a month. I read through their treatment, told them that it was the kind of thing I could only write in collaboration with someone who'd actually experienced the honeys-in-daisy-dukes, barbecue-in-the-street, '64-Impala-cruising frenzy of Freaknik or one of the similarly themed spring Greekfests.

K had long been fascinated by the craft of screenwriting. I'd shown him the scripts to *Raging Bull* and *Taxi Driver* one day in my apartment. He flipped through them, asked me to explain the arcane terminology, wanted to learn how a finished film is built around these sketchy blueprints. We'd even made an abortive attempt to write a script about his teenage years as a Brooklyn drug dealer; but I gradually lost steam with the project. Didn't have the heart to tell him that I found all his autobiographical stories of guns and drugs too dark and disturbing.

I gave him the first draft of *Freaknik* to take home and appraise; he called me, sounding disgusted, having read just the first few scenes.

"This muthafucka ain't *black*, right?"

No, I told him, he was a forty-something white Californian, best known for directing a Sir Mix-a-Lot car-wash titty-fest called "Put 'Em on the Glass." No wonder, K said. He had no flavor for real hip-hop slang (the characters were always calling each other things like "chucklehead"); worse, everyone in the script, from old Southern grandmothers to nerdy college kids, talked like they were running around barefoot on some plantation. Who the fuck were they supposed to be? Kunte Kinte and Kizzy?

K was a natural for this kind of over-the-top comic material. Like most casual movie buffs, he had an intuitive understanding of scene structure. Never got a handle on the technical camera terms—he'd always say PAN TO when he really meant CUT TO—but the loose banter of the Southern characters rolled off his tongue in various distinct accents and cadences. He didn't write so much as *act,* meditating for a few minutes and then freestyling the dialogue, hamming up each scene as if he was doing a one-man show for my tape recorder.

He'd come by and meet me at *The Forward's* offices after business hours. We'd start working on a few scenes together in the office library. Then we'd walk down to the Barnes & Noble on 21st Street and write a few more scenes in the upstairs Starbucks. Even recorded a few of the scenes sitting in Life's apartment in East New York one night, but I could hardly hear that tape clearly because Life kept guffawing at the countrified voices K was putting on. His most inspired scene was when the film's central character, a goody-goody college freshman named Tyrone, finds himself locked up for a night in the Fulton County jail next to some hardened criminals. K loved acting out the role of the tough guy called Steve, an Atlanta drug dealer who befriends Tyrone in Fulton County, protecting him from the other inmates until the college kid can make bail.

It was a sight to see him strolling around the offices of *The Forward* with his hair pulled back in gangster braids. Sure, he was aware he was scaring the shit out of people. Told me how the little old ladies would recoil from him in the elevator, pressing themselves against the wall, wishing they could disappear from view.

Late at night, after everyone else had gone home, he'd stand transfixed in front of the paintings of the Yiddish paper's founding fathers, the old-time socialists and labor leaders like Meyer London. Had a thousand and one questions to ask me, things he'd never understood about Judaism. What was the difference between a Zionist and just plain Jewish? Why did some Jews wear black fedoras and some only beanies and some nothing at all? And what about that word *Jewish?* Didn't the *ish* sound a bit demeaning, as in *boyish* or *childish?* He thought the word *Jew* sounded much more forceful. Like the fearless cats in *Escape from Sobibor.* Yes, if he'd been born a Jew, he'd want to be known as a Jew.

One night he picked up a copy of the Yiddish paper and asked me to translate the week's headlines for him. I stumbled pitifully through a couple of words.

"*Cleen-ton—Cleenton zogt*—Clinton says—I don't know, some shit about the U.S. policy toward Israel."

"That's Hebrew right there?"

"Yiddish."

"What language did Louis Lepke and them cats talk? Yiddish or Hebrew?"

"Yiddish."

"Yo, could you teach me some Yiddish?"

"Why would you want to know Yiddish?"

"Muthafucka, *you* know what I'm sayin' when I talk Jamaican— why can't *I* know Yiddish? That's like some type of secretive shit with y'all?"

"What *possible* use could you have for knowing Yiddish?"

I pictured him trying to eavesdrop on the conversations of all those huddled Hasidim as they rushed down Eastern Parkway, striving for a moment of "cross-cultural understanding" . . . but, as usual, he had a darker purpose in mind.

"Ain't no black muthafuckas in Brooklyn know Yiddish. Muthafuckas can understand when you talkin' Jamaican—a little Spanish, pig Latin. But peep it. If ya clique could all be conversatin' in *Yiddish,* ain't a muthafucka out there could understand what the fuck you was sayin' . . ."

No, I told him, I didn't know enough Yiddish to teach him. The only phrases I remembered were things like *I am a little Jewish boy* and *I miss you very much, Grandma.*

He shook his head slowly. "All right, dun. But I *know* ya holdin' out on me, muthafucka."

A few days after we'd completed the *Freaknik* rewrite, K called me at *The Forward* sounding breathless. "You'll never guess who I got sittin' right here next to me!"

"Who's that?"

"Wise-Islam! Nigga came *home,* duke!"

Tales of this long-lost Wise had been swirling around Brooklyn for months. Well, he hadn't actually been *lost*—he'd been doing time in various facilities upstate. K and Wise had known each other as kids—they'd crossed paths in the Goshen Secure Center and in the juvenile unit at Elmira. Now K was asking me if he and Life and Wise could swing by *The Forward* to meet me and hang out that day.

I had a better idea. What about slices of pizza?

Three hours later we were all sitting in the Sbarro across from Madison Square Garden. Wise had only been home for a few days, still living in a halfway house in Queens. He apologized to me for seeming out of it, said he was having a hard time readjusting to non-jail society. Reality was still speeding by too fast for him to take in.

He had cornrowed hair and a neatly trimmed beard, contoured close to the jaw, shaved clean on the cheeks. Wore the frozen look of a guy who, though terrified of flying, reluctantly agrees to board the plane, leaning back, strapped in tight, clutching the armrests as the pilot begins taxiing down the runway.

Wise was justifiably confused. He wasn't just coming home from a long stretch behind bars; he was coming home from *Clinton.* The hellhole that had turned K's older brother Toño into an invalid. Though not as infamous as Attica or Sing Sing, on the streets of Brooklyn no upstate joint is more feared than the Clinton State Correctional Facility at Dannemora. Clinton's traditionally been the end of the line for troublemakers, the place where all the incorrigible badasses are transferred. An old brutal citadel just off the Canadian border, temporary residence to many a badman, from Lucky Luciano to Tupac Shakur.

"That's a bad joint up there," Wise told me as we sat over our steaming slices in Sbarro. "When you get to Clinton you besta have your groove on. Or, trust me—somebody'll *put it on* for you."

Housing some three thousand inmates—more than twice the civilian population of the town of Dannemora—Clinton is the largest maximum-security prison in the state of New York. Three quarters of the prison population is comprised of inmates like Wise, blacks and Latinos from New York City. The staff of corrections officers, Wise told me, are nearly all French-Canadians, many from the same extended family, cousins to one another. "Hatin' niggas is in they *blood*," he said.

K and Wise were talking in that clenched-teeth style, lips barely moving, a stream of heavy Ss, like the hissing of charmed snakes. Seemed to be the universal mode of private communication among black convicts or former convicts. K later explained that it was based on function more than fashion; the way you learned to talk when you were "ox-carrying"—sleeping nights with a razor blade tucked against your gums.

Wise said he'd been hanging with Tupac inside Clinton; a bunch of other notorious cats too. At one point, he began smirking and telling me how, before being transferred to Clinton, he'd been locked up in Comstock with Robert Chambers, the Preppie Murderer. In general, he said, white pretty boys like Chambers have nightmarish bids, getting stabbed, forced to drink piss and wash other inmates' underwear; but Wise explained how Chambers was getting weed smuggled in to him; and with that weed he was able to buy off a crew of Jamaican rudeboys to protect him and bodyguard him at all times.

We got up to leave Sbarro and were all standing by the entrance to the Seventh Avenue subway, across the street from Madison Square Garden and Penn Station—Wise dazed and disoriented by the flickering glow of Manhattan. Staring at the multicolored, ever-changing signboard in front of the Garden, he turned to me with an embarrassed whisper. "Yo, Doug—we in *Queens?*"

ife loves watching sweat-soaked warriors beating each other un-conscious. He boxed at a much lighter weight himself—has a nice col-lection of fight tapes in his apartment out in East New York. One video contains all the permutations of the glorious Hagler-Leonard-Hearns '80s. Sitting in his one-room place in the Boulevard Houses, we spend a rainy Saturday watching all those championship fights in one sitting—Life jumping to his feet during that explosive third round of the Hagler-Hearns bout, crumpling his perfectly good Newport in excitement, letting out a joyous war cry—

G'night, muthafucka! Good! Night!

Of all the Franklin Avenue clique, Life's the only guy who did fed time. Fed time, he tells me after the Hagler-Hearns fight, that's a whole different ball game from Rikers or the state penal system.

"You seen muthafuckas on the street that probably look ruthless to you, right? Naw, I seen some of the most ruthless people on the *earth,* believe me. When you get to the big penitentiaries, them big su-permax pens, you see some muthafuckas that just don't give a fuck. Mass-murder muthafuckas that done got over a hundred years and really don't care if they live or die."

He served nearly two years for gun-running in a string of federal pens: Atlanta, El Rino, Terre Haute, Lewisburg, Steelwater, Leaven-worth. They kept moving him every few months because he was clas-sified as a violent offender. Ended up doing most of his bid in the penitentiary at Sandstone, Minnesota. "That shit was like a concen-tration camp—everywhere you go, got you under surveillance twenty-four hours of the day."

He lights up another Newport, rises from the kitchen table, heads to the closet, looking for one of his most prized possessions. Inside the small wooden frame is a vellum certificate from his classes in Sandstone, indicating that Life's licensed to do professional electrical engineering work. "What the fuck," he mutters, can't find his other certificate, the one he earned after the welding classes.

"I was doin' electrical work before I even went in, and when I went in I pursued the electrical classes. Then when I felt I had learned enough about the electrician work, I jumped into welding, and I stayed in welding until I got that certificate too.

"So now that I'm on the street, when you present these certificates to certain jobs and they look on it and they see FCI Sandstone at the top, they be like, 'Damn, where this shit came from? Oh shit, *Federal Correctional Institution.*'

"They be like, 'Bet, we'll give you a call.' Muthafuckas never call. Certificates ain't worth shit really—it's like you put in all that hard work for nothin'."

He lives in that little apartment with his longtime girlfriend, Neecie. As a teenager, she was a booster, one of the F.A.P. girls division; now she's an aspiring R&B singer who wears her hair in a short afro, dyed platinum-blond. A blue tattoo of a panther leaps up her smooth caramel calf muscle. The symbolism? Yeah, a bit of Huey Newton, but something more too. "To me, it just represents what a panther is—capable of killin', but it attacks people only when it feels like it's bein' threatened."

One afternoon, waiting for Life to get home from his security job, I go with Neecie to the nearby supermarket. She always calls Life by his other street alias: Rufus. A name he picked up while running with a Jamaican crew on Lincoln Place. Rufus—in honor of a notorious gangster of the same name, a now-deceased gunman from the Kingston ghetto called Concrete Jungle.

"Rufus done changed—he really has," Neecie says, wheeling her shopping cart down the frigid supermarket aisles. "Back in the days, when they was heavy into Five Percent, they all woulda *hated* you. And it probably woulda been a problem if they woulda been drunk or high—they woulda kicked your ass just 'cause they *felt* like it. But thank God they changed.

"Now he realizes that just like there's a lot of white people out here that's devils, there's a lot of black devils too. Your own people that'd stab you in the back and won't think twice about it. Now Rufus just treats you like you treat him."

She stops to examine the prices of different-sized boxes of Count Chocula and Cocoa Pebbles.

"Life really eats this crap?"

"What? He *loves* it. Tell you somethin' 'bout Rufus—he just a big kid, really."

A big *scary*-looking kid, perhaps. Gold front in his smile, redwood of a neck, furry brown Kangol tucked down on a treacherous rudeboy slant.

"He been through a lot," Neecie tells me. We're splitting the grocery-carrying duties on the way to Schenck Avenue. "You had to be there—or be him—to understand . . .

"Me and him been on job interviews together in the rain and snow. Before he got locked up, we went on so many job interviews together. One time I got the job, but he didn't get the job. I mean, Doug, he tried so *hard*. It's like they couldn't understand the type of person he was—tryin' to change his whole life around and start lookin' for work. Just fucked up his ego, fucked up his pride and everything. Made him feel, like, why does he even *try?* He should just keep on continuin' to sell drugs—robbin'—stealin'—whatever.

"Oh man, it was terrible. That day when he didn't get the job, he went crazy, he was buggin'—*bezerk!* We was on the train and he was like, 'I *hate* these fuckin' white people! These muthafuckas—word to *mutha*—I don't even want 'em breathin' on me! Smellin' like *dogs!*' And everybody on the train gettin' scared—white people was runnin' away from him. He was sweatin' like a bull. Sweatin' and hollerin' and carryin' on."

One hot Saturday in the middle of June, I met Life at the New Lots station, the last stop on the Brooklyn-bound Number 2 line. Rudeboy

stood waiting for me on the elevated platform—there'd been a change
of plans, he said. He had to swing by Wise's place on Bedford in
Crown Heights. Wearing that furry brown Kangol, below-the-knee
black jean-shorts with a white towel hanging, roughneck-style, from
his back pocket.

Somewhere on the ride between Saratoga and Sutter, Life started
sniffing loudly, accused me of letting out a stealth fart and—despite
my vehement denials—stomped to the other end of the car, guffawing, pointing his finger, telling complete strangers that a rat must've
crawled up my ass and *died*. At Utica Avenue, still protesting my innocence (which, by the way, I maintain to this day), we jumped
aboard a West Indian dollar-van, heading deep into the heart of Flatbush, speeding and swerving and blasting the heavy reggae strains of
Sugar Minott the whole way.

Life left me inside a McDonald's that was so Jamaican you could
forget you were in Brooklyn, forget you were in *America*—the place
felt like the humming island heat of Halfway Tree in the heart of
Kingston. Life had to drop something off across the street. Couldn't
take me along—I'd be fucking up his image—rudeboys would take
me for an undercover beast. When he came back he decided it would
be faster for us to take a gypsy cab to Crown Heights.

He flagged a gypsy cab on Utica and Winthrop. The African driver asked Life to extinguish his cigarette. Life shot him an angry look,
cursed under his breath, then snuffed out his just-lit Newport on the
sole of his basketball sneaker. Started haggling about the rate to Washington Avenue. The African wanted eight dollars. Life said, "That's too
much, man! Should be about six!" The African came down to seven.
Life exhaled in disgust. The gentle-voiced African asked Life to please
roll his window back up—air conditioning, you see. Life shot me a
look: he despised the African. Began noisily sniffing and clearing his
throat. More accusations of malodorousness—

"*Stinks* in here, man!"

"I have the AC."

"I ain't worried about the AC—I want some air to come up in this muthafucka! Stinks like a bunch a wild muthafuckin' monkeys!"

"No, if it stinks, it is because someone brought in his cigarette."

"Hell naw—it ain't no cigarette! Somebody ain't wash they *ass!*"

The African screeched his Lincoln to a stop in the middle of traffic. "So why don't you just take another cab?"

At last we reached Wise's mother's building in Crown Heights. Life holding his thumb on the buzzer for a good minute. Finally Wise came bounding downstairs. He was so changed from the quiet guy with the shell-shocked eyes who'd been sitting across from me in Sbarro pizzeria a few months back. Laughing crazily, shirtless, parading his bulging, sinewy, jail-hardened physique. As he ran back up, leaping three steps at a time, I saw the NATURAL BORN KILLA tattoo arching across his powerful back. Got that during his stretch inside Clinton.

On the way over, Life had warned me that Wise was back to his old wild ways. He tried to explain why the guy could never relax and keep a low profile in Brooklyn.

"Shit, Wise got plenty of enemies. He fucked up so many people in jail it's incredible. I mean, Jamaican dudes, he done cut they dreadlocks out they head, made some dudes drink piss. Just fucked people up and made they whole bid a nightmare. Cut some dudes and they got scars on they bodies for life.

"Now, you liable to run into these people at any point on the streets. That's why he gotta keep his mentality at a certain level of being crazy—so if some shit ever does come to him, he don't take it as no surprise."

Wise's mother had a spacious, well-kept railroad apartment; Life and I sat by the window, drinking water and cooling down in front of an oscillating fan, watching as Wise's teenage sister Tashina put a finger-wave treatment in another young girl's hair. Wise was busy on the phone, trying to find out if there was a branch of Western Union still open for business at this hour.

"Yo Wise!" Life said. "Hurry up! I gotta make a call!"

Wise didn't even turn his head to acknowledge the remark. "It's *my* time, muthafucka."

"You ain't in fuckin' jail no more!"

Wise flashed Life a chilling glare, held it for a long moment, then broke into a big smile. "Word, Doug, come ask me can you get on the phone, you goin' to the *clinic.*"

He set down the receiver momentarily, then started shouting for his mother to bring him a big cold glass of water.

"I ain't goin' down that hallway again," his mother sighed from her bedroom.

"Nigga think he got slaves in here," Life grumbled.

"She mad, Wise, she *mad,*" Tashina warned. "You betta leave her alone."

"I don't care. Ain't nothin' but a feelin'. She'll get over it. Just like Life'll get over that feelin' 'bout his watch."

Earlier in the day Life had learned that, during a seemingly friendly visit to his apartment in East New York, Wise had stolen his favorite Guess? watch. This was an ongoing exchange of playful larceny that apparently started when Life stole a Method Man tape from Wise's bedroom.

"Yo, you played me like I was a herb!" Life said, suddenly jumping to his feet.

"Yo, you played me like I was a Twinkie, nigga!" Wise countered.

"Yo, I'm a *bag* you so hard! Yo, what else you took?"

Wise shrugged. "Wasn't nothin' else to take."

"You took somethin' else, nigga," Life said. "I'm a find out when I go to the crib."

Finally, Wise got off the phone and sat down across from me. He produced an enormous fresh tobacco leaf which he smoothed and stretched and then filled with a quarter ounce of prime herb. This was the Chronic, he said. So named for the weed's propensity to push whoever smoked it into a somewhat sick frame of mind.

Wise inhaled deeply, leaned back, spliff dangling from his lower lip. Looked me long and hard in the eyes. "Lemme ask you this now—you know how to roller skate?"

Wise had a regular driver who was going to chauffeur us down to the roller rink on Empire Boulevard. Like our earlier cabbie that day this driver was an African. But he was not soft-spoken and Muslim and fussy about people smoking in his air-conditioned car. This driver was a refugee from that murderous civil war in Liberia. He was blasting a reggae tape, one continuous loop of the hottest rhythm to come out of Jamaica that summer, Capleton's "Tour." Kept rewinding a song that sounded like "Tour"—but with a militant chorus urging all true Rasta soldiers to—

> *Light up de chalice*
> *Mek we bu'n down Rome!*

But before anyone could burn down Rome—or even lace up a pair of rented roller skates—we had to make a stop at a Western Union. Time was getting tight. Stopped by one Western Union somewhere in Flat-bush but they weren't able to do the transaction Wise needed to have done. Only twenty minutes to make it all the way across Brooklyn to some gas station in Greenpoint. The Liberian driver took this time constraint as a challenge to his manhood.

Suddenly all of Brooklyn was flying past at breakneck speed. We were slashing and screeching to that hard-pounding dancehall beat. Whenever the traffic was clogged, the Liberian would look both ways, then gun it through the red light, flying over curbs and sidewalks and anything else that stood between him and Greenpoint. I felt I was riding shotgun with the bad guys in an episode of *Starsky and Hutch*. Life was loving the joyride, kept hollering his encouragement to the Liberian: "Yush! *Badbwoy* drivah!"

Wise turned around with a big grin on his face. I could see that his hand was casually resting on his .45.

"Yo, Life, why you figure these niggas in the Ack clockin' us so hard?"

Life turned to stare at the three sunglass-wearing hardrocks in the Acura.

"Wise, *chill!* They just clockin' *Doug.* They like, 'What the *fuck* is whiteboy doin' rollin' with them rowdy-ass niggas? They holdin' him *hostage* in there or somethin'?'"

An hour later, we all found ourselves inside the crowded Empire Roller Rink. Back in the '80s, the Empire had been known as a bad-boy's hang out, famous for shootouts and late-night mayhem. But on this particular Saturday, the rink had been booked for an afternoon of "Gospel Skating" by some Brooklyn Baptist church. We decided to crash the Gospel day; Wise was treating, pulled out his fat coil and peeled off a twenty. Life and I were both pathetic skaters—that powerhouse weed of Wise's wasn't helping my coordination much—but Wise could skate with a dancer's rhythm and a feline grace. In a tank top showing off the striations in his shoulders and arms, with his gold tooth gleaming and his dreadlocks tied up in a blue bandanna, Wise kept skating up to the high-cheeked church honeys, smiling, asking them to dance, macking them for their phone numbers. As if the glint in his eyes was that of a churchboy and not a stonehearted gunman.

"My sister, my sister! Praise the Lord, my sister!"

"Oh shit! Wise out his muthafuckin' mind!" Life laughed. "These bitches thinkin', What church do *he* go to?"

Wise raced by us, gliding backward, yelling victoriously: "But I got them *digits,* muthafucka!"

Later on, standing in the back of the roller rink, holding a hot dog in each hand, Wise turned to me with a cynical smirk. "They all in here tryin' to raise up to the Lord—but when they bust they ass, who they closer to: God or the devil?"

*   *   *

Around midnight, walking back to the Franklin Avenue subway station with Life, we ran into Big Kap from the Flip Squad and some of
the old Posse guys and we heard talk that K had been looking all over
for us. He'd been driving a small yellow Nissan convertible with Jersey plates; a sexy-looking girl in the passenger seat. They'd driven
around Franklin and Washington Avenue searching for us.

Word was they were headed for Coney Island.

"Who that bitch he rollin' with?" Life asked me.

I shrugged. I couldn't keep tabs on all the man's activities.

K called me the next morning wanting a rundown of my day and
night with Life and Wise. I told him about the insane Liberian For-
mula 1 driver and Wise's roller-skating antics inside the Empire. K
turned suddenly serious. Advised me to think very carefully before I
got into a moving vehicle with Wise. "That nigga fuck around and
catch a body, you ain't a journalist no more, my friend. You ain't no
kind of eyewitness or accessory neither. You ain't heard? Once you in
a car with a muthafucka, y'all actin' *in concert*. He fuck around and
catch a body, you be facin' a nice little manslaughter bid."

"So what else Wise was talkin' 'bout?"

"Not a lot. All the parties he's been going to all summer. Something about the Mike Tyson pool party out in Jersey. It was 'off the
hook.' Everything with Wise was 'off the hook.' He asked me how you
were doing—"

"And what you told him?"

"Not much. Told him that you'd been in the studio a lot. That you
had your promo on the radio now, Red Alert's playing your song on
Hot 97. Then he said, 'So is the nigga still a *thug* or what?'"

"And what you told him?"

"Told him no. What would *you* have told him?"

He didn't answer. Paused. Continued with his own interrogation.

"What Wise said then?"

"I don't remember."

"What he said?"

" 'Tell my nigga I said he *slippin'*.' "

The phone went dead. His son Little K had a habit of yanking the cord out of the wall whenever we were talking. But no, Big K was still on the line, breathing very softly. Now I realized I should never have opened my mouth about Wise.

"Oh, so now I'm slippin'? I'm fuckin' *slippin'*? Word, I'm a see Wise about that shit—trust me . . ."

One scorching midsummer day Life called me to tell me about a big block party taking place on Washington Avenue. I met him on Washington and we walked through the street fair, sampling the various hot West Indian foods and drinking cold beer and listening to the hip-hop and reggae they were playing on the portable bandstand.

In the crowd, Life ran into Buckshot, the up-and-coming rapper, once part of the F.A.P. boosting crew. I'd never met Buck in person but I owned his CDs. Had his voice blasting in my Walkman headphones on the Brooklyn-bound Number 2. Buck was the first MC to rhyme about the F.A.P. on tape or vinyl. Half the songs on his first album, *Enta Da Stage* (recorded with his group Black Moon), made reference to the Posse and the badboy heyday of Franklin Avenue. All of the hip-hop magazines had acclaimed Buck as one of the most inspired and original lyricists to emerge in the '90s. With his sinewy laid-back delivery, voice always lurking somewhere behind the beat, Buck possessed the most sought-after trait in an MC: a lyrical flow unlike anything that'd come before. He'd recently done a guest spot on the title track to the Spike Lee film *Crooklyn,* paying homage to his block and his crew:

I'm feelin' another part of reality
Hit me when I represent the F.A.P.

As we talked with Buckshot on the shaded corner of Washington and St. John's, we were joined by an immense guy called Sha whom I'd never seen around before. (I later learned why: he'd been upstate on an eight-year robbery bid.) Built like a defensive end, at least 260, with slablike lats and biceps that popped up like polished croquet balls. Wore a too-small sky-blue T-shirt to accentuate his admirable musculature. On the back of the shirt was a giant playing card. Ace of Spades. Sha wore Malcolm X glasses and was slightly cross-eyed and talked with the trace of a lisp. He told me he was working as a bouncer. Rumor had it he was also performing around town as a male stripper.

I caught a whiff of Sha's ninety-proof breath, watched as he wobbled back and forth on his heels, leaning his weight into my chest, telling me, a little too loudly, that I looked like somebody from TV. He couldn't place my face but he was sure I was somebody he'd seen on Channel 9. Or was it Channel 11? Then he started leaning into Buckshot and telling him that he wanted to start working for Buckshot's new record label, Duck Down, as a bodyguard. Not a request; Sha was basically *telling* Buck to hire him.

A few minutes later Sha whacked me on the back so hard that my Heineken foamed up and spilled all over my shoes. Now he accused me of being some guy from Def Jam Records he'd met the other week at a club in Manhattan. And no matter how many times I told him no, Sha was squinting down at me, convinced that I was a little liar.

We left the Washington Avenue street festival around four. Life was still laughing about Sha. "Tell the truth, ain't that nigga just a little *too* bugged out?"

Life had a notion to take me by the spot on Lincoln Place where he used to sell weed. His career as a weed dealer dated back to high school. Used to keep so much herb on him that he started carrying a .25 on his way to the Sarah J. Hale school—just in case someone tried to rob him for his stash. In '84, he was busted for the stash and the illegal handgun and sent to Rikers.

"Where I was takin' it to be some kind of adventure, the shit just bounced me back to reality and let me know this is a different side of the world that most people don't get to see. You can make friends on the Island—but the friends that you make, they gotta understand that you got guidelines that they gotta respect. Don't never let 'em ever feel like you trust 'em—don't never let 'em ever feel like you *like* 'em—don't never let 'em feel like you wouldn't split they head open at any God-given time."

Coming down Lincoln Place, Life spotted the old crew of gunmen he used to run with—a bunch of hard bearded faces rolling conical spliffs on some cracked concrete steps. Members of that infamous posse called the Junglies—gunmen hailing from Kingston's Concrete Jungle. Life stopped to bump fists and talk to the Junglies for a few minutes. *Yes dready! I-mon deh 'pon a mission, yunnoseeit?* Life didn't have a drop of Jamaican blood in him, but like many Crown Heights hardrocks, he could "fling patois" like a born Kingstonian. He introduced me to the Junglies as a "producer" from Manhattan. Life always told strangers I was a record producer; gangsters don't take kindly to scribblers lurking in their midst.

We continued down Lincoln and came to the building where Life used to sell weed. "This used to be one of the biggest weed spots in Brooklyn. Used to have big lines up in this muthafucka." Pushing open the unlocked lobby door, he was astonished to find that the front door of his old ground-floor weed spot—an ordinary apartment door with a tiny peephole and slot for shoving in cash—had remained unchanged after all the years. "The kitchen is just to the right of the door, and we used to have the stash in the floor. We carved up the wood and made a trapdoor that goes down to the basement. We had the weed in a big garbage bag on a string, so we could drop it in the basement when the cops came. Plenty of times I had to jump out the back window runnin' from jakes . . ."

From the window of the stairwell landing, we could see straight inside the window of the old weed spot. Life hadn't been back here since '89, but the apartment was untouched, abandoned: a weed dealer's time capsule. Life could see his Ferrari and Run-DMC posters on the walls, his weight set, bench, rowing machine.

"I probably still got clothes in there."

Despite his burly build and well-trimmed goatee, Life moved like a ten-year-old kid in baggy black shorts, white socks and black Adidas basketball shoes. He suddenly asked me to help lower him out the window to a little ledge so that he could do a cat burglar scamper over to the window of his old weed spot.

"You think you can follow me?"

Did I look like Spiderman? The drop to the ground was a good twenty feet, but Life said he'd done this move a thousand times before. With some difficulty, I managed to lower his 225-pound frame out the window, and he began to inch along the ledge toward his old spot. But before he was even halfway there, a snarling pit bull came charging around the corner of the back courtyard—and Life realized that there was no possible escape route by ground. "That shit'll have to wait for another day," he said, inching back to the window.

"Yo," he said, back inside the stairwell, his breath still labored from the aborted climb. "I told you how one of my friends died in that apartment? He drowned himself in the bathtub. His girl used to fuckin' be pressurin' him, knowmsayin'? She didn't want him workin' in there, but he had a kid he was tryin' to support. He just couldn't handle the pressure and he drowned himself. Drowned himself in the tub. I came in and found him there. His name was Tattoo."

The summer of Brooklyn street parties hits its crescendo every Labor Day, the wildest weekend on the Brooklyn calendar. After a full year's planning, the city's Caribbean community pours forth in its raucous burst of Carnival. By Monday morning a mob of some two million people clogs the parade route along Eastern Parkway, dancing and grinding to the calypso bands and the reggae sound systems, sampling the spicy curry goat and roti and the ice-cold Red Stripe Beer.

On Labor Day '95 I find myself out on Washington Avenue with Life and Neecie and Wise. Wise has his little son with him, a sweet-faced kid who keeps smashing—at precise intervals—another little boy's head with an inflatable baseball bat.

Wandering off on my own to get a Tastee beef patty, I'm swallowed up in the creeping Carnival mob, can't move in any lateral direction, sucked a full block down the parade route against my will. Eastern Parkway has become a sea of sparkling festival costumes, mobile steel drum bands, shirtless middle-aged men grinning and doing their belly-jiggling dance, long-limbed schoolgirls in lime-green outfits hopping down the Parkway, gold glitter falling from their little laughing faces.

Then, doubling back down Washington Avenue, I nearly get stuck up by some guy named Razor who used to run with K's older brother Toño and the Ave-Ave Crew. I'm oblivious to the danger, chomping on my Tastee patty, a clueless gazelle to Razor's lurking leopard. He spots me from his corner lair—is heard murmuring, scheming, wondering if I'm fair game for robbery.

"Who dat? Yo! Who dat?"

Fortunately for me, it's Life who overhears his murmuring. Big, broad Life, grabbing Razor by the neck, wrestling the criminal plot away from him. I walk up with my half-eaten patty and catch them butting foreheads. Life using his leg power to walk Razor backward, shouting: "That's my *peeps*, nigga! Don't even *think* about it!"

Razor's eyes roll back lazily. Oh well. Lemme find some next vic. With his long thin dreads pinioned back, sporting a beige linen vest and matching baggy shorts, I watch him staggering, half dancing on the corner, drunk out of his skull.

A few minutes later, K shows up on the block; Life grumbles something in his ear about Razor wanting to rob me. This sends K into a rage. Races over to talk to Razor about it, but then Razor begins to shout, loud enough for the whole block to hear: "Oh shit, Little Toño! Little Toño! You ain't too big for me to spank ya ass, nigga!" K glares at Razor hard, grinding his teeth—turns away at last, lets his anger fizzle and smoke. Yeah, Life's right. Razor is just too drunk to know what the fuck he's doing.

It was only at my insistence that K showed up at all today. Told him he couldn't miss the last blowout party of the summer. He wanted to stay home, said he couldn't stand to be in Brooklyn for the parade. "Even if you ain't lookin' for no drama on Labor Day, drama will come *find* your ass."

On a wall at the corner someone's mounted a bottomless blue milk crate; three kids dribbling a small green-and-blue basketball, shoving each other, dunking, dreaming of being like Mike. Another little boy runs past and loses his ice cream on the pavement. "Aw ya done did it *now!*" bellylaughs his sister.

Now musclebound Sha shows up on Washington Ave, wheeling a plastic garbage can filled with bottles of Heineken submerged in ice water. He has a thick roll of cash in his hand, says he's made a killing today. I find three singles in my pocket, step over to buy another Heineken from him.

"Mike!" he shouts happily, slapping my back with his bear paw.

"I'm not Mike," I tell Sha.

"You told me you was fuckin' Mike."

"I never told you I was Mike."

He has an evil gleam as he stares down at me through his Malcolm X glasses. Once again, Sha's convinced I'm trying to play him for a fool.

I glance over at K on the corner, eyes glazed with a faraway look I've come to recognize well by now, the look he gets thinking about "all the niggas who ain't here," all the badmen dead before their time: original F.A.P. heads like Snake, Rome, Kool Aid, Infinite . . . his cousin Nesto . . . his older brother Julio . . .

Around seven P.M., with the parade winding down and the sun glowing red on the horizon, word filters through the crowd that Razor's life is in imminent danger. Evidently, I'm not the only one he's been sizing up for stickups. The previous weekend Razor robbed the Dominican bodega on the corner and now, I'm told, the Dominicans have taken out a contract on him. K points out the stone-faced Dominican hit man in a backward Yankees cap, blocking the doorway, hand on a large bulge in the back of his waistband.

"They just waitin' for all the police to leave before they dust Razor's ass. Trust me, them Dominican niggas don't be playin'."

A festive mood is still draped over the neighborhood; people all around me laughing and playing and dancing. But the unspoken tension is as thick as the milky Irish Moss that Life's slowly sipping as he leans his back against the bogeda window.

Not just the Dominican hit man but half of Washington Avenue seems to be holding heat. K has trusty Scobey on his hip. The automatic in Wise's waistband standing out bold as a morning erection.

K and Life keep trying to persuade Razor to go home, but he remains too proud, or too drunk—planting himself in front of the Dominican bodega, daring the hit man to shoot him in broad daylight.

Now K starts insisting that we get the fuck off Washington Ave. Life wants to linger, show support for Razor. K yells for Life to leave it the fuck alone. "That nigga hard of hearing?" he asks Neecie. "He hard of hearing? He ever picked up lead before?"

Finally K grabs my shoulder and says, "Yo, I gotta get you off the fuckin' block 'fore niggas start blazin'." We leave everyone else behind without even a nod goodbye, walk up Underhill Avenue, past a deafening reggae sound system blasting the latest rudeboy anthem out of Kingston:

> *What will yu say if yu comin' from dance an' yu red*
> *Hear a voice say, "Bwoy, nuh move else yu dead!"*

A sinister curtain has descended on the block. Someone's shot out one of the streetlights. The corner is pitch black and dotted with silk-shirted gangsters openly brandishing pistols.

A palpable feeling hovers in the warm summer wind: I think it's death.

"Do me a fuckin' favor—walk *inside* me!" K snaps. Figures I'll be less likely to be hit by the spray of gunfire away from the curb. He's agitated about Razor; but he's more concerned that we get out of Crime Heights before the loud tattoo of popping pistols.

"It fucks me up because I grew up with the nigga. But I can't do nothin' 'bout it—I'll be damned if I'll kill myself, stop my plans—worst of all—stop my fuckin' family, for his ass. Raze don't know enough to recognize the fact that: *Yes, these muthafuckas is gonna kill me.* Right now, he's drunk, he's in good spirits, or maybe he's not even hearin' what the fuck people are sayin' to him . . ."

We walk up through the reggae ruckus of Underhill Avenue, K pausing to bump fists—"Yes, ragamuffin, yes!"—with a one-eyed Jamaican badman leaning by the wall holding a bottle of Dragon Stout in one hand and something dark and metallic in the other.

"Why rob a store on your own block?" K is asking himself as we come down the now-darkened Parkway toward Grand Army Plaza. "Back in the days, sure, we had it like that. Raze just came home from up north—he been locked up since '78, '79—he must think that shit's still the same. But things change. When he was out here, him and Toño, we was all fightin' with *fists*. What the hell Raze know 'bout guns?

"Nigga's probably up there thinkin': *Oh, I'm a be some kind of hero.* But a hero ain't nothin' but a muthafuckin' sandwich. Ya gonna die, they gonna come to ya funeral—and two or three days after that they won't know nothin' 'bout no Razor. *Who the fuck was Razor?* Niggas don't remember a muthafuckin' thing. Forget you as easy as pie."

Away from the danger now, walking through Park Slope, he points out the site of a store that his brother Julio once robbed at gunpoint. Back in the days of the Tomahawks. The days when Julio and the Tomahawks had half of Brooklyn under pressure, when they could rob almost any store with total impunity.

"El General was one bad muthafucka."

I've never asked him the details of how his brother died. Now he tells me.

"Julito and his crew was steady doin' stickups, right?* *He went up north in '83 on an armed robbery bid, caught a five-to-fifteen. Came home in '88 after serving the five years in Elmira. He told us he was gonna be coming home; the next day he called us collect and said he was in Arlington, Virginia. They'd picked him up right outside the gate at Elmira and taken him down to deportation court in Virginia. Said they was gonna start deportation proceedings against him to send his ass back to Panama.*

"They had him in St. Elizabeths, this mental hospital-type place in D.C., right off Martin Luther King. Actually, we was right around the corner, slingin' our shit. We was right on Martin Luther King and Mellon; we had a spot near Orange Street.

"I paid for a lawyer; I also paid some guys and a couple of girls to come up there to the court and act like they was all part of our family. And we managed to get him off from that deportation shit. But I remember the judge tellin' him: 'Look, if I see you in my courtroom again, for any kind of crime, I'm deporting you to Panama.'

"Four months after they let him out he got caught with an eighth of a key in Brooklyn. 'Round that same time I had got arrested for that gun shit and they had us together in the same jail, C-95 on Rikers.

"He was in Cell 24 and I was Cell 26. We spent sixteen months up on the Island together. That was my best time in jail. Then they sent him up north again to serve his one-and-a-third-to-four. That was in the ending of '89. When he finished that bid, right away they snatched his ass up and took him to Varick Street. The INS Detention Facility in Manhattan. He used to call me beggin' me to come see him at Varick Street. I couldn't visit him 'cause I was boxing—that's the year I was out there in Vegas.

"Used to call me and I used to send things up there, but I never went to visit him. I'm sorry I didn't go visit him now.

---

*These recollections about his brother, Julio, come from a taped interview with K conducted on January 15, 1997.

"One day they took him out of Varick Street and sent him, back to Panama. He got to Panama just as all hell was breakin' loose, just in time for that fuckin' U.S. invasion. After that, nobody really knows what happened to him. What's been said is that when Julio got to Panama he got down with this anti-American faction that was part of Noriega's regime. He was down with them cats, doing all this anti-American gangster shit for them. His payment for puttin' in the work wasn't supposed to be no money; it was supposed to be that they would smuggle him back into the United States, usin' fake papers, down some road in Texas, that type of shit.

"Gotta understand one thing about my brother Julio: he was a real fuckin' pest. He was the type of muthafucka that would aggravate the shit out of you. He'd keep on pesterin' you until you lost your fuckin' mind. What's been said is that he aggravated them Noriega cats—kept askin' them when they was gonna fix his papers—to the point that they just got tired of him pesterin' them all the time. And they killed him. Chopped him the fuck up. They found one part of his body in Panama and the other part in the Zone. Couldn't even give the nigga a decent funeral. That's how they killed El General. That's how they killed my fuckin' heart."

And with that, my Brooklyn summer came to an end. One Friday night in early September, K called me to say he was back in Crown Heights, hanging with Life and a bunch of the old Posse on the street. Even True was there. True from the mosque? Weren't there still hard feelings between True and K? Naw, he said, the beef with True was squashed. True was no longer working at When Worlds Collide so he really didn't give a fuck about K's gunslinging incident.

"You should roll through," K told me cheerily.

I begged off. No time to roll, had a tight deadline on an article for the newspaper, Krazy Glued to my desk until it landed. K kissed his teeth, told me I was *wutless—a bumboclaat pussybwoy,* handed the phone to True so he could say what's up.

The next morning K called again, said it was a good thing I hadn't rolled through. Said he was fed up, wasn't fucking with the Crime Heights knuckleheads anymore. Said the night ended up with him and Life and Sha all hanging out in the park by the Brooklyn Museum. K had been rhyming and Life had been doing his human beatbox accompaniment and Sha had just been sitting there drinking beer. Sha was nothing but an overgrown drunk. K finally had to leave them alone because Sha was acting the fool.

"Acting the fool how?"

"Like, 'Nigga, how come you don't never call me?' I says, 'Sha, I ain't even got ya muthafuckin' number!' Writes down his digits. 'Nigga, *now* you ain't got no excuse. You don't fuckin' call me *now,* next time I see you, we gon' fight.' 'Sha, shutdafuckup. Stupid-ass muthafucka. Ya *know* ya ain't really want no part of me.'"

I heard something in Life's voice I'd never heard before. Fear. He sounded like he was in a sweat, afraid his phone line might be tapped. "Yo, I don't know what the fuck is goin' on. Fuckin' DT just calls me at the crib askin' do I know a Tony Harrison."

"What'd you say?"

"I said, 'Hell naw—I don't know no fuckin' Tony Harrison.'"

"Who's Tony Harrison?"

"I don't know no fuckin' Tony Harrison!"

K, when I talked to him, sounded a little less stressed. "Yeah, beast called me this mornin' askin' a bunch of muthafuckin' questions— sayin' some muthafucka had my number in his pocket or some shit . . ."

"What'd you tell them?"

"Not a muthafuckin' thing! I don't *know* no fuckin' Tony Harrison."

*　　*　　*

Mystifying. Until I went out to the corner store Monday and bought all my morning papers. There, plastered on newsprint in the *Times,* the *Daily News* and the *Post* were photos of musclebound Sha.

SUSPECT IN SERIES OF RAPES IS ARRESTED IN PARK SLOPE—POLICE SAY HE WAS ABOUT TO ATTACK AGAIN . . . COPS: RAPE SUSPECT NABBED AS HE STALKED HIS SIXTH VICTIM . . . BOUNCER HELD IN BROOKLYN RAPES . . .

> A man who the police believe is responsible for attacking or sexually assaulting several women in brownstone Brooklyn neighborhoods was arrested early Saturday morning as he was about to attack another woman, the police said.
>
> The man, Tony Harrison, 26, of 418 St. John's Place in Prospect Heights, was under surveillance by the police and, they said, was seen following a woman into an apartment building on Union Street in Park Slope shortly before he was arrested about 5:20 A.M.
>
> The police said Mr. Harrison had preyed on women in Park Slope and Boerum Hill for the last 10 months, raping, robbing or attacking them in the lobbies of their apartment buildings, usually after midnight. According to the police, the rapist threatened women with a gun or a knife and told them that he would kill them if they screamed . . .

My thoughts turned immediately to one of my colleagues at the newspaper, a young brunette who lived in Park Slope and who'd been terrified for months to walk home from the subway station at night. Young ladies were linking up, she'd told me, walking home in tandem, watching every moving shadow for the vicious Park Slope Rapist. I remembered the smell of Sha's beery breath as he leaned into my chest. *Mike! You told me you was fuckin' Mike!* The lazy eye calling me a liar.

With Sha's arrest, I came to see firsthand the curious place that sex offenders occupy in the criminal hierarchy of the streets. A man could be convicted of armed robbery, aggravated assault, murder—a host of violent crimes that would only enhance his status as a badman; but a *rapist*—shit, no one wanted to be seen talking to a rapist! He was only a step above a child molester in the cellar of reprobation. When I told K that I'd seen Sha's face in all the morning papers, he grew livid, called Sha a "pervert," said that having a rapist in their midst was going to fuck up the crew's image. "Don't *never* mention that muthafucka's name to me again! He gonna get his ass carved up real nice when he get on the Island."

Talking to Life's girl, Neecie, that night, I noted that she gave little credence to the psychological theory that rape was not a crime of sexuality but of brute aggression, of one man's need to exert his physical power over a weaker human being. "Sure he was kinda funny-lookin', sure he had that lazy eye," Neecie said, "but don't tell me he couldn't get himself a girlfriend like everybody else . . ."

So the verdict of the street was in—guilty as charged. Still, I had no inkling whether or not Sha had actually committed the string of heinous crimes; in my presence he'd seemed little more than a drunk, a swaggering, obnoxious drunk, but hardly the most menacing man I'd ever met on the streets of Crown Heights.

For weeks, Life kept getting desperate phone calls from Sha in the Brooklyn House of Detention, a frightened Sha, maintaining his innocence on all charges. The cops were trying to frame him, he said. Sticking him with needles, drawing blood for their DNA tests without having the proper court orders.

"Yo, Doug," Life said, "Sha really wanna talk to you."

"Why does he want to talk to *me*?"

"He wants a journalist to come interview him in Brooklyn House, hear his side of the story."

I was reluctant to look any deeper into this abyss. Sha began asking Life for my home phone number (Life wouldn't give it to him), making so many frantic calls to Life's apartment that finally, just to keep Sha from hassling Life (and Life from hassling me), I agreed to take the subway down to Brooklyn House on Atlantic Avenue and hear his side of the story. Life and I tried to line up an available day, but Sha's visiting schedule conflicted with Life's work schedule, and then Sha was abruptly transferred out to Rikers, which made any plans for a visit even more of a nuisance. One Wednesday we made arrangements for a visit to the Island but then, without notice, Life was called into work and he called off our early morning rendezvous on 125th Street.

Sha's frantic phone calls became less frequent. Soon, I was almost able to forget about him, allow his once-razor-sharp image to blur in my memory. I didn't hear his name again for many months, when Life told me he'd got word that Sha had tried to commit suicide, tried to hang himself in his cell. Someone from Brooklyn had caught sight of him on Rikers, reported that Sha's hulking physique had wasted away; the former bouncer and male stripper was now so haggard and skinny that no one would recognize him in the street.*

By early November, K had fallen into a lingering depression. All structure had crumbled from his daily routine. His whole world was turning sour and dark. After putting in all those hours in the studio with Terror, he'd shown up one day and found the door boarded shut. All the recording equipment was gone; no furniture; no sign of life inside.

Finally, K tracked Terror down at his father's home off White Plains Road. It seemed Terror was no longer Terror—he'd gone back

---

*On January 27, 1997, Tony Harrison was convicted in Brooklyn Supreme Court on multiple counts of first-degree rape, first-degree sodomy, sexual assault and menacing. The judge meted out a century of prison time.

to being Barrington Daley. Cut off his dreadlocks and shaved his goatee. Wearing a shirt and tie and carrying a palm-sized Bible in his right hand. The Lord's work, that's all he talked about now. Hip-hop, that was Satan's work. Regretted having strayed from the Church for so long to walk through the wilderness with Satan and his firm-breasted consorts. Satan, the master of temptation. Soon he would be leaving New York to travel to Australia and New Zealand as a Pentecostal missionary.

Perfect timing.

K now lost his weekend job at Swatch. Showed up for work one Saturday and was told he was superfluous. He'd done his job so well that he'd put himself out of business. The owners of the three boutiques hadn't been robbed in months. They thanked him for having done such good work scaring the shoplifters and stickup men off the block.

I wasn't sure what he was doing with his time. Sat home all day, arguing with Faith, watching TV, waiting for me to call. If I didn't call him all day he'd call me in the night asking me why I hadn't called him all day. If I told him I was busy with work, his response was surly. Kept asking me what the fuck was happening with that fucking *Freaknik* screenplay we'd written—when would that be made into a fucking movie? More importantly, when would we get all that fucking cheddar they owed us? We no longer had any control over the matter, I told him. Julio and Marcus had stopped returning my phone calls; I had no idea whether they'd even managed to find anyone interested in financing their Southern-fried booty flick.

"What's the point writin' somethin' to have it just sit in a fuckin' drawer?"

"I told you before we started—it's always a thousand to one against them actually making a movie."

Then he got very quiet and began to mumble some vague remarks about how pointless everything was—why was he even trying to go legit? why even try to fight the inevitable? He was born to be a fucking hoodlum and, yes, he was going to die a fucking hoodlum.

What did he want me to do—*talk* him out of it? Remind him about that thin strip of orange plastic that had finally deteriorated, fallen from his wrist, wound up in a garbage dumpster somewhere in midsummer Crime Heights?

"You don't gotta remind me about *shit*, muthafucka. Lemme tell you somethin'—you can't make me do a muthafuckin' thing that I don't wanna do. I'm a be a *real* muthafucka till the day I fuckin' die."

A freezing Wednesday night in late November, writing in my office until after two A.M., on impulse, instead of telling the cab driver to take me down to 21st Street, I decide to swing by Columbus Circle to see Life at the Trump International construction site where he's doing security work. Creeping up on him, trying to surprise him as he sits there in the unheated security shack on the side of the site that faces the Mayflower Hotel. But Life's senses have been honed by the years of hustling and prison time. Hears the faint crackle of footsteps and looks up at me with a smile.

What a boring-ass job. Nothing to do but smoke Newports, listen to Hot 97 on the tinny little radio, phone into headquarters every hour on the hour with the all's-clear report. Once in a blue moon a homeless guy tries to sneak into Mr. Trump's construction site and Life will threaten to bumrush the guy if he doesn't vamoose.

But I catch something more than boredom in Life's eyes. He doesn't sound as depressed as K, but he's edgy, at a lower ebb than I've ever seen. I sit beside him in the cold little shack and, just like K the other day, Life's now murmuring about the criminal temptations that keep clawing at him. Some cats he knows are making a move down to Florida, want to know if he'll get down with the hustle. Set him up with half a brick and a tool and then everybody'll split up and do their own thing.

He cracks a match and sucks another Newport aglow, says, what the fuck, he knows it makes more sense to stick it out with this legit life. But sometimes, man, sometimes it just seems futile. He's bringing home $350 every two weeks—working full time on the graveyard shift. Even with Neecie's paycheck added in, they're barely able to cover the rent and lights and phone bills. The other night, he says, lowering his voice and his eyes in shame, they both had to jump the turnstiles just to get to work because neither one of them had money for tokens. Shit is humiliating, he says. If we head to his crib right now, look in his kitchen cupboards, we won't see anything besides Combat roach trays.

But it's not the present tense that has Life worried; it's scoping down the horizon at the big picture: realizing how he's fucked up, made too many wrong turns, and now so many of life's byways have been permanently barricaded to him. At today's crossroads he sees a choice between one of two paths. "It's either you work and take this little bit of money you gettin'—or g'head and take ya ass out there raw-dog style and get locked up. 'Cause they damn sure got some-place for ya ass."

A place Life knows a little too well. In those eerie early morning hours, chain-smoking Newports, he remembers hearing the threat in the back of the ATF car. Thirty years. Thirty fucking years.

Gunrunning had seemed such an easy and victimless hustle. He and Grim thought they'd nailed it down to a science. Head down South, pay someone with a clean criminal record to go into a licensed gun dealer and buy the firearms. Then once they're paid for, have your confederate call in a report that his guns have been stolen.

The profit margin in gunrunning was *strong*. Down in Virginia, you could get yourself a .380 for $90, come back up to Brooklyn and move it for $450. A .357 you could buy for $200, come up here and sell it for $750 or $800. Tec-9s they were paying $300 and some change, brand-new, still in the case, bring it back to Brooklyn and get $2,000.

Transporting was the tricky part. He and Grim would rent a van, take out the seats and the interior, carefully pack the boxes of guns in-side and then tighten up all the screws in the paneling. Nine times out of ten you'd have a third guy with you. The van packed with guns would be driving in front—always in the front of the decoy car—and you'd have your radar inside the van so you could detect when any police were nearby. If you did sight any jakes, tap your brake lights twice, make the decoy guy in back pass you and start speeding, doing eighty or ninety, have the police stop him, write him his ticket while you kept humming along at fifty-five.

They thought they were so slick, thought they'd got over. They were somewhere on I-95 in Chesterfield County, Virginia, when Life saw the blue ATF car fly past doing about 110. On this run, they were too cocky, didn't have a decoy driver trailing them. Life was eating Popeyes chicken and Grim was rolling up a big spliff from the bag of weed that he kept tucked in the side of his Timberland boots. Life glanced back now and saw more ATF cars in back, and then the blue car in front screeched off on a diagonal and blocked the highway ahead. Life dropped the half-eaten drumstick in his lap, looked at his partner and said: "Yo, Grim, we goin' away for a *long* time."

In the back seat, Grim's girl, Michelle, started shrieking hysterically. Life screamed back at her to shut the fuck up. The ATF agents knew Life and Grim were heavily armed and they weren't taking any chances. "Put your hands out the door! Put your hands out the fuckin' door!"

When they stepped out of the van, they were made to lie belly-down in the gravel as the agents started to search the van. They kept them lying on the highway while they searched, and the search was taking so long that Life felt a flicker of hope—maybe the feds couldn't find the shit.

But then one fat cop in the back of the van called out for a special screwdriver to undo the van's paneling; now Life knew that the game was over. A lady ATF went by the side window, pried the panel back, saw all the boxes of guns and bullets. All the agents got excited, shouting, congratulating each other like they'd just won a game of hoops: *Yeah!*

They took a clean white sheet, spread it on the side of the highway, started laying all the guns in a nice arrangement for the photo shoot. They took pictures of the guns, took pictures of Life and Grim and Michelle with the guns. Then the sheriffs split them up, took each of them in a different ATF car, began the interrogations.

"You can make shit lighter on yourself," the fat hillbilly-looking ATF agent told Life. "Why don't you just tell us who's the head man behind all this?"

"Look, you can talk me to death but I ain't gonna tell you a muthafuckin' thing until my attorney's present."

"All right, we got us one of them hardheads—don't wanna cooperate." The big hillbilly ATF agent laughed his shit-smelling breath in Life's face. "Boy, we gon' see how tough yer ass is—'cause the minimum y'all facin' is thirty years."

"Thirty years. When he said that, I felt like shittin' on myself. Actually, I got a ball in my stomach: it felt like my heart bust. I just sat there, tryin' to let that shit hit me, tellin' myself that this was reality, that your ass was in the midst of gettin' thirty years."

But the feds couldn't nail Life on a gun-transporting charge (the van hadn't crossed state lines yet), and he took the plea bargain offer: making false statements to a licensed gun dealer. "They didn't have me as an actual buyer, so they charged me with conspiracy. They had six counts on me altogether, and Grim had thirteen counts against him. My charges carried one to five years. If I woulda went to trial I was facing that full thirty years. And I wouldn'ta beat it, either."

But like so many criminal cases, it all came down to the bottom line. The feds calculated that it was going to cost them too much money to take Life to trial so they let him plead out to conspiracy.

Around three A.M. we're standing in the hollow belly of the Trump construction site. I've never been inside an under-construction skyscraper; I stand staring up through all the unfinished floors, hypnotized by the Erector set connection of the massive girders overhead. Hard to imagine, Life says, but in two years' time this joint is going to be Manhattan's most exclusive condominium and hotel tower. In two years' time the mound of dirt and rubble we're standing on will be the hotel lobby: nothing but gleaming gold and marble and mirrors. And the apartments above us: nothing but movie stars and Wall Street billionaires. The penthouses, he's heard, complete with panoramic Central Park views, are on the market for more than five mill a piece.

Five mill, I'm thinking, trying to imagine how *any* apartment could be worth that amount, exploring through the rubble of the construction site; suddenly I rear back at the loud scratching next to me and then I see a huge raccoon rummaging through the overloaded dumpster. Must've wandered in from Central Park. Shouting, but not loud enough to panic the raccoon, I inform Life about the furry mammal trespassing on Donald Trump's property.

Life claps his hands with relish, takes it upon himself to go raccoon hunting, using just a fat wedge of broken concrete and a sharp length of metal rod.

Rabies, I warn him, backing away, preparing to make a lightning dash through the rubble.

"Fuck that. Gonna make me a hat."

The raccoon's the size of a small pit bull, its bared teeth probably just as lethal, but this doesn't deter Life from cornering that frightened striped creature in a jumble of cinder block and scrap metal.

"Come outta there, muthafucka!" he says, trying to jab at his quarry with the metal rod. "Only gonna be one of us walkin' outta here tonight!"

In early December, K and I were back in the Palladium, at a gala launch party for Duck Down, the label and management company owned by Buckshot and his longtime partner Dru Ha (Drew Friedman, a twenty-three-year-old Jewish hip-hop entrepreneur). A few weeks earlier, I'd dropped in on Buck at the Duck Down offices on West 18th Street. He sat back at his big executive's desk, looking out at the view of Manhattan, outlining the big plans he and Dru had for their label, telling me how he'd learned to navigate the treacherous waters of the music business by studying the hustling ways of the Franklin Avenue Posse.

"The music business is still hustlin'. Even when I used to be a little scrunt, even when I used to be boostin' and sellin' my oils on Franklin, I used to watch niggas runnin' shit on the block. You can hustle for short change, you can hustle on some real run-around-the-block shit, but if you workin' for short change, you gonna get short change.

"How does a muthafucka go from doin' that to doin' *this?* By organizin'. This ain't no muthafuckin' surprise world—no secret world. It's a fuckin' office in Manhattan. How d'you get an office? By elevatin' your shit until you *need* a muthafuckin' office!"

Many of the original F.A.P. heads were there at the Palladium party, stone-faced, standing off against some pillars rolling up blunts and getting high on Chocolate Thai. K and I stood in the middle of the Palladium's dance floor, watching Buck, Dru Ha, Heltah Skeltah, Smif-N-Wessun* and the rest of the Boot Camp Clik pacing the stage, throwing promo T-shirts and tapes into the audience, getting the whole mob chanting in unison to "Bucktown," Smif-N-Wessun's ode to the life of the Brooklyn badman:

I walk around town with the pound strapped down in my side
No frontin', just in case I gotta smoke somethin'
Round here heads don't act they age
Ya might be another dead bwoy 'pon page

---

*Smif-N-Wessun now record and perform as Da Cocoa Brovas; the popular Brooklyn duo changed its name after being threatened with a lawsuit by the venerable Massachusetts-based firearms manufacturer.

Enter the cipher, with ya lighter
L's are ready, prepare for another allnighter
But keep a watch for the cops cuz they rock Glocks
Comin' on the block tryin' to rock knots

Pigs be actin' like they bigger than us niggas from the streets
Cuz we stalk mad-deep and them walk beats
I guess them hold a grudge cuz I won't budge
Playin' tough, starin' down the judge with my hands cuffed

Standing there with my nappy hair and my dirty gear
I'm a warrior—now I'm up outta here
Pigs look me up and down with a frown
Is it because I'm down—or is it because I'm from—
BUCKTOWN!

K and I left the Palladium party early; he had to go back to the Bronx to get his luggage. He was catching an early morning Amtrak for Atlanta.

He'd decided that he needed to leave New York before the first of the year. Going down to Atlanta to stay with his brother Pacho. He'd heard from Pacho that the pace of life in Georgia was much more mellow. Pacho'd said you could relax in Atlanta, get your mind situated properly in Atlanta. Hopefully, K said, in a few months' time his mind would be situated properly and he could send for Faith and his kids.

Walking down 14th Street in the freezing wind, he told me that he'd accepted something. It would be impossible for him to stay out of trouble in New York. Too many temptations here. Too many evil thoughts.

TEN

duppy or gunman

> But these men lie in wait for their own blood, they set an
> ambush for their own lives.
> Such are the ways of all who get gain by violence; it takes
> away the life of its possessors.
> **—Proverbs 1:18–19**

Down South living seemed to agree
with him. Atlanta was becoming the new mecca for hip-hop, he said.
Seemed like half of Brooklyn was relocating to Atlanta. Yes, his mind
was becoming properly situated; he had a new game plan, had decided to work with his older brother Pacho on starting up an independent rap label. Pacho supposedly had some investors in South
Florida who were interested in such a business proposition. Within
weeks their brother Craig had come down to Georgia too; they were
all living together in one small apartment in the College Park section.

Early in January I called down to College Park to tell K that
there'd finally been a business development with our *Freaknik*
script—the project had been taken over by Freddy DeMann, head of
Maverick Picture Company, Madonna's film division, and in a few

---

dup•py [dəpē] *n.* a haunting spirit of the dead conceived in the folklore of the West Indies as a usu. malevolent shadow or immaterial body. [West African, per. Bube *dupe* ghost]

days they were going to have to FedEx both of us a batch of new contracts to sign—but while we were talking I kept hearing these strangely mesmerized murmurings in the background, like someone preaching in a Panamanian accent, then distinctly caught the words *so-called Jews.*

"What's that?"

"That Black Israelite bullshit," K snapped. "Fuckin' Craig comes down here with all these Black Israelite books and now he's got Pacho readin' that shit too."

"The guys from Times Square?"

"Same muthafuckas."

I'd long noticed the Black Israelites around midtown Manhattan, standing behind barricades, shouting aggressively at passersby, dressed in flowing robes with Hebrew letters embroidered in the fabric, holding up signs claiming things like THE REAL JEWS ARE BLACK!

One day, as I passed the Marriott Hotel on Broadway, they'd screamed in my ear. *What are you?* I stopped walking and told them I was Jewish. They pointed their fingers and chuckled. *Who told you that? Your rabbi?* Told me I was just an impostor Jew whose hairy ancestors had crawled out of the caves of the Caucasus mountains to usurp the identity of the true brown-skinned Jews of the scriptures . . . They held up an elaborate chart indicating that the black peoples of the New World were the real Twelve Tribes of Judah. *So where did the slave ships set sail from?* I wanted to ask. *Sixteenth-century Palestine?* But you couldn't argue with those Black Israelites. You couldn't even ask them a question. They'd shout down anything you had to say and start spouting things in bastardized Hebrew or quoting some out-of-context passage from the Bible about the bronzed feet of Jesus . . .

K was pissed at his brothers and it wasn't just their Black Israelite studies. Said that all his brothers wanted to do was sleep until noon, and when they did wake up, they'd start grumbling first thing about *Whitey-Kincaid-this* and *peckerwood-that,* always trying to blame the *Other Man* for all their fucking problems. And then when they weren't doing that, they were arguing amongst themselves or Craig was threatening to put an automatic pistol to his own temple and end it all.

Said it was making him sick; he regretted moving to Atlanta; but maybe, just maybe things would get better as soon as Faith came down with the kids and they could start looking for their own place to live.

Life was just struggling to keep his head above water. He'd stopped working graveyard shifts at the Trump International construction site. Hadn't moved too far, though, was now working days as an in-store security guard, preventing any theft of books from the Barnes & Noble near Lincoln Center; and evenings as the doorman at a large apartment complex off Nostrand Avenue in Crown Heights. I asked him how he was managing to hold down two jobs six days a week. Said he'd conditioned his body to get by on only two or three hours of sleep.

I stopped by his place in the Boulevard Houses in East New York on one of his rare days off. He kicked disgustedly through the spent 9-mm casings and crack vials on the lawn outside. The elevator took forever to open: when it did the walls reeked of numerous, fermenting sprays of human piss.

"I don't wanna raise my kids up here, man. I don't give a fuck; I wanna raise my kids up in the suburbs, knowmsayin'? Someplace where it's so quiet, you could hear a rat piss on cotton. Someplace they'd have more time to situate their mind and focus on different things in life. Out here, once ya mind gets clogged with a certain level of corrupt—it's like, fuck it, then ya programmed to living' into that lifestyle. And once ya old enough to realize it, now ya just tryin' to patch up shit that you shoulda been workin' on in ya youth days . . . just seems hard as hell, seems like it ain't no light at the end of the tunnel . . . it's either ya gonna be strong enough to fight the shit out, or ya gonna turn your life back to crime . . ."

C alling down to College Park one afternoon to check in with K, I heard Faith's voice answering the phone in Pacho's apartment. There was a great din of shouting and cursing in the background, and Faith whispered that something very strange was going on but she couldn't talk about it right now—the only thing she could tell me was that the police had just taken K away in handcuffs.

She called me back later that day to explain. She said that ever since she'd arrived in Atlanta there'd been problems with Pacho and Craig. They'd all been bickering constantly. On Saturday morning Pacho's four-year-old daughter had been hitting little one-year-old Keisha, and Pacho and his girlfriend were sitting there watching, not doing anything to stop it, and Keisha started screaming so loudly that K came running into the room. When he saw that his daughter was crying, in pain, he turned and pushed Pacho and Pacho fell and said he'd hurt his leg and then someone called the cops and when the cops showed up K started yelling at the cops and they put him in handcuffs and that's how K ended up in the Fulton County jail charged with domestic assault.

But, Faith said, she was very suspicious about the whole episode. Because the minute K was out of the house, Craig and Pacho started packing up their clothes—boxing everything and carrying it out of the apartment—and she heard them all whispering things which led her to believe they'd arranged another apartment someplace else in Atlanta but they didn't want to tell her where it was.

And then, quite suddenly, they were gone. K was in jail and Faith was left alone, with her two little kids, in an empty apartment, in a city she knew next to nothing about. They'd taken all the furniture with them. The kids had to nap on the bare floor. Faith had spent her last cent on food for the kids; they even took *her* baby food out of the refrigerator. They had all the power in the apartment turned off. Broke, she had to walk with the kids all the way from College Park to downtown Atlanta where the Fulton County jail was. She said she thought Pacho and Craig had been plotting for some time to have K thrown in jail because their mother was moving down to Atlanta in a few weeks and they wanted to move to the new place without K knowing where it was.

Later that same day Craig called me collect from Atlanta. I thought he was going to hit me with his version of events but he just started screaming at me—"You still fuckin' with my brother? You still fuckin' with him? You better leave my fuckin' brother alone!"

I tried to ask him a question, but he interrupted, shouting: "My brother ain't nothin' but a piece a shit! My *brother's* the reason me and my family always be havin' problems—that muthafucka ain't nothin' but trouble . . ."

Faith said that Pacho had come down to the courthouse to try to drop the charges, telling the police that it was all a misunderstanding. But it was too late: the state of Georgia was picking up the charges now. Faith had some jewelry she was able to pawn to raise his bail money and get him out of the Fulton County jail after a few days. They were left stranded in Atlanta with the two little kids and no money. Had to go to a homeless shelter to get food and milk because the kids kept crying with hunger.

I called Western Union and wired Faith enough money to buy a few days' worth of food and the one-way train tickets back to New York. K called me a few minutes later, promised he would pay me back someday. He said he now considered himself an orphan and—except for his older brother Toño, wasting away in a Bronx nursing home, suffering from some mysterious brain injury—he no longer had any family.

In mid-April I got a call from a friend in the film business who told me there'd been an article about the *Freaknik* project in *Daily Variety*. I logged onto the Nexis database and printed out a copy of the article.

VAUGHAN, NEW LINE, 'FREAK' OUT, read the headline. According to the article, New Line Cinema had sent a camera crew and a "musicvid director" named Jesse Vaughan to join "100,000 partying African-American college students in Atlanta late last week to document Freaknik, the annual, massive, Dionysian spring break bash." The studio was planning a low-budget, reality-based feature in conjunction with Madonna's Maverick Picture Company. A new Writers Guild rewrite guy had been hired by the studio and his name (misspelled, actually) was the only screenwriting credit listed in the article.

Sitting at my desk in *The Forward*, K read the *Daily Variety* article over and over. He didn't really care about the fact that our names hadn't been listed as screenwriters. Other questions bothered him more: *What exactly is preproduction? When they say this director cat was filming second-unit footage, isn't that shit considered preproduction? And, if so, didn't the contracts we signed say that they owe us some muthafuckin' money upon commencement of preproduction?*

Actually, I said, the terms of our contracts specified that we would be paid in full upon *notification* of preproduction. But Julio and Marcus hadn't notified us; Maverick Picture Company hadn't notified us; New Line Cinema hadn't notified us. These guys were clever: they wouldn't notify you; and when you tried to call them, they wouldn't accept your phone calls.

What! K said, jumping up from my desk. Were they trying to pull some kind of slick three-card monte hustle? If so, maybe it was time for *him* to step to somebody's mustache. Maybe it was time to round up the clique and handle this shit *Brooklyn*-style!

No, I said. That wouldn't be necessary.

He rolled his eyes. What a life! Here he was flat broke, homeless again, never sleeping, his kids had been diagnosed with sickle-cell anemia, and he's waiting around to be *notified* that some slick-ass motherfucker's going to pay him the money he's owed . . .

He looked horrible: worn-out, haggard, angry. I could see where this was headed. Walking down 34th Street that night, I talked to him about going to see someone, working through his rage, perhaps get a prescription or two for his manic depression. In the past whenever I'd mentioned the issue, he would become defensive—"Whatcha tryin' to say? I'm fuckin' *crazy?*"—but now he looked me dead in the eye and nodded. "Yeah, you right. Can you help me find somebody for that? Jesus knows, I don't want no more problems . . ."

My friend Jack tipped me to a moderately priced mental health clinic on the Upper West Side. K asked me to accompany him to the first session. He brought along Nina, one of his old girlfriends—it made him feel a little less unmanly going to see a shrink if he had some sexy female companionship along for the ride.

Nina was a big voluptuous Brooklyn girl with her hair pulled back in a ponytail; she'd been with K during the days of both drug dealing and prizefighting. Always called K by that other alias: *Gato.* Her amorous, gun-wielding, long-limbed Panamanian cat. Now she worked as a dental hygienist for a Jewish dentist on the Upper East Side. The minute she met me she started examining my teeth, spreading my lips with her fingers, gazing into my open mouth, nodding. Said she could tell I'd never smoked crack. "How's that?" She said the teeth were the first telltale sign with a rockhead: the sickly, yellowish hue in the teeth.

On the Number 2 train up to 96th Street, she and K were laughing about his days boxing out in Vegas, how she'd flown out there one day to surprise him and shown up at the Top Rank gym in some tight minidress with no panties or bra underneath, strutting around the gym in her pumps, and all the fighters in training stopped working on the speedbags and heavybags to stare at her *seriously* jiggling form.

Nina, K announced, was one armed-and-dangerous bitch. She laughed and tossed her ponytail in my face as K painted the mental picture. "Word, Gato, I did look *bad* that day, right?"

She told me that she'd had her eyes on K for a long time before she'd ever met him. The first time she'd seen him he was standing in front of the Empire Roller Rink kicking it with Mike Tyson. The second time she was coming to the Love People disco and there'd been a big shootout inside and K came running out with his Tec in his hand and dove in through the passenger window of a moving car. The third time she saw him she was down in the Franklin Avenue subway station: he was saying goodbye to his baby-mother, kissing his little daughter goodbye, and as soon as they were on the train, pulling out of sight, K whirled around, started macking Nina *hard,* trying to get her phone number.

"I was like, 'No this nigga *didn't!* I know he not tryin' to talk to me *two seconds* after sayin' goodbye to his baby-mother!'"

Strangers in the nearby subway seats were smiling as Nina hollered. I could see why K liked to have her around. Nina made everybody laugh.

When we got up to the mental health center, K was very tired and irritable, and Nina helped him fill out all the paperwork. Finally a cheerful small white girl with long red hair came and asked him to accompany her to a private intake session. He said he'd feel much more comfortable if Nina and I could be there with him. The girl said this was highly unusual—it was supposed to be a confidential intake session—but finally she relented.

We all sat in a small white room and the little red-haired girl was taking notes and K was letting it all spill forth: how he'd just come out of jail, how he'd been brawling with all the COs down in Fulton County, how he didn't want to have any more violent outbursts, how those Prozac and Zoloft pills had been helping him think clearly and stay calm when he was locked up in Essex County and the Tombs.

Whoa, whoa, whoa!—she asked him to go back a bit, start with his childhood perhaps. And then K was talking about the first time he'd seen a dead body and the first time he'd shot somebody and the first time his body had been ripped open by automatic gunfire—and the girl stopped taking notes and stared at Nina and me, studying our reactions, thinking, I suppose, that K was delusional, making up all these violent war stories about himself.

Nina caught the white girl's suspicion; she let out a loud laugh: "*Shit!* You ain't even heard the half of the *half* of how wild Gato used to be!" Well, said the little red-haired girl, standing up with her clipboard, she'd now have to consult with one of the doctors about whether they could actually take on someone with such a violent case history because, she said, therapy tends to bring out all sorts of painful memories and whichever doctor is assigned the case would need to know the full history of violence and feel confident, or at least reasonably secure, that he wasn't putting himself at any physical risk dealing with such a violent patient.

A few weeks later the clinic called K and said that they'd arranged for his first appointment. He went by himself this time. Called me from a pay phone immediately after the session. Said the psychiatrist had been a young white guy who reminded him, vaguely, of me. The guy liked hip-hop; they talked for a few minutes about the Wu-Tang album.

Then the shrink had listened patiently as K talked about all the things that had happened with his father and mother and brothers as a kid in Brooklyn, how he knew he was supposed to have been an abortion, how he knew that no one in his family had ever loved him or wanted him, and then he started crying uncontrollably and it seemed like he cried like a baby for the remaining forty-five minutes and when he came outside it had been raining hard but now it had stopped and the streets were clean and wet and the trees were sweet-smelling and he said he had never felt cleaner and sweeter in his whole fucking life.

*　　*　　*

He continued going to the clinic every few weeks. He kept asking the shrink about getting the antidepressant pills but the shrink said he didn't feel that K was suffering from true clinical depression and therefore an antidepressant prescription wasn't necessary in his case.

A few weeks later, when I asked K how the therapy was progressing, he said he'd decided to stop going.

"Why?"

"Because. Shit stopped workin'."

In early May K heard from his baby-mother Candice that his son Tino was having disciplinary problems in school. He asked me to come with him to P.S. 316 in Crown Heights, said he'd made an appointment to speak to Tino's schoolteacher and the school principal.

"This is where all the trouble started right here," he said as we walked the halls of his former grade school, superficially a clean, safe-feeling institution—until I noticed, on the bulletin board, the WANTED posters for two late-thirtyish black men accused of arson and child molestation in the playground. The school staff initially mistook K and me, in our baseball caps and jeans, for a pair of undercover detectives, a fact that had K laughing aloud in the principal's office. "Picture *me* bein' beast!"

Candice had told K that Tino was acting out in class, hitting other children. The school psychologist was contemplating putting him in a special ed program. "I don't want him goin' into special ed," K mumbled. "That's the route I went, and I know that only leads you down one path—gettin' with a whole bunch of ruthless little cats and then turnin' your life to crime . . ."

As we sat waiting in the school office, K said that one of the biggest mistakes of his youth was constantly playing Casanova, having all these kids by all these different baby-mothers. The domestic situation for Tino was particularly complicated. Tino's mother, Candice, now had three children by three different fathers, and was legally married to a fourth man serving a bid upstate.

Not surprisingly, all the domestic turmoil had already taken its toll on little Tino. His first-grade teacher, Mrs. Mack, talked of Tino as a frightened, intensely shy six-year-old. Mrs. Mack was one of the only adults Tino would confide in. And when he did open up to her, she said, he could be such a gentle, affectionate and intelligent boy. "He's obviously gone through some very traumatic experiences in his young life. Was he present when his mother was shot in the face?"

"No, that happened long before he came along," K told her. In the Posse's heyday, Candice had been one of the leaders of the F.A.P. girls division, dubbed Two-Gun Candy, known for packing two .45s everywhere she went; she was shot in the face by another female gangster during a dispute.

Tino's teacher had never met K before that day, but she knew immediately who he was: in every aspect, from his deep-brown complexion to the darting playful eyes, little Tino was a dead ringer for his dad. The fear Mrs. Mack described seeing in Tino's eyes was also eerily familiar. "I used to be afraid of everybody too," K told her. "It's the fear that turns to rage and has you wildin' out."

His own father was never there to give him any guidance or discipline, K told Mrs. Mack. Mrs. Mack nodded; many of the young boys in her class have never known fathers. Then her eyes brightened momentarily. "But *you* have a chance to break the cycle. You're *here* today—and that's a start."

"It's so hard for me to get him to open up to me. He won't even talk to me when I ask him what's wrong—he just looks away."

"What do you expect?" Mrs. Mack said. "He doesn't even *know* you."

Mrs. Mack had no idea why Tino wasn't in class that day. Neither did the school principal. K and I left P.S. 316 and went on a mission of trying to locate his son. We stopped by Candice's apartment; she wasn't home. K was starting to get very agitated. Someone on the street called out to him—"Speng!"—but he didn't even turn his head. I glanced back at the Yankees-cap-wearing caller, who shouted "Speng!" again, then I asked K why he didn't acknowledge him. "I don't answer to that fuckin' name no more!" he snapped at me, striding resolutely up the block.

He led me to another apartment building; we went up to the second floor and started banging on the door. Several pit bulls inside began to snarl. The door creaked open. It was a young white woman, visibly pregnant, smoking a cigarette. K said, "Tino here?" Shy-eyed little Tino emerged with a little white boy and an older white girl. The kids stepped unafraid past the unmuzzled pit bulls. We all went downstairs, and I noticed that the white boy and the white girl kept calling each other "nigga."

Once we got outside K took Tino aside and asked him why he wasn't in school that day. Tino wouldn't answer. Then K asked Tino where his mother was. Wouldn't answer. Then K put his arm around Tino and we walked to the bodega and K offered to buy Tino a soft drink and some corn chips. The little white kid named Kevin had run ahead of us and then he came darting out of the bodega, having stolen a handful of candy. The Arab store clerk shouted angrily at him. Little Kevin laughed back: "Suck my dick, stupid muthafucka!"

K took Tino to sit on the benches in the park near the Brooklyn Museum. He seemed very embarrassed by the state of his child's clothes. Everything Tino had on was dirty, food-stained, tattered. The boy's face needed to be washed and his hair needed trimming. K promised he'd come by and buy him some new things as soon as he got some money together.

"Pops," K said to his son. "You know you can always talk to me. Don't be scared to talk, Pops. Say what's on your mind. Nothin' you could ever say will make me mad at you—you understand that, right? Say whatever is on your mind, Pops—you hear me? You can yell at me, scream at me, say *fuck!* say *shit!*—say *I hate you!*—I don't care what words you use, so long as you say what's on your mind . . ."

Tino stayed silent. Kept staring off at the sprinklers and the other six-year-olds playing. There were a couple of Hasidic kids doing circles on their little banana-seat bikes. That made Tino smile at last. He also enjoyed playing with my Walkman. I set the radio to Hot 97 and put the little insert headphones in his ears. When a rap song came on that he recognized he would mouth all the words perfectly. His smile was getting bigger. But he still wouldn't speak. And he wouldn't look into his father's eyes.

My hip starts vibrating, Skypager humming frantically. Finding a pay phone, I learn I have an assignment from the paper, a late-breaking news story, right here in Crown Heights: the Jews on Kingston are rioting, engaged in a running street battle with the cops of the 71st Precinct.

What happened? I quickly catch up on the facts. Two members of the Shomrim, a Hasidic citizens patrol group, have been arrested for using their walkie-talkies to beat a black man whose eight-year-old nephew, according to police reports, the Hasidim falsely accused of stealing a bicycle. Following the arrest, a mob of Hasidim gathered in the streets, besieging the beating victim's home on Empire Boulevard, clashing with police in riot gear in front of the 71st Precinct House, demanding that the two Shomrim men be released immediately.*

Now, in the aftermath of the disturbance, the leaders of the Lubavitch Hasidim have publicly accused the 71st Precinct cops of brutality, a refrain which has long been voiced in the black neighborhoods of Crown Heights. These tensions between the Crown Heights Hasidic community and the police have been simmering for five years now. Many Jewish residents have never forgiven the NYPD for its ini-

---

*To many Orthodox Jews in Crown Heights, the Shomrim are viewed as a necessary breakwater against the surrounding sea of violence and crime; while in the African- and Caribbean-American community, the unarmed citizens patrols are often denounced as lawless vigilante groups with a long history of beating and stomping innocent black residents.

tial hands-off policy during the 1991 riots, those three nights of violence and looting which catapulted Crown Heights into international headlines as a symbol for black-Jewish enmity. Nor has anyone in the tightly knit Orthodox enclave forgotten the fate of Yankel Rosenbaum, the twenty-nine-year-old Holocaust scholar from Australia, stabbed to death on the night of August 19, 1991, chased by a mob of young men chanting, "Kill the Jew!"*

I talk to my editor on the pay phone, outline my plans for the afternoon's reporting: he tells me to go by the Seven-One precinct house, try to get a statement from the cops, walk down to Kingston Street, talk to some of the angry black hats. But first, I have an idea of my own, decide to get some quotes from the other side of the Crown Heights fence. I start at a familiar spot: upstairs in Shabazz's apartment on Eastern Parkway—the old Franklin Avenue Posse headquarters. Shabazz's mother is a small frail woman whom everyone in the Posse affectionately refers to as Miss Mary or simply Moms. Miss Mary isn't doing too well these days. She had a heart attack in the winter of '95; she's also afflicted with hypertension, diabetes and glaucoma. With Shabazz still finishing his sentence in Sing Sing, she is trying to scrape by on her Social Security checks. Nearly blind, she lives a precarious existence, rarely leaving the apartment. The high point of her week is Shabazz's collect call every Sunday from Sing Sing; her only other companionship, the mewing of her two underfed cats.

Born down in South Carolina some seventy-five years ago, Miss Mary worked her whole adult life as a domestic for a Jewish family on the Upper East Side. She only stopped working for them a few years ago, when her health began to fail.

---

*Three hours earlier, a driver in the motorcade of the Lubavitch Grande Rebbe had lost control of his car, jumping the curb at the intersection of President Street and Utica Avenue. The vehicle struck and killed a seven-year-old black first-grader named Gavin Cato who had stopped on the sidewalk to adjust his bicycle. (Many in the black community were outraged when a grand jury later declined to indict the driver of the vehicle, Josef Lifsh, for vehicular manslaughter.)

She's been living in Crown Heights, in this same run-down, crime-plagued and, yes, Jewish-owned building, since the days of the Brooklyn Dodgers. I ask her to tell me her views of the Hasidic community down on Kingston Avenue. She shrugs as she pours a glass of Kool-Aid in the kitchen, says that she only sees those Jews when she goes down to the welfare office; there are always a lot of them at the welfare office. Then she says something else that I've often heard before.

"They don't want you to live in that neighborhood down there. And they got police watchin' them all the time, guardin' them all the time. Why should the police guard *them* all the time and they don't guard the other people all the time?"

"Yup, that was right field right there," says I-God, gesturing off in the direction of a half-empty parking lot. A hot sunny day on McKeever Place, and I keep thinking that fifty years ago this very spot would have been the throbbing spiritual heart of Brooklyn—fathers and sons would've been streaming from all corners of the vast borough, riding the Franklin Avenue trolley line to see their beloved Bums playing a doubleheader against those despised uptown Giants . . .

But now the only baseball being played is by two little shirtless boys equipped with a Day-Glo green bat and orange tennis ball, fielding pop-ups in the concrete Jackie Robinson playground, in the shadow of the massive Ebbets Field Houses.

On our walk down to the 71st Precinct House on Empire Boulevard, K has said that, rather than taking the circuitous route, avoiding the despised Ebbets Field projects, we might as well take the shortcut, march straight through Ebbets Field. During our previous walks down Franklin Avenue, toward the old funeral home that was once the infamous Love People reggae disco (now a Pentecostal church), down Empire Boulevard, K has always made a point of steering clear of the Ebbets Field projects. Now today we are walking straight toward them. Won't the beef erupt again? I ask. Won't some of the old-timers recognize him? K shrugs and continues his nonchalant gait.

It's ten years since war broke out between Franklin Avenue and

Ebbets Field, a war that brought countless shootouts to the neighborhood and made it unsafe for members of either camp to venture onto the other's turf. Unlike Franklin Avenue, whose faces seem to change with every passing season, whose badmen seem to vanish for years at a time, K notes that "these Ebbets Field niggas" stay put in their housing project fiefdom; the same boys who played in the concrete playground in the '70s are now hardened, dreadlocked, gold-teethed men in their thirties, standing by parked Lexuses and Acuras, blaring Ron G. mixtapes and Biggie Smalls remixes from powerful Bose speakers.

K stands talking to one pretty young girl named Kristal, who, leaning against the fence, recalls how K used to come up to see her in her Ebbets Field apartment, openly brandishing a .45 pistol in each hand. "That's how thick the beef was," she says with a laugh.

"But I-God here was always the peacemaker," K tells me, smiling at the thin bespectacled guy in a red Fila sweatshirt and red Texas Rangers baseball cap. "He was the only one we used to let walk through Franklin unmolested."

A Toyota with tinted windows lurches to a stop and out of the back seat leaps a short stocky brown-skinned guy in a flowing white T-shirt.

"Oh shit!" K yells. "Sudan!"

"Yo, I thought that was you, nigga!"

Sudan and K hold each other in a long powerful hug and I think back to the day in the mosque when K and Dante danced around the stage together in a similar reunion clench—here, under the massive Ebbets Field Houses, two former enemies, holding each other by the nape of the neck like long-lost brothers, yet another Malcolm X-meets-West Indian Archie love-hate tango.

"Last time I seen you," Sudan says, "we was down in Virginia. Back in '87, '88."

"Word!" K says. "Bustin' mad shots at each other."

The sun's setting by the time we walk up Empire Boulevard to the 71st Precinct House. K starts to re-create for me one of his childhood crime sprees, pointing out how, when he got into trouble, the cops used to impound his Honda XL-80 dirt bike—but he would always come and sneak in the back of the precinct and steal his bike back, right from under the clueless cops' noses.

Entering the precinct house, I pull out my reporter's notepad, hand the sergeant on duty my business card from *The Forward*. But none of the cops in the precinct house will give me a comment about the latest charges of police brutality. The sergeant stares hard at K and then refers me to some useless prerecorded police information hotline. The "Jewish Riot" is turning out to be one of the week's top stories: outside the precinct house, a couple of reporters from *Newsday* and the *Times* are scribbling; a camera crew from Channel 4 is setting up to shoot an update for the eleven o'clock news.

I tell K I need to walk down to Kingston Avenue, to the heart of Hasidic Crown Heights. He arches one eyebrow at me. "All right, but if some shit pops off just make sure and tell 'em I'm with *you*."

As we veer up Kingston, I quickly see the reason for his apprehension. In an instant the tables have turned: *his* is now the strange face on the block. He nods in the direction of one young Hasid speaking into a walkie-talkie. "You don't see him up there, talkin' 'bout 'Baruch ha-Shem' "—he still remembers his one line of Hebrew from the days working for the Israelis at Raspberry Sport—" 'we got one of them big—one of them big *shv*—' Yo, what's that word, again?"

"*Shvartze*."

" 'We got one of them big *shvartzes* coming up the block with some little fuckin' turncoat in a White Sox cap.' "

We aren't really under intense Hasidic surveillance, I know; but things would no doubt be different were K to stride up the block unaccompanied. We pass a string of colonial mansions on Union Street. K shakes his head admiringly. Says that those homes look like something out on Long Island. Who'd believe you're in the heart of Brooklyn?

On Eastern Parkway we pass a pink-cheeked thirty-something Jew—still buttoned up in his black Orthodox garb—who's diligently fixing his front stoop with a blue bucket of cement and a trowel. The Jew stares at K, then quickly turns his eyes away, back to his masonry work.

"You know somethin'?" K says. "If black people took half the pride in they buildings that these Jewish cats do, we wouldn't be livin' in such fuckin' shitholes all the time."

Suddenly, across one of the groomed lawns, two Jewish boys in black-felt yarmulkes come chasing after some kind of whirling purple saucer. The plastic saucer sails toward us, hovering, before landing with several skittering clicks on the pavement. K leans down, retrieves the purple saucer, handing it to the littlest boy—a milky face with soft curling sidelocks, staring up at him, stunned, speechless.

"Say thank you," I tell the boy, but he remains mute.

"Shorty's fuckin' scared of me," K says, shaking his head, as we proceed up Eastern Parkway. "Scared to even take it from my hand. How's a little kid like that already know to be scared of black people? Somebody's gotta *teach* him that shit . . ."

I don't bother to remind him about his previous confession that afternoon, how as a young boy he had often accompanied his brother Toño and the Ave-Ave Crew as they rolled down to Kingston to vic some rich Jews—perfect robbery targets in those distinctive black fedoras, renowned for carrying excessive amounts of cash in their pants pockets and for favoring expensive Rolex and Longines watches on their wrists.

The encounter with the frightened milk-faced boy leaves K in a sullen mood; we walk on in silence for some time. "A little kid is innocent," he says finally as we cross Nostrand Avenue back into the black section, *his* section, Crime Heights, USA. "I would never do nothin' to no little kid."

One steamy Saturday in early August I hop the J train out to the Cleveland Street stop in East New York, K having invited me to dinner in the apartment he and Faith have been living in since late June. "Yo D, wait till you *taste* this shit," he says, unlocking the front door of the second-floor walk-up. "Word is bond, ask Faith—I started cookin' at like *ten* in the morning." Faith smiles at us, tablespoon in hand, finishing a small carton of vanilla ice cream as we enter the long, narrow railroad apartment. In the center of the beige living room carpet, stretched out head to head, Little K and Keisha lie sleeping, shirtless, Keisha in her diaper, Little K in a pair of blue-and-red Power Ranger underpants.

"Little Man!" K says. "Ain't you gonna say what's up to Uncle Doogie?" But the boy's eyes remain tightly shut, despite his father's booming baritone and the high-pitched squawking of the TV. Earlier in the week, Little K and Keisha both came down with runny noses and ear infections—routine enough for most toddlers, but potentially life-threatening for kids with sickle-cell anemia. K and Faith had to rush them down to the sickle-cell specialists at Bellevue Hospital; I glance down at Little K's arm, still bruised from the intravenous needles.

"You know what tomorrow is, Doogz?"

"No. Should I?"

He reminds me that tomorrow his son will be turning three years old.

Faith cracks the cord of spaghetti in two and drops it in the boiling water. K stands with a red-stained wooden spoon, heating up the homemade pasta sauce—complete with turkey sausage and razor-thin garlic slices—that is his prized culinary creation.

It's been a difficult few months for K and Faith; since returning from Atlanta, he's gone looking for security work but still hasn't been able to find a regular day gig. Seems the old stores on Fifth Avenue are using only licensed security guards these days. I've often wondered how they're managing to make ends meet here in East New York; Faith's been getting WIC money for the kids, I know, and has applied to get monthly Social Security checks for Little K and Keisha—payments for which children with sickle-cell anemia can apparently qualify. K, meanwhile, has been drifting through more weeks of desperation and depression; there's some talk that he may start managing a run-down barbershop on Washington Avenue in Crown Heights, fixing it up, bringing in business, though I'm not sure how financially viable such an arrangement could possibly be for him.

All the more reason, then, for this frenzy of celebratory kitchen activity—the arrival, two weeks earlier, of a couple of checks from New Line Cinema in Los Angeles, payment, at long last, for our rewrite and polish work on *Freaknik,* the Atlanta-based booty flick. After many months of waiting, the head of business affairs at New Line finally notified me that the film was in preproduction and that he would be FedExing K and me checks in the promised amount: $19,161 each.

One bizarre hitch in the payment process: K had no photo ID proving who he was, and New Line wouldn't cut his check without proof of citizenship. He brought me his original birth certificate, his original baptismal papers, the paperwork from some temporary driver's license he had out in Las Vegas when he was boxing. "How can you not have one *single* piece of photo ID?" He laughed at my question; like many an outlaw and gunman and mafioso before him, he'd been living his entire adult life under the premise that it's safest to remain invisible, keep no driver's license, documentation or paperwork on your person—just in case "some shit pops off" and a sudden alias is required . . .

Holding up my coffee mug filled with ginger ale and tinkling ice cubes, I offer a toast to K and Faith's new apartment, to the U.S. passport he's applied for and his forthcoming New York State nondriver's license, to the new bank account and CDs he's opened at Carver Federal Savings (that was a *pride* thing: wanted to keep his hard-earned cheddar in the city's oldest black-owned bank).

Keisha keeps rubbing her eyes and staring at me, looking as if she might start bawling in the middle of my boring speech. Little K sits listless, picking at the coiled noodles with his fingers. "He won't eat the sauce," K explains. "He very seldomly eats meat."

K himself has no such reservations. Across the table from me, noisily slurping up his spaghetti, he sits in a huge white tank top which somehow still looks too small for his torso. I think back to those meetings in the dank visiting room of the Tombs, of how much K has altered since those times. Gone are the gangster braids—his hair is now cut close to the scalp, razored down the sides in a rather conservative fade; gone also is the jumble of colorful santería beads around his neck. K now thanks the Lord Jesus before each meal and keeps a miniature copy of the New Testament in his back pocket. Gone even—and this I find hardest to believe—is *Scobey:* the trusted Colt .45 now lies buried in a patch of earth somewhere in Georgia.

After dinner, K and I decide to go out for a walk down Fulton Street. In the stairwell, a young Hispanic teenager in fluorescent Nikes sprints up the stairs ahead of us. K shows an evil scowl. "He goin' to get the yay-yo," he says, gesturing with his clean-shaven chin, upstairs to the third-floor apartment, a drug fortress with a newly installed solid-steel door.

Sometime in mid-July, K explains as we head downstairs, this quiet stretch of Fulton Street went through a sudden metamorphosis. When he went to bed one night the bodega outside his window was abandoned and boarded up; at eight the next morning, it boasted a brand-new sign, gleaming neon lights, its shelves fully stocked with dry goods and groceries. Girls in short skirts with hoop earrings and bright lipstick profiling outside. And parked on the street, all in a row: a small fleet of Town Cars with tinted glass, hooked-up Range Rovers, Infinitis and Lexuses that signaled the arrival on the block of a drug don.

Or, more accurately, the return. A big-time kingpin, out of state for months, had returned overnight to the neighborhood. K soon learned that the kingpin owned not just the bodega, but the laundromat under the elevated J train (surely the only coin laundry in the city complete with HBO movies on a giant-screen projection Sony), several grocery stores and the fleet of Lincoln Town Cars (each emblazoned on the front with the words ALWAYS HAPPY and on the back with the warning DON'T MESS WITH ME).

Later that afternoon, workmen showed up at K and Faith's building and replaced the decrepit front door with a new one made of solid steel—impossible for the cops to break down—and then the superintendent, who must have been down with the drug don, issued everyone in the building new keys. They next went to work with blow torches on the third-floor apartment above K and Faith's, converting it into an impenetrable safe house. K heard the workers in the night, stomping up the stairs with garbage bags filled with the rattling mayonnaise jars they would use to cook the beige powder into hard smokable rocks.

The next day at noon, K walked into the bodega to see the top dog himself. He spotted the kingpin—a short man in his fifties, with salt-and-pepper in his hair—standing at the counter eating a plate of arroz con pollo, silk shirt unbuttoned to his belly, one leg up on a small stool.

"Yo, pardon me, duke." He tapped the kingpin gently on the shoulder. "Talk to you for a minute?"

The little drug don didn't even look up, didn't say a word. Skillfully sucking the marrow from a cracked chicken bone, he finally muttered two quiet words. "Know you?"

As soon as he said that, five other Dominicans, all strapped, suddenly stepped in and surrounded K.

"Mira, papi," said the first lieutenant, a lanky kid with a heavy Spanish accent and a large diamond-encrusted medallion around his neck. "Anythin' you got to say to him, you could say to *me*."

"Oh, it's like that?"

"It's like that."

One of the other drug workers started to smirk and K stepped hard into his chest.

"You laughin'? Somethin' funny to you? I'll lay ya bitch ass out right *here!*"

"Yo, papi, chill!" the kingpin now said, putting down his plate of food. "It don't gotta be like that. What is it you got to say to me?"

They walked off into the corner of the bodega to converse with more privacy.

"Dig, nigga, I ain't tryin' to knock ya hustle or nothin'," K said, the kingpin's fearless gaze locking tight with his own. "I just want you to know—I *live* in that buildin' where you got ya safe house at. My wife and my *kids* be up there, duke. Do what you gotta do out here in the street, knowmsayin'? But you bring any drama into my buildin'— check it, duke—I'm a *kill or be kilt* for those kids."

"Yo, papi, don't worry 'bout nothin'," said the little kingpin. "You have my word nothin' is gonna happen to your family, nothin' is gonna happen on this block. Period. This block is *mine*. I got it like that." He held up two tightly crossed fingers. "I got kids, too, papi, so I know what you sayin'."

As we continue our walk down Fulton Street, the little kingpin is nowhere to be seen. Even drug dons, K reminds me, take Sunday as a day of rest. "I gotta give him his props, though," he says, gesturing to the kingpin's fleet of luxury cars with their flashy BBS chrome rims. "He real smooth with his shit." The crew of Dominicans has congregated on the corner underneath the Cleveland Street elevated subway station; dozens of Dominican flags waving, the frenetic thumping of merengue blaring from a parked Range Rover. The crew's trademark is the distinctive colorful chain earrings that dangle from their right earlobes. "But the Big Man, he got like five or six in his ear."

As we pass by the posse, the Dominican lieutenants and workers nod respectfully to K; one shouts out to him in Spanish; here they all know K as *Pana*.

It's hot, I'm thirsty, I stop to buy a Jamaican cola champagne from the Korean fruit market next to the train station; I leave K on the street, with the promise that I'll call when I get to Manhattan.

The J train pulls into the elevated platform, and through the graffiti-etched window, sipping my cola champagne, I catch a last glimpse of K—white muscle shirt gleaming on deep-brown skin—disappearing into the hurlyburly of Dominican flags and blaring merengue, gangster-strolling unmolested through that posse of partying drug dealers, back home to Faith and his two sleeping kids.

By the end of the summer, when Crystal and I have to be out of our apartment in Chelsea, K, ever solicitous, volunteers to help us with our dreaded chore. A one-man moving team. Better than Moishe's Movers—or any other foursome of Israeli army vets. I'm astonished, not just by his sheer strength, but by how efficiently he can load the U-Haul. So methodical and analytical in the way he stacks boxes and shifts furniture, building a solid foundation, then sturdy middle tiers, wedging everything tightly in place as if completing an IQ test, some complex, three-dimensional jigsaw puzzle, leaving no corner of the U-Haul wasted.

"How do you know so much about moving?"

"From my moms. I told you—she used to have us movin', like, every three months back in the day." He laughs aloud at the memory. "She was steady not payin' the rent, steady gettin' evicted every three months like clockwork. Word, that's one thing she taught me—if nothin' else—how to load up a van with boxes and fuckin' furniture."

At the end of the long day's move, we're left with some bookshelves and mirrors Crystal wants to donate to the Salvation Army; but K says, *hell no!*—he and Faith will happily take them. We all set out for his place in East New York in the middle of the night. Crystal is at the wheel, swerving the big rattling U-Haul deftly, like she's charioting a tiny Fiat. A kick-ass driver, she can navigate her way through every side street and shortcut in the Bronx or Manhattan—but Brooklyn, hey, only the dead know Brooklyn. As soon as she crosses over the Brooklyn Bridge in the U-Haul she turns to K in confusion, becomes a little Catholic schoolgirl again. *Help.* Laughing—*Go straight, sis!*—K directs her the whole way out to East New York.

She parks on Fulton Street, in the eerie darkness beneath the elevated train tracks, K and I unloading the bookshelves and mirrors, banging our knuckles, trundling them upstairs. It's almost three in the morning; we must look like criminals, a couple of crooks unloading swag. Only a handful of crackheads wander the street, watching, waiting, eyes glowing like deadly yellow beacons in the night. The Dominican kingpin's fleet of ALWAYS HAPPY Town Cars is double-parked along the corner. There is a vacant lot next door—through the trash and debris, overfed rats are noisily scurrying in the dark, scampering boldly across the sidewalk, taking their sweet time, like barrel-chested Teamsters jaywalking across 34th Street. Faith told me that their whole building is infested with these fat rodents: she can hear them partying inside her walls and dancing on the ceiling overhead. And their nasty little cousins, dozens of disease-carrying mice, are multiplying exponentially in their apartment. One night Little K woke up crying because a mouse was sharing the bed with him, tickling his Power Ranger underpants. He refused to get back into his bed, demanded to sleep with Mommy and Father in the big bed.

Coming downstairs, jumping back into the U-Haul, in the ghostly stillness under the elevated tracks, Crystal speaks to me in hushed tones. "I knew they were living in Brooklyn—I knew they were living in East New York—I didn't know they were living like *this.*"

"How'd you think they were living?"

She doesn't answer, just mumbles the names of the old crew, those old friends of hers who lived in similarly ghostly sections of the Bronx—desolate blocks in West Farms and East Tremont—where murder in the street is as common as a game of frozen tag.

"How can he let his kids grow up like this? He has to get them out of here. Look around you. What good could *possibly* happen to anybody in an environment like this?"

Dinner with a gangster. It's a hot summer night on Flatbush Avenue, crackly Tito Puente records blaring from the jukebox; I watch scarfaced K digging voraciously into his favorite dish, a steaming plate of Panamanian-style tripe called modongo. A dish which, to the uninitiated palate, smells like a hearty home-cooked blend of several unsavory bodily functions. I think back to the night, four summers earlier, our chance meeting in a tiny East Village nightspot called the Nuyorican Poets Cafe. His gangster glare, his arrogant smirk. *So be a journalist—ask me a fuckin' question.*

"If you had it to do over again—?"

"If I had it to do over again, I'd be a goin'-to-school, goin'-to-church, book-readin' muthafucka. I'd still be doin' some little mischievous shit on the side probably. But knowin' what I know now, I wouldn't never wanna get into the drug game."

"When you look back on it all, what do you feel? You ever feel—"

"Remorse? I'll be honest with you—some things that I did, I got no remorse for. It was a muthafucka who I *know* woulda done the same shit to me, a nigga that woulda clapped me up in a heartbeat, then I really don't feel too much remorse. He knew what time it was, just like me. We was both playin' by the same muthafuckin' rules . . .

"Then there's *other* shit that I do feel remorse about. To this day I have bad dreams about some of the shit that I did. I know I done made many a nigga's mother cry. That's what gets to me. To this day, I think about it. I think: would that person have changed his ways if I didn't push him off the fuckin' earth? He'd still be here today, and what would he be doin'? Would he have got his shit together and changed his muthafuckin' ways?

"And then too, I always think about what if, when I went to push him off the fuckin' earth, he was just a little bit better than me—and he had someone come push me off the earth? That's when I think about how stupid we was. I coulda died many a fuckin' day over some *real* bullshit . . ."

Sipping my too-sweet café con leche, I remind him about the morning we went to see his son Tino's first-grade teacher, Mrs. Mack, at P.S. 316 and she told him that Tino seemed afraid of everything, and K replied that he used to feel the same way—it was always a fear at first, *fear* that turned to violence—

"See, back in the days, if somebody used to tell me, 'Yo, that's Badboy Blue over there—he one *bad* muthafucka,' I would go and fuck with Badboy Blue—because *I'm* supposed to be the baddest nigga. See, in reality, I'm scared of you now, because a muthafucka that respects me done said that *you* the baddest. I'm gonna fuck you up—I might lose my life behind that shit—'cause I don't want you to live on this fuckin' earth with me. That's how I walked; that's how I *used* to walk . . .

"Nowadays, I still be feelin' it sometimes, when I'm on the train, when I see a muthafucka that looks real mean, I still get tempted . . . But lookin' back, hindsight shows me that it was some ignorant bullshit. It makes more sense to walk away from a muthafucka than start wildin' and beefin' over nonsense . . .

"But then again, if it didn't happen, you and me probably wouldn't be sittin' here havin' this fuckin' conversation, right?"

Another night. Another meal. The Greenwich Café on Greenwich Avenue. K looks out of his element tonight; this is the West Village, after all, where you're apt to see things you're not likely to witness on Flatbush Avenue. Just as our food arrives, the two good-looking white girls at an adjacent table lean forward and exchange a tender lip-to-lip kiss.

"Look at that shit," K hisses, so nauseated by the display of lesbian love that he won't touch his meal for a few minutes. "Yo, why you gotta bring me down to these Sodomite joints, yo? What's the deal? I'm startin' to wonder about your affiliations, dun. Word. You might fold under questioning."

But it's not the Sodomites I want to discuss tonight; I'm more curious to know about K's own affiliation with Father Allah's so-called Five Percent Nation, wondering what it must've been like to be a member of that elect and righteous Nation of Gods and Earths.

"You mentioned about you and Mecca in Medina."

"Word, my first parliament—my first summer home, yo. I'll never forget the day. Had on a yellow Izod tennis shirt with some beige suede Clarks and beige khakis. In them days the diamond-patterned argyle socks was the *shit,* and I had a pair of yellow-and-black-and-tan argyle socks.

"I was with Mecca; she was my lady at that point; she was my Earth. She was from Franklin and Sterling. At that time, I wasn't even thinkin' of sellin' drugs. I had come out of Elmira with no thoughts of sellin' that shit at all. Like I told you, I came home a virgin—the one thing that was on my mind that summer was pussy.

"It happened in Fort Greene Park every last Sunday of the month. They called it a parliament. There was hundreds of people in the park. A black man's heaven, yo. To see all these young ladies with turbans and long three-quarter dresses. The trees were in bloom, the whole park smelled of flowers. All the crime that day was gone. I can recall thinkin' to myself: *damn,* I wish it could be like this all year round. 'Cause it looked like we'd stepped into the Garden of Eden.

"Little kids was sittin' in ciphers; they had all kind of food, free food; over to the left of me, I could see people jammin' to some music; while over on the right there was a lecture going on, as far as the Five Percent mathematics, solar facts and actual facts and so forth.

"At a certain point you could see ten ciphers at one time going on, and big lectures upholding the name of Allah. I was in awe. I'm in the Five Percent Nation now—I been called Knowledge Born for two years, since Wonderful and Pure Life gave me that name in Goshen—but my only contact so far was in jail. This was my first real parliament.

"You saw all your homeys, and there was no beef—it was all love. I saw Sudan and I-God from Ebbets Field—*Peace, God. What up,*

God—my man Uni, Tizlam, Shabazz was there, Star-Asia, True-Allah, Jamal, a bunch of fuckin' people. Plus, it was a lot of old Gods and old Earths. Well into their fifties and sixties. I thought it was just a young person's phase, the Five Percent thing, but there was mad old people there. I walked around, got into two or three ciphers, manifestin' today's mathematics."

"Why today's mathematics? What's that mean?"

"Every day has a different mathematics. The reason it's called mathematics is that in Five Percent every number has a concept to it. It goes from Knowledge to Born, and Born back to Knowledge. One is Knowledge; Two is Wisdom; Three is Understanding; Four is Culture or Freedom; Five is Power or Refinement; Six is Equality; Seven is God; Eight is Build or Destroy; Nine is Born; and Zero—well, you know—Zero is the Cipher.

"So if it was the twentieth of June, the date would be expressed as Wisdom Cipher. One of the other Gods would say to you—'What's today's mathematics, God?'

"You'd say: 'Today's mathematics is Wisdom Cipher. Wisdom being the black woman that is secondary—secondary only to Knowledge, which is the basic foundation of all things in existence. Just as the man is the basic foundation of his family; and the sun is the basic foundation of the solar system. Wisdom can also be said as Knowledge-Knowledge, God, 'cause from the shaft of the Knowledge given to the Wisdom brings forth that third thing, and that third thing is Understanding: the child, the cream of the planet earth. One, two, three. Man, woman and child. Knowledge, Wisdom and Understanding.'

"Then he'd start to build on what you said, expandin' from where you left off, bring forth *his* own understanding . . .

"I remember that parliament like it was yesterday. It was just love. *Mad* love. People was servin' food; you'd just say, 'Fix me a plate, God. Fix me a plate, Earth.' And no money was exchanged. After a while the police came to bust it up. Me and Mecca was gettin' ready to jet and I was like, 'Damn, baby, I don't even wanna leave. I wish it could be like this forever.'"

"Do you still have a copy of the Five Percent Lessons?"

"Hell no."

"Can you get me a copy of the Lessons?"

"Doug. You could get me a copy of the Torah?"

ife. Life manifested: Life is the Love of Islam for Ever. Life, gold-tooth-grinning, bounding down the stairs with his powerhouse sprinter's gait.

"Yo, what's the *deal,* rudebwoy!"

"Been a long time, eh?"

"Word is *bond!*"

Life's landed on his feet though: took some night classes, wrote the exams, got the upgraded security license he needed. He's now working at the Macy's in downtown Brooklyn—wears a huge red single-breasted blazer, has full medical benefits and a fairly flexible schedule. Even got himself a credit card or two. Yo, man, he's trying, he's *really* trying.

He's excited today because he and Keith, the building super, have put together their own private weight room in the basement. Life's mother's neighbor recently moved down South, left Life and Keith in charge of a complete set of York free weights.

I come down to the concrete dungeon on this cold Crown Heights night. The only light is one bare blinding bulb dangling overhead. All the barbell plates are covered in rust. A pit bull locked up in the next room, snarling and clawing at the metal door, lathering itself into a frenzy, threatening to gnaw its way through cold solid steel. Life, ever the prankster, starts messing with my mind: "I think he can *smell* you, Doug. Word up—that dog don't like white people!"

No, Keith laughs. The fucking canine is a marshmallow. The storeroom was broken into a few months back and Killer didn't even bite the burglar on the ass.

Heavy work boots stomping down the stairs. Another massive lifter on the scene. It takes me a minute to make the connection: dreadlocked Razor, the self-same drunkard who'd wanted to vic me at the Labor Day Parade, the same stickup man whom the Dominicans had been gunning for that night. Apparently, they'd missed. Can't keep a badman down.

Razor is the demon of the dungeon. Phenomenal power—can bench-press over four hundred pounds, more weights than actually exist here in Life's dark little world. Razor keeps saying that this is *his* show to run and, in Razor's Dungeon, there will be no smiling, no idle chitchat, no frivolous sitting or resting. Razor refers to everyone as *baby*. Keeps barking out commands like a dreadlocked drill sergeant. And, true, we all defer to him, because this is one musclehead who clearly knows what he's doing. Weight-lifting technique is one of the few things Razor mastered during his dozen-year tour of upstate New York.

Razor watches the world through a permanent sidelong squint. Always scheming, ready to pounce. I recall the words I once over-heard on Washington Avenue: *Razor, he was a treacherous one.*

Razor—prostrate on the bench, effortlessly repping a barbell laden with every rusty plate we can muster—seems a most perfect embodiment of the American nightmare. Prison didn't punish him. Didn't rehabilitate him. Prison simply turned Razor into a more densely muscled and brazen stickup artist.

We're joined by children, Keith's nephews, wannabe strongmen—*Don't mess with that, junior!*—picking up dumbbells and trying to swing them overhead, talking about the latest Tupac rumor to hit the Brooklyn street: that the wily little rapper (having faked his own murder in order to escape his slave-wages contract with Death Row Records) has been spotted partying down in Jamaica with Treach from Naughty by Nature and a bunch of gorgeous redbone honeys in thongs.

"It's true, kid, it's *true!* Wasn't no autopsy! Wasn't no funeral! Ain't nobody see the nigga's *body!*"

The street loves tricksters. Like Brer Rabbit or Anansi or *Black Bart Simpson* T-shirts. Elegua with his box of robustos. 2Pac the indomitable. *Jack Mandora mi nuh choose none.*

Life hits the play button on his boombox, blasting his mixtape to get himself psyched for his turn on the bench, rhyming in unison with Meth:

Hey you! get off my cloud!
You don't know me an' you don't know my style!

My turn to prostrate myself, lay myself down at Razor's mercy. He leans forward, spots me through dumbbell flies—grunting, imaginary-tree-hugging, I gaze up at the jailhouse tattoo on his chest, the word RAZOR scratched out in boxy uneven lettering. The muscles of his arms so thick and defined, they jut at nearly square angles.

Touching my elbows lightly with his calloused palms, Razor leans over me, hollers down at me—*C'mon, baby! Rock wit' me, baby! Good money, baby!*—breath reeking of stale Newports and sleeplessness. A single droplet of sweat pools on his forehead, dangling, for a seeming eternity, before splattering in my eye.

I am blind.

Getting up from the bench, dropping the dumbbells to the concrete, dizzy, trying to rub back my vision, I see Life's sister standing on the staircase, snickering, staring at Life's black leather weightbelt cinched tight around my waist. "You look like Barney Rubble!" she says, pointing, laughing her way back up the stairs.

Upstairs, K is sitting at the kitchen table with Life's mother.

"Yo, why you ain't come downstairs, muthafucka?"

"Yo, why you ain't *wait* for me, muthafucka?"

"What's the deal, nigga?" Life loudly slaps the hardened meat of his pectorals two times. "Scared to fuck with this?"

K gets up from the table, follows Life into the narrow hallway. They throw up their fists, slap-boxing, sparring with their whirling fifty-two hand-block technique. Razor sits watching them from the sofa, eyes narrowed in the treacherous squint. I listen to the titanic rumbling of the sparring partners, wonder what it would be like to see them fight someday in earnest.

His final burst of energy now spent, Life lets out a relieved grunt, lights up one of his Newports, shares another with Razor. Who wants to fuck with him? Pulls out a pack of playing cards, starts doing his cardsharp routine, undetectable sleights of hand. *Now turn over ya card!* head thrown back joyously, laughing about all the motherfuckers he herbed for their commissary in Sandstone with that trick.

He has shot glasses lined up on the kitchen table, starts pouring out sloppy ounces of 151-proof Puerto Rican rum. K shoots me a screwface. Razor's lost in his devious thoughts. Life shoves a shot glass of rum in my hand. His mother says we're both nuts to touch that firewater.

Strangely mellowed, throwing back one last shot of overproof, Life sails away into reggae crooner mode. Sings in a crystal-clear tenor, a beautiful gliding voice I've never heard before. Turns himself into a rudeboy jukebox, taking requests from all corners, running down the biggest hits from the heyday of the Franklin Avenue Posse, all the lovers' rock and boom-tunes that echoed from the speakers in the Empire Roller Rink when the Posse would gather to party on a wild Friday night.

Now special request goin' out to all original gunman dem!

He uses his empty shot glass as an echo chamber, neck arched, head thrown back in his sweet reggae serenade. *"Bumbohole!"* K barks, forming a two-fingered pistol, mimicking the sound of celebratory gunfire overhead.

Must be a duppy or a gunman
I-man noh find out yet

I'm late for my journey to Sing Sing. By the time I reach Grand Central Station, shouldering my way against the morning rush-hour flow like some salmon with a confused body-clock, the huge timepiece overhead indicates that I am precisely two and one half minutes late. I spot K and Miss Mary standing up by the information desk. K greets me with his screwface and his Teflon-piercing glare.

"What's the matter?"

"We been waitin' here a fuckin' hour! You *know* Ma can't be standin' up for no long time like that."

"So why'd you get here an *hour* early?"

We agreed we were going to take the 9:20 to Ossining; still have a good fifteen minutes before the Metro North train departs Grand Central. K keeps scowling, doesn't answer my question. I purchase three round-trips and we begin to make our way down to Track 28. Miss Mary shuffling very slowly, not able to see ten feet in front of her, holding on to K with one hand and her wooden cane with the other.

"You heard my page?" K says.

"No."

"I had them muthafuckas pagin' you for 'bout fifteen minutes. *Dick Hedd report to the information desk please. Dick Hedd report . . .*"

He cracks a mischievous smile at last—starts complaining about not having had any breakfast this morning. Didn't budget his time properly, left the house too early and missed out on Faith's scrambled eggs, toast and fried turkey sausage.

Miss Mary laughs. "Knowledge, you big ol' elephant, you always hongry." She looks up at me. "This one—it like he two years old, always talkin' 'bout, 'I'm hongry, Ma, I'm *hongry.*'"

"I'm losin' weight, Ma."

"You losin' weight? You *need* to lose weight, you big ol' elephant. Get any bigger they gon' put you in a *zoo.*"

"That's my Ma. I *love* my Ma."

*   *   *

Taking our seats on the Metro North train, Miss Mary is chuckling, telling me about the near-disastrous incident K set off earlier this morning as they tried to get on the subway at Franklin Avenue. Miss Mary showed the transit worker inside the token booth her senior's pass and then asked which entrance she should use. The transit worker barely looked up, grunted something she couldn't understand. Miss Mary had to ask him again and again. He kept grunting incomprehensibly.

Then K started banging his hand angrily against the token booth window, telling the guy to hurry up and give Miss Mary a proper answer.

"The man starts talkin' all this mess to Knowledge, you know, thinkin' he safe behind all the big glass, and Knowledge says to him, 'Come out from behind the glass if you wanna talk junk!' and then the transit guy, you know, he *scared,* and he call these two police over. So hear Knowledge now: 'You think I'm scared of them little ol' poe-*leece?* You think I'm scared of *them?*' So the police come over and I thought for sure they was gonna lock this big ol' elephant up."

K and I stare at each other for a long time without talking.

"Can't let nobody disrespect my Ma," he says. "*Fuck* that. 'Scuse me, Ma. This lady been more of a mother to me than my own mother. I'll go back to jail before I let some little punk *disrespect* this lady right here."

He's writing a rhyme the whole way to Sing Sing. Jots the first two verses on pieces of looseleaf, folded into quarters, and the third verse in one of my reporter's notebooks (bogarted from my desk at the office, the cover of which he's now labeled with the words *All This Shit Is Dope*), oblivious to the lurching of the train, bobbing his upper body to the rhythm of his own head, blocking out the stares of the sweet-faced Puerto Rican girl with her thick thighs squeezed into too-tight straight-legged jeans and the Wall Street–type reading *How the Irish Saved Civilization* and the old black guy who keeps shuffling through a set of neatly scripted index cards with misspelled self-help aphorisms (*Lifes like hills & valleys, theres always ups & downs*), K rocking to his own ups and downs, shouldering heavily against me, re-working his own syllables, changing the emphasis of the quarter notes and triplets, shuffling those words like so many mental index cards.

> *The sense greater than the sender*
> *I'm that wack-rhyme ender*
> *I come in a mob as if my name was Tony Bender*
> *While I'm taxin' and relaxin'*
> *You's an improper fraction—*

"Tony Bender?"

"From *The Valachi Papers.*"

"Who's he?"

"Damn, you don't know a muthafuckin' thing about crime, d'you, homeboy? . . . Tony Bender, he was a lieutenant with the Genoveses. A treacherous muthafucka—the cat set old man Genovese up for a narcotics bid. Then when he was locked up Genovese figured out who it was that back-stabbed him and he had Tony Bender whacked."

Maybe I don't know Tony Bender, but I *have* heard a few things about Sing Sing. I know it's the place that zapped the life out of Louie Lepke, where Julius and Ethel Rosenberg walked their last lonely walks. By mid-morning I find myself sitting inside the fortress walls, in the brightly lit visiting room, waiting for the corrections officers to bring Shabazz down from his cell.

"Where Bighead at?" K keeps mumbling, glancing back with impatience. "Where they got Heliumhead?"

At last Shabazz appears at the far end of the visiting room, smirking, gangster-limping in his prison green. I hardly recognize him. Neither does K. "Damn," he whispers, "homeboy grew into his head." In the summer of '92, the last time I saw him, Shabazz was a whippet-thin DJ, wizard-scratching vinyl on his Technics 1200s. Now he stands thick and broad across the chest and his neck looks like a toughened collection of cords. His hairline has receded. There is little trace of youth left in his face.

"Word, Headus," K says. "Gotta admit. You lookin' kinda diesel."

"Benchin' 360." Shabazz shrugs. Says that his one obstacle to growing bigger is that he refuses to eat any of the filth prepared by the pigs in their mess hall; most of his protein must come from self-cooked meals of canned octopus.

"You can't get no Allah Food?"

"Naw, they cut that out, man. Pataki and 'em cutting out e'rything."

For the first fifteen minutes of the visit, Shabazz talks about his case—why all his appeals have been denied. He can't understand it; he's been a model prisoner, going to school every day, taking vocational classes in barbering. But every time he comes before the board, they stamp his shit *denied*. Looks like he's going to end up serving his max right here in Sing Sing. "Muthafuckas sent me up here on a one-way Amtrak ticket," he grumbles. "Railroaded my ass."

"Bazz, I don't wanna remind you 'bout a certain conversation when one of us was in C-95—back in '89—don't wanna remind you what *my* advice was 'bout takin' that DA's plea bargain . . ."

Shabazz told us how the ADA got up in court, pointing a finger, saying: "Aren't you a member of a notorious street gang known as the F.A. Posse?" And then one of the cops testified that Shabazz had been struggling so wildly and with such superhuman strength that the cop was convinced—well, this was only conjecture, Your Honor—that the accused had been smoking angel dust. "Angel dust! Ain't that some shit! I ain't never seen no angel dust in my muthafuckin' life, right, K?"

He begins to expound on the distinction between *inmates* and *prisoners:* an inmate is someone who follows the pigs' orders, gives in to the crushing power of the system; a prisoner remains an untamed rebel, incarcerated against his will.

"You understand the difference, Ma? I'm a *prisoner* here. I ain't no inmate."

"That's nice," Miss Mary says.

*   *   *

K sits with his checkbook sticking up out of his shirt pocket—as ostentatious as any rose boutonniere.

"Nigga, you tryin' to *impress* me?"

"Why I gotta be tryin' to *impress* you?"

With a sudden slashing motion Shabazz snatches the checkbook from his friend's pocket. Flips it open, studies it closely. "Goddamn government name and the whole nine. Shit. Don't tell me you got them credit cards too?"

K nods proudly. Tells his old partner-in-crime that he has recently been accepted by the membership department of the Writers Guild of America.

"The fuck you talkin' 'bout?"

"It's this bunch of screenwriter muthafuckas—a union—yo, I told you me and him did this fuckin' rewrite for New Line Cinema?"

"Now I *know* it's either you smokin' that shit or you tryin' to impress me, nigga."

For my benefit K begins to reenact the blow-by-blow of the only fistfight he and Shabazz ever had, on the corner of Franklin Avenue and the Parkway.

"Shabazz ain't gonna tell you this," K stage-whispers to me, "but *he* wasn't the one who won that fight."

"What?"

"Bazz! Who won the fight?"

Shabazz just cradles his chin in his hand and shakes his head slowly.

"Bazz! Tell the *truth*—you wasn't cryin' for it to stop?"

Shabazz turns to me with an ironic smile. "Do you peep the *ego* on this nigga? He wanna be the *sun* and everybody else gotta be like little *planets* circlin' round him."

"Bazz, I ain't got no big ego. I just don't want you perpetratin' no fraud here. Who won the muthafuckin' fight?"

Shabazz turns to his mother with arched eyebrows; Miss Mary confirms her son's diagnosis: "Knowledge sho-nuff got a big head. Don't think nobody could ever beat him."

Two tables in back of us sits a tall late-twentyish guy with a classic square-jawed Sicilian face; the only white inmate I've seen in the Sing Sing visiting room all day. Wearing a gorgeous cream-colored cashmere turtleneck with a thin gold chain around his neck. His father and brother flank him at the visiting table. None of them speaking; all three staring off at different bored angles. The father wears his thick silvery hair swept neatly back, dressed in a black cashmere mockneck and gray slacks with sheer black socks and black suede shoes. I watch them as furtively as I can, keep hearing that line K was rhyming in my ear on the Metro North ride. *Come in a mob as if my name was Tony Bender.* After nearly half an hour of stony silence, they all get up from their table, walk out of the visiting room with a dignified familial strut.

"They look like Mafia," Miss Mary says loudly.

"Shhh!" Shabazz says. "Ma, what you think they *is?*"

His eyes turn suddenly bright. "Yo, dun, didn't I see you on TV a few years back, on the *Donahue* show with Khallid and a bunch of Crips?"

K shakes his head.

"That wasn't you?"

"It *was* me. Big muthafuckin' mistake."

"Why you say that, dun?"

"I thought he was somethin' he wasn't."

"What's that?"

"He not really tryin' to serve no justice to black people."

Shabazz gazes hard at K, doesn't look convinced. Evidently Khallid still has a loyal following behind the walls of Sing Sing.

"Lemme tell you the truth about Khallid and them," K says, lowering his voice, leaning forward on the table. "I seen this shit with my own fuckin' eyes—used to bodyguard him. He ain't really on no upliftment business. The only thing he tryin' to uplift is his own *name*. He just like any other badboy, dun. He strictly out for self . . ."

"Don't know 'bout that."

"So where that money went from the Million Man March? They was passin' round that plate two, *three* times down in D.C. Where them millions went to, yo?"

I get up and walk back to the long bank of vending machines to get another cup of synthetic coffee and another package of Nutter Butter cookies for Shabazz to take back to his cell. When I return to the table, I notice that the conversation has turned to the subject of Jews. K is maintaining that Farrakhan and Khallid don't really hate the Jews; it's simply a matter of jealousy.

"Sure they jealous," Miss Mary says. "Who got the money?"

"Ma, it ain't the *money*. Money ain't got a thing to do with it. They jealous of the unity they got."

I sit down and K slaps me on the arm, nearly spilling my sweet reconstituted coffee. "Word, I seen it with my own eyes. I been to this muthafucka's newspaper. You wanna know how *organized* the Jews is? They had this election over there in Israel and muthafuckas from Brooklyn was *killin'* themselves to get to JFK in time, just to fly to Israel so they could vote in that election over there in Jerusalem. I'm *tellin'* you—that's what Farrakhan and 'em would like to see happen with us—have that level of fuckin' unity within *our* ranks."

Shabazz chuckles without smiling. K mentions a certain Reverend Fat Ass, a so-called civil rights leader for whose camera-seeking antics he has no patience.

"Now you look at Giuliani—Giuliani might be a dickhead, right? but muthafuckas *respect* him. Why? Because he's dead fuckin' serious about everythin'. He ain't walkin' around with no processed hair, lookin' all fat and stupid, talkin' a bunch of bullshit that don't even mean nothin'."

Shabazz is smiling now. "When you got so political, dun?"

K seems enraged, mesmerized, lost in his rapture. "All we got for leaders nowadays is a bunch a comic-relief muthafuckas. And most of us, we be brainwashed into thinkin' that if they throw us a bone, just make a grab for it. Shit! Throw a Jew a bone, he's like, *Fuck that! Where's the other half of the carcass? Why you throwin' me a bone? Where the prime rib at?"*

The CO calls Shabazz's government name over the PA and, pocketing his pack of Nutter Butters, he rises from the table. Hugs his mother and K. Then he hugs me.

"I don't want to come see you in here again."

"Naw, next time I'll come see you."

L ate in the winter of '97 Little K had another sickle-cell crisis. I stopped by to see him in the pediatric unit of Bellevue.

"Powah-*rain*-jah!" the round-faced toddler was yelling when I came into his hospital room; his favorite Japanese superheroes were, at that very moment, karate-fighting on the little overhead black-and-white set. I sat down on the corner of the window ledge. The boy still smiling broadly at me, despite the intravenous needles and tangle of tubes snaking around his arms.

"Ya hurt me? Ahtolyah Gednyabad!"

"Ayatollah *who?"*

"Ya hurt me? Ahtolyah Gedny*abad!"*

I looked to Faith for a translation.

"That's what we be sayin' to him. *Ya heard me? I told you—get in ya bed!"*

"Yo, I wanna show you somethin'," K said.

His son's latest crayon drawing. K held up the sheet of paper for me to examine, so proud of his little man's artistic abilities.

"Dat Faddah!" Little K said with obvious glee.

"What's he doing in the picture?" I said. "It looks like he's yelling."

"Yuh!"

"I ain't *yellin'!"* Father yelled, snatching the drawing away from me. He pointed out the fact that, in his son's rendering, he was standing quite peacefully and with a big upturned grin on his face.

K and I left Bellevue together. He wanted to go to the Woolworth's on 23rd, find a frame to put his little man's drawing in. Wanted to hang it up in the apartment as soon as he got home. Walking down First Avenue he told me that the sickle-cell doctors had just informed him of some distressing news.

"What's that?"

"Said my little man's gonna be all right. He gonna get better from this. But then he said that with kids like Little K, most kids with sickle-cell, they very seldomly live to see twenty-five."

"But you knew that, didn't you?"

"No, I never knew that."

I thought I remembered overhearing him having a long phone conversation with Crystal about the diminished life expectancy of children with sickle-cell anemia. Perhaps I was mistaken.

"I don't know what I'd do without my babies. I don't think I'd wanna keep on livin' without my little babies."

In the next few days, Little K made a strong recovery. A week later he was back to being his old rambunctious self. Next time I saw him, he was sitting over a Happy Meal in a McDonald's on Sixth Avenue and K was teaching the boy the fundamentals of boxing. When K would say the words *get set!* the strapping three-year-old would curl up his fists, hold them tight against his chin, waiting for further instruction. Then K, crouching down, would call out *right!* and *left!* and the boy would plant the corresponding punch to his father's face. K would close his eyes and purse his lips and let his little man pummel his face until he had Little K screaming with delight.

oño was ready to throw a fit. When we got out of the elevator at
the Bronx Lebanon nursing home, Big Tone was positioned in his
wheelchair, planted right by the elevator doors, twitching, eagerly
awaiting our arrival.

"You don't see him gettin' ready to start actin' the fool?" K
shouted. He was always shouting in regard to his older brother. "Tone!
What the fuck happened to your *hair?*"

"I just got a cut, Kev," Toño replied softly.

K was terribly embarrassed by his brother's rudimentary hospital
haircut. "Aw man, look at the way they chopped my nigga's head up.
Tone—I gotta take you out next weekend to get another Caesar."

"I'd like that," Toño said.

We wheeled Toño down the hall to his bedroom. He shared the
room with another wheelchair-bound former gangster who was blasting R. Kelly's "Summer Bunnies" at such volume that the tweeters of
his little boombox were in danger of shredding. The roommate had a
big Ferrari poster over his bed. Also a vivid doggy-style centerfold
from *Black Tail* magazine. The nurses must've *loved* that.

Toño kept contorting his face in palsylike spasms. Every few seconds his mouth would curl up as if was going to yawn—I kept waiting patiently for him to yawn—but, no, he was only thinking. His
eyes pointed in two different directions.

"How are you feeling today, Toño?" I knelt down and spoke directly into his ear.

"I have good days and I have bad days. Today is a good day." He
reached back, started waving his arm frantically, trying to get his little
brother's attention. "Kev! Did you remember to bring me my cigarettes?"

"Nigga, I ain't givin' you no more muthafuckin' cigarettes! You
just be givin' them shits away to every nigga up in here."

No, I couldn't stand to see Toño sitting there twitching and craving his nicotine release. I left the hospital and went across the street to a Puerto Rican bodega and bought Toño his pack of Newports. When I came back upstairs, K grabbed the cigarettes and tossed them furiously at his brother's chest.

"There! Smoke 'em and give 'em away to *whoever* the fuck you want!"

I knelt down next to Toño and spoke directly into his ear again. "You remember me?"

"I remember you, Doug. You had brought me a pair of Jordache pants back when I was stayin' by Kev and Faith in the Bronx. I still appreciate that."

None of the doctors in Bronx Lebanon could accurately diagnose what was wrong with Toño. He'd obviously suffered some kind of brain trauma while incarcerated all those years in Clinton, some nerve damage that had decimated his nervous system, robbed him of all muscular control. There was also the general deterioration of his vision. Some days, K had told me, Toño would sit there, completely blind to his surroundings.

I asked Toño how his vision was today. He said he could make out some of the colors in my Nautica ski jacket: some gray and some black and, yeah, some blue too. Said that the doctors had told him that the problem with his eyes would *never* get better; the back of the eye sockets no longer connected to the eyes.

"That happened in Clinton?"

"That happened on Rikers Island."

"The guards?"

"Naw, I was havin' a fight with a cat who was a whole lot bigger than me. He hit my head and now the back of the socket don't connect to my eye."

He sat there in the hallway, leaning hard to one side, enjoying the minty flavor of his Newport. His lifeless legs had shriveled up to the size of an eight-year-old boy's. It was hard to reconcile his body with that of the fearsome bareknuckle brawler and stickup man I had heard so many legends about. I told Toño that I'd seen his old crimey

Razor. Razor, the demon of Life's dungeon. Told him that Razor still talked respectfully about Big Tone's streetfighting prowess.

"Yeah." Toño smiled. "My fifty-two blocks. I was pretty nice with my fifty-two blocks."

Down the long hallway someone began to shriek—whether in pain or confusion I couldn't determine. When I looked closely at Toño, I saw that he was crying.

"I wanna get better, Doug. I wanna come home and leave this place. This is no place for me."

K had used some of his New Line money to buy an '86 Volvo. A jet-black turbo sedan, in decent shape, very little mileage, just one small dent in the side door. Told me that he'd bought it on Staten Island, paid only $2,000 for it.

It was raining hard when we drove back to Manhattan from Bronx Lebanon. K was telling me that Toño was so lonely in the nursing home that he'd even called his father and asked him to come visit him.

"Who's his father?"

"This Panamanian muthafucka that be at the Maximillian on Nostrand Avenue. Toño called him the other day beggin' him to come see him and the nigga said he ain't comin' *nowhere* to see Toño. He a real piece of shit, man. I ever see him on the street, word is bond, I'm a smack the shit out of him. His whole fuckin' life, Toño never asked that muthafucka to do *nothin'* for him . . ."

He raced down the FDR for a while without talking, turned up his tape of the latest rockers riddims from JA. The rain was coming down in heavy pattering sheets.

"Just like my own pops," he said finally. "I never asked that muthafucka for *shit* neither. All I ever asked him for was love—and he couldn't give it to me."

He was in such a bad mood after seeing his debilitated brother, he said the only thing that would cheer him up was driving out to Flatbush to get a nice beef roti. I nodded. As we drove up the on-ramp to the Brooklyn Bridge he asked me if I'd been following the news stories of the Jewish guy in Jersey who'd murdered his own children because— get this—he didn't want his ex-wife to raise them as *Christians*. I said, yes, unfortunately, I'd been reading all the articles about that bizarre double homicide case.

Crossing the Brooklyn Bridge he turned to me with a frown.

"Ay yo, can I ask you a serious question?"

"What's that?"

"Naw, nothin'—never mind—it was stupid . . ."

He drove halfway across the bridge before saying anything more.

"You ever wonder why God put you on this fuckin' earth?"

"I'm not sure I follow—"

He chewed his lower lip for a moment, searching for words, a more precise meaning.

"I mean, do you ever think that the world would be a much better place if you had never been born? If your parents had never met— never kissed—never fucked? *No?* I get that feelin' all the fuckin' time."

Crystal prays her rosary. At the kitchen table on a windy spring night. Staring blankly at the wooden floor, the thick blue and black binders of her dissertation research stacked high in front of her. The black cordless phone resting in her lap—over a No. 2 pencil, forming the sign of the cross. A few jagged shards of graham crackers scattered on the pale blue tablecloth, slowly ground, with the movement of her forearm, into tiny piles of beige dust.

Standing in the shadows, trying not to be heard, I study the steady progress of my fiancée's long bronze fingers over blood-red beads.

She won't tell me what happened, won't even look up. But *something* happened: why else would she be praying so fervently, so silently for someone's soul?

Lips moving silently, fingers moving silently over blood-colored beads.

Finally, pausing, looking up, she says the name.

Tommy.

Bronx-born badboy. Prom-date-turned-gunman-turned-stalker-turned-convict.

"What, he came home from jail?"

She nods slowly—with gravity, sadness, release.

"He called you?"

Red beads rub against her knuckles, and against my palms. She exhales a dry little laugh. A cold dry wind, clawing at my ignorance. "Called me from *where?*"

As soon as her cousin said it, Crystal cut the conversation short. She didn't need to hear any more. Tommy's dead. That's enough.

How did it *happen?* How does it *usually* happen?

She plots the points simply, connects the lines quickly, as if using a metal straightedge and a few slicing strokes of a razor-sharp pencil. While Tommy was in jail, Van, another of her childhood memories, another of the old Crotona Avenue crew, started messing with a Puerto Rican girl down in the Tremont section. The girl's boyfriend got jealous and came and found Van and shot him dead.

Yes, this part of the story I already know: Crystal had been pretty broken up when she heard about Van's murder. Van had always been like a kid brother to her. Van wasn't *really* bad like Tommy, she said. He'd been to jail, of course, but he wasn't an instigator—wasn't a gangster—more of a joker and a lover—a follow-the-crowd kind of guy.

Tommy learned about Van's murder while he was still in prison. Swore that as soon as he came home he was going to exact revenge on whoever'd murdered his homeboy. Went down to Featherbed Lane and got into a beef with a crew of Boricuas. Typical Tommy. As it turned out, it wasn't even the right guys. Quickly came to a shootout.

Tommy shot one of them and was shot himself. He died in the street, gun in hand.

No, she says, she's not going to his wake tonight, nor returning to White Plains Road for his funeral next week. What would be the point? Her face is now bloodless, no tears in her eyes. Too many tears wasted already. Now she can only pray her rosary. Perhaps light a votive candle for the salvation of his soul. No, the real Tommy, she says, her first true love, that bright-eyed churchboy she once knew on Crotona Avenue, buried himself too many years ago.

ELEVEN

badman business

I'm not very strong for praying . . . I do believe in God, but his ways seem so strange to me sometimes. I know right from wrong and I intend to do right when I get out . . . lots of love to all . . .

—John Dillinger,
writing to his niece from the Indiana State Prison,
Christmas Day, 1929, while serving a nine-year
sentence for a botched armed robbery

K called me one sunny day in early May saying that he wanted to swing by and meet me that afternoon. He was flying down to Atlanta the next morning—had to go to court and close out that bogus domestic assault case with his brother.

"What's so important that you've got to see me today?"

"I gotta give you your birthday present before I bounce."

I met him in the Village, on the corner of West 12th Street and Greenwich. He pulled up in his newly washed and polished Volvo, tires fresh and Simonized, blasting the latest DJ Clue mixtape from his powerful sound system. The dent in the side door was fixed. He was conservatively dressed in a dark blue shortsleeve shirt, untucked, and plush iron-gray corduroys, wearing his matching two-tone blue-and-gray suede British Walker loafers. Color-coordinated as always. He pulled a small gray box from the glove compartment.

"I know you don't wear no jewelry. But I saw this shit and I thought you should have it."

"I hate to break it to you—I'm already engaged."

I popped the top off the little jewelry box. Lifted the square of protective cotton. A small pendant: a silver Star of David on a fine silver chain.

"Why this?"

"A muthafucka oughta be proud of his peeps. What, you don't like it? I ain't givin' it to you if you ain't gonna wear it—you gonna keep it in the box like them fuckin' British Walkers I got you? Yo, that's *another* thing—why you don't never wear them fuckin' dope-ass Britishers?"

"They didn't fit. You got me a ten—my foot's barely a nine."

"See, you's a real piece of shit, D. Fuck you. Give 'em back to me if you ain't gonna wear 'em. I'll give 'em to Bazz or Life. You ain't down no more."

He unclasped the silver chain, reached around my neck, fastening the Star of David in place. Then he tucked it down under the neck of my T-shirt so that it could remain hidden from view. He said this Star of David was something private; I should never let strangers stare at it.

"See, the good thing about this being silver is that if somebody's thinkin' evil shit about you—well, I forgot, you don't believe in that spiritual side of things—but *we* believe that if somebody's thinkin' bad thoughts about you, you'll *know* it, because the silver will start changin' color."

"You mean a warning?"

"Yeah, like a warning."

We drove down to Gray's Papaya on West 8th Street to get a few fifty-cent hot dogs. Standing side by side at the crowded counter, chewing our franks, sipping orange drinks, he said that as soon as I could take a break from my writing schedule he wanted me to come out to Brooklyn and meet some Jamaican rudeboy called Rat.

"Word, but when you meet Rat, don't never call him Rat. Everyone calls him Jay now. And don't never stare at the scar on his face. Them niggas ain't like me, y'know. They ain't get around a bunch a white muthafuckas and change they fuckin' ways."

"Why do—why *did* they call him Rat?"

"Why you think? He looks like a fuckin' rat!"

Had he just befriended this new rat-faced Scarface?

"What? I been knowin' Rat from the Vanderveer days. Rat's one of the original V.I.P.—old-time Vanderveer International Posse. Rat and them practically raised me up. Rat ain't no young kid, you know. Rat's a grown man. Rat's older than Tone. He 'bout to turn forty fuckin' years old."

"What does he do these days? Work?"

"*Rat?*" He let out a low chest laugh, nearly choking on his last bite of sauerkraut and frankfurter. "Bwoy! Yuh *mad?* A pure gun-hawk dem! *Wuhk?* Rat and dem strickly pon some *badman* business . . ."

We walked down West 8th Street toward his parked Volvo.

Told him I thought I would pass on meeting Mr. Rat.

K paused to try to get the phone number of a full-figured homegirl bouncing toward us in tight jeans. She was licking a vanilla ice cream cone with the tip of her tongue.

"That looks *so* good, sweetheart—could I get some? Ice cream, I mean."

She gave him a flirtatious once-over, then replaced it with a look of mock disgust, snubbed him, kept walking, exhibiting her Gaultier-encased onion with an exaggerated wiggle.

"You tryin' to hurt a nigga's feelings?" he yelled after her.

I slept one night with the Star of David pendant around my neck. The next morning when I went to shave, lathering up, looking in the bathroom mirror, I saw that the entire chain had turned an ugly greenish black. Even left an ugly greenish hue on my skin. I unfastened it and

telling him to drop by the ceremony on the way to the airport. And then: "Naw, man, it's *your* day. Today's the day for you and Crys to do *y'all* thing . . ."

I was walking around the apartment with the cordless phone on my shoulder, chewing on a cold toasted English muffin, looking everywhere for my cummerbund—until I remembered I wasn't supposed to wear a cummerbund; I'd rented a vest instead—and as he was talking, I kept picturing him at the other end of the line, out there in East New York, at the very fringes of Brooklyn, and now when I thought of him I saw some kind of giant matrioshki doll, each layer popping open to reveal yet another persona.

I wondered which of them I was talking to today . . . Kevin Antonio Thomas, the witty script doctor, leaving a Writers Guild preview screening of *Sling Blade* in his dashing navy blue greatcoat and navy blue Eton cap, strolling down Broadway quoting back verbatim passages of dialogue in a pitch-perfect imitation of that simpleton-murderer's Arkansas drawl ("Some people calls it a Kaiser blade, but I calls it a sling blade, *mmmmmmm*—") . . . or American Dread, the ridiculously irresponsible rapper, rushing back to our table in Pronto Pizza, hissing, "Yo, we gotta break the fuck outta here—*now!*" and I'm thinking, Did he just *rob* the place? But, no, all he did was drop such a massive bowel movement that he clogged up the shop's only toilet—leaving us mere moments to flee the scene before the entire restaurant runs awash with the flood of his horrible shitwater . . . or was it Knowledge Born, the crazed Brooklyn gangster, drawing out his .45 in the lobby of When Worlds Collide, struggling with Justice and Life, ready to gun down drunken Mighty in front of a mob of fifty eyewitnesses . . .

Did he have a map? I heard myself asking. Did he think he could find the small chapel on the far end of the Columbia University campus?

"Yeah, I got the map. Yeah, maybe I'll roll through . . . I dunno . . . but if I do, I'll just be wearin' a fuckin' sweat suit."

And then I saw him as he'd looked the previous summer, walking down Fulton Street in his muscle shirt, bumping his way through the put it back in the jewelry box. Put the box in the back of my dresser drawer, laughing away his evil-thoughts theory. He was always ignoring the simplest explanation. Inexpensive silver turns green.

We didn't talk again until my wedding day in June. He and Faith had been invited to the wedding, but the weeks passed and we didn't get any RSVP card from them. Crystal kept going through her invitation checklist, asking me, "Is your friend coming or not?" and I could only shrug and tell her to hold him a place at one of the tables, because you never knew with K—well, she'd said it herself, hadn't she? As soon as you expected one thing from him, he'd surprise you by doing the opposite.

By the week of the wedding, all my friends and colleagues who'd met him over the years were asking the same question—"Is Big K coming?"—and I could only say, "Well, he's got his invitation—"

I woke up before dawn on my wedding day, still hungover from the night before, fumbling around for Crystal on her side of the bed—so disoriented I'd forgotten that my wife-very-soon-to-be was staying in a hotel room uptown with her mother. The phone kept ringing every five minutes, there were all sorts of questions and crises: the tuxedos we'd rented didn't fit one of my nephews, the rabbi-and-priest tag-team calling to confirm the time and place of the ceremony, the air conditioning still wasn't turned on in the reception hall, Crystal sounding hysterical, in tears because the place settings still weren't done properly—and then just after nine A.M. when I clicked over the call waiting it was K shouting at me: "Yes, dogburger! So today's the big fuckin' day! What, you nervous or somethin'?"

"No, not really—I just can't find my cummerbund."

"Chill the fuck out, dun. Shit's gonna go good."

Then I finally asked him: "Are you coming today?"

He started to mumble a sheepish apology, something about being standby on a flight to Atlanta later that evening. I pressed him again, mob of Dominican drug dealers, shoulders lowered, ready to go to war with all the demons of the present and the ghosts of the past.

"Do me a favor now—don't bust that ass."

"What?"

"Comin' down the aisle today—don't bust your fuckin' ass. Try and keep your faculties, man. Don't fall to fuckin' pieces."

It was one of those strange conversations that we had every so often, both of us talking in circles, not sure what the other was trying to say. The call waiting started its insistent beep again. He said he'd better let me go.

"One love," he said, in lieu of goodbye.

A few days after the honeymoon, back in New York, I got a call from Justice, Life's older brother, the man who'd come back and rescued Jeff and me when we were trapped inside the mosque on Flatbush Avenue. Big Justice, hollering hello, congratulating me on "jumping the broom." He'd been living out on Staten Island, found work on a construction crew, landed a spot on a minority coalition working a site out in Williamsburg. Said it was brutal, backbreaking work—handling a jackhammer, starting before six in the morning—but he was so grateful just to have an honest job and a wife who'd stuck by him and now he was concentrating on saving up money for his son's back-to-school clothes. Soon he was going to leave the black coalition; the Italian GC—general contractor—had offered Just a job when work on the site wrapped up, wanted to bring Just to a new project in Queens, and Just was hoping to get his union card, union hardhat and full health benefits.

"Yo, Doug E. Fresh!" he said excitedly. "You got any chess skills for me?" Justice loved playing chess and was looking for someone to give him a decent game on a regular basis.

"Sorry," I told him. "My six-year-old nephew can checkmate me in five moves."

I thought about the mysterious rumors I'd heard about Just, how he and K had had "mad beef" back in the flashing D.C. heat of the drug wars, back when youthful greed and arrogance and egotism had riven the Posse in two.

Then Justice said that he'd "bucked up on" (bumped into) K in Crown Heights one day recently, on Washington Avenue, that K was driving someone else's Montero.

"I don't know, man," Just said. "Rudeboy was movin' kinda fast . . ."

I knew that Justice was not referring to the speed of the vehicle.

K and I spoke several months later, in early August—he called to say that there was some confusion with the billing on his Writers Guild quarterly dues. We talked a bit about stories in the local news recently, about how Malcolm X's grandson, fourteen-year-old Malcolm Shabazz, had burned his grandmother to death, how the authorities were now debating whether the boy should be incarcerated in a juvenile jail or in a mental institution, and K said: "Well, you know what I think—jail can't *cure* a muthafucka of his violence; jail's where a muthafucka learns to *perfect* his violence."

And then, speaking of violence, he told me that he and Rat kept seeing Mike Tyson out on Ninety-Five (95th Street in Crown Heights); he said Mikey T was driving around on some kind of exotic three-wheel Honda superbike. "It's *bugged!* I don't know how that shit can be street-legal—but he says he got the papers to make the shit street-legal. You should *see* this fuckin' thing, duke."

I asked him how Tyson seemed to be handling this period of indefinite suspension from boxing—since savagely biting the ear off Evander Holyfield in June—if the former champion seemed depressed about his latest public disgrace. "*What?* Mike don't give a *fuck.* That's one thing I can say about him—Mike still a *real* muthafucka at heart."

*   *   *

A few days later, he had Faith leave me a message on my machine—some vague question about penny stocks that K had been reading about in the paper—but I didn't call him back about it because, well, I really didn't know the first thing about the stock market. Then on Saturday I woke up to hear two messages from Faith before nine A.M. How *urgent* could this question about penny stocks be?

I took my time, fixed a big pot of black coffee, read the Saturday *Times* and the *Daily News* before calling her back.

"What's the problem?"

"He got locked up last night."

"What happened?"

"They arrested them in the Rite Aid on St. John's Place. Said they was tryin' to rob the place."

I thought she was joking, kept waiting for K to pick up the extension—cackle wildly in my ear. *Gotcha! Stupid muthafucka!*

Robbing the Rite Aid? That wasn't even his MO—weren't Julio and Toño the family's stickup specialists?

"I got the call from the 77th Precinct first thing this morning. I was beepin' him all night but he never answered me. They said they holdin' him down there. He goin' to Central Booking this afternoon. Then my mother called me 'cause she seen it on TV. Turn on New York 1—you got New York 1? They showin' it every thirty minutes—it says four Brooklyn men held the manager of the Rite Aid at gunpoint, tellin' him to open up the safe."

I had to flick off the stereo and turn on the TV. On Hot 97, the DJ was scratching up a "radio-friendly" version of a hardcore street ode by Crooklyn's Finest, the late lamented Biggie Smalls.

On the road to riches and diamond rings
Real niggas do real things

I clicked the TV over to the twenty-four-hour New York news channel.

"It's gonna come on any minute now," Faith predicted.

Yes, it was. A small cartoon revolver in the top corner of the screen. Lower down, all the day's vital statistics: 87° 11:38 AM Saturday August 9.

BROOKLYN—SAMARITAN STOPS ROBBERY

The alert actions of a Good Samaritan helped foil an attempted armed robbery of a drugstore in Brooklyn. The manager of the Rite Aid on St. John's Place was closing up the store last night when four men came in, held a gun to his head and demanded all the money in the safe. Police say there were several customers at the store at the time, and one of them was also held at gunpoint. Just then, someone walking outside noticed what was happening and flagged down a passing patrol car. Police say all four suspects were arrested.

I drifted away from the anchorwoman's reading, mind cluttered with other words and phrases picked up over the last five years: metal filings sucked to a magnet. *Crime Heights. Original Crooks. Badman business.*

Through the heavy haze I saw him clearly now, a lonely figure atop a distant citadel, fishing deep in his pocket, deeper still, *deeper—* then tossing away the key to his life as haphazardly, flippantly, as the next man might extinguish a match.

The silence between us was painful. "What were they doing, Faith? Trying to make it to *America's Dumbest Criminals?*"

She let out a laugh. A long hard laugh. No humor in her voice, though. Just another hard woman laughing out her pain.

"Know anything about it?"

"I just know he was supposed to take the kids to Sesame Place yesterday and he couldn't go. I had to take the kids without him."

"Stephanie who?"

"*Sesame* Place. You know, in Langhorne, Pennsylvania. We was plannin' this from back in July—Little K and Keisha keep talkin' 'bout the waterslides at Sesame Place. So I kept sayin' to him, 'Don't forget we gotta take the kids to Sesame Place on Friday,' and he goes, 'Yeah, right, I won't forget'—this, that and another. Then yesterday morning Little K comes into my bedroom cryin': 'My father not takin' me to Sesame Place?'

"I said, 'What happened? You forgot we was goin' to Sesame Place?' Hear him: 'I can't go now, mami. I got somethin' important to do at seven o'clock.'

" 'You got somethin' *important* to do at seven o'clock? Whatcha gotta do that's more *important* than takin' your kids to Sesame Place?'"

When I hung up the phone with Faith, I walked straight to the bookshelf. Started sifting through a thick stack of folders, several disorganized sheafs filled with all his handwritten lyrics and letters, Polaroids, black-and-white contact sheets, jailhouse commissary receipts from the Tombs and Essex County. Looking for one of those letter-poems he'd been writing while he was down in Atlanta. He'd been very depressed in the months before he'd gone to Fulton County jail. He'd written one scathing letter-poem called "Owed to My Father"—wanted to mail it to his dad, but then he'd decided against it. He'd written one to his son called "That Time." Given it to me and asked me to give it to Little K—should anything bad ever happen—once the boy was old enough to understand. I finally found "That Time." It was folded up at the bottom of one of the manila folders.

> *What shall I leave for you, my seed*
> *When it comes time for me to pass into the land of the dead?*
>
> *What shall I leave for you, my seed*
> *When I have nothing for myself in the land of the living?*

When all my life I've procrastinated, saying TOMORROW
When TOMORROW *wasn't mine to promise*

When fear and anger stopped me from reaching my goals
While they kept me in their harness

What, my seed, shall I leave you of insight
When I myself am always confused as to life, religion and where I
  belong?

What shall I give you in the way of space
When I myself don't fit in?

What is there in the way of heirlooms
That I may give to you

Other than the sickle-cell
That I've already passed to you and your sister?

LOVE?

I give this free
So it doesn't count

The letter went on to ask a few more rhetorical questions, list a few
more of his paternal failings—how he'd never taken his son to see a
Yankees game, or shown him how *real* men are supposed to "gel"—
before ending with a wish:

To strive and excel
To accomplish everything that life has to offer
I leave this, as a curse, on you

I folded the letter back up into quarters, returned it to the middle of
the manila folder. Then, when I went to put the folder back on the
shelf, something else slid out, something thin and shiny and smooth.
The little laminated card of Elegua, the dark-faced orishá, lover of Ap-

pleton Rum, Cohiba robustos and all things sweet. Hadn't even known he was in there. I was surprised to see that the trickster god still possessed the power to scare me after all these years. He slipped between my feet: a small dark face on the floor, regal chin held high, dark shadowed eyes gazing up at me. I stared back for a long time before reaching down to put him away.

EPILOGUE

cipher
complete

The king of my kingdom
Completin' a cipher . . .
—**Big Daddy Kane**

I arrive at the hearing in Brooklyn
Supreme Court, Part 10, on Monday, September 17. Court is already
in session. Stern-faced Judge Firetog rustling papers, considering a
defense motion. Over the judge's head, carved into the wood of the
courtroom wall, I read an immense aphorism:

> THE VOICE OF THE LAW
> IS THE HARMONY
> OF THE WORLD
> —HOOKER

Owing to the tardiness of one of the defense attorneys, the cowboy-
boot-wearing Melvin Krinsky, the Rite Aid armed robbery case has
been postponed for several hours; I leave Faith sitting in the Part 10
hallway, return to the courtroom alone, quietly. Three white courtroom cops are sitting at the table, studying something intently: it appears to be a building blueprint. I approach, clear my throat, softly

asking them if the first docket on the sheet—the seven-count indict-
ment of penal code violation 160.15—has been pushed back until a
later date.

"And you would be?" one of the cops asks, without looking up,
stiff reddish blond eyebrow arched in suspicion.

"Someone who knows one of the defendants."

"You *know* one of the defendants?"

"Yeah."

The blueprint rustles down, settles over the table like a snowy
blanket. Three shocked cops look up, ruddy-cheeked, clean-shaven—
three separate shades of piercing pale blue cop eyes, fixing hard on
me.

"You better get some new friends."

I didn't see K in court that day, nor did I see him face-to-face after his
release from Rikers Island. (He was freed in October 1997, on
$50,000 bond, Faith's mother having put up her house in Staten Is-
land as collateral with the bail bondsman.)

I didn't see him; but he was in my mind often, as when I opened
the *Daily News* on December 13 and saw a full-page article under the
headline:

SLAMMING DOOR ON AN ERA:
SPOFFORD SHUTTING DOWN

Spofford Juvenile Center, the city's infamous
juvenile jail whose name once summoned images of
childhood misery, will close this spring, officials told
the Daily News.

The announcement came amid a News
investigation into deteriorating conditions at the bleak,
white-brick Bronx jail, including severe crowding,
complaints of abuse by guards and vermin
infestation . . .

So the state was finally closing down the forty-year-old SJC, the place K had often described as a badboy's screening program, a requisite freshman-year course in the college of adult criminality? My ears still echoed with his words on the subject:

> You may find this a little bit disturbin' but back then—to us—it was somethin' like a muthafucka gettin' into Princeton. How's it feel when you open up your mailbox and you find that letter sayin' they accepted you to an Ivy League college? You're elated, right? How do your friends feel when you tell them? They're elated for you, right?
>
> That's how it was for us juveniles goin' to jail. That was our ghetto status symbol, man. Goin' to Spofford, goin' to Brace, goin' to Goshen.

And so the cipher keeps rolling. *From Knowledge to Born, from Born back to Knowledge.* The doors of a decrepit, roach- and rat-infested Bronx juvenile jail slam permanently shut—while upstate and across the nation, the gates of countless brand-new, high-tech, maximum-security penitentiaries swing open . . .

New cells, new beds desperately needed to house those swelling ranks: over 1.7 million incarcerated, an exponentially growing population, now greater than *all* the United States armed forces combined . . .

Life gave me his own Brooklyn spin on America's "correctional-industrial complex" one afternoon in the winter of '96, sipping a bottle of that milky, stamina-building Irish Moss while we were walking the desolate, wind-whipped blocks of East New York.

"Open your eyes—the fuckin' jail system is one of the biggest, multimillion-dollar businesses this country got right now," he told me. "Everybody knows that shit. It's so obvious—to muthafuckas that use they *cap*, knowmsayin'?

"If you notice, a lotta rich muthafuckas is not buying real estate no more; they not buyin' grocery stores no more; they investin' in prisons . . .

"See, muthafuckas ain't stupid—they figure there's no way possible that they gonna have a crime-*free* America. *Never.* With all the alcohol they put in the stores, with all the drugs and guns out here in these streets, they know they always gonna have a bunch a *crazy* muthafuckas runnin' around, doin' some *crazy* shit . . ."

The day after Christmas (I'm conditioned, from my boyhood in Canada, to think of it still as Boxing Day), I got a voice-mail message from Life's older brother Justice, calling me from his job on the construction site in Queens.

"Yo, Doug," he said, "see if you can pick up a copy of today's *New York Times,* then look at the Metro section, then give me a call when you've seen it. Peace out."

I threw on my hat and coat. What now? I wondered. What new piece of "badman business" would I see splattered on today's newsprint?

But no, walking down 34th Street, fluttering through the Friday *Times* in a wildly gusting wind, I broke into a broad smile, seeing the prominent picture of Justice and his wife, Helga, in the neonatal intensive care unit of Long Island College Hospital in Brooklyn.

JUST A HANDFUL, PREMATURE GIRL IS A TINY GIFT

This should not have been Kayla Groce's first Christmas. She was scheduled to emerge, healthy and heavy, in February. Instead, she arrived, prematurely on Nov. 9, her gestation interrupted, her life precarious. She weighed 1 pound 4 ounces—less then the smallest of the McCaughey septuplets, about as much as a large grapefruit.

I stood on the corner of 34th and Eighth Avenue, in the midst of all the post-Christmas shoppers, reading the boxed feature story with its description of tiny Kayla in her incubator unit, the tubes snaking from her mouth, nose and chest, the miniature Bible, opened to the 23rd Psalm, wrapped in plastic, keeping her company.

> The newborn's weight was so low that doctors were at first pessimistic, but Kayla is alive and literally kicking, offering testimonial to the technological advances that have made the simulation of the womb and the preservation of fragile life possible.

The winter wind howled; the newspaper flipped up into my face, the passing bag-carrying sale-fiends were staring at me like I was a madman. I laughed out loud when I read the *Times* reporter's description of Justice, a "construction worker, [holding] his first daughter delicately in his bulky arms."

> "She's smiling," he said to his wife. "She's softening me up already."

E ndgame: New Year's Day '98. Justice and Helga and their thirteen-year-old son, Kendin, drop by the impromptu open house Crystal and I are hosting; or, more properly, that Crystal is hosting: I'm being antisocial, ignoring my visiting in-laws, trying to focus on the Michigan Wolverines battling Washington State in the Rose Bowl.

When Justice shows up, though, I give up on the football game. They've been shopping for a car seat for little Kayla, who's due to come home from the hospital in February, when she reaches the four-pound threshold.

Around dusk, Just and I sit down with a deck of cards. He's promised to show me a couple of poker variations he picked up "inside"—Follow the Queen, Fifth Street, Seven Card No-Peek, Michael Jordan (twos and threes wild); but I'm having a hard time following his rules; most of these jailhouse card games involve several wild cards that switch unpredictably in the middle of a hand.

Poker isn't really Justice's game anyway. He's brought along his chessboard, and he begins setting it up, telling me that he wants to see what kind of skills I've got for him.

Just gives me the advantage of playing white. The match opens tentatively. I'm having a hard time concentrating. The Rose Bowl's blaring in the background (did Woodson pick off that pass?); I'm eavesdropping as Helga, who works as a receptionist at American Express, and Crystal's mom, who works in a bank down on Wall Street, swap office stories. Justice moves a pawn, then compliments Crystal on her spicy collard greens, asking Helga to get the recipe. (Helga's from Belize, where collard greens aren't part of the national cuisine.)

Seeing the confusion in my eyes, Crystal's cousin Little Rudy—a burly seventh-grader who is "little" only in relation to his six-foot-five former-basketball-star-father—comes and stands at my shoulder, shaking his head, trying to offer me advice.

"Easy meat," Justice says, winking at Little Rudy, rocking back and forth on his size eleven, wheat-colored Timberland work boots. I move my knight; he lets out a relieved sigh and then laughs at my blindness: I've overlooked his big blunder, missed a chance to "touch the girl," snatch up his unprotected queen.

He soon puts me in check. Panicking, I shield my king, trying to stave off the inevitable, but Just slashes through my ineffectual defense with his queen and bishop and knight.

"Mate," he says suddenly. We've been playing for less than ten minutes.

"That's it?" Crystal laughs. "I thought you knew how to play." Justice smiles at her boyishly, exposing his two sparkling gold caps; we reset the chessboard so that Justice's son can go up against Little Rudy. Perhaps these two soft-spoken, bespectacled thirteen-year-olds, one

Bronx-born, the other a Brooklynite, can give each other a better match than I could offer Justice.

"Yo, rudeboy," Just says, leaning forward, lowering his voice so as not to cause me any further embarrassment. "Thought your game'd be a bit tighter than that."

Note on the Names

This book contains no fictional or composite characters. However, for various reasons, certain proper names as well as aliases have been altered.

As we went to press, K indicated that he did not wish his real name to appear anywhere in the text. It does not. Nor does the rap moniker or nickname by which he may be familiar to some people. I have also altered the proper names, nicknames and aliases of his immediate family members, children and former girlfriends in accordance with his wishes.

With some individuals, I've changed aliases, and certain physical characteristics, in order to mask their true identities and provide them with a degree of anonymity. These include the men I refer to as Dante, Wise and Razor. (The code of the street is fairly explicit on this point: As Albert Fried wrote in *The Rise and Fall of the Jewish Gangster in America*, regarding Louis "Lepke" Buchalter's arrest and ultimate downfall at the hands of a well-intentioned colleague, "Gangsterdom recognizes no unwitting acts of treason.")

A number of other character names have been altered: Bunny, Drévon, Rayshaun, Terror, Trigga Trigg, True, Fox, Porter, Davis and Hanes.

Though I never had occasion to meet my wife Crystal's childhood sweetheart, I've rendered the facts of their relationship exactly as she described them to me, and corroborated the date and place of his death with police reports. His name was not Tommy.

Acknowledgments

This book could not have been written without the support and assistance of numerous individuals. I'd like to thank my editor, Rick Horgan, for his unflagging enthusiasm, astute advice and sharp editorial eye. Thanks also to the entire Warner Books team: Heather Kilpatrick, Jimmy Franco, Airié Dekidjiev, Jackie Meyer, Bob Castillo, Jody Handley, Fred Chase.

I'm particularly grateful to my agent, Sloan Harris, who took a sketchy book proposal, shepherded it into shape, and then, throughout the writing process, provided me with that curious blend of handholding and ass-kicking so invaluable to a writer working on a tight deadline. Thanks also to Alicia Gordon of ICM in Los Angeles for her longstanding support and enthusiasm for the project.

Jeffrey Goldberg was a generous friend for allowing me to dramatize his role in this story, for reading an early draft of the manuscript and offering shrewd journalistic suggestions. My colleagues at *The Forward* were kind enough to give me a place to hang my hat and a desk at which to burn the midnight oil. Thanks to Jerry for his longstanding faith and encouragement (dating back to the days of 185 Nassau Street); to Bill at Mouth Almighty, for advice and support beyond the call of duty; to Phil and Bernie and Seth (nice to have lawyers for friends); to Jack-o, always ready to answer my crazy boozy questions, down in some L.E.S. bar, shouted into his ear over the incessant thump of drum 'n' bass.

Finally, but really foremost, I am indebted to K and all the men and women of Crime Heights who allowed me to "enter their cipher" over the years: Life and Just (*rudebwoy deh bout yah!*) . . . Buck (big-ups to Duck Down) . . . Bazz (welcome home) . . . Miss Mary (rest in peace), who took me into her home and gave me Kool-Aid on those hot summer days . . . Big K, key to the kingdom, gangster-poet and street-memoirist, sitting for countless hours of taped interviews with varying degrees of patience ("Fuckin' Doogzilla, boyee! Do I *stutter*? *What* did you *not* understand, D?"), helping me recollect moments which we'd experienced together but which may have been lost—for me at least—in a haze of alcohol, adrenaline or fear-induced amnesia.

It would have remained impenetrable, this *reino de las calles,* without the help of so many skilled and willing guides.

"Franklin gon' always be Franklin," Buck told me one afternoon in his Duck Down Records office. "Franklin Avenue gon' be there when you dead and gone."

Yes . . . and to all Original Heads, all F.A. massive, past, present & future:

Maximum respect.

Glossary

AUTHOR'S NOTE: *The argot of the New York streets changes rapidly and unpredictably; a slang term which is de rigueur in mid-June may be wholly obsolete by summer's end. The following definitions provide a mere smattering of the argot current during the time frame covered by this book: mid to late '90s. Regarding New York's ongoing cultural cross-pollination and the vagaries of ethnicity in Brooklyn (the borough with the city's largest and most densely concentrated African-American and Caribbean-American populations): words of West Indian origin are often understood and used on the Brooklyn streets by people not of Caribbean descent.*

Babylon—*(n. Jamaican)* used by Rastafarians to mean: (1) the corrupt political system; church and state; (2) any policeman.

batty—*(n. Jamaican)* backside, not considered vulgar (in contrast to *raas,* below).

battyboy—*(n. Jamaican)* homosexual; variants include *battyguy* and *battyman*; also *maama-man.*

beast—*(n. Jamaican)* policeman; a reference to the evil seven-headed beast of the Book of Revelation.

bid—*(n.)* prison sentence; stretch. ("To my homeboys in Clinton max, doin' they bid.")

biscuit—*(n.)* a handgun. Slang heard often in old gangster movies. Also *burner, rings, steel, tool.*

bitch—*(n.)* term of extreme disrespect and derogation for one's adversary; by no means necessarily a female.

blank—*(v.)* to murder someone.

bloodclaat—*(n. Jamaican)* very offensive curse word. Literally "blood cloth," from the rag which would be applied to a slave's shredded back after a severe punitive whipping.

blunt—(*n.*) White Owl, Phillie, Dutch Master or other inexpensive cigar which has been emptied and refilled with marijuana.

bomb, the—(*n.*) superlative; the best.

Boogie Down—(*n.*) the Bronx: the birthplace of all hip-hop culture.

books—(*n.*) in jailhouse context, means the inmate's account, on which cash can be left for purchasing goods from the correctional facility commissary.

botánica—(*n. Spanish*) a store which specializes in providing santería supplies such as charms, herbs, potions, musical instruments and other materials used by devotees.

bounce—(*v.*) to depart or flee.

Boricua—(*n.*) a Puerto Rican.

brick—(*n.*) a kilo of cocaine; also know as a *key.*

brujería—(*n. Spanish*) witchcraft; black magic. Known in Jamaica as *obeah.*

buck—(*v.*) to shoot.

bumboclaat—(*n. Jamaican*) vaginal cloth; menstrual rag; (*adj.*) a modifier of extreme intensity, offensiveness or confrontation.

bumrush—(*v.*) to charge an adversary; to stampede or crash an event to which one has not been invited.

burner—(*n.*) gun; also *biscuit, rings, steel, tool.*

cheddar—(*n.*) cash money. See also *cheese, dead presidents.*

cheese—(*n.*) filthy lucre.

clap—(*v.*) to shoot.

clock—(*v.*) to watch or stare.

crimey—(*n.*) partner-in-crime; not always used in a criminal context: can also mean homeboy or buddy.

cuz—(*n.*) cousin; in the context of L.A. gang culture, a term of address used only by Crips to identify fellow Crips; *never* uttered by Bloods.

dead presidents—(*n.*) cash; hence the variations: *Benjamins* for C-notes; *Grants* for fifties.

dickbeaters—(*n.*) fists; a '70s coinage, no longer in general use.

diesel—(*adj.*) powerfully muscled.

dime—(*n.*) ten dollars' worth of marijuana or cocaine. Also *dime sack.*

dope—(*adj.*) excellent.

DT—(*n.*) detective; occasionally truncated to *D.*

duke—(*n.*) a term of affectionate address for friends or family; can also be combined with another pronoun as an intensifier, e.g., *Ma Duke, Mom Dukes.*

dun—(*n.*) a term of affectionate address for one's homeboys or partners-in-crime.

duppy—(*n. Jamaican*) ghost. (See note p. 336.)

Earth—(*n.*) female affiliate of Five Percent Nation. See also *God.*

Elegua—(*n. Yoruba*; sometimes *Elegba* or *Eleggua*) a powerful orishá within the santería pantheon, Elegua is sometimes called the Lonely Spirit (Anima Sola). In Yoruba culture, he is described as the messenger of the gods and the lord of all the crossroads. His blessing is required before any magic spell can be executed and he must be fed or offered sacrifice before any other orishá. He is a master magician and his spells are impossible to break; he metes out justice as only he sees fit. He carries with him many of the characteristics of a young boy—capricious, fond of playing tricks and making mischief. Elegua is usually represented as a stone head with eyes, ears and mouth made out of cowrie shells and is usually kept behind the front door to guard the household. (See musical santería prayer recorded by Celia Cruz, Cuba's queen of salsa: "Elegua Quiere Tambo.")

fifty-two hand-blocks—(*n.*) a fistfighting style unique to the New York streets. (See note p. 57.) Sometimes truncated as *fifty-two.*

fish—(*n.*) a homosexual.

Five Percent Nation—(*n.*) also known as the Nation of Gods and Earths; hence: *Five Percenter.* (For details on origins, see note p. 87.)

flip the script—(*v.*) turn the tables on or surprise someone. In some contexts—but by no means always—implies a violent outburst.

flow—(*n.*) a hip-hop term to describe an MC's distinctive rhyme scheme, cadence and style of delivery. ("Yo, kid got a *ill* flow!")

front—(*v.*) to lie, dissemble or otherwise perpetrate a fraud.

German—(*n.*) Rikers Island slang, used by black inmates to denote a Puerto Rican. (See further explanation, pp. 198–199.)

God—(*n.*) male affiliate of Five Percent Nation. See also *Earth.*

gorgon—(*n. Jamaican*) (1) particularly fierce or impressive dreadlocks; (2) any top-ranking ghetto badman, dreadlocked or not. Often *don gorgon.*

gorilla—(*n.*) the most massive, menacing adversary imaginable. ("You ain't no gorilla!")

grill—(*n.*) face. ("Guard your grill!")

gun—(*n.*) in a jailhouse context means *not* a firearm but an extremely large *shank* or stabbing implement.

gun-hawk—(*n. Jamaican*) ultimate badman of the streets; i.e., a bird of prey armed with an automatic. (See Pennie Irie's song "Gun Hawk.")

hardrock—(*n.*) a gangster, tough guy, gunman; someone hardened by prison time.

herb—(*v.*) to play someone for a fool; to beat them or outsmart them.

holdin' heat—carrying a concealed firearm.

hole—(*n.*) a jailhouse or prison term for isolation or solitary confinement.

in full effect—at fullest potential; not to be trifled with.

Island, the—(*n.*) Rikers Island prison facility, located in the East River, just off La Guardia Airport—the largest municipal correctional complex in the world.

Jah know—*(Jamaican)* God knows.

jake—*(n.)* a cop.

jam—*(n.)* a party, often in an outdoor park; largely a defunct, old-school hip-hop term.

jook—*(v. Jamaican)* to stab. Hence, as expected, a secondary sexual connotation.

key—*(n.)* a kilo of cocaine; also known as a *brick.*

knock—*(v.)* to arrest.

knot—*(n.)* head. To *rock his knot:* clobber someone's cranium.

L—*(n.)* marijuana; variants include *lye* and *la.* Abbreviation of *lifted.*

lifted—*(adj.)* high on marijuana.

maama-man—*(n. Jamaican)* see *battyboy.* (See also note p. 138.)

man—*(n.)* (1) manslaughter as defined under New York Penal Code 125.15, 125.20; (2) a life sentence, e.g., "twenty-five to man."

mark—*(n.)* a punk or sucker. Slang peculiar to L.A. street gang culture, *never* used in this manner on the streets of New York.

MC—*(n.)* preferred term for a rapper, abbreviation of *master of ceremonies* (or in the words of Rakim, the greatest of all MCs, a microphone fiend who *moves the crowd*).

Medina—*(n.)* Brooklyn. From Five Percent Nation terminology. (*Mecca,* by contrast, refers to Harlem, on whose streets the sect originated in 1964.)

mouth murderer—*(n. Jamaican)* one who talks tough but cannot back up his words with actions.

nickel—*(n.)* five-dollar bag of marijuana.

nuh?—*(adv. Jamaican)* a nebulous query implying agreement or emphasis; i.e., *isn't it true? will you do as I'm saying? get to the point!*

1&2s—*(n.)* the two Technics SL-1200 turntables and cross-fading mixer used by a hip-hop DJ; also *wheels of steel.*

Original Man—(*n.*) any black man. From Nation of Islam ideology (see p. 87).

orishá—(*n.*) one of many gods of the Yoruba people (from present-day Nigeria) which survived slavery's brutal Middle Passage to the New World; the slaves, immediately baptized and converted to Roman Catholicism, outsmarted their masters by cloaking the identities of the traditional nature spirits and rituals under cover of Christian imagery: while pretending to worship St. Barbara, they were secretly praying to Changó, the god of thunder; paying homage to St. Anthony of Padua, they were really calling on Elegua, the trickster orishá, messenger of the gods and lord of the crossroads.

ox—(*n.*) a jailhouse razor concealed (often orally) for use in slashing other inmates.

paloff—(*v. Jamaican*) hang out, communicate, socialize; a variant of Standard *palaver.*

Pana—(*n.*) affectionate abbreviation for *Panamanian.*

peace, God!—a greeting used exclusively by members of the Five Percent Nation.

peel a cap—shoot someone in the head; not to be confused with *bust a cap,* to fire a gun.

peep it!—to look closely at something; to follow one's meaning.

perico—(*n. Spanish*) cocaine (literally, a parakeet).

phat—(*adj.*) excellent, admirable, skillful, stylish.

player—(*n.*) man who prides himself on his ability to maintain simultaneous relationships with numerous women while avoiding detection or domestic strife.

pound—(*n.*) (1) a handshake; hence (2) the number five, e.g., "the pound" or "four-pound"—.45-caliber handgun.

props—(*n.*) respect; short for *propers.* Often intensified as *mad props.*

raas—(*n. Jamaican*) arse. A vulgarism; generally used as an exclamation of surprise, more closely approximating *damn!* or *shit!* Intensified, like many West Indian curse words, by adding "cloth," hence: *raasclaat.*

raatid—*(adj. Jamaican)* damned; a mild expletive. From archaic English *wrothed,* moved to intense anger.

ragamuffin—*(n.)* a rough youth of the Kingston shantytowns; see *rudeboy.*

ratchet—*(n. Jamaican)* German-made switchblade popular among '60s rudeboys.

raw dog—*(adj.)* a state of complete and utter wildness; with total disregard to the consequences of one's actions.

rings—*(n. Jamaican)* a gun; also *biscuit, burner, tool, steel.*

rock—*(n.)* crack cocaine.

rude—*(adj. Jamaican)* bold, rough, ruthless. Used as a compliment or term of admiration. ("Mi bwoy rude, nuh?")

rudeboy—*(n. Jamaican, early '60s)* (1) gangster, gunman, renegade youth of the midnight ghetto streets (see Desmond Dekker's "007 (Shantytown)," an ominous yet celebratory ode to the invincible rudeboys of Trenchtown); (2) on the streets of '90s Brooklyn, a term of affectionate greeting and respect among peers; e.g., *"Yeow, rudeboy!"*

said speed—*(adv. Jamaican)* literally "at the speed of speech," i.e., no sooner said than done.

santería—*(n. Spanish)* literally "the Way of the Saints," a syncretistic religion of Caribbean origin which combines the gods, goddesses and beliefs of the Yoruba and other Bantu peoples of southern Nigeria, Senegal and the Guinea coast with the saints and Holy Trinity of Roman Catholicism. Many of its adherents today are uncomfortable with the name "santería" and prefer to call their religion "La Regla Lucumi."

selector—*(n.)* within reggae context, the loose equivalent of the hip-hop DJ; the man who selects records to play at a dance.

(Whereas the *DJ* in reggae culture wields a microphone, chats lyrics and is the rough equivalent of hip-hop's *MC*.)

serve—*(v.)* (1) to be sentenced by a judge; (2) in hip-hop context, to beat, better or humiliate one's adversary.

shank—*(n.)* jailhouse knife or razor.

Sodomite—*(n. Jamaican)* a homosexual. Like *raatid* (see above), many contemporary Jamaican expressions make reference to the language of the King James Bible.

spliff—*(n. Jamaican)* a large conical marijuana cigarette.

spot—*(n.)* (1) a nightclub or party; (2) when used in drug context, a place where crack or marijuana can be bought but never smoked.

star—*(n. Jamaican)* a term of affection for one's friends or comrades, e.g., "Wha'ppen, star?"

steel—*(n.)* a gun. ("I keep it real like a piece of blue steel.")

throw down—*(v.)* to fight.

tool—*(n.)* a gun; also *biscuit, burner, rings, steel.*

trey-bag—*(n.)* three-dollar bag of marijuana.

vic—*(v.)* to victimize someone; also *(n.)* a victim.

wack—*(adj.)* weak; corny; of no intrinsic value.

what's poppin'?—a friendly greeting: *what's goin' on? what's the latest?*

where you from?—State your gang affiliation or neighborhood; an extremely confrontational query, unique to L.A.'s territorial gang culture, *never* used as such in New York—approximate Brooklyn equivalent is: *Who you wit'?* (See p. 173.)

word!—expression of strong agreement. Also *word up!*

word is bond—my word is my bond.

word to mother—I swear on my mother's name.

ya ain't said shit—you have done little or nothing to impress me.

Yard—*(n.)* the island of Jamaica; from Kingston's communal

tenement dwelling arrangements known as *yards* ("Dreadlocks
cyaan live inna tenement yard"); hence:

Yardie—*(n.)* a citizen of or immigrant from Jamaica; also *Yardman*.
(In Great Britain during the late '80s, the mass media
erroneously and hysterically seized on *Yardie* as a term to
denote Jamaican drug gangsters. Among Caribbean-
Americans—and in Jamaica itself—the term has no such
criminal connotation.)

yay-yo—*(n.)* cocaine.

yunnoseeit?—*(Jamaican) don't you see my meaning? isn't it so?*
Variants include: *seen?*

yush!—*(Jamaican)* universal greeting of respect among rudeboys.

The author gratefully acknowledges permission to quote the excerpts of K's previously unpublished lyrics and poetry that appear on pages 5, 8, 39, 45–6, 112, 189, 207, 371, 393–4. All material quoted by permission.

Grateful acknowledgment is made to the following for permission to reprint material:

Lyrical excerpt of "Tougher than Tough" by Derrick Morgan © 1967 Island Records Ltd/Blue Mountain Music Ltd. Reprinted by permission of Polygram International Publishing, Inc.

"Many Thousands Gone" copyright © 1955, renewed 1983, by James Baldwin, from *Notes of a Native Son*. Reprinted by permission of Beacon Press.

The Gangs of New York by Herbert Asbury, copyright © 1927, 1928 by Alfred A. Knopf, Inc. Reprinted by permission of Random House, Inc.

Transcript excerpts of *CBS This Morning* television broadcast © 1993 CBS Inc. All rights reserved. Originally broadcast on September 3, 1993, over the CBS Television Network.

The Autobiography of Malcolm X copyright © 1964 by Alex Haley and Malcolm X; copyright © 1965 by Alex Haley and Betty Shabazz. Reprinted by permission of Ballantine Books, a division of Random House, Inc.

"Only the Dead Know Brooklyn," reprinted by permission of Scribner, a Division of Simon & Schuster, in *From Death to Morning* by Thomas Wolfe. Copyright © 1935 by Charles Scribner's Sons; copyright renewed © 1963 by Paul Gitlin Administrator C.T.A.

Lyrical excerpt from "Crooklyn" by Buckshot of The Crooklyn Dodgers © 1994 MISAM Music, Inc./Target Practice Music (ASCAP). Reprinted by permission.